D1272122

The Future of Worker Representation

The Future of Work Series

Series Editor: **Peter Nolan**, Director of the ESRC Future of Work
Programme and the Montague Burton Professor of Industrial Relations
at Leeds University Business School in the UK.

Few subjects could be judged more vital to current policy and academic
debates than the prospects for work and employment. *The Future of
Work* series provides the much needed evidence and theoretical
advances to enhance our understanding of the critical developments
most likely to impact on people's working lives.

Titles include:

Julia Brannen, Peter Moss and Ann Mooney
WORKING AND CARING OVER THE TWENTIETH CENTURY
Change and Continuity in Four Generation Families

Geraldine Healy, Edmund Heery, Phil Taylor and William Brown (*editors*)
THE FUTURE OF WORKER REPRESENTATION

Michael White, Stephen Hill, Colin Mills and Deborah Smeaton
MANAGING TO CHANGE?
British Workplaces and the Future of Work

The Future of Work Series
Series Standing Order ISBN 1–4039–1477–X

You can receive future titles in this series as they are published by placing a standing order.
Please contact your bookseller or, in case of difficulty, write to us at the address below with
your name and address, the title of the series and one of the ISBNs quoted above.

Customer Services Department, Macmillan Distribution Ltd, Houndmills, Basingstoke,
Hampshire RG21 6XS, England

The Future of Worker Representation

Edited by

Geraldine Healy
Edmund Heery
Phil Taylor
and
William Brown

E·S·R·C
ECONOMIC
& SOCIAL
RESEARCH
COUNCIL

First published 2004 by
PALGRAVE MACMILLAN
Houndmills, Basingstoke, Hampshire RG21 6XS and
175 Fifth Avenue, New York, N.Y. 10010
Companies and representatives throughout the world

PALGRAVE MACMILLAN is the global academic imprint of the Palgrave
Macmillan division of St. Martin's Press, LLC and of Palgrave Macmillan Ltd.
Macmillan® is a registered trademark in the United States, United Kingdom
and other countries. Palgrave is a registered trademark in the European
Union and other countries.

ISBN 1–4039–1759–0

This book is printed on paper suitable for recycling and made from fully
managed and sustained forest sources.

A catalogue record for this book is available from the British Library.

Library of Congress Cataloging-in-Publication Data
    The future of worker representation / edited by Geraldine Healy ... [et al.].
        p. cm. – (The future of work)
    Includes bibliographical references and index.
    ISBN 1–4039–1759–0 (cloth)
        1. Labor unions – Great Britain. 2. Industrial relations – Great Britain.
    I. Healy, Geraldine (Geraldine Mary) II. Future of work (Series)

HD6664.F88 2004
331.88′0941—dc22   2004050428

10   9   8   7   6   5   4   3   2   1
13 12 11 10 09 08 07 06 05 04

Printed and bound in Great Britain by
Antony Rowe Ltd, Chippenham and Eastbourne

Contents

List of Tables and Figures

Tables

Figures

Acknowledgements

This book presents findings from research projects funded under the Employment Relations stream of the ESRC's *Future of Work* programme. The idea to develop the book was hatched at one of the periodic workshops organised during the programme and took further shape at a day-long conference organised jointly with and hosted by the Trades Union Congress early in 2002. It was decided at this point to invite contributors from outside the *Future of Work* programme, particularly to ensure coverage of the important theme of worker representation through non-trade union bodies.

In putting the volume together we have incurred numerous debts of gratitude. We owe a lot to Peter Nolan, Director of *Future of Work*, who encouraged us to produce the book and agreed with Palgrave that it would be published as part of a dedicated series. We also owe a lot to our publisher and the supportive (and patient) editorial team that shepherded the book through to completion. Finally, and as ever with a volume of this kind, we owe a very heavy debt to our contributors. They have provided excellent chapters to a person when there were multiple competing demands on their effort and time. They have also been extremely helpful and tolerant throughout the editorial process and put up with its occasional glitches with good humour: they are all still speaking to us (we hope). We hope that they are as pleased with the finished product as we are.

Foreword

The representation gap in contemporary UK workplaces has, since the haemorrhaging of collective bargaining and trade unionism in the mid-1980s, been a source of growing public policy concern. With fewer than 30 per cent of employees currently represented by trade unions, there are serious questions about channels of communication, democracy and participation in UK workplaces. What is the future for the collective institutions that once played a prominent role in ensuring that workers' voices were heard and respected?

Have the employers that allowed their former channels of communication with unions and their employees to wither put in place new structures in their organisations that enable sensible dialogue about the key decisions that affect working lives? Is the accent on partnership in some organisations likely to produce mutual gains, and what is the status of non-standard employees, part-time workers and low-paid ethnic minority women in the new arrangements? Much has been written about the emergence of a new economy, but what is the position of workers in new and expanding industries such as software and call and contact centres, and how are employers responding to the new organisational boundaries that are increasingly fragmenting and blurring traditional lines of responsibility and obligations to workers.

This timely new book, which brings together leading researchers in industrial relations, sociology, management and economics addresses these and other questions about the character of employment relations in UK workplaces in the first years of the new millennium. Taking as a reference point the national survey data generated in the late 1990s (WERS 1998), it moves the analysis forward on the basis of new research studies conducted under the ESRC Future of Work Programme.

Launched six years ago, the Programme has supported the work of more than one hundred researchers at 22 UK universities. Its objectives were to test established wisdoms, generate new data, and refine theory and concepts. The contributions to academic, policy and practitioner debates have restored work and employment issues to the top of the social science research agenda and have displaced the futurology that predominated a decade with a secure evidence base and sound theoretical foundations to navigate changes in the character of employment relations in the future. This new series by Palgrave Macmillan brings together the leading researchers on the changing world of work and represents the most authoritative input into contemporary debates for many decades.

PROFESSOR PETER NOLAN
Director, ESRC Future of Work Programme

List of Abbreviations

ACAS	Advisory, Conciliation and Arbitration Service
ACTSS	Administrative, Clerical, Technical and Supervisory Staff
AEEU	Amalgamated Engineering and Electrical Union
AFL-CIO	American Federation of Labor – Congress of Industrial Organizations
AFSCME	American Federation of State, County and Municipal Employees
ASTMS	Association of Scientific, Technical and Managerial Staff
ATL	Association of Teachers and Lecturers
AUEW	Amalgamated Union of Engineering Workers
AUT	Association of University Teachers
BDC	Biennial Delegate Conference
BECTU	Broadcasting, Entertainment, Cinematograph and Theatre Union
BIFU	Banking, Insurance and Finance Union
BME	Black and Minority Ethnic
BT	British Telecommunications plc
BUILD	Baltimoreans United in Leadership Development
CAB	Citizens' Advice Bureau
CAC	Central Arbitration Committee
CBI	Confederation of British Industry
CIETT	International Confederation of Private Employment Agencies
COF	Citizen Organising Foundation
COHSE	Confederation of Health Service Employees
CRE	Commission for Racial Equality
CSP	Chartered Society of Physiotherapy
CSR	Customer Service Representative
CWU	Communication Workers' Union
DTI	Department of Trade and Industry
EAT	Employment Appeal Tribunal
EC	Executive Council
ECJ	European Court of Justice
ERA	Employment Relations Act, 1999
ESRC	Economic and Social Research Council
ETUI	European Trade Union Institute
EU	European Union
EWC	European Works Council
FRU	Free Representation Unit

FTC	Fixed-term contract
GLA	Greater London Authority
GMB	Britain's General Union
HASWA	Health and Safety at Work Act
HPWS	High performance work system
HR	Human Resource(s)
HRM	Human Resource Management
IAF	Industrial Areas Foundation
IDS	Incomes Data Services
ILO	International Labour Organisation
IPA	Involvement and Participation Association
IRRU	Industrial Relations Research Unit
IT	Information technology
LAGER	Lesbian and Gay Employment Rights
LFS	Labour Force Survey
LLA	Lifelong Learning Advisor
MSF	Manufacturing, Science and Finance
MU	Musicians' Union
NACAB	National Association of Citizens' Advice Bureaux
NALGO	National and Local Government Officers' Association
NATFHE	The University and College Lecturer's Union
NCU	National Communications Union
NEC	National Executive Committee/Council
NGH	National Group on Homeworking
NGO	Non-Governmental Organisation
NHS	National Health Service
NUJ	National Union of Journalists
NUPE	National Union of Public Employees
NVQ	National Vocational Qualification
OLS	Ordinary least squares
ORS	Organization Resources Counselors Inc
PLI	Public liability insurance
PPP	Public–Private Partnerships
R2L	Return to Learn
SLTG	Stephen Lawrence Task Group
SME	Small and Medium-sized Enterprise
SNB	Special Negotiating Bodies
SOG	Self-Organised Group
TELCO	The East London Communities Organisation
TICE	Transnational Information and Consultation of Employees
TGWU	Transport and General Workers' Union
TUC	Trades Union Congress
TUPE	Transfer of Undertakings (Protection of Employment) Regulations

UCATT	Union of Construction, Allied Trades and Technicians
UCW	Union of Communication Workers
ULF	Union Learning Fund
ULR	Union Learning Representative
USDAW	Union of Shop, Distributive and Allied Workers
VEA	Vocational Education Advisors
WEA	Workers' Educational Association
WERS	Workplace Employee Relations Survey

List of Contributors

Brian Abbott is Senior Lecturer in Industrial Relations and Organisational Behaviour at Kingston Business School, Kingston University.

Peter Bain is Senior Lecturer in the Department of Human Resource Management at the University of Strathclyde, Glasgow.

Harriet Bradley is Professor of Sociology and Dean of the School of Social Sciences and Law at the University of Bristol.

William Brown is Master of Darwin College and Montague Burton Professor of Industrial Relations at the University of Cambridge. He is a Council member of the Advisory, Conciliation and Arbitration Service (ACAS), a member of the Low Pay Commission and Chair of the TUC Partnership Institute's Advisory Board.

Hazel Conley is Senior Lecturer in Human Resource Management at Bristol Business School, University of the West of England.

Andy Danford is Reader at the Business School, University of the West of England.

Rick Delbridge is Professor of Organisational Analysis at Cardiff Business School and a Fellow of the Advanced Institute of Management (AIM).

Jan Druker is Professor of Human Resource Management and Head of the Business School, University of East London.

Gregor Gall is Reader in the Department of Management and Organisation at the University of Stirling.

Kay Gilbert is a Lecturer in the Department of Human Resource Management at the University of Strathclyde, Glasgow.

Mark Hall is Principal Research Fellow at the Industrial Relations Research Unit at Warwick Business School and co-editor of *European Works Councils Bulletin*.

Geraldine Healy is Professor of Employment Relations at Queen Mary, University of London.

Edmund Heery is Professor of Human Resource Management at Cardiff Business School and Chief Editor of the *British Journal of Industrial Relations*.

Jeff Hyman is Professor of Human Resource Management at the University of Aberdeen.

Fang Lee Cooke is Lecturer in Employment Studies at the new Manchester Business School, University of Manchester.

Cliff Lockyer is Senior Research Fellow, Fraser of Allander Institute, University of Strathclyde.

Mick Marchington is Professor of Human Resource Management at the new Manchester Business School, University of Manchester.

Abigail Marks is Lecturer in Human Resource Management at the University of Herriot Watt in Edinburgh.

Nupur Mukherjee was Research Officer on the ESRC-funded project on Double Disadvantage, based at the University of Bristol.

Anne Munro is a Reader in the Business School at Napier University in Edinburgh.

Sarah Oxenbridge worked as a researcher at the University of Cambridge between 1999 and early 2003 and has since worked as a Senior Researcher at the Advisory, Conciliation and Arbitration Service (ACAS) in London.

Helen Rainbird is Professor of Industrial Relations at University College, Northampton and is co-editor of *Work, Employment and Society* from January 2005.

Mike Richardson is Senior Researcher at Bristol Business School, University of the West of England.

Jill Rubery is Professor of Comparative Employment Relations at the new Manchester Business School, University of Manchester.

Dora Scholarios is Reader in the Department of Human Resource Management at the University of Strathclyde, Glasgow.

Melanie Simms is Lecturer in Human Resource Management at Canterbury Business School in the University of Kent.

Celia Stanworth is Reader in the Business School, University of Greenwich.

Paul Stewart is Professor of the Sociology of Work and Employment at Bristol Business School, University of the West of England, and editor of *Work, Employment and Society.*

Stephanie Tailby is Principal Lecturer in Employment Relations, Bristol Business School, University of the West of England.

Phil Taylor is Reader in the Department of Management and Organisation at the University of Stirling.

Mike Terry is Professor of Industrial Relations at the Industrial Relations Research Unit, Warwick Business School, University of Warwick.

Martin Upchurch is Reader in International Employment Relations, Bristol Business School, University of the West of England.

Jane Wills is Reader in Geography at Queen Mary, University of London.

1
Representation at Work: Themes and Issues

Edmund Heery, Geraldine Healy and Phil Taylor

Introduction

One of the most striking social changes to have occurred in the life times of contributors to this book has been the substantial collapse of a system of worker representation founded on trade unions and collective bargaining – what Henry Phelps Brown (1990) described as the 'counter revolution of our time'. Three decades ago, more than half the UK workforce were members of trade unions and collective institutions regulated the terms of employment for most of those in paid work (Brown *et al.* 2003: 199; Waddington 2003: 220). These arrangements have been heavily eroded in the intervening period. Trade union membership has stabilised in recent years but fewer than 30 per cent of UK employees are now members and in the private sector union density has dropped below 20 per cent. The majority of employees are no longer covered by collective bargaining and unilateral decision by the employer is now the most frequent method of setting the terms of employment (Cully *et al.* 1999: 108). Moreover, where collective bargaining survives, it is often a 'hollow shell' exerting negligible influence over managers (Millward *et al.* 2000: 179–83). These developments have raised concerns about the emergence of a 'representation gap' (Towers 1997). The right and aspirations of workers to participate in the governance of enterprises are being frustrated it is felt, by the decline of representative institutions.

How might the representation gap be filled? Those seeking an answer to this question have offered two main solutions, both of which have stimulated considerable debate and a substantial programme of research. The first proposes the revitalisation of trade unions. There has been a spate of books in recent years concerned with the 'rekindling', 'renewal' or 'revitalisation' of the trade union movement, which start from the premise that unions can re-build their status as representative institutions if they undergo an effective process of change (Frege and Kelly 2004; Cornfield and McCammon 2003; Fairbrother and Yates 2003; Bacharach *et al.* 2001; Turner *et al.* 2001). Advocates of this position differ widely in their interpretation of the challenge facing unions and the necessary adaptation they must make; their views are often bitterly opposed. But they are united in seeing a continuing role for trade unions and collective bargaining in representing people at work.

The second position is less frequently and often less clearly articulated but identifies a role for new or alternative institutions of worker representation. There is a managerialist version of this argument, which claims that employee involvement and other programmes devised by managers are sufficient for the expression of worker voice (see Kaufman and Taras 2000: 540–1). A very different version accords priority to advocacy, campaigning and mutual assistance organisations that operate in civil society and which frequently are grounded in the new social movements of identity (Osterman *et al.* 2001: 131–47; Abbott 1998a). A third version points to the state as the critical vehicle and stresses the value of statutory systems of worker representation that endow citizens with rights to participate in the governance of their employing organisations (Frege 2002; Adams 1995: 180). A central question that arises for all versions of the second position concerns the relationship between alternative institutions of worker representation and trade unions. Proponents of a replacement thesis suggest that alternative institutions can replace trade unions though there is a sharp division between those who welcome and those who decry this claimed effect. Proponents of a complementarity thesis, in contrast, believe there is scope for fruitful interaction; that unions can work alongside and in concert with other institutions. The two solutions to the problem of the representation gap can therefore overlap as the task of union revitalisation is defined in terms of integration with other institutions of worker voice (Hurd *et al.* 2003: 106–8; Verma *et al.* 2002: 379).

This book consists of 12 empirical investigations into the current state of worker representation in the UK that seek to test these arguments. Eight chapters deal with trade unions and consider the prospects for union representation in the new service industries, the steps unions have taken to represent a more diverse workforce and recent experiments with labour–management partnership. The remaining chapters examine forms of nonunion representation. Four alternatives are considered: statutory works councils, employment agencies, which place workers in employment and claim to act on their behalf, advocacy and advisory organisations, and social movement organisations campaigning for workplace justice. These last two types are investigated through case studies of the Citizens' Advice Bureaux (CAB) and the East London campaign for a living wage, respectively. Institutions of worker participation created by employers, such as involvement or profit-sharing schemes, are not considered, mainly because a substantial research literature already exists (see Heller *et al.* 1998; Hyman and Mason 1995). The purpose of this chapter is to provide a background against which the later, more focused contributions can be viewed. To this end, it surveys the debate and research on the future of worker representation, considering union revitalisation and alternative forms in turn.

Union revitalisation

Recent work on trade unions in Britain and other developed countries is both voluminous and highly variable in terms of subject matter, method and argument. One way of imposing order on this variation is to sort accounts of union revitalisation on the basis of their main level of analysis. We recognise that the different levels of analysis may in practice overlap and interrelate to one another, but suggest that making these analytical abstractions brings into sharp focus the differences between the approaches. Thus, societal models of revitalisation hold that unions must adapt to long-run changes in society and economy, which require a 'new unionism' matched to the interests of a changing workforce. Institutional models, in contrast, suggest that the task of revitalisation is to adjust union activity to the structure of opportunity provided either by the institutions of industrial relations narrowly conceived or the broader institutional matrix of different 'varieties of capitalism'. With organisational models, the task of revitalisation is internalised and is dependent upon changes in union government to allow more effective management, greater democratic participation or the expression of diverse interests. Finally, actor-centred models emphasise the need to renew the population of leaders and activists occupying representative positions in unions, the underpinning belief being that unions can exercise strategic choice and that different choices will be made by representatives with novel characteristics. In what follows we review each of these types of argument. We set out what we believe are the central assumptions of the different versions of union revitalisation and illustrate them with recent contributions to the literature. In each case we also examine the responses of critics to all four positions and identify the types of argument that have been used to counter each.

Society

At the heart of the societal argument is the belief that unions are under a growing selective pressure to adapt or evolve. The source of this pressure lies in deep-seated changes in economy and society that are altering the structure of interests and preferences that workers bring to their employment and, by extension, to trade unions. This, in turn, requires a new form of unionism better matched to the requirements of a changing workforce. Unions must perforce adapt to their environments, in this essentially evolutionary viewpoint, or cede their niche to other representative institutions and ultimately become extinct. If unions are unable to develop new forms, according to Kochan (2003: 177), then they are unlikely 'to avert the downward trend in union representation, influence and contribution to the welfare of the British workforce and society'.

The nature of the adaptation posited by advocates of the societal argument varies, depending on the underlying theory of social change to which they subscribe. Three versions of the argument are presented below though others are readily identifiable in the literature on trade unions (Heery 2003: 279–83). A particularly influential version of the argument suggests that unions are under pressure to change their relations with employers and strike a fresh bargain founded on partnership or 'mutual gains' (Kochan and Osterman 1994: 147–65). In one formulation of this argument, favoured by North American writers, the pressure for co-operation with employers emerges from fundamental change in methods of work organisation (Bélanger *et al.* 2002: 45; Appelbaum and Batt 1994: 123–45). The spread of high performance work practices requires employers to invest in high commitment management to secure necessary levels of worker skill, commitment and flexibility. This, in turn, provides new scope for identifying shared interests between employers and employees. Within the high commitment workplace regime there is opportunity for workers to realise their interests in development, involvement and job satisfaction (Appelbaum 2002). Accordingly, a new unionism can emerge that centres on these previously neglected or latent interests and which co-operates with employers to embed new forms of production, and their associated management practices, within the economy (Frost 2001b).

The theoretical reference point for adherents to this position is theories of post-industrialism or post-Fordism, with their relatively benign interpretation of changing patterns of work organisation. The reference point for a second, less upbeat formulation, favoured by British writers, is theories of globalisation. According to Brown and colleagues (Oxenbridge *et al.* 2003: 324–32; Brown *et al.* 2000: 616–19; Brown *et al.* 1998: 73), exposure of domestic markets to international competition has effected two broad changes in interest representation. On the one hand, distributive bargaining to secure either a wage premium or restrict effort levels has become less tenable. On the other hand, the heightened competitive threat encourages workers and their representatives to develop a 'productivity coalition' with employers, in which security of employment is exchanged for flexibility. Therefore, although the structural trigger is different the perceived effect is similar: a broadening of shared interests between workers and employers.

In both formulations of the argument a central adaptive response of unions that is identified is the development of labour–management partnership at enterprise level. Accounts of formal partnerships suggest that they usually consist of a substantive element, with unions seeking to reinforce high commitment management through agreements on worker security, single status, fair treatment, training, development and involvement, and a procedural element that promotes consultation on business strategy and joint-working on business operations and de-emphasises distributive wage bargaining (Terry 2003a: 462–7; Heery 2002: 22–4). The essential point, however, is that these changes in union representation are seen as part of a long-term adaptation to the changing needs of workers, founded in the transition to a new production regime, new conditions of global competition or a combination of both (Knell 1999: 9–11).

The second version of the societal argument adopts a different take on the evolution of employment relationships and emphasises the transfer of risk from employers to employees and the growth of contingent work. Worker interests are being transformed, in this interpretation as employers divest themselves of traditional obligations to their employees under the pressure of more intense competition. The restructuring of public services under the influence of the 'new public management' provides an additional source of change, resulting in the growth of sub-contracting and precarious work in a sector previously characterised by stable employment (Hebson *et al.* 2003; Allen and Henry 1996). The theoretical reference point for this version of the societal argument lies in notions of an emerging risk or network society, characterised by the hollowing out of large bureaucracies, the decay of internal labour markets and their replacement with, frequently short-term, market exchanges (see Nolan and Wood 2003: 165–7). Unions, on this view, must adapt to a terrain, in which long-term, secure employment is giving way to new forms of contingent work, defined by their insecure status (see Chapter 4).

One consequence that has been suggested is that unions must shift their primary site of representation from the workplace or enterprise to the external labour market. For Cobble (1991), 'worksite unionism' is no longer appropriate to the needs of a 'post-industrial workforce' and unions must organise workers either on the basis of occupations or geographical communities (see Heery *et al.* 2004a; Wills 2002c; Cobble and Vosko 2000; see also Chapter 6). This 'extra-enterprise' representation of workers, in turn, has been seen to require three elements. First, the exclusion of workers from enterprise-based systems of welfare and skill formation suggests that unions themselves should meet these needs through the expansion of individual services. Attention has been focused on union benefit systems, training and development schemes and systems of labour market information, all of which can directly support contingent workers in a mobile career (Osterman *et al.* 2001: 111–19; Benner and Dean 2000). Second, the level at which collective bargaining is conducted should be shifted upwards to the multi-employer level to allow the broad regulation of contingent labour markets. The function of multi-employer bargaining, moreover, should be to establish minimum conditions that support worker mobility between firms without penalty and to ensure the provision of public goods within regional or occupational labour markets, such as the supply and accreditation of training (Wial 1994). Third, in both British and American writing on contingent work, there is an emphasis on unions forming coalitions with political agencies, community and advocacy organisations, in some cases to press for protective regulation and in others to better facilitate provision of labour market services (Erickson *et al.* 2002; Wills 2002c). Partly this arises from the lack of bargaining power of contingent workers, by virtue of their contingent status, and their need to draw on the resources of other groups and institutions. Partly too it arises from the requirement for representation beyond the enterprise, which of itself draws trade unions into joint work with other organisations that operate within civil society (Frege *et al.* 2004). In the network economy, unions may have to become networking organisations.

The final version of the societal argument summarised stresses the fragmentation of worker interests and the need for unions to represent diversity. The material basis for this change is seen to lie in the feminisation of the workforce and other changes in workforce composition, such as an increase in migrant or ethnic minority labour. It is seen to lie, too, however, in the strengthening of social identities grounded in gender, ethnicity, sexuality, disability and other characteristics (Ledwith and Colgan 2002: 1–2). For this version of the societal argument, the pressure for change arises in the overlaying of the labour movement with new social movements, with the associated articulation of demands for equal treatment and freedom from discrimination to which unions must respond. In this case the point of reference for at least some versions of this argument lie in theories of post-modernity, with their emphasis on the decline of traditional solidarities (and associated grand narratives) and the fracturing of social identity (Selmi and McUsic 2002).

The conception of changing worker interests that underpins this position has several components. At its core is acceptance that there are multiple, equally legitimate interests to which unions ought to respond: that the needs of women, minorities or identity groups should not be subordinated to a putative general or class interest. This in turn implies that women and minority workers have an interest both in equal treatment, the removal of discrimination, and in 'diverse treatment', an acceptance of their specific, particular needs (e.g. that, women may require particular forms of employment, such as properly regulated part-time work). The adaptive responses that are believed to be required of unions flow from this conception. If unions are to respond effectively to a more diverse workforce then they must accept women and minority groups as part of their constituency, withdraw from discriminatory practices, promote equality of opportunity and engage with diversity (Dickens 1998: 29–36; Ledwith and Colgan 2002: 9–21). This, in turn, will require internal changes to systems of union government and management to give voice to women and minority workers (see Chapter 5). It will also require external change, such that unions pursue equal treatment or entitlement to diverse treatment in their political, legal, collective bargaining and servicing activity (see Chapter 7). If unions are to adapt effectively to a changing workforce, on this view, then they must undertake a twin reform to allow both the expression of diverse interests and intervene more effectively in the system of job regulation to ensure those interests are realised.

Response

Critics have developed two broad responses to societal models of union revitalization. On the one hand, they have attacked the presumed sequence of underlying change in economy and society, transformation of worker interests and adaptive union response. This line of attack, in turn, has generated three types of argument. First, it has been suggested that economy and society are more stable, and worker interests less fluid, than has been suggested. Thus, critics of partnership have pointed to the limited diffusion of high performance work practices and the continuing prevalence of traditional forms of work organisation (Danford 2003; Waddington and Whitston 1996; see also Chapter 8), while critics of the need to adapt to contingent work have pointed to the persistence of long-term employment (Rainnie 1998). It is incontrovertible that there has been a feminisation of paid employment and there is very broad acceptance of the need for unions to respond to this change. But some have questioned the distinctiveness of the interests of women workers with the implication that union form and function need not radically alter (Waddington and Whitston 1997: 534–5; Kelly 1990: 37). The hallmark of this critique therefore is that the core structural features of capitalist societies are relatively enduring and that as a consequence worker interests are relatively fixed and undifferentiated. Those who hold to this position often accept that unions must undergo a process of revitalisation but they do not accept that this must comprise a radical evolution of union form to cater to a rapidly changing set of worker interests.

The second position accepts the societal change argument but claims that its elements have been wrongly specified. Critics of the partnership thesis, in particular, have often advanced a radically different interpretation of the evolution of worker interests that stresses the degradation of work and erosion of employment standards (Upchurch and Danford 2001: 115; see also Chapter 3). Unions must adapt to change on this view but this requires the rediscovery of militancy to counter the imposition of new types of management control, characteristic of a malign phase of neo-Fordism (see Chapter 8). The third position shifts the focus of attention to union responses and holds that these arise from causes other than a functional adaptation to long-run economic or social change. Once again, this argument has arisen particularly in the response to the partnership thesis. Thus, Heery (2002: 24–5) has suggested that many formal partnership agreements represent a short-run adaptation to immediate crises of business performance, while for Kelly (1999) they have emerged from a cyclical process of employer counter-mobilisation. The essential point is that adaptive responses on the part of trade unions are seen to arise from immediate contingencies or cyclical processes rather than deep-seated, directional change.

The other response to societal models of union revitalisation emphasises cross-sectional variation. One version of this response emphasises variation within national economies. Thus, Roche (2000) in a commentary on theories of the 'new industrial relations' has questioned the coherence of recent change and averred that the dominant pattern is one of 'contingency as trend'; that is the increasing fragmentation of national systems (see also Katz and Darbishire 2000). For Roche, there is an increasing diversity in patterns of management and employment relations that reflects the variable exposure of sectors to the world economy. In some industries, the importance of competition based on quality and value-added can provide the basis for union revitalisation through partnership but elsewhere the material basis for this strategy is lacking. Essentially, this position rejects the implicit claim in much societal argument that there is 'one best way' to revitalise the labour movement and holds instead that there should be increasing variation in strategies of interest representation; that unions should become portfolio planners rather than repositories of best practice (see Jarley 2002: 228–33).

Another version of the cross-sectional critique stresses variation between national economies (Thelen 2001: 71–2). American proponents of the societal argument, in particular, have tended to use the single case of the US as a basis for making general claims about the evolution of worker representation in 'post-industrial' societies (e.g. Cobble 1991). The risk inherent in this method is that the particular can be mistaken for the general; that the challenges facing American trade unions may reflect a particular inheritance or institutional context that are not found elsewhere. The suggestion that representing contingent workers requires the re-creation of multi-employer bargaining may carry less force in countries that have never experienced the collapse of bargaining at this level; the suggestion that unions should represent diversity by pressing for improved conditions for part-timers may have less relevance in countries where there is better child-care and a higher proportion of women take full-time jobs. What this critique suggests is that the task of union revitalisation is, in part, specific to particular national contexts and it is this belief that lies at the core of the institutional models to which we now turn.

Institution

Institutional accounts of union revitalisation contend that unions must match their form and practice to the prevailing institutional context, usually though not exclusively within individual nation states. That context itself tends to be viewed as a structure of incentives, as providing a series of opportunities and constraints, which union representatives can read and to which they must adapt. Two main versions of this argument are current. The first suggests that union revitalisation rests on a successful adaptation to the immediate institutions of industrial relations, particularly the structure of collective bargaining. The second, in contrast, builds upon the 'varieties of capitalism' literature and argues that union strategic choices are constrained by the wider institutional forms of co-ordinated and liberal market economies. Particularly in this second current, it is assumed that the pattern of revitalisation must vary from national case to national case; that national union movements will differ in terms of the methods used to restore their fortunes. In some institutional contexts there may be a heavy reliance on organising to re-build membership and collective organisation but elsewhere, political action or renewed relations with employers may assume greater importance (Frege and Kelly 2003: 10–11). National institutions matter, in this line of analysis, and this implies a variable pattern of union revitalisation.

The first version of institutionalism found its classic expression in Clegg's (1976) argument that 'trade union behaviour' varied in accordance with the structure of collective bargaining. Union membership, structure, government, workplace organisation and strike activity, according to Clegg, derived from the distinctive pattern of bargaining that had emerged in each national economy. This line of reasoning has reappeared in the recent literature on union revitalisation, rather curiously, in the influential 'union renewal' thesis pioneered by Fairbrother (1996; 2000). In an analysis of public sector trade unionism in Britain, Fairbrother (2000: 323) has argued that the decentralisation of collective bargaining to workplace level can potentially stimulate the 'renewal' of trade unionism. This is so for two main reasons. First, under devolved bargaining the agenda of union representation is more likely to reflect the immediate concerns of workers and so provide a stronger basis for democratic participation and activism. Union renewal for Fairbrother comprises the re-creation of active workplace trade unionism. Second, and relatedly, decentralisation is likely to stimulate necessary union militancy because it provides an opportunity for workers who directly experience 'coercive social relations' (2000: 5) to vent their frustration. Under the preceding, centralised arrangements, in contrast, union activity was dominated by senior, paid representatives, who were themselves removed from alienating conditions of labour, and who favoured an accommodative or 'reformist' form of trade unionism. Decentralisation of bargaining, therefore, provides an opportunity for renewal, understood as the combination of a more combative union policy and a more participative form of union government.

If the renewal thesis stresses the opportunity afforded by institutional change, the second type of argument tends to emphasise constraints. A defining argument of the varieties of capitalism literature is that there is a pronounced synergy across the various institutional domains of each main form of capitalist society (Hall and Soskice 2001). In 'liberal market' economies, like Britain, there is a reinforcing logic that runs through modes of business finance, the institutions of corporate governance, corporate structures and strategies and systems of labour management (Gospel and Pendleton 2003). This logic embraces the short-term management of business assets and a bias towards arms-length, relatively adversarial relations, between financiers and business, between businesses and between business and labour. In 'co-ordinated market' economies, like Germany, in contrast these same elements display a different combination, which encourages management for the longer term and greater reliance on high trust relationships. Applied to the question of union revitalisation in Britain, this set of claims has supported the argument that union strategies will not succeed if they fail to match the prevailing institutional context. In particular, it has been argued that union attempts to revitalise by seeking more co-operative relations with employers will have limited success if other institutions, such as modes of business financing, promote short-term, adversarial relations (Heery 2002: 25–6). Partnership on this conception may only be fully capable of development in co-ordinated market economies, where there are appropriate institutional supports (Turnbull *et al.* 2005; Streeck 1992). In liberal market economies a more adversarial form of trade unionism may be better suited to the institutional environment, with attempts at revitalisation focused much more on building the collective capacities of labour through aggressive organising campaigns (Heery and Adler 2004).

Response

One response to institutional argument has been to accept its basic parameters but to suggest that the implications of a particular set of institutions for union revitalisation have been wrongly specified. Critics of Fairbrother's renewal thesis, for instance have suggested that devolved bargaining encourages adoption of narrow, economistic goals and hinders the co-ordination and cross-subsidy of union activities that is essential if unions are to reach out to new groups of workers (see also Heery 2003: 289–90; Terry 2000). It has also been pointed out that decentralised bargaining structures are associated with wider income inequality and a wider gender pay gap because they allow economic insiders to maximise returns to their bargaining power (Almond and Rubery 1998; Whitehouse 1992). One commentator's opportunity, therefore, can be another's constraint and there is continuing debate over the precise implications of bargaining structures for union behaviour and bargaining outcomes.

The second response to institutional argument has been to point to and seek to explain variation within a common institutional framework. The core propositions developed here are that institutional constraints may not prove absolute, may be susceptible to the influence of trade unions and other industrial relations actors who can help refashion their institutional context and that scope remains for strategic choice (Gospel and Pendleton 2003: 571–5). Formal and informal partnerships are a feature of enterprise employment relations in the UK (Oxenbridge *et al.* 2003: 324–6; see also Chapter 9), despite the seemingly inhospitable institutional context, and this raises the question of what conditions promote experiments of this kind. It may be that partnerships are likely to emerge in particular types of organisation, possibly in integrated businesses that are relatively immune from the threat of hostile takeover, which have a strong personnel function and an inherited management style that emphasises consultation. The structural characteristics and ideological character of the enterprise union might also be significant. Partnership may be found where the union is weak or dominated by an unrepresentative oligarchy (Taylor and Ramsay 1998) or where the influence of the wider union has altered the character of representatives (Samuel 2005) or developed their capacity to shape business restructuring (Frost 2001a). Whatever the precise feature that is identified, however, the key point is that within-system variation may be explained by reference to the internal structures of trade unions and the characteristics of representatives. It is to these variables that we now turn.

Organisation

The third type of union revitalisation argument identifies the reform of the system of union government as a central task. The aim is to shift the locus of control over union policy and decision-making, typically to allow the expression of hitherto neglected interests. The system of union government is viewed as a screen that can amplify or diminish the voice of competing groups within unions, whether these are rank-and-file members, paid officers, senior representatives, women workers or members of minority groups. If union government is reformed through changes in the formal structures of democratic participation or the union's management structures and processes then new voices will be heard, leading to an adjustment in policy and activity and a necessary revitalisation of trade unions. This argument comes in a number of different forms. In perhaps its classic, but still very influential form, there is a critique of oligarchic or bureaucratic control of unions by unrepresentative paid officials. In this version, a prerequisite for revitalisation is a challenge to oligarchic domination of unions, typically through the mobilisation of rank-and-file members. In a second, increasingly influential version there is a stress on the need to secure the articulation of different levels of union government, such that activity at workplace level is supported and co-ordinated through action at higher levels. In a third version there is an emphasis on the need for union government to represent diversity. The key features of reform that are advocated here, include strengthening the position of women and minorities in formal union democracy and the adjustment of union management systems to ensure the greater responsiveness of decision-makers to the interests of women and minority union members.

Critics of trade unions, from both left and right, have repeatedly made the argument that union behaviour, what unions do, is a function of union form, how unions are governed. The Conservative critique of trade unions in the 1980s rested on this kind of argument; that unrepresentative union leaders were engaging in militant or excessively political action, which was contrary to the interests and preferences of ordinary union members. The prescription that followed was that union government should be changed to allow greater member voice through the medium of secret ballots to determine the composition of union executives, strike action and the creation of political funds (McIlroy 1995: 169–71). More recently, left critics of labour–management partnership have developed an argument that possesses the same underlying structure. It is argued that partnership agreements are contrary to the interests of workers in that they have failed to secure notable improvements in terms and conditions and have often been the means through which business restructuring or the intensification of work has been effected. Given this mismatch between interests and activity, it is suggested that partnership must stem from a failure of union democracy and typically it is presented as the work of a detached hierarchy of representatives or paid officials, out of tune with rank-and-file members (Danford *et al.* 2002). On this line of argument, the revitalisation of unions requires a more militant policy and the rejection of partnership, which in turn requires member mobilisation and wider democratic participation. There is an obvious overlap here with the union renewal thesis outlined above: the devolution of bargaining gives an opportunity for renewal precisely because it allows union members more readily to control bargaining activity. Where this occurs, where the union hierarchy is dissolved in the membership, then a more combative policy, fully reflective of worker interests, can result (Fairbrother and Stewart 2003: 173–5).

For many left critics of union bureaucracy it is axiomatic that the 'development of more vibrant and participative forms of union…must come from within the workplace rather than from outside the union, from a political group, or from above, at the national level' (Fairbrother 1996: 142). A second position, however, suggests that revitalisation requires a closer integration of union activity at different levels and concedes a more significant role for the union centre in supporting, co-ordinating and, *in extremis*, controlling union activity at workplace level. The defining recommendation of this position is that the revitalisation of unions requires a closer articulation of union activity at different levels, particularly in liberal-market economies with a devolved pattern of industrial relations. Thus, Frost (2001a) has argued that the effective negotiation of work organisation at enterprise level requires local unions to be integrated into the wider organisation and able to draw upon the expertise of the union centre if they are to develop more than a reactive stance to management initiatives. Similarly, in the literature on union organising there has been a stress on the value of articulated national and local activity. Voss and Sherman's (2003: 69–74) research on organising locals in California, for instance, identifies a strong connection to the centre amongst those that have undergone the most thoroughgoing revitalisation. A feature of much of this work on articulation is an emphasis on management processes in providing the link between the union centre and its periphery. It is through union training, performance management and planning and review mechanisms that the centre supports and guides its constituent branches (Colling and Claydon 2000; Waddington and Kerr 2000; see also Chapter 7). Indeed, Heery *et al.* (2000a: 1004) have characterised recent organising initiatives in Britain as a form of 'managed activism', in that they use project management and human resource development techniques to develop an activist-based organising capacity at local level.

Where there is articulation there can also be contradiction and another feature of this position is preparedness to countenance central control of lower levels as a means of resolving intra-organisational conflict. Thus, in studies of organising in the US it has been observed that policy has led to the suspension of local unions that were opposed to increased investment in organising activity (Waldinger *et al.* 1998: 113). On this view, the national leadership of the union can embody a general interest (targeted in this instance on growing the union and drawing new groups into membership) and legitimately overrule representatives at lower levels who act to defend sectional interests. The privileging of interests that emerge and which are expressed at workplace level, which characterises the renewal model, here gives way to a greater recognition of the problem of sectionalism within unions. For the articulation school there is a stress on the need to forge and pursue a general interest at the centre of unions, on occasion, against internal opposition.

The third version of the union government argument emphasises the need to adapt systems of democratic participation and management to the interests of women and minorities. Some advocates of this position have drawn upon theories of union oligarchy and stressed the need for women workers to challenge a male-dominated bureaucracy (Healy and Kirton 2000: 343–7; see also Chapter 5). For others, there has been an overlap with the case for articulation, with commentators suggesting that progress towards equality requires greater co-ordination of union activity and a restraint of the autonomy of male-dominated bargaining groups (Colling and Dickens 2001: 151; 1998: 401). Whatever the precise form of the argument, however, there is a strong common emphasis on the need for 'internal equality' within unions, if 'external equality' is to be secured by collective bargaining and other interventions in the labour market (Dickens 1998). Internal equality itself is seen to be advanced through measures that reform formal union democracy, together with union management systems. There is an emphasis, that is, on measures that promote the election of women and members of minorities to representative positions with significant decision-making powers, together with management changes that include the appointment of women's and equality officers, the arrangement of training in equality bargaining for union negotiators and provision of group-specific training for women and minority activists (Greene and Kirton 2002; Colling and Dickens 2001: 139–43).

It is also generally believed to require measures that include 'radical' as well as 'liberal' equality initiatives, particularly to advance the interests of minorities (Kirton and Greene 2002: 171; Cockburn 1989). Liberal equality initiatives are defined in terms of the removal of barriers to equal participation in trade union activity by women and minorities and include provision of childcare and the scheduling of meetings to facilitate attendance, women- and minority-specific training to provide a basis for wider participation and gender and equality monitoring of union membership. Radical initiatives, in contrast, focus on equality of outcome and are designed to ensure that decision-making is exposed to new influences. Steps recommended include a commitment to proportionate representation for women and minorities in union structures, the creation of reserved seats on representative bodies and the establishment of dedicated committees and conferences with an input into union decision-making (Kirton and Green 2002: 159). A third theme that has come to the fore and which has shaped union government in UNISON is the principle of 'self-organisation', providing funding and support for women and minorities to devise their own form of organisation within the union while retaining a connection to the wider system of government (McBride 2000; see Chapter 5). This principle encompasses both liberal and radical conceptions of action in that self-organisation furnishes a supportive platform for women and minorities to participate in general union government, while also guaranteeing a degree of influence within union decision-making beyond the self-organised group.

Response

Central to all organisational versions of revitalisation is an assumption of a tight linkage between worker interests, union form or system of government and union behaviour; behaviour that is congruent with worker interests is dependent on an appropriate form of government that allows those interests expression (see Fairbrother 2000: 324–6). A common response accepts this basic framework but seeks to explain failings of union behaviour despite seemingly appropriate forms of government. Thus, Conservative critics of unions in the 1980s noted the failure of initial legislation to alter the character of union leadership and so pressed for further refinement of the individual balloting procedures that they favoured. The result was legislation that required unions to rely upon postal, not workplace ballots, despite the fact that the latter guaranteed a higher level of membership participation (see Undy *et al.* 1996: Ch. 4). Advocates of the renewal of trade unions through decentralised government and member mobilisation have similarly reacted to the failure of workplace militancy by noting the 'bureaucratisation of the rank-and-file' and the need to further renew workplace trade unionism by widening participation, collapsing hierarchies and generating fresh mobilisation against incorporated elements of workplace leadership as much as the external union (Hyman 1989; Beynon 1984: 371). Finally, feminist critics of gender-based participation have complained of tokenism or noted the limited impact of changes in government on the bargaining behaviour of unions (McBride 2001). The main response has been to call for the superseding of liberal forms with ever more radical systems of participation that will guarantee favourable outcomes. In this kind of 'internal' critique of union government, therefore, there is a prescription for the refining of union forms to permit the stronger expression of member voice and ensure that failings of union behaviour are eradicated. Union government is flawed on this view but never irremediably so and it is believed that a final reform can ensure union behaviour is fully reflective of members' interests.

Other responses depart from the underlying assumptions of the organisational model. It has been suggested, for instance, that there is no one-to-one relationship between worker interests and union form; that there is no essential system of governance that allows expression of workers' essential interests (Heery and Kelly 1995: 157–8). One implication is that there may be two or more ways of governing unions that allow an effective link to be made between the needs of union members and the behaviour of their representatives. The interests of women and minority trade unionists are seemingly advanced by a system of union government that promotes their activism and guarantees access to decision-making positions (Colgan and Ledwith 2002; Healy and Kirton 2000; see also Chapter 5), although it is recognized that such 'guarantees' may be thwarted by traditional cultures and practices. But they may also be advanced by 'union managerialism'; by market research into the preferences of niche union consumers and systems of human resource development and performance management that require paid officers to engage with these preferences (Heery 1996: 180–8). Seemingly very different activist and consumerist reforms of union government may combine therefore to ensure a change in union behaviour and they may both do these by opening up direct lines of communication between women and minority workers and union leaders that circumvent the traditional system of member participation.[1]

A second implication is that the contribution of a single form of government to the revitalisation of trade unions may vary over time or from context to context. A decentralised pattern of union government that accords wide autonomy to workplace unionism may facilitate member participation, lay activism and challenges to state incomes policy or employer-led restructuring in a context of full employment or sheltered product markets; arguably the situation in UK manufacturing in the 1970s. Where these conditions are absent, however, as they are in the present context, the isolation and weakness of workplace organisation may become apparent, leading to compliance and passivity: 'wildcat cooperation' not militancy (Heery *et al.* 2003: 104–5). Another source of variation may be the attitudes, ideologies and characteristics of union representatives. The reform of union government may facilitate the access of women trade unionists to positions of power. But individual women will use those positions differently depending on their ideology, connection to factions and in the light of their own experience (Colgan and Ledwith 1996; Ledwith *et al.* 1990). It is to a consideration of factors of this kind that we now turn.

Actor

Actor-centred models of revitalisation focus on the characteristics and attributes of union leaders and activists and contend that renewal is dependent on drafting in a fresh cohort of representatives who will behave differently. Once again, this argument comes in different forms though in all cases there is an underlying belief that unions have scope for strategic choice. There is a voluntarist assumption at the core of these models: the characteristics of leaders and activists matter because they influence the choices that are made (Heery 2003: 290–5; see also Smith 2001: 21–3, 189–95). Union leaders at all levels are believed to have the capacity to interpret their roles in an active sense, with major implications for the pattern and outcomes of union behaviour. And there has been a focus in research on the ideology, identity and experience of representatives, which are believed to underpin this interpretation.

Ideology has been the focus of the first, neo-Leninist, version of this argument. The key characteristic of union representatives that is identified in this formulation is whether or not they subscribe to a left-wing ideology, which in turn may be associated with membership of a socialist, communist or Trotskyist political party. In McIlroy and Campbell's (1999: 23) words, '[t]he activities of "politically motivated men" (and women) should be restored to the history of industrial relations' (see also Calveley and Healy 2003; Darlington 2001; 1998). The functions of such representatives have increasingly been discussed in terms of the mobilisation framework developed by Kelly (1998: Ch. 3; see also Darlington 2001; Gall 2001). Kelly identifies four primary tasks, all of which contribute to the mobilisation of workers in collective action. Leaders can promote a sense of injustice by attributing grievances to action by employers, promote group cohesion and identity, persuade workers of the benefits of collective action, such as striking, and, 'defend collective action in the face of counter-mobilising arguments that it is illegitimate' (Kelly 1998: 35). All of these actions are more likely to be taken by left union leaders because of their 'overtly ideological and solidaristic…commitment to trade unionism' (Darlington 1998: 70), that is, because of their left affiliation. They can contribute to revitalisation because it is an axiomatic belief of neo-Leninists that union militancy is the most effective means of protecting and advancing workers' interests (Darlington 2001; Kelly 1996a). If unions are to restore their fortunes, for these writers, they must re-build their capacity for collective action and this will require a prior strengthening of the traditional left and its activists.

Identity is the focus of the second version of the actor-centred argument. The core argument here is that revitalisation requires leaders who are more representative, particularly of the female and minority workers whom unions must increasingly attract into membership (Kirton 1999: 213; Kirton and Healy 1999: 31). It is representativeness that is the key characteristic of union leaders in this formulation; they must share the identity of those they seek to represent (see Chapter 5). Representativeness is considered important for several reasons. First, it is likely to shape the attitudes and behaviours of representatives themselves. Having women representatives or representatives drawn from minorities can 'make a difference' (Heery and Kelly 1988), in the sense that they are more likely to identify with those who share their characteristics and accord priority to their interests in their activities as organisers, bargainers and lobbyists. They are likely to be 'equality aware' (Colling and Dickens 1989: 32). Second, it may also shape the response to trade unions of those workers who are represented. Women and minority workers may be more likely to join unions if they are recruited on a 'like-to-like' basis. They may also be more likely to identify with unions if representatives are similar to themselves and more likely to become active if there are role models with shared characteristics (Kirton 1999). It follows that union revitalisation requires increasing the proportion of women and minority leaders at national, intermediate and workplace levels. In the well-known formulation of Colling and Dickens (1989: 32), if issues relevant to women (and minorities) are to appear 'on the table' then women (and minorities) have to be 'at the table', with the opportunity to negotiate on their own behalf. That relevant issues do appear on the bargaining table is important for the reasons advanced above; the feminisation of the workforce and the strengthening of diverse identities amongst the working population. Making union leaders more representative of the new, emerging workforce may therefore be a precondition of revitalisation.

The final version of the actor-centred argument emphasises the prior experiences of union representatives. The assumption here is that the values, beliefs and skills of representatives are formed largely before they assume their representative role and that altering the source of recruitment to representative positions will substantially shift the pattern of leader and activist behaviour. This argument comes in a variety of forms. Kelly and Heery (1994) have suggested that there are significant generational differences in the values and behaviours of union representatives, which reflect conditions during their initial socialisation into the labour movement. Their research on paid officers indicated that those who entered unions during the period of rank-and-file mobilisation in the 1960s and 1970s but who were studied in the 1980s, a period of labour retreat, were often more militant in their response to employers than the workers they were representing. Representatives in trade unions, as in other organisations, therefore, may be socialised into a particular 'strategic recipe' that is applied even in altered circumstances.

A more recent version of the argument has stressed the innovative role of activists recruited to representative positions from new social movements beyond trade unionism. For Turner (2003: 40–7), a critical element of the recent (partial) revitalisation of American trade unionism has been the infusion of activists from other movements who have displaced conservative officials and pushed the American Federation of Labor – Congress of International Organizations (AFL-CIO) and several major unions towards a greater focus on organising. Indeed, for Turner, mature social movements, like labour, can only revitalise themselves if they experience a transfusion of this kind; renewal must always involve fusion and learning from beyond the institutional frame of the labour movement. A similar argument has been developed at a lower level of analysis by Voss and Sherman (2003: 65–9) in their analysis of union locals in California. A distinguishing feature of revitalised locals, they report, was the presence in key leadership positions of activists with experience of other movements, such as community organising, Central American solidarity groups and anti-apartheid. These activists prompted revitalisation in several ways but two themes stand out. The first is that they brought a reinvigorated sense of movement to trade unionism, a passion and a commitment that was lacking in established, routinised bargaining and grievance-handling. Their contribution therefore has been to try and recreate trade unionism as a social movement: to 'put the move back in the labor movement'. The second theme has been their knowledge of new ways of organising, drawn from the campaigning upfront style of some of the new social movements. In other words, they have brought knowledge and skills to trade unionism and allowed unions to draw on the 'repertoires of contention' (Tarrow 1998: 20–1) developed by younger, fresher waves of protest.

Response

The primary response to actor-centred arguments has been to claim that structure trumps agency; that the autonomy and scope for choice of leadership and activist cohorts is limited (McIlroy 1997: 116–17). Thus, Charlwood (2004) has suggested that the election of a new set of left officials to leadership positions in British unions is unlikely to result in a return to militancy because the constraints of the environment in which they operate are too strong. He points to the failure to truly ignite of the firefighters' and postal workers' disputes of 2002–03 as signal examples of the limited capacity of ideological transition at the apex of unions to trigger change. A similar argument has been made by McBride (2000) in her critique of gender-democracy in UNISON. The increasing presence of women in representative positions, she argues, has had only a modest impact on the union's 'external' behaviour because an internal structural constraint – the insulation of largely male bargainers from the system of representative democracy – limits their influence. Arguably this type of critique of actor-centred models of renewal can be made from the vantage of any of the other three models. Changing the population of union representatives may fail to trigger revitalisation if the long-run trend in society and economy is running against trade unionism, if the institutional environment is hostile and if the internal structures and processes through which representatives operate have been subject to insufficient reform. Actor-centred arguments rest on a belief that leaders have scope for strategic choice but this invites sceptics to question that scope and point to limiting conditions.

More nuanced approaches recognise that it is the interrelationship between structure and agency that leads to the reproduction or transformation of the rules and resources that shape the conditions of work. For example, Healy and Kirton (2000) drew on the availability of power resources to consider the ways that women may challenge union oligarchy and Kirton and Healy (2004) provide evidence of particular conditions that may lead to passive union identities to become politicised. Equally, Kirton and Healy recognise that the context in which trade unionists work and live will be critical in enabling or constraining mobilisation. Within this approach, just as actors may be constrained, structures should not be viewed as determining.

Summary

We have suggested that four types of prescriptive model for the revitalisation of trade unions can be identified in current literature. However, while all four are strongly prescriptive – they suggest how the labour movement must change if it is to survive – they can also be presented as theoretical models from which a research agenda can be derived. The societal models, for example, suggest that new forms of union organisation will first be manifest at the leading edge, where there is strongest pressure on unions to adapt to changing worker interests. If the three examples outlined above are used then the following testable propositions can be derived: that partnership will be found and will work most effectively either in organisations that are exposed to global competition or in those applying high performance work practices; that unions will shift their locus of representation 'beyond the workplace' and seek to compensate for diminishing worker security when they are seeking to recruit or have a sizeable body of contingent workers in membership; and that unions will seek to represent diversity when their job territory is diverse. A second type of proposition can also be derived from this literature. The societal models have an evolutionary cast; underlying them all is the belief that unions face a selective pressure to develop new forms. What this suggests is that adaptation will be found where pressure is strongest. In other words that declining unions, or union movements facing crisis, will be most prone to innovate and develop new methods of representation, whether these rest on partnership, contingent work or diversity (see Chapter 6).

The institutional models suggest one of two things. The first is that change in trade unions will flow from change in the institutional environment. Fairbrother's renewal thesis has already been treated as a testable proposition in this way with authors seeking to establish the impact of devolved bargaining on union behaviour and vitality, with rather mixed results (e.g. Colling 1995). The second is that unfavourable institutional contexts will undermine non-concordant innovation. Work of this kind is best undertaken through comparative research and Turnbull *et al.*'s (2005) evaluation of partnership agreements in the British, Irish and German airline industries is a notable example. This research evaluates a common innovation in different institutional environments and suggests that experiments with partnership are more productive in co-ordinated, not liberal, market economies.

The research agenda that can be derived from organisational models focuses on the link between union government and union behaviour: is it the case that particular, desirable behaviours are associated with particular forms of government? In some cases this question has been pursued through evaluation of changes in union government or management systems, assessing their impact on other aspects of union activity. For the critical issue of gender and diversity this has taken the form of establishing whether changes in 'internal equality' generate further change in 'external equality', in union bargaining behaviour (e.g. Kirton and Greene 2002; McBride 2000). In other cases, research has focused on innovative behaviours, practical examples of union revitalisation, and traced backwards. The aim here has been to identify the systems of union government from which significant innovation has emerged (Heery 2004a). A focus on behaviour is also implied by the fourth, actor-centred model. The key issue here is whether union representatives with particular characteristics 'make a difference' in the sense of fulfilling their representative roles in significantly distinct ways. To date, both survey and qualitative research has been used to this end, seeking to establish the particular contribution to revitalisation of representatives with distinctive ideologies, identities and experiences (e.g. Calveley and Healy 2003; Voss and Sherman 2003; Healy and Kirton 2000; Darlington 1998; Colgan and Ledwith 1996; Heery and Kelly 1988; see also Chapter 6).

The empirical propositions that can be derived from the four types of model are, to a degree, competing. They each refer to a particular level of analysis and this raises the question of which is most important: is the revitalisation of unions determined critically by broad social and economic change, the institutional context, systems of internal government or the characteristics of representatives? Indeed, some of the core debates in industrial relations analysis have concerned the relative importance of influences operating at different levels. For example, there is an established and ongoing debate over the relative contribution of economic trends, the institutional framework and union strategy to the aggregate level of union membership (Mason and Bain 1993). But the four types of argument can also be seen as complementary and interrelated. Arguably any satisfactory programme of research into union revitalisation must proceed at all levels and consider the impact on unions of broad social change and institutional patterns, while also examining internally generated change arising from new forms of government or new cohorts of representative. Moreover, we believe the real task of revitalisation for unions must embrace action at all levels. Unions must engage, that is, with the changing nature of the workforce and pursue strategies that are congruent with the existing institutional framework. But as part of such engagement they should also pursue internal reform and draw in fresh cadres of activists.

Non-union representation

The decline of trade unions has generated interest in other institutions of worker representation (e.g. Osterman *et al.* 2001; Freeman 1995: 519–20; Chapter 5). Arguably, union decline has both created a need and furnished an opportunity for other organisations and movements to fill the representation gap and provide a fresh channel for representing workers' interests. Moreover, and in more speculative vein, it may be that long-run change in the composition and organisation of capitalist societies is leading to the fragmentation of the system of representation. A plurality of institutions may better match the requirements of a society, in which there are multiple and competing identities seeking representation at work, a cardinal theme in postmodern accounts of social change (see Kelly 1998: 114–16). They may also reflect a more disorganised phase of capitalist development (Lash and Urry 1987), characterised by the break up of encompassing and authoritative representative institutions of both capital and labour.

Whatever the precise cause and long-term significance of non-union representation, which are inevitably controversial, we feel the issue is worthy of systematic consideration by industrial relations researchers. In what follows we seek to assist this process by performing three preliminary tasks. The first is to map the range of non-union institutions of worker representation, using the UK as a source, and identifying the particular characteristics of different types of representative body. The second and third relate to the relationship between non-union institutions and trade unions. We consider in turn the argument that alternative institutions can replace trade unions and so act as barriers to their revitalisation and the contrary claim that revitalisation is dependent on unions forging alliances with other types of representative institution.

Types of non-union institution

It is possible to identify three broad types of non-union representative institution, distinguishing each in terms of their point of origin. There are bodies that seek to advance workers' interests that have been created respectively by employers, by the state and by NGOs and other voluntary bodies in civil society. In some cases these institutions are of long standing. There is a very long history, for example, of employers creating staff associations and establishing non-union consultative committees. In each type, however, there has been recent innovation with new organisations being created or established organisations assuming an expanded or more significant role. Both employment agencies and voluntary organisations, like the Citizens' Advice Bureaux (CAB), have become more significant labour market actors in recent years (see Chapters 11, 12). There is no authoritative research that demonstrates we are witnessing a shift from a union-based to a plural system of representation: it may be that union decline simply results in the decay of worker representation *per se*. But innovation suggests that change of this kind may be taking place and provides an additional reason for examining non-union institutions.

Employers have always created institutions of worker voice, often in response to a rising challenge from trade unionism (Ramsay 1977). Staff associations have been established as channels of communication within individual enterprises and non-union consultative forums remain common: indeed, the statutory recognition procedure introduced by the Employment Relations Act (ERA) 1999 has stimulated fresh use of bodies of this kind as employers try to forestall unionisation (Heery and Simms 2004: 6). According to the Workplace Employee Relations Survey (WERS), consultative committees are found in just under a fifth of non-union workplaces and in the private sector 58 per cent of workplaces without union representation report the presence of a non-union worker representative, up substantially from the 1980s (Gospel and Willman 2003: 151–2; Millward *et al.* 2000: 115). There have also been developments at the multi-employer level. While there has been a secular decline in employers' associations in recent decades there has been the emergence of issue-specific employer forums, several of which seek to promote the interests of identity groups within the workforce. *Opportunity Now* advocates the cause of gender equality within the business community, *Race for Opportunity* does the same for race equality and there is an *Employers' Forum on Age* and an *Employers' Forum on Disability*. A final type of institution that can be placed in the employers' camp, are labour market intermediaries, such as employment agencies. Clearly these are profit-seeking organisations whose primary orientation is to the needs of business clients but they do discharge a representative function for workers in certain respects. This is most obviously the case when specialist entertainment agencies or other agencies dealing with skilled workers, find work, negotiate pay and promote the careers of worker-clients (Purcell *et al.* 2004). Organisations of this kind serve the labour market needs of workers to the extent of bargaining on their behalf. Agencies may also deal with qualitative interests that arise in the labour process. According to Druker and Stanworth (2004: 66; see also Chapter 11), they can provide a degree of worker voice, resolving minor grievances that arise on work placements.

It is difficult to generalise about such a range of institutions but we believe that representative bodies created by or associated with employers are likely to display a series of characteristics. First, they are likely to have a unitarist rationale, emphasising the shared interests of workers and employers: the employers' forums for instance have emphasised the business case for equality at work (Dickens 2000b: 144). Second and related, they tend to promote integrative forms of representation, information-sharing and consultation, not bargaining. Third, the substantive agenda they promote may be relatively costless for employing organisations: encouraging equality for women and ethnic minority managers while neglecting inequality arising from low pay (Dickens 2000b: 153). Fourth, they are likely to advocate voluntarism and reject advancing worker interests through the closer legal regulation of business activity. Some of the employers' forums have advocated strengthening law and the larger employment agencies are happy to see legal regulation if it drives out low cost competition (Purcell *et al.* 2004). But generally, representation of worker interests through employer-created bodies is assumed to require no more than a voluntary response from employers themselves.

The second type of non-union institution consists of state-created representative bodies. In the UK there has been a marked increase in the number, and arguably the significance, of such institutions and the formal institutions of worker representation are moving towards the pattern seen in much of continental Europe, where trade unions exist alongside statutory works councils. Statutory institutions of worker representation can be classified along two primary dimensions. The first of these is the range of interests that they are allowed formally to represent and a distinction can be drawn between issue-specific representative bodies and those with a more general representative remit. Examples of the former in the UK include non-union health and safety committees and representatives, arrangements for consultation on collective redundancies and the provisions in the Working Time Regulations and Maternity and Parental Leave Regulations for the negotiation of 'workforce agreements' to provide for flexibility (see Chapter 10). Institutions that allow for more general representation include European Works Councils (EWCs) and the regulations that will shortly implement the 2002 EU directive on information and consultation in national undertakings. The latter will allow a system of statutory works councils to be established across UK business for the first time.

The second dimension relates to the powers of statutory institutions. State-created representative bodies may have complete control over certain issues (e.g. social programmes within the enterprise), a right of veto or codetermination over others (e.g. health and safety), a right to consultation (e.g. on collective redundancies) and a right to information (e.g. on business performance). The typical pattern is for councils to be given stronger rights when they deal with vital interests of workers (e.g. protection from hazardous working practices) or with interests that are of secondary concern to employers (e.g. provision of sports, leisure and welfare facilities). Their powers generally become more attenuated as the agenda of representation moves towards the vital interests of the employer and deals with business planning, performance and finance (Hyman 1996: 71). In the UK, general institutions of worker representation have been endowed with relatively weak rights of representation, restricted to information-sharing and consultation and have been denied the strong rights of codetermination seen in Germany. It remains to be seen, whether this will adversely affect their functioning as representative institutions.

What are the distinguishing features of statutory worker representation? Most obviously they confer rights upon citizens (unlike legislation that 'licences' the activities of voluntary bodies like trade unions) and, as such have universal coverage. Indeed, this principle of universality was established in the UK by a decision of the European Court of Justice (ECJ) in 1994, which ruled that Britain's transposition of the directive on collective redundancies was unlawful because it restricted rights of information and consultation to recognised trade unions (see Chapter 10). However, the principle of universality is qualified both in European and UK legislation. In particular, coverage by regulations is restricted by workplace or company size and the new rights to information and consultation are confined to undertakings with 50 or more workers. This threshold is regarded as high by many and as representing an unacceptable qualification of citizenship rights in the interests of 'flexibility'.

The traditional rationale for statutory participation has focused precisely on the question of citizenship and the need to extend democratic participation of citizens from the political to the economic sphere. Works councils have been viewed as institutions of industrial democracy. Increasingly, however, this democratic rationale has been supplemented by or even given way to a business case rationale. Workforce agreements that allow for the tailoring of working time and other regulations to the needs of particular companies are advocated because they allow flexibility and reduce the negative effect of state regulation. The final distinctive feature of statutory participation is that the representative institutions created are regarded as serving an integrative purpose. This can be seen in the pattern of issue-specific powers conferred on works councils and equivalent bodies, which seeks to balance the respective interests of employers and workers. It is also seen in the balancing of rights with obligations: works councils typically operate under a peace obligation and are charged with co-operating with the employer. There is a formal even-handedness underlying legislation of this kind, in which the (ideally) neutral state balances the respective and equally legitimate interests of worker-citizens and their employers.

The third type of non-union representative body comprises voluntary, charitable, mutual aid and other NGOs formed within civil society. There are many organisations of this type with an interest in employment relations, which display quite diverse characteristics (see Chapters 12, 13). They can be classified in a number of different ways. Thus, a distinction can be drawn between membership organisations, often created for purposes of mutual support, and advocacy organisations, which speak on behalf of an identifiable constituency but which rely on public and corporate donations and subventions from the state to undertake their representative function. Examples of the former include the Indian Workers' Association, small, local organisations that offer mutual support to those suffering from asbestosis and other conditions and the homeworking projects that provide advisory and other services to homeworkers under the framework of the National Group on Homeworking (NGH) (Gilbert 2002). There are many examples of the latter. The CAB is of this type (see Chapter 12) and there is a multitude of campaigning and charitable organisations that provide representation for particular groups of workers, including well-known organisations like Age Concern, Mind and Oxfam. Some organisations assume a hybrid form, in which services are provided to members but support is also derived from donations and grants. Examples include the London and Manchester Hazard Centres, the Maternity Alliance and the Institute of Employment Rights.

Another distinction can be drawn between organisations that are focused on the issue of employment and those which encompass it within a broader representative purpose. Thus, Lesbian and Gay Employment Rights (LAGER) is an advisory and representation service for lesbians and gay men that focuses specifically on discrimination and problems at work, whereas Stonewall has a much more general remit that covers all aspects of gay and lesbian identity, including employment. In the area of international labour standards a similar division can be seen. Oxfam campaigns broadly for the eradication of poverty and includes within its focus the protection of workers in developing countries and marginal employment. Labour Behind the Label has worked with Oxfam, for example, on a campaign to highlight the exploitation of workers manufacturing sports clothing in the run up to the 2004 Olympic Games (*The Guardian* 4 March 2004), but is an organisation focused specifically on the protection of clothing workers. A final distinction can be drawn between unitary organisations, like Oxfam, and federal organisations. Many campaigning organisations, such the Maternity Alliance and Labour Behind the Label are of the latter type: they have been created by a number of primary institutions, including charities and trade unions, to campaign on a specific issue, perhaps for a fixed period of time (see Chapter 13).

Because of their diversity it is difficult to specify the defining characteristics of voluntary representative organisations. However, one tentative generalisation relates to the levels at which they perform their representative role. Organisations of this kind very frequently provide services to individual workers, including distributing information, providing advice and representing workers before courts, tribunals and other types of hearing. In many cases this work is confined to workers belonging to a particular identity group or possessing a particular interest for which representation is required: gays and lesbians and those experiencing homophobic discrimination in the case of LAGER and Stonewall. Voluntary bodies also frequently represent worker interests at the level of the state and seek to obtain changes in government policy and legislation, relating to their specific constituency. Thus, both LAGER and Stonewall have advocated stronger legal protection for gays and lesbians and have supported this position through research, publicity and lobbying. Oxfam and other organisations with an interest in development have done the same for international labour standards, while the Maternity Alliance campaigns for stronger state support for working parents. There is a tendency to a bifurcated strategy of representation amongst voluntary organisations, therefore, that targets individuals on the one hand and government on the other (see Chapter 12).

This generalisation is not absolute, however, and it is possible to identify instances of voluntary organisations engaging in other types of representative work. For example, in some cases they seek to organise workers collectively, often on a particular issue or for a particular campaign (see Chapter 13). This is particularly apparent in mutual-aid organisations, such as those concerned with homeworking or industrial disease. Commitment to collective action may also include promoting trade unionism. In developing countries NGOs have sometimes played an important part in union-building (Rock 2001: 26–7) and in Britain groups like NGH have advocated union organisation for the workers they represent (Gilbert 2002; see also Chapter 13). Relations with trade unions may also embrace attempts to influence their policy and practice. A proportion of voluntary organisations target other institutions, including trade unions but also employers that are involved more directly in the formation and regulation of employment relationships. These efforts can include arranging training for managers and trade union representatives, providing advice and issuing model policies or standards of good practice. The whistle-blowing charity, Public Concern at Work, for instance, offers training and advice to employers (and trade unions) on the effective management of information disclosure. A final point at which voluntary bodies may seek to represent workers' interests is through public campaigns targeted at consumers. This has been a feature of recent Fair Trade campaigns, in which voluntary organisations have both used consumer pressure to influence employment practice in the supply chains of large, private sector firms like Adidas and Nike, and created new companies of their own to guarantee acceptable employment standards. The bifurcated pattern may be dominant therefore but breaks down in particular instances, depending on the nature of the organisation's mission and objectives.

A second area in which voluntary organisations may be distinctive is in terms of their conception of purpose. Compared with employer- and state-created bodies they are much more likely to regard themselves as partisan, as created to advance the interests of their constituency or membership rather than a putative general interest. LAGER and Stonewall are committed to securing justice and improved employment conditions for gays and lesbians: other interests such as those of employers are secondary. Again, however, there is variation. Public Concern at Work advises individuals on how to disclose information and may provide support in cases of victimisation. But it defines its mission in terms of promoting the public good through the effective management of information disclosure; an activity which it regards as benefiting all parties to the employment relationship. The Hazards Centres in contrast side much more definitely with the interests of workers: they exist to a large degree to improve health and safety through campaigns against bad employers (see also Chapter 13). Variation on this dimension, we feel, is likely to reflect the origins of voluntary organisations and the extent to which they have an institutional connection to the labour movement. The Hazards Centres are closely linked to trade unions and employ the discourse of trade unionism and share its conceptions of purpose. Public Concern at Work, in contrast, has emanated from the consumer movement and as a consequence is less 'unionate' in its ideology or activities.

Like most empirically derived typologies our classification of non-union representative institutions is fuzzy around the edges and, to a degree, the different categories overlap. Thus, voluntary organisations have worked closely with employer-led campaigns and, indeed Age Concern was involved in the creation of the Employers' Forum on Age (Duncan *et al.* 2000: 220) while Help the Aged is a member organisation. Many charities concerned with representing people at work (including the CAB) also receive subventions from the state. There is also overlap with the system of representation through trade unions. The Trades Union Congress (TUC) is also a member of the Employers' Forum on Age and individual unions receive funding from the state for a number of their activities through the Union Learning and Partnership Funds (see Chapter 7). In 2004, moreover, the UK Government announced the creation of a union Modernisation Fund, reflecting the role of unions in delivering a number of state policies. Finally, unions have co-operated with and are among the primary backers of many voluntary organisations that focus on employment. As we have seen not only the Hazards Centres but also LAGER, the Maternity Alliance, Labour Behind the Label and the Institute of Employment Rights are voluntary organisations which rest on union support. This overlap raises the question of alliance-building and the extent to which union and non-union institutions of representation complement one another. First, however, we wish to consider the alternative view; that alternative institutions pose a danger to unions and threaten to supplant their representative role.

Replacement

The replacement thesis has been developed in two main versions. On the one hand, advocates of replacement of unions by new institutions have argued that unions are deficient vehicles of representation, at least for some groups within the workforce. On this line of argument, the emergence of new institutions of representation represents a functional adaptation to the (changing) interests of workers and is both necessary and desirable. On the other hand, defenders of single-channel representation through unions have questioned the effectiveness of non-union institutions. The argument here is that unions are independent institutions that have been developed by working people and are the best means to promote their interests. Alternative institutions of representation, in contrast, have been created by other actors in the employment system and operate frequently against the interests of workers; they exist primarily to serve other, contradictory objectives.

An example of the first type of argument can be found in the work of Crain and Metheny (1999). Its starting point is an observation that unions have often failed to deal with, and indeed been complicit in, sexual and racial harassment by co-workers. In the US this has led to a recurrent pattern in cases of this kind, in which:

> ...the victim complains directly to the employer, causing the employer to take disciplinary action against the harasser. The union then often files a grievance on behalf of the harasser protesting the discipline, and the victim becomes the key witness for the employer. Thus, the common scenario finds the female victim of discrimination or harassment pitted against her union and her co-worker harasser(s), and represented by a nonlabor group, by the EEOC [Equal Employment Opportunities Commission], or by the employer itself. (Crain and Metheny 1999: 1553)

Harassment, it is further argued, is a manifestation of deeper conflicts of interest and intra-class exploitation that are masked by trade unionism and the 'united front' ideology on which it rests. It follows that greater scope must be allowed for women and minorities to form their own separate organisations, even their own unions, or rely upon non-union, identity groups to advance their interests at work. In the US context, in which the argument has been made, this further requires the reform of American labour law to remove the principles of majority rule and exclusive representation for majority unions that form part of the Wagner Act framework. Crain and Metheny are not antagonistic to trade unionism *per se* but they envisage a multi-institution framework of worker representation that allows greater scope for non-union organisations to represent and bargain on behalf of competing interests. This is necessary, they contend, if the interests of those who need representation most, women and ethnic minority workers, are to be advanced.

An example of the second kind of argument can be seen in Kelly's (1996b) critique of works councils. Unlike other evaluations of statutory worker participation, this is developed explicitly from the perspective of employees and unions and is concerned with the capacity for works councils to fill the 'representation gap' in the UK labour market. Kelly argues forcefully that they will not. He points to the weak, largely consultative powers of works councils, which are likely to be particularly apparent in Britain, questions whether employers will embrace councils and work co-operatively with them and sees them as bearers of a debilitating ideology of social partnership. The latter is believed to be particularly harmful in a context of employer militancy and will help undermine the vigorous defence of workers' opposed interests through trade unionism. Kelly also feels that works councils may forestall union revitalisation: 'if ... there were a recovery of union membership and militancy, it would be utter folly to derail such a movement by colluding with employers in the promotion of weaker forms of worker representation' (1996b: 60).

Both of these versions of the replacement thesis have drawn responses from critics and there is a continuing debate over the relationship between trade unions and other forms of interest representation. Thus, Selmi and McUsic (2002) have replied to the call for separate organisation for women and minorities by arguing that this directs attack away from the primary source of oppression at work, the employer, divides labour's house and neglects the scope for the internal reform of trade unions to embody a more inclusive conception of solidarity. For Selmi and McUsic the need to recognise and represent diverse interests implies the kinds of union revitalisation strategy described above; not separatism.

Kelly's critique of works councils, for its part, has elicited a response from Hyman who has suggested that statutory participation may offer the, 'least-worst option for British unions' (1996: 62; see also Chapter 10). Central to Hyman's argument is the belief, based on the experience of councils in Germany that unions can operate effectively through systems of statutory participation, which provide them with access to the workplace. For a weakened union movement, like Britain's, statutory support for collective organisation may be necessary to help unions gain a foothold in companies from which they previously have been excluded. They provide a means of requiring employers to respond to worker representatives when unions lack the power to ensure this response themselves. Hyman also makes the point that works councils are often reliant on unions: they require the expertise, network and supporting ideology that unions can bring to their operation in order to become effective. In other words, the two types of institution can achieve a concordant, not competitive, relationship.

Complementarity

Hyman's argument is a variant of the complementarity thesis; that unions can work co-operatively with other institutions of representation to mutual advantage. This argument also comes in a number of different variants. First, it can be argued that unions and non-union institutions fulfil distinct functions and represent discrete, non-overlapping interests of workers. Thus, it has often been suggested that the dual channel of representation in continental Europe through works councils and trade unions, allows the pursuit of integrative, co-operation with management at one level and the pursuit of distributive goals through collective bargaining at another (Clegg 1976: 83). The two institutions of representation allow workers to follow different, non-competing aims. Another example of this division of labour can be seen in union backing for voluntary and campaigning organisations. The latter may permit unions to address issues that extend beyond their core competence of bargaining and representation at work, such as environmental protection or international labour standards, through organisations that have greater legitimacy, expertise or are better suited to the work of campaigning or lobbying. The essential point is that the different types of representative institution are used to serve different purposes.

Second, it has been argued with increasing frequency that unions and other forms of representative institution can form alliances or coalitions (Clawson 2003: Ch. 4; Ledwith and Colgan 2002: 20–1). Labour–community coalitions have been an important feature of the recent wave of living wage campaigns in the US and, more latterly, Britain (see Chapter 13) and coalitions have also been formed in the context of industrial disputes, union organising, anti-globalisation and anti-sweatshop campaigns (Frege *et al.* 2004). In the latter cases, unions' coalition partners, in the US, have often been student organisations, reflecting a new wave of campus radicalism. But unions have also worked with faith, community, ethnic and consumer organisations. The defining feature of coalition is that unions and their partners engage in joint working, perhaps under the shadow of an umbrella or federal campaigning organisation. The relationship therefore goes beyond working in parallel to embrace working in concert.

The purposes of coalition are various. In part, coalition reflects a change in union goals and a greater convergence of goals with those of new social movements. As unions have responded to pressure to represent new social identities within their own ranks so they have been drawn to co-operate with external bodies that are also concerned with representing the interests of women, ethnic minorities, older, disabled and gay and lesbian workers (Frege *et al.* 2004). Coalition also arises because unions and other organisations may be able to exchange resources: the different types of institution have distinctive but complementary competences. For unions, for example, the benefits of coalition with voluntary organisations include access to the following resources: expertise, physical and human resources, connection to new constituencies, capacity to mobilise social protest, and legitimacy (Frege *et al.* 2004). Working in coalition is one way in which unions can sidestep the perception that they are a non-legitimate special interest.

Third, it has been argued that unions and non-labour organisations can go beyond coalition to create a more symbiotic relationship, in which there is an effective fusion of the two types of institution. Hyman's defence of works councils points to this kind of relationship. In Germany, he argues works councils and trade unions have become integral to each other's operations. Unions 'capture' works councils by winning elections and thus acquire a presence (with associated legal supports) in the workplace. Works councils, for their part, rely upon the support of unions, their expertise, training and networks, to function effectively as organs of representation. Another example of this kind of overlapping relationship might be the entry of new social movements into trade unions, where they participate in union politics and act effectively as pressure groups seeking to tilt union policy towards the needs of their constituencies. Unions, in turn may benefit from this relationship by acquiring a line of connection to groups who previously stood outside labour's ranks but whom unions now need to organise. The relationships between unions and the women's movement (and its associated organisations) and more recently gays and lesbians and organisations of the disabled, arguably provide models.

There is very broad support for the complementarity thesis amongst academic commentators on trade unions at present that arguably reflects the increasing receptiveness of unions themselves to working with non-labour organisations (Heery 1998). There is also recognition, however, particularly in the literature on coalitions, that co-operation with non-union bodies can prove difficult. The relationship between unions and environmental, feminist and development organisations has often been fraught, reflecting the fact that the interests of these movements may overlap with those of unions but are not the same. Stronger environmental protection or fairer access to and treatment at work may impose costs on union members and the ethos, culture and forms of practice of single-issue campaigning bodies are often alien to trade unions. These problems can be overcome and there are many instances of successful labour–community coalition (Clawson 2003: Ch. 4; see also Ch. 13). It may also be, however, that the most enduring coalitions emerge when they deal with issues that are relatively remote from the core interests of trade unions and their members. Joint work, that is, may be easier to develop when issues have relatively low salience.

Summary

In this section we have described some of the main forms of non-union institutions of worker representation and reviewed the debate over the relationship between these institutions and the trade union movement. As with our review of the theme of union revitalisation, the focus has been on prescriptive argument, on the case made for unions working with or avoiding entanglement with non-union bodies. Again, however, we believe that the review also sets out a research agenda. One line of inquiry that we feel should be pursued with some urgency is to carry out a fuller mapping of the different forms and functions of non-union worker representation. The WERS series has allowed this to be done for employer-created representative institutions that operate at workplace level (Gospel and Willman 2003). But there is a need to look in greater detail at non-workplace and non-employer created bodies, particularly the very large group of campaigning and voluntary organisations that now have an interest in the employment relationship. Part of this mapping exercise could usefully look at trends over time: is it the case that we are moving towards a more pluralistic system of worker representation and, if so, what are the causes of this development? Answering this question would allow employment relations researchers to connect with a much wider range of social theory that is concerned with social identity and its transformation.

A research agenda can also be constructed from the competing arguments about union relationships with non-labour organisations. Both the replacement and complementarity theses are ripe for empirical testing, we feel, for different types of issue and different types of non-labour body. As part of such a test, it may be possible to identify the conditions under which productive coalition or ruinous rivalry, emerge. Already American scholars have engaged with questions of this kind and, for example, have identified the key role of 'bridge builders' who link unions with non-labour campaigns (Rose 2000; Brecher and Costello 1990). More work of this kind is needed. The UK appears to be moving very definitely towards a dual system of worker representation based on statutory works councils and trade unions and it is vital that researchers identify the patterns of interaction and effects of these two types of institution (see Chapter 10). There is also a particular need to research the relationship between unions and voluntary organisations. An overdue feature of recent work on trade unions has been the greater emphasis on questions of equality, diversity and identity (e.g. Ledwith and Colgan 2002). Developing this theme, we believe, of necessity implies looking in detail at the relationship between unions and specialist, non-labour bodies that offer representation to workers on these issues.

Contributions

The 12 empirical chapters that follow fall into four clusters. The first cluster consists of chapters that examine the issue of union revitalisation by examining the prospects for unionisation amongst three groups of workers who are often seen as emblematic of the 'new economy'. Jeff Hyman, Cliff Lockyer, Abigail Marks and Dora Scholarios report research into the attitudes to work and trade unionism of software workers. Peter Bain, Phil Taylor, Kay Gilbert and Gregor Gall perform the same task for call-centre workers but also examine recent attempts at union organising in call centres. And Mick Marchington, Jill Rubery and Fang Lee Cooke assess the efficacy of partnership and organising approaches to the representation of workers who work across organisational boundaries; temporary workers and sub-contractors.

There is rather scant encouragement for those who hope for union revitalisation in any of this first set of chapters and in combination they underline the scale of the challenge facing unions in Britain. The bleakest prospect is found in Hyman *et al.*'s chapter on software workers for whom unionisation is low and declining, who display little commitment to collective action and who, in many cases, have the human capital to navigate the labour market successfully as individuals. Amongst call-centre workers, in contrast, support for unionisation is quite high and there is a solid core of unionised workers in call centres established by unionised firms. But Bain *et al.*'s study points to the weakness of union organisation and identifies powerful structural constraints (e.g. tight management control and high labour turnover) on union-building. Finally, Marchington *et al.*'s study of workers in multi-agency environments questions the relevance of attempts at revitalisation that seek either to build partnership with the employer or build effective organisation through aggressive organising, because both are predicated on continuous employment in a single enterprise.

Despite attesting to the difficult context faced in the new industries, the authors of all three chapters point to opportunities for trade unions. These are construed differently in the different cases, however, and what emerges from the group of studies is the likelihood that there is no single route to union revitalisation but that, strategies of organising and representation, have to be tailored to the structural properties of different forms of employment (see Jarley 2002: 228–33). Thus, Bain *et al.* argue forcefully that the thorough application of an organising model is required to unionise call centres. Hyman *et al.*, in contrast, recommend labour market organising and the need for unions to develop forms of representation that are appropriate to the needs of mobile workers, many with significant human capital, who may value support in maintaining their skill set and finding employment. Chapter 4 by Marchington *et al.* also recommends organising at the level of the labour market but stresses that a basic requirement for this to occur is a change in the structure of employment law, which currently licenses and largely confines union activity to the workplace (see also Heery *et al.* 2004a).

If the starting point for the first cluster of chapters is to examine workers, the starting point for the second cluster is to examine unions and their policies and practices. In Chapter 5 Geraldine Healy, Harriet Bradley and Nupur Mukherjee examine the activities of black and minority ethnic women trade union activists against the background of broader attempts by unions to represent a more diverse workforce. In Chapter 6 Edmund Heery, Hazel Conley,

Rick Delbridge, Melanie Simms and Paul Stewart look at attempts by unions to accommodate the interests of workers in non-standard employment, including part-timers, agency workers, freelances and those on fixed-term contracts. Finally, Anne Munro and Helen Rainbird use a case study of UNISON to examine union responses to the lifelong learning agenda and examine the newly established role of Union Learning Representative.

This group of chapters intersects with the wider debate on union revitalisation at a number of points. The chapters by Healy *et al.* and Heery *et al.* are concerned with tracing union responses to what are often seen as significant long-term shifts in the labour market, an increase in diversity and the growth of contingent work. All three chapters, moreover, examine the response of unions to a changing institutional context and trace developments in union policy and practice to the changing opportunity structure afforded by state policy. This is particularly marked in Chapters 5 and 7. Union engagement with the interests of black and ethnic minority workers has been stimulated by the Stephen Lawrence Report (MacPherson 1999) and the subsequent amendment to the Race Relations Act. Unions' increasing engagement with workplace learning has stemmed from developments in training policy and the growing propensity of the state to use trade unions as agents of policy delivery in this area through the Union Learning Fund and other initiatives (Ludlam and Taylor 2003: 736). In both cases, the opportunity afforded by the state has accentuated processes of functional specialisation in trade unions, seen most graphically in the creation of the new roles of Union Learning Representing and, in UNISON, Lifelong Learning Advisor (LLA).

All three chapters in this group emphasise the link between internal, organisational change within unions and the development of 'external' policies. They stress the interconnection between both sides of the union representation process. All three also emphasise the importance of articulation and the need for developments at workplace level to be supported by changes at higher levels in trade unions. Thus, in Chapter 5 there is a stress on the importance of self-organisation and union-wide networks in providing support for activists from black and minority ethnic groups, while in Chapter 7 there is a very strong emphasis on the need for Union Learning Representatives to be integrated with the wider union. This is vital, it is argued, if the work of these representatives is not to fall under the sway of management and if the learning and training policies they develop are to reflect the independent development needs of workers, as opposed to the training needs of employers. Finally, Chapters 5 and 6 emphasise the identity of union representatives and the fact that individual differences influence the way in which representative roles are performed. In Chapter 5, in particular, evidence is presented of the important part played by black and minority ethnic activists in promoting trade unionism within their communities and in challenging racism at work.

The third cluster of chapters deals with the vexed question of labour–management partnership. A critical take on partnership is offered in the chapter by Andy Danford, Mike Richardson, Paul Stewart, Stephanie Tailby and Martin Upchurch. Their chapter dissects an experiment in labour–management partnership in the aircraft industry and states trenchantly that partnership works against the interests of workers and union. Their conclusion echoes that of Kelly (1996a) that the restructuring of employment in the context of globalisation requires militant trade unionism, not partnership, because the scope for shared interests between employer and employee is diminishing. Sarah Oxenbridge and William Brown adopt a more favourable position in Chapter 9. Their evaluation of partnerships in a number of organisations identifies two broad clusters: there are 'shallow' partnerships, often in the service sector and inscribed in a formal partnership agreement, and more 'robust' relationships, which are also often informal (see also Kelly 2004). Although Oxenbridge and Brown believe that partnership can offer a means to revitalise unions they offer a nuanced position. Even in successful partnerships, they argue, union representatives can be placed in a difficult position because the benefits to the union of co-operation with management may be relatively intangible while workers have to surrender significant concessions.

The final cluster of chapters deals with representation through non-union institutions. In Chapter 10, Mark Hall and Mike Terry review the evolution of statutory forms of worker participation in Britain since the 1970s and provide an assessment of the likely impact of the new regulations on informing and consulting workers, which give effect to the Information and Consultation Directive 2002. In Chapter 11, Jan Druker and Celia Stanworth examine the activities of employment agencies and use original research to assess the extent to which they represent the workers they place with client organisations. In Chapter 12, Brian Abbott presents a novel assessment of the work of the CAB and, again, seeks to identify the specific characteristics of, and evaluate, its role in representing people with workplace problems. Finally, in Chapter 13, Jane Wills examines the East London campaign for a living wage and argues strongly for this kind of community-based coalition to advance the interests of the most marginalised and exploited workers in Britain's urban labour markets.

All four of these chapters have something to say of relevance to the replacement and complementarity theses. The case for replacement emerges strongest from Druker and Stanworth's chapter which, again, makes uncomfortable reading for those who espouse union revitalisation. The authors are under no illusion with regard to the partial and compromised nature of the 'representation' agencies afford to the workers they place in employment but they do describe a process of grievance-handling which contributes to the very low level of demand for union membership identified amongst the agency workers they researched. Their findings echo the results of other research which has pointed to the effect of employer-sponsored voice in damping demand for union representation (Fiorito 2001; Rundle 1998). The other three chapters offer more hope for complementarity. The East London living wage campaign has been developed with the active support of trade unions and Wills argues that involvement in campaigns of this kind offers an opportunity for unions to engage with the interests of contingent, low-paid workers. Abbott similarly describes joint working between the CAB and trade unions and argues that the representation-work of both institutions serves different constituencies and can be regarded as operating in parallel to a very large degree. Finally, Hall and Terry argue that the new works council legislation offers an opportunity for British unions to rebuild influence within the economy and can reinforce other initiatives that seek to develop labour–management partnership. Albeit in different ways and with different emphases these chapters make the case for a pluralist system of worker representation based on trade unions interacting positively with non-union institutions.

Employment relations research in Britain is now largely concentrated in business schools and with few exceptions the contributors to this volume are business school academics. Unlike other subjects taught in business schools, however, employment relations has never accepted the primacy of employer interests or framed its research agenda solely in terms of the needs of managers. The separate and equally legitimate interests of workers have always provided an alternative starting point. This can be seen very definitely in the present volume. The representation of the interests of workers has always been and must always remain central to the subject of employment or industrial relations. In the real world of work, however, that task of representation is undergoing significant change marked by the decline of trade unions, attempts at their revitalisation and the seemingly increasing significance of non-union institutions. Our book we feel is true to the established concerns of the field of employment relations. But it also reflects this changing context and in this way, we hope, points to the future.

Acknowledgement

We would like to thank William Brown for helpful comments on this chapter.

Note

1. However it may be that these reforms emerge from and require the continued mobilisation of women and minority activists if they are to be sustained. They do not emerge in a vacuum (McKenzie 2003; Healy and Kirton 2001). The agency of particular union members and activists in challenging and sometimes changing union form and structure should not be underplayed.

2
Needing a New Program: Why is Union Membership so Low among Software Workers?

Jeff Hyman, Cliff Lockyer, Abigail Marks and Dora Scholarios

Introduction

In the near 600 pages of Castells' seminal *The Rise of the Network Society*, two meagre paragraphs are devoted to trade unions. In the first, they are dismissed as being too institutionally enfeebled in their representational and organising capacities to respond effectively to organisational restructuring strategies and in the second, as victims to the ability of information technologies to 'assemble and disperse labor on specific projects and tasks anywhere, anytime...' (2000: 301–2; see also Dawson 2003: 143–5). Software workers could help develop and apply the information technologies to support organisational plans for workforce dispersal and fragmentation which in turn may influence prospects for employee collectivisation. Nevertheless, we know very little about the identification of this rapidly expanding and highly strategic section of the workforce towards management or their orientations and behaviour towards trade unions and unionisation. We do know though that union membership among software workers is low and declining. This chapter draws upon data collected from five software companies located in the central belt of Scotland in order to examine the orientations and experiences of software workers toward trade unions. For, whether union members or not, we know very little about the overall predispositions of these workers to trade unions and as a growing occupation, located firmly in the 'knowledge economy', these may be able to provide valuable indications for future union vitality.

We can identify two main interlocking organisational dimensions with regard to union behaviour. The first of these is the character of the employees themselves and their orientations, attitudes and propensities towards unionisation and relationships with management. In this chapter we explore these attributes and also enquire whether there may be alternative foci to trade unions for software workers in terms of their work identification and cohesiveness as an occupational grouping. The second dimension covered in this chapter concerns employers and the extent to which they can influence the behaviour of software employees.

In terms of employee characteristics, software workers represent a particularly fascinating and important group of workers to explore in terms of their behaviour towards unions. They represent an expanding cohort of so-called knowledge workers in the UK and other countries, many possessing considerable latent power through their proximity to and involvement with electronic means of production and accumulation. An early study of technical workers' unionism by Smith (1987) provides evidence that computer personnel possess at least some of Batstone *et al.*'s (1978) four potential sources of industrial power, namely: skill scarcity, strategic position, immediate impact on production and potential to create uncertainty (Smith 1987: 104). Other writers, however, have hinted that software workers are no less immune to management pressures to routinise and Taylorise their work than are any other group of skilled workers (Beirne *et al.* 1998; Kraft and Dubnoff 1986). Software workers also enjoy familiarity with information technology, an increasingly effective tool in organising union membership both in the US (Fiorito *et al.* 2002) and the UK (Diamond and Freeman 2002).

Employer influences on patterns of union membership may be described as structural or behavioural. Structural factors include size of enterprise and the sector in which it is located. There appears to be a direct relationship between size of enterprise and union membership. Whilst many work for large organisations, both in the private and public sectors, considerable proportions of software workers are employed in small- and medium-sized enterprises (SMEs) (ONS 2001) not generally regarded as fertile ground for union recognition and activity (Hyman, R. 1991; Cully *et al.* 1999: 109). The behavioural context in which employee orientations and propensities are nurtured is also highly relevant. Historically, levels of union recognition and membership in an organisation have been directly associated with employer strategies and policies (Bain 1970).

This chapter therefore raises a number of research issues regarding software workers and their attitudes towards unions which we intend to explore through five case study companies. This approach allows us to examine perspectives of both employees and employers and especially to note factors which encourage or inhibit expressions of collectivism among software workers. Following a brief review of employment and union membership trends in the sector, the literature pertaining to each of these factors will be outlined, following which the chapter will present an analysis of software workers derived from the case studies.

Growth of software work – falls in union density

Software has been the largest global knowledge-based industry, with the European software market, at least until 2001, growing at about 10 per cent annually (Ramsay 1999). In the UK, according to the Labour Force Survey (LFS), between 1996 and 2000 the numbers of economically active core software occupations (including computer systems managers, software engineers and computer programmers/analysts) rose by 39 per cent to 726 200. The rapid growth between 1996 and 2000, compared to an increase of 2 per cent in the economically active population, prompted major Government polices to alleviate skill shortages and a number of measures, including simplifying the allocation of work permits to non-EU software workers, were introduced. Disaggregating these figures, during the same period, the numbers of software engineers in the UK virtually doubled to just under 200 000. Numbers of computer systems managers and computer analysts also grew, though not quite so spectacularly. The largest growth was found in the general 'business services' sector, which employed over two-thirds of software engineers by the year 2000.

In Scotland, where the present study was conducted, the rate of growth was even higher at 15 per cent annually during the late 1990s. The sector employs around 25 000 and contributes £1.4 billion to the Scottish economy (Scottish Enterprise 2001). Although Scotland has a growing software industry, there are few large indigenous firms. Approximately 38 per cent of all software employees in Scotland are employed in indigenous software firms the largest of which employ about 200 people. The remaining workers are employed within autonomous software divisions of large organisations (45 per cent), are sole traders (2 per cent), and individual contractors (15 per cent). It is predicted that by 2005 there will be 50 000 software professionals in total employed within Scotland. Notwithstanding current fluctuations, software is clearly a long-term growth industry.

Whilst software employment has increased over the past five years, and in some cases substantially, union membership growth has been virtually static and as a proportion of the employed software workforce, has actually declined. Between 1996 and 2000, whilst LFS data indicates an overall increase of 14 000 in union membership amongst software workers the percentage of those organised fell from 16 to 12 per cent, with the proportions organised ranging from 5 per cent of software engineers to 15 per cent for computer analysts. However, of the 14 000 additional union members almost 11 000 were in the public sector.

Trade union density amongst the software occupations in the private sector fell from 13 per cent in 1996 to 8 per cent in 2000. In contrast, union density amongst software staff in the public sector remained resilient, easing only slightly from 42 per cent in 1996 to 40 per cent in 2000. However, whilst the proportions organised among computer systems managers and computer analysts/programmers remained virtually unchanged, union density amongst software engineers fell from 44 to 31 per cent (all figures from LFS Autumn 1996; 2000).

Again disaggregating, LFS data indicate that for the UK in 1996, slightly fewer than 10 000 software engineers were union members, representing approximately 10 per cent of the employed software labour force. By 2000, absolute numbers of union members declined very slightly, but during this time, the overall numbers of engineers doubled, thereby reducing union density to a mere 5 per cent. Either software engineers were not joining unions or alternatively there has been rapid membership turnover during this period.

Software jobs and alternatives to collectivisation

Whilst we know that union membership among software workers is low, there is considerably less agreement about possible reasons. In general terms, professionally related occupations have been problematic groups for explanations of white-collar union trends since the 1960s (Bain *et al.* 1973; Bain 1970). These explanations of white collar and professional trade union membership have traditionally combined mainly structural and attitudinal factors. Trade union legislation together with government economic and employment policies are identified as the defining factors in the increasing union membership trends in the 1970s and, together with sectoral restructuring, the sustained decline in membership in the 1990s. Following from the political policies of the 1980s, attention has been directed, particularly within the labour process debate (Kelly 1998: 20), towards the policies of employers as a second structural influence (see Kelly 1998: 43). These include reduced or restricted patterns of union recognition, growth of small greenfield sites where union presence is unwelcome (and from the union perspective, difficult to organise), preference for alternative representative arrangements, such as staff associations as in some parts of the financial services sector, and in establishing and consolidating unitarist techniques such as employee share schemes and performance related pay. A further set of structural factors has focused on the characteristics of the sector and workforce, with higher levels of union membership associated with large establishments, public sector employment, long established sectors and workplaces in which other groups of employees are organised, and with older rather than younger employees.

The influence of attitudinal factors towards trade union membership has proved more difficult to categorise. The dominant and mainly institutional approach has been to link social status, images of society and the orientations of employees themselves to collective institutions and behaviour. Writing in the 1960s Goldthorpe, Lockwood and their colleagues noted the non-unionised images of non-manual workers (Goldthorpe *et al.* 1968: 146). Kochan's (1980) behavioural model attempted to link employees' satisfaction with pay, working conditions, the utility of non-union voice mechanisms and attitudes to the union's ability to affect pay and conditions with employees' perceptions of the 'utility' of union membership versus individual action. Though this model may be accused of oversimplifying both motivational and identity issues it does offer scope to identify the principal influences on patterns of union membership. In the 1990s Kelly's ambitious model drew on Tilly's (1978) mobilisation theory to integrate employee interests, organisation, mobilisation, opportunity and different forms of action (Kelly 1998: 25).

Attitudinal explanations for union decline are perhaps the most contentious, and the question of the orientations of employees to collective institutions and behaviour forms a central focus of our enquiry in this chapter. Bradley and her colleagues present the issue in stark terms: 'the extent of the decline in membership raises the question of how far the weakening of trade unionism is an expression of broad social change, especially the shift away from class-based collectivism towards greater societal individualism' (2000: 155). This raises further questions on the meaning and character of collectivism, which is still heavily disputed. In its more radical version, collectivism can be seen as an expression of class interests (Bain *et al.* 1973: 16). A pluralistic interpretation treats collectivism as an instrumental route for employees to pursue specific sectional interests. Following this tradition, Purcell (1987) sees collectivism as one end of a continuum of management style which at one pole embraces union representation and at the other, are adopted highly individualised policies in which collective representation plays no part (Deery and Walsh 1999). Nevertheless, commentators have adopted different positions within this broad configuration. Thus Storey and Bacon (1993) equate collectivism with unionism and individualism with non-unionism, but classify practices such as team-working and what Deery and Walsh (1999: 248) term 'participative group methods of work' as representative of a 'new collectivism' (1993: 8). Other commentators suggest that by incorporating management inspired techniques within a collectivist framework, distinctions between the domains inevitably break down and that it is definitionally and analytically preferable to reserve collectivism as the preserve of independent groups of employees seeking to protect their interests (Kessler and Purcell 1995). This distinction is important, for membership of a work team or professional identification may have implications for union orientation or membership but nevertheless may still be compatible with latent adversarial feelings towards management.

Deery and Walsh further point out that in this debate the perspective of the employee has been rather overlooked, though it is vitally important to question the orientations of employees towards union membership and their attitudes towards unions if we are to gain more critical understanding of these institutions and their future relevance (1999: 246). This understanding is especially pertinent when the occupations are becoming prominent features of the economic and labour market landscape, as is undoubtedly the case with software workers. Nevertheless, as we indicate below, the scope for expressions of collectivism (however defined) lies not just within the realm of employees themselves: the attitudes and behaviour of employers may also determine the extent to which employees' orientations may find expression.

In the remainder of the chapter, we first introduce the research context and empirical study which forms the basis of our exploration of worker orientations towards unions. The findings of the study then form the focus of analysis which attempts to explain the relative absence of union awareness or orientation amongst software workers, and for the majority of our case study and other software organisations, the complete absence of union organisation. We draw on both attitudinal explanations for the absence of collectivist orientations as well as structural explanations based on organisational and employment context.

Research context

Large-scale surveys such as LFS are able to provide useful indications of union membership trends but are not designed to explore the orientations, attitudes and behaviours which contribute to these trends. The present study offers in-depth case studies and survey data of software employers and workers selected to be representative of the Scottish software sector. Drawn from a larger project examining meanings of work for people employed in two high growth sectors in Scotland, namely, call centres as well as software development, five software houses were selected as representative of the profile of the sector in Scotland, taking into account location, size, and product or service. These comprised a unit of a substantial telecommunications concern (Beta), two medium-sized independents (Omega and Gamma), and two smaller independent firms (Pi and Lambda).

Between May 1999 and December 2001, background data on company history, operating procedures, employment policies and employee characteristics were gathered as part of an intensive programme of case study analysis and observation involving research teams based in each company for about four months. This process included a total of 86 exploratory interviews with employees and senior management and 73 semi-structured interviews with a representative sample of employees in each case study. Towards the end of each period of company study all available employees within the case study organisations received a questionnaire. A total of 541 surveys were distributed directly to all technical employees by a team of researchers over a four-week period. 328 completed surveys were returned, representing an average response rate of 69 per cent, although where direct contact between employees and the research team was not possible, as in the case of Gamma where most developers worked off-site, the response rate was much lower at 25 per cent. From the surveys returned, 288 were used in the present analysis. These responses represented employees who replied that they regularly used skills or knowledge related to a technical role (i.e. programming, testing, systems analysis, business analysis, software design or user/application support) and excluded employees subcontracted from Indian companies.

The key characteristics of the case study organisations are presented in Table 2.1. In terms of union organisation, the case studies represent at least three contrasting contexts. Beta, which is a software engineering division within a former public utility telecommunications company, was the only one of our case studies which recognised unions and had significant levels of union membership amongst its software employees. Both the Communication Workers' Union (CWU) (acting for 64 000 Beta employees worldwide) and Connect (acting for 16 000 employees) were represented in the software division, although Connect was the specialist union for managerial and professional grades – the majority of our software workers – for whom Connect had negotiated a collective bargaining agreement. Connect represents about 40–50 per cent of Beta employees within the UK, and recently has attempted to widen its membership to large blue chip companies including Fujitsu, T Mobile and Vodaphone. In our Beta sample, 54 per cent reported being members of the union. These numbers are relatively low given that the union maintained a high level of visibility within the workplace, and that consultation principles were publicised on the employee intranet, along with full information on a range of industrial relations issues.

None of the other four case study organisations recognised Connect or any other union. The medium-sized owner-managed companies (Omega and Gamma) were either negative or indifferent towards the suggestion of a union representing software workers. Omega, which was founded by two women who had previously worked for another female-oriented organisation, explicitly promoted the recruitment of females and use of previous employment networks. Several employees also were related to the owners. As such, the owner and some managers perceived little need for a union believing trust within the organisation to be high. Other employees appeared divided on this issue. One of the managers was pessimistic about his future with the company citing an 'autocratic regime at the top' and the company's failed attempts to 'shake off the small company culture' (Omega, Manager). Another employee raised the culture of openness in the company as some compensation for the lack of a union: 'I wouldn't say there is no demand for it but it has just never cropped up ... There is an element of consultation but not a lot' (Omega, HR officer). It should be noted that Omega was the only case study organisation that refused to allow us to ask questions about union membership in our questionnaire.

Gamma, like Omega, provided a range of services to varied clients and was one of Scotland's largest and most successful independent owner-managed software firms. It also had informal, haphazard and rudimentary HR policies and procedures. There was no formal pay structure although they were in the process of implementing a 'reward and remuneration package' at the time of the research. The organisational structure was flat, with few specialisms, and largely project-driven around product releases with some gaps

Table 2.1 Description of case studies

	Beta	Omega	Gamma	Pi	Lambda
Union presence in company	Yes	No	No	No	No
Total number of employees[a]	275	248	150	50	20
Year established	Former public sector utility; restructuring of software centre 1999	1985	1986	1977/1999	1996
Product/service	Bespoke telephone operations; robotic tools; database integration; financial systems	Applications development, resourcing, testing, client support; AS400 technology	Systems integration of front and end operations; open systems development; bespoke CRM systems; subcontractor linking major platforms for clients	Legal and business software development testing, support, training and maintenance.	Health and safety recording software
Primary market	Telecommunications; internal clients	Public sector, health services, financial services	Major database users, initially manufacturing, but in recent years financial and business services	Law firms	Insurance: or IT multinationals
Major business direction	Providing a range of business solutions for external clients	IT services and solutions largely for public sector; developing into English market	New release of software; shift from C++ to Java	Client server and web server versions of software	Client server and web server versions of software
Development of HR policies and practices	Sophisticated and highly centralised	Informal; HR given low priority	Informal; no formal pay structure	Emerging; high status and active HR officer	Informal; shareholder incentives

[a] Establishment sizes are approximate due to workforce fluctuations during the period of the research. The figure for Omega includes 111 contractors. In Gamma, 50 questionnaires were distributed by email.

between development and deployment. Employees were generally deployed in clients' offices and seldom in the company's head offices.

The two smaller organisations (Pi and Lambda) had experienced rapid recent growth centred on a core software product which could be modularised and customised to client needs in a specific sector. Both were non-unionised with informal cultures and flat management structures – Lambda's MD described a 'relaxed atmosphere' and Pi's CEO a 'peer to peer oriented culture' with the 'values of camaraderie and close relationships'. There were no formal written policies and practices, although, as the companies began to grow, some attempts in the direction of formal procedures were evident. Pi represented the most visibly emerging HR strategy with a recently appointed and active HR officer who attended senior management meetings. She had implemented several new initiatives centred around formalising policies and practices, and described the organisation as extremely supportive of employees, to the degree that the company would back them over clients. Many of Lambda's employees had some association with trade unions as the company had been formed following a management buyout in 1996 of the IT support and project management division of a former heavy engineering company with a history of union membership. Those unions (Amicus and the AEEU) were of little relevance to the software workers and managers of the new company, however.

Software employees views on work, unions and employers

Views of employees regarding unions and collectivist orientations were obtained from two principal sources, the employee survey and from interviews. Survey responses provide data on general attitudes whilst case study interviews illustrate those factors which sustain employee and employer orientations towards individualism or collectivism. These in turn help to explain the low profiles of union membership and activity in all the companies, and in the case of the four smaller companies, the absence of a union at all. Five key dimensions can be identified: first, individualism as a behavioural trait; second, levels of satisfaction with work; third, levels of satisfaction with pay and grievances associated with pay; fourth, awareness of unions and attraction to their activities; and finally, the significance of employment context. In each case, the findings of the questionnaire study (see Table 2.2 for a description of the respondent sample) are used first to examine the extent to which these themes explain software workers' attitudes to collectivisation.

Individualism

Our examination of attitudes to collective representation through the questionnaire study confirm adherence to individualist values. Although the responses indicate that there is still a general acceptance of a role for collective representation and action, the majority of software workers perceive this to be an *unimportant* aspect of their own jobs. Table 2.3 summarises the

Table 2.2 Research design and survey respondent characteristics

	Software division of unionised co.	Non-unionised, medium-sized, independent		Non-unionised, small startups		Total sample
	Beta	Omega	Gamma	Pi	Lambda	
Exploratory interviews	33	34	5	10	3	86
Semi-structured interviews	20	21	17	16	3	73
Questionnaires distributed	163	170	139	49	20	541
Questionnaires returned (response rate)	117 (72%)	129 (76%)	22 (24%)	43 (88%)	17 (85%)	328 (61%)
Questionnaires used in analysis	97	119	36	36	14	288
Respondent characteristics						
Males	81 (84%)	76 (67%)	16 (80%)	24 (67%)	9 (64%)	206 (73%)
Females	16 (17%)	38 (33%)	4 (20%)	12 (33%)	5 (36%)	75 (27%)
Age: 30 or less	34 (35%)	37 (32%)	8 (40%)	11 (31%)	11 (79%)	101 (36%)
Age: 31–40	39 (41%)	41 (35%)	7 (35%)	14 (39%)	3 (21%)	104 (37%)
Age: 41 or over	23 (24%)	39 (33%)	5 (25%)	11 (31%)		78 (28%)
Management roles	25 (26%)	32 (27%)	1 (5%)	13 (36%)	8 (57%)	79 (27%)
Contractors	9 (9%)	21 (18%)	1 (5%)	0	0	31 (11%)
Tenure (months)	97 (128.49)	119 (37.84)	22 (31.18)	36 (63.06)	14 (29.36)	274 (68.3)
Intend career with company	46 (47%)	51 (43%)	11 (50%)	20 (56%)	12 (86%)	140 (49%)
Intend career elsewhere	40 (41%)	54 (45%)	8 (36%)	12 (33%)	2 (14%)	116 (40%)
Intend to change career	11 (11%)	14 (12%)	3 (14%)	4 (11%)		32 (11%)

Table 2.3 Attitudes to collective representation (percentages)

Variables	Overall n=281		Beta n=96		Omega n=115		Gamma n=21		Pi n=35		Lambda n=14		Beta union members n=54		Beta non-union members n=43	
	D	A	D	A	D	A	D	A	D	A	D	A	D	A	D	A
Management should have the right to manage their organisation without interference	49	25	52	22	46	24	38	33	54	29	50	29	52	24	52	19
People have the right to take industrial action in order to get a fair deal	17	58	14	69	19	51	24	43	23	60	7	57	7	80	21	55
Independent employee representation is a very important part of any job for me	71	8	58	14	82	4	65	5	76		64	14	40	22	79	5

Notes: D 'Disagree/Strongly disagree', A 'Agree/Strongly agree'.

responses to three questions we selected to reflect attitudes to potential union organisation. Approximately half the total sample strongly disagreed or disagreed with the statement, 'Management should have the right to manage their organisation without interference', with the other half of the sample split between a neutral position and the more extreme position of agreement with this statement. Only in Gamma where the response rate to the questionnaire had been low were attitudes more favourable to management. Over half the sample, again with the exception of Gamma, strongly agreed or agreed that: 'People have the right to take industrial action in order to get a fair deal.'

However, these responses need to be taken in a context in which collective values are not strong. Hence, in response to the statement, 'Independent employee representation is a very important part of any job for me', 71 per cent of respondents overall strongly disagreed or disagreed. In Beta, the only one of our companies which recognised a union, the percentage was lower at 58 per cent on average strongly disagreeing or disagreeing. This still reflects the majority of software workers in a former public utility company where union awareness and the opportunities to join the union might be expected to be high. When this response was broken down for union members and non-members, even 40 per cent of the existing union members in our sample did not feel independent employee representation to be important. The effects of age, tenure, job status and perceived mobility on these attitudes are suggested in the correlation coefficients presented in Table 2.4. Supportiveness for the rights of management to manage uncontested increased with age ($r = 0.13$, $p < 0.016$). Not surprisingly, independent employee representation was less important for those with people or project management responsibility ($r = -0.16$, $p < 0.008$).

Our qualitative data supports the findings of much earlier studies which found that strong individualised instrumental orientations to work among white-collar and technical workers were associated with both loose organisational bureaucracy (which in particular typified our four non-union companies) and with strong market conditions for employees (which were evident in all five companies). Hence, the absence of bureaucracy offered Kuhn's American engineers in 1963 with 'ample opportunity for individual bargaining' and in consequence little attraction to a union whilst a third of the unorganised engineers and scientists in Riegel's 1959 study also took the instrumental view that a union was unnecessary owing to their individual market strength (both reported in Bain *et al.* 1973: 135). Very similar individually materialistic and instrumentalised views were evident among our contemporary sample of software workers. Thus a typical comment when asked about the lack of interest in the union at Beta was:

> I guess people feel more independent ... there's a perception to look after themselves in the large part, and I guess the labour market being as it is

Table 2.4 Job satisfaction (percentages)

Variables	Overall n = 281		Beta n = 96		Omega n = 115		Gamma n = 21		Pi n = 35		Lambda n = 14		Beta union members n = 54		Beta non-union members n = 43	
	Sat	Dis	Sat	Dis	Sat	Dis	Sat	Dis	Sat	Dis	Sat	Dis	Sat	Dis	Sat	Dis
Extrinsic satisfaction	70	27	64	33	68	29	86	14	71	26	100		63	35	65	30
Intrinsic satisfaction	84	11	82	13	80	11	81	14	97	3	100		85	11	79	16
Satisfaction with hours/shifts	88	6	93	4	89	4	76	14	79	9	86	7	93	2	93	7
Satisfaction with pay	64	31	58	38	69	25	71	14	59	41	64	36	61	36	53	42

Notes: Sat 'Moderately, Very or Extremely Satisfied', Dis 'Moderately, Very or Extremely Dissatisfied'.

in this sector, with lots of opportunities, is the major part (Beta, software engineer and personal development manager).

This individual bargaining strength is further illustrated in the following observations from software workers in the same (unionised) company:

> I wouldn't trust a union to represent my views to Beta. I'd rather represent my views myself ... If I went in tomorrow and said JP Morgan have offered me another £5000, if you give me another £2000 though, I'll stay.... (Beta, software engineer)

and:

> I think there is the attitude within the software industry that if you don't like the conditions you've got, go somewhere else where the conditions are better ... I know that if I walked out the door today I could be in another job by the end of next week. (Beta, applications support analyst)

At non-union Gamma, the response was similar:

> ... as an employee you have a lot more leverage, a lot more bargaining power, just as an individual, you can go in and say well, if you don't give me another £5000 I'm going to go.... (Gamma, software engineer)

Frequent reference to the role and importance of personal initiative was made by several of the software staff interviewed: if a problem arises, 'I sort it out' (Gamma, principal software engineer) or 'I'd do something about it, I'd do it myself' (Gamma, business development manager), and at Lambda: 'I would speak to my boss about it' (software engineer).

Satisfaction with work

Notwithstanding the apparent willingness of software employees to act on their own behalf, at the time of the study, there appeared to be few intractable problems for the employees to resolve either individually or collectively. There is evidence that satisfied employees are less likely to join a union than unsatisfied workers (Charlwood 2002; Premack and Hunter 1988) and previous studies indicate that IT workers are generally satisfied with their working lives (May *et al.* 2002). In short, we may expect software workers' attitudes to collectivisation to be related to their job satisfaction given the employment conditions which they have come to expect. In return for long working hours when required (Perlow 1998), software workers tend to expect a high degree of autonomy and generous rewards whether financially or in terms of skill acquisition and career progression (Barrett 2001).

The results of the questionnaire do reveal relatively high levels of satisfaction with different aspects of the job across the sample. In particular, using 18 items from the short form of the Minnesota Satisfaction Questionnaire (Weiss *et al.* 1967), we created variables measuring four different dimensions of job satisfaction: extrinsic satisfaction (work conditions, supervision, management relations and effectiveness, career prospects, and policy towards performance assessment) (Cronbach alpha reliability of scale $\alpha = 0.86$); intrinsic satisfaction (job variety, influence, sense of achievement) (Cronbach alpha reliability of scale $\alpha = 0.78$); satisfaction with pay (single item); and satisfaction with working hours and shifts (single item).

Table 2.5, which summarises the levels of satisfaction and dissatisfaction overall, for each company, and for union members/non-members in Beta, shows approximately 80 per cent moderately to extremely satisfied with intrinsic aspects of the job and hours of work and shifts. This varied little across the companies, as one would expect – autonomy, variety and sense of achievement are an integral part of the profession which software developers would expect in any company. Satisfaction with extrinsic aspects of the job (e.g. management relations, supervision, policies) and pay was lower, although 70 per cent and 64 per cent respectively still responded that they were satisfied with each of these. Extrinsic satisfaction was higher in the smaller companies (Pi and Lambda) and the company with the low response rate (Gamma). The differences in satisfaction levels between union members and non-members in Beta were marginal and not statistically significant.

In terms of how satisfaction affected attitudes to collective action, only dissatisfaction with hours and shifts seemed to matter enough to shift opinion about management's right to manage without interference. Table 2.5 shows that satisfaction with hours was significantly inversely related to support of management across the whole sample ($r = -0.15$, $p < 0.009$). Rather, dissatisfaction with either extrinsic or intrinsic factors were both significantly related to intention to pursue their career elsewhere ($r = -0.23$ and $r = -0.17$ respectively). As interview quotes readily confirm job mobility is clearly a preferred and perhaps more effective solution to dissatisfaction with working conditions than reliance on a union.

These correlations provide no indication that dissatisfaction with any aspect of work would be related to the importance of independent employee representation for these individuals. This is perhaps not surprising given that levels of satisfaction, especially intrinsic satisfaction, are so consistently high; but these correlations alone are rather blunt at capturing possible differences across companies and the effects of employment context. For example, the aggregated results obscure the third of the sample in Beta, Omega and Pi who expressed low levels of extrinsic satisfaction and the even larger proportion in Beta, Pi and Lambda dissatisfied with pay. Further analysis presented below examines the potential consequences of this dissatisfaction for stimulating interest in collective action.

Table 2.5 Means, standard deviations and correlations between the main study variables

Variable	M	SD	1	2	3	4	5	6	7	8	9	10	11
1 Management should have the right to manage freely	1.76	0.83	1.00	-0.14	-0.05	-0.03	-0.02	-0.15	0.03	-0.08	0.13	0.01	0.11
2 People have the right to industrial action	2.41	0.77	-0.14	1.00	0.15	0.00	-0.02	0.01	-0.05	0.01	-0.11	0.04	0.01
3 Independent employee representation important to me	1.37	0.62	-0.05	0.15	1.00	0.04	0.02	0.04	-0.04	-0.06	-0.07	0.04	-0.16
4 Extrinsic satisfaction	4.38	0.94	-0.03	0.00	0.04	1.00	0.35	0.24	0.28	-0.23	0.01	-0.08	-0.01
5 Intrinsic satisfaction	5.00	0.91	-0.02	-0.02	0.02	0.35	1.00	0.22	0.16	-0.17	0.06	-0.02	0.13
6 Satisfaction with hours	5.49	1.12	-0.15	0.01	0.04	0.24	0.22	1.00	0.21	-0.02	-0.12	-0.01	-0.01
7 Satisfaction with pay	4.38	1.39	0.03	-0.05	-0.04	0.28	0.16	0.21	1.00	-0.09	0.12	-0.05	0.02
8 Perceived mobility	0.39	0.40	-0.08	0.01	-0.06	-0.23	-0.17	-0.02	-0.09	1.00	-0.29	-0.25	-0.10
9 Age	1.92	0.79	0.13	-0.11	-0.07	0.01	0.06	-0.12	0.12	-0.29	1.00	0.35	0.16
10 Tenure (months)	68.33	85.04	0.01	0.04	0.04	-0.08	-0.02	-0.01	-0.05	-0.25	0.35	1.00	0.20
11 Management	0.27	0.45	0.11	0.01	-0.16	-0.01	0.13	-0.01	0.02	-0.10	0.16	0.20	1.00

Notes: $n = 252$; correlation coefficients are Kendall tau values; values above 0.12 are statistically significant at $p < 0.05$.
Attitudes to collective representation measured on scale of 1–3. Satisfaction variables measured on scale of 1–7. Age 1 '<30', 2 '31–40', 3 '>40'.
All other variables measured as 0/1.

A previous study based on the same group of software workers reported their experience of long and unpredictable hours, intensity of work and potential intrusion of work into their domestic lives (Hyman *et al.* 2003). Despite this, many respondents explained that the considerable satisfaction which they derive from their work stems from the autonomy and freedom offered to them. At Beta an engineer explained that:

> I would say what's particularly important is the working environment and we are allowed to get on with our job without any real interference. We are allowed to take decisions. (Beta, applications support analyst)

A Lambda software worker explained that:

> I am happy where I am and I'm quite glad with the free rein that we've got as well which I don't think would be there in a lot of other companies or large companies. (Lambda, UK business development manager)

The importance attached by managers and employees to *individual* skill development was evident. Thus at Beta, a management development specialist explained that:

> The emphasis in skills development lies very much with the individuals... what we do is to make sure we give them as much support we can ... We'll support it by turning it round in terms of authorisation and budget provision as quickly as possible.

Satisfaction with pay

As already noted, at least 60 per cent of the questionnaire respondent sample overall and in each company reported being moderately to extremely satisfied with pay, but approximately a third reported being dissatisfied. The correlations in Table 2.5 indicate a positive relationship between satisfaction with pay and age ($r = 0.12$, $p < 0.029$) suggesting greater dissatisfaction amongst younger employees. This group was also more mobile; that is, more likely to pursue their career in other companies ($r = -0.29$, $p < 0.001$) – specifically, 56 per cent of those under 30, compared to 41 per cent of 31–40s and 17 per cent of over 40s saw their current jobs as part of a career that would take them elsewhere. Thus, although pay dissatisfaction was not itself related to greater perceived mobility, there is a suggestion of alternatives to union action offered by labour market power for those who experience dissatisfaction with pay.

Dissatisfaction with pay can be a factor in stimulating union membership. There is evidence, for example, that low-paid workers are more likely to be active in a union or to endorse union activity (Reed *et al.* 1994). In our study, however, three factors became clear. First, the majority of survey respondents were satisfied with their pay. Second, if software workers did have grievances over pay, they would often be prepared to take action. The third point is that owing to their strong market position, their response to grievance would entail an individual approach to management, as we saw above, or to exploit their labour market strength through job mobility, as explained by one Beta employee: 'If things got bad or something then people would just leave'. A colleague from the same company added: '...I think there is an attitude within the software industry that if you don't like the conditions you've got, go somewhere else where the conditions are better' (Beta, software engineer).

Rather than try and negotiate higher pay with an existing employer, to which loyalty in any case is tenuous:

> It's become very clear to me as long as ten years ago that the way to make salary increases is to move job. You do not make salary increases by staying in a job. (Beta, technical architect)

Awareness of union

Bain *et al.* (1973) pointed out that one obstacle for unions that want to attract non-manual employees is lack of awareness of their existence. In our case studies we found that awareness of unions was generally low and where there was awareness, union membership held few attractions. Moreover, the 'services' offered by unions held little attraction or relevance for staff.

Unions were recognised only in Beta, which provided an opportunity to use the questionnaire responses from Beta employees to examine attitudes towards the existing union in that company more closely. On a positive note, union awareness in Beta was high with only 16 out of the 97 respondents (16 per cent) unaware of the union's presence. The 54 per cent of our sample who were members of the union also expressed slightly more positive attitudes about the union's general effectiveness, as might be expected; however, this was not unanimous. Only 45 per cent of union members rated the union as generally effective, with the majority either unsure or more negative with regard to its overall performance. All of the 43 non-members in Beta were either unsure or more negative about its effectiveness.

When asked about the union's effectiveness in dealing with specific issues, union members were positive about its record on health and safety matters (64 per cent rating it as effective) and individual member grievances (57 per cent rating it as effective). Half of the members, however, rated the union as ineffective in pay negotiations, while 34 per cent responded that it was ineffective in recruiting new members. Although on most issues, non-union members responded that they were unsure about the union's effectiveness, on pay negotiations and recruitment of new members there was striking agreement with the attitudes of union members: 57 per cent of non-members rated the union as ineffective in pay negotiations and 38 per cent as ineffective in recruitment.

Interviews at Beta demonstrate its perceived impotence among staff. The inability of the union to gain concessions from employers in the contemporary workplace was a commonly expressed frustration:

> There is a union but neither Brian or I are in it. Well, I'm not in it because I think they are completely ineffectual, I don't see anything. The union fees are actually quite high and I don't see what they are doing for this vast amount of money they take in. They appear to have minimal influence over Beta management. I really don't think they are really very good. (Beta, software engineer)

And the alternative approach of offering discounted commercial services treated with disdain by the same person:

> They sometimes come out and try to kind of 'selling union' type job ... all they seem to tell you is if you join the union you can get ten percent off the AA or the RAC. They don't actually say here are the things that we've achieved for employees in Beta.

In terms of awareness at the non-union sites, one Gamma employee expressed his ignorance of unions in the following explicit terms:

> They sound so old fashioned and ancient that I don't really know of anything to do with them apart from sort of the miners; that was the last I heard about them. (Gamma, software engineer)

At Omega, another non-unionised workplace, previous negative experience of a union deterred any further interest for one software worker:

> Well, I was in the union at the bank, but it did nine-tenths of nothing when I was made redundant. So I've never thought it worth pursuing since then. In theory they were there to protect you but they didn't do anything. It's never been an issue here. I wouldn't say there is no demand for it but it has just never cropped up. (Omega, HR manager)

Colleagues at the same company and at the unionised Beta pointed to the positive physical and cultural contexts in their companies as key deterrents to unions:

> ...I don't really reckon they are as important in an organisation like Omega, where you have predominantly professional people working in

good, clean working conditions. So there is less for unions to actually campaign for and do anything about and individuals have the right to appeal against things that happen to them in the workplace ... So I guess it works for us. I don't think there are many grievances from people that would indicate that something like a trade union or staff association would actually help. (Omega, manager)

There is a fair amount of stuff goes around to do with the union but they don't seem too active in our area. I think because we are in the sort of job that gets reasonably treated anyway.... (Beta, software engineer)

In response to falling membership some unions have adapted the instrumental attractions of a union to advocate a servicing role for their members as opposed to the more collectively orientated approach where union membership is viewed as a committed expression of collective interests in 'which members actively participate and "become" the union through their collective organisation and activity' (Heery *et al.* 2001). Surprisingly perhaps, the more instrumental service role for unions held little attraction for many of our respondents and in consequence suggests that this may not be a fertile route for union revitalisation. Thus in Beta one union member complained that:

Our union seems to just spend most of their time trying to sell me insurance rather than talking to members, they are turning into financial advisers and that's basically another string to their bow to try and make some money, and that's basically all that we seem to get ... so that's where I see them going. (Beta, software engineer)

Nevertheless, this approach is not one rejected by all respondents. One (ex-union) Beta interviewee pointed out that the union refocusing, 'on trying to be a service to members rather than a conduit for comment to and negotiation with employers is one that I think is a very positive one ... Actually through providing benefits and information and all of these sorts of things ... I think there's a future' (Beta, software engineer and personal development manager). Nevertheless, the same employee did not expect to rejoin the union and this view tended to be a minority one.

Organisational culture and context

There has been a considerable literature which links attempts to link ideological, structural and behavioural factors among employers to patterns of union recognition. Ideology has been noted as a factor, especially when linked to holding families or dynasties whose ideological positions have inclined towards unitarism or paternalism (Cully *et al.* 1999: 257; Purcell and Sisson 1983). Unitarist values have also been associated with North American transplants operating in the UK (McLoughlin and Gourlay 1994).

Structural influences include size, with SMEs especially prone to non- or anti-unionism (Rainnie 1989). The 1998 Workplace Employee Relations Survey (WERS) indicated that union recognition among small enterprises was low, especially where working owners were present at the workplace (Millward *et al.* 2000). In these circumstances, only one in a hundred owner managers were in favour of union membership (Cully *et al.* 1999: 265). In each of the four SMEs covered in the present study, working owners were present and took active executive roles at their workplaces. Low union membership has also been noted in private sector services (Cully *et al.* 1999: 92).

With four of our companies sharing common characteristics of small to medium size, private services sector and active owner participation, it is perhaps not surprising that unions were not recognised. Bearing in mind the vital role of the active executive owner, a further component needs also to be considered in the context of union endorsement, namely owner views on enterprise, management and work relations. With the four private sector companies, a unitarist orientation is clearly evident. This approach is apparent in individualistic approaches to pay, communication from the top downwards and as we show below, a strong company ethos based on informality but underwritten by charismatic personalities and unwritten codes of conduct typified each of the SME case studies. In common with the non-union companies studied by McLoughlin and Gourlay (1994), there was little sign of sophisticated systems of Human Resource Management (HRM), with few written policies and little evident sign of attempts to link business strategy with employment strategy. Interviews with senior management at Beta, however, indicated a different and more structured style of management, one largely derived from its origins as a large public sector corporation.

At Lambda, where recruitment was mainly for graduates, a sense of mission and of enterprise was readily evident. The owner insisted that he wanted to recruit people 'who want to join the club, not with a 9–5 mentality'. He was concerned that too many graduates 'want everything on their plate' and turn out to be 'not that motivated to go places'. After five years with the company, employees become shareholders and the club-like emphasis was reinforced by days out for all staff, barbecues and raft races.

At Omega, interviews with the chief executive quickly established that unions would not be welcome, notwithstanding the relative size and continuing expansion of the company. No union questions were permitted on the employee questionnaire and an element of autocratism was apparent through interviews with both senior and junior staff. As with Pi below, there was a strong emphasis on recruiting former colleagues and close acquaintances to the company. A senior manager pointed out that the culture is entrepreneurial, with a flat structure but 'the managerial style is control' and in the words of another: 'the owners have had a problem letting go... we pay lip service to giving over authority and responsibility, but...'.

Communication was tightly controlled from the top and consisted mainly of twice-yearly formal evening meetings addressed by the Chief Executive and in which little audience participation occurs, echoing Bacon and Storey's (1996: 43) point that: 'direct communication by a company or an organisation with its workforce implies individualism'.

A more benevolent or paternalistic form of autocratism was apparent at Pi where the owner insisted that much of his ownership excitement derived from 'having control over my own destiny'. A flat and informal structure was established in which 'the doors are kept open so that people can come and talk all the time ... I go to the pub every Friday night with them'. Recruitment was originally among former business colleagues: 'I knew them personally. I knew their families. I knew what they are capable of and I brought them into the business'. He insisted that to maintain a 'family' culture 'we've created mechanisms for that ... we've created traditions' such as 'a boys' golf outing ... we've gone to the same place every year and very few people from outside the company are invited'.

At Beta, union membership was estimated at about 40 per cent by the Connect branch official. Amongst our questionnaire sample, the figure was slightly higher at 54 per cent. The Software Centre manager at Beta indicated that notwithstanding a move towards informality, Beta's identity as a company is rooted in its traditions: 'When I joined it I was amazed. I walked in and everybody was wearing a shirt and tie. Where I worked before the software guys ... came in sandals, kaftans and all that kind of stuff, ponytails. Then coming in here and having a dress code seemed to be absurd'. The company has more of a structure and operates more by formal written codes than the smaller independent software firms. There are formal appraisal systems based on 'competencies': '... a set of behaviours the business has decided that our people must exhibit. And that's what we use to measure performance. There are paragraphs to tell you how people should behave and get certain marks'.

In summary, with the exception of Beta, where a union is recognised, there appears to be little encouragement from owner-managers for employees to join unions and coded messages from them of organisational cultures incompatible with union organisation or activity.

Discussion: potential for union intervention

Recent editions of the *European Journal of Industrial Relations* (March 2003) and *British Journal of Industrial Relations* (September 2002) were dedicated to union revitalisation problems, potential and prospects in different European countries. In one paper, Heery and his colleagues offered a summary of union attempts in the UK to gain members and achieve employer recognition. These initiatives include: efforts to recruit and retain workers in workplaces irrespective of union recognition by the employer; to gain recognition from employers through direct approaches to them; to merge with other unions; to establish coalitions with other interest and campaigning groups; through political pressure; and through social partnership arrangements with employers (Heery *et al.* 2003). In his summary of European trends, Visser (2002) concludes with the pessimistic message that continued decline across Europe can be expected unless unions can reach 'new workers' and workplaces and offer sufficient incentives for employees to join and remain with the union through the diverse employment trajectories which typify new work in the contemporary economy (2002: 425). In software, an archetypal 'new' industry and in which union density continues to decline, there was little evidence in our study of concerted union efforts to adopt systematically any of the above approaches. Nor was there any clear indication of areas of potential growth or influence available to unions.

Moreover, if we consider the main explanations for propensity to join unions offered by Kochan (1980), the prognosis for unions in the software sector is not promising. McLoughlin and Gourlay developed Kochan's 'critical determinants' for a propensity to unionise to include job satisfaction, participative utility and perceived ability of union to secure additional benefits (1994: 94). In other words, if employees are satisfied, happy with existing communication channels and have little expectation that a union can secure additional benefits, then propensity to unionise will be low. In addition, there appears to be little evidence in our study for the so-called 'representation gap' identified by Towers (1997), which purports to offer unions with opportunities to expand their membership following the recent years of decline and subsequent 'frustrated demand for union membership among non-union members' (Charlwood 2002: 463).

Indeed, the sense which emerges from employee interviews and questionnaire study is that employees are generally satisfied with their work, and that individual autonomy is especially valued. Any shortcomings in the job would be treated through individual intervention with the ultimate sanction of exiting if job and salary expectations are not met by the company. Unions appear to have little substantive role in meeting these expectations, with the common view being that they lack sufficient authority to intercede on behalf of the software workers. In Beta, the one company which recognised a union and where the union was actively involved in pay negotiations, even union members were despondent over its effectiveness in this respect. Most of the software workers in our study appear to lack commitment to collective action and at the same time consider that unions offer little instrumental capability to satisfy their labour market requirements. In consequence interest in unions and their activities is low. Kochan's broad critical determinants are clearly not met in these circumstances. Even if union interest were higher, employees would face substantial barriers in persuading owner-managers to recognise unions in their enterprises, whilst in Beta, where unions are recognised, activity seems to be maintained at a subdued, and essentially individualist level. It appears that union vitality is sustained by both structural and attitudinal factors and when the trajectories of both coincide, as has been the case with software workers, opportunities for union organisation become heavily circumscribed.

Thus, from this study it appears that opportunities for unions to expand membership in software are limited. Current union organising initiatives in the sector appear to be very low profile and inconsequential. These pessimistic conclusions may perhaps be mitigated by two emergent factors, though the first of these offers scant comfort to software workers in that their labour market has loosened significantly in the past couple of years. Promoted established posts are now scarcer and software workers wishing to enhance their salaries and conditions may not be able to manipulate their individual mobility with the same freedom as was available during the period when the research was undertaken. Internal advancement (or consolidation) and security may become preferable or more feasible objectives. Any ambitions towards union presence may be helped by the statutory recognition procedures offered by the Employment Relations Act 1999, though our early study showed few if any signs of increased activity among software workers during the three years following the Act (see also Charlwood 2002: 488). It appears, though, that even under these changing conditions, there is no evidence as yet that software employees are turning to their sector unions to defend or advance their interests. Nor is there much likelihood that employers, now operating within a more favourable (to them) labour market, will be more welcoming to union representation.

Nevertheless, a second possible opportunity derives from this labour market volatility and resides with the unions themselves. It is clear both from available union statistics and from the findings of this study that few unions with interests in the sector are making headway in terms of recruitment and recognition. Arguably unions may need to examine alternative approaches to securing membership, especially if direct recognition from employers is an unlikely source of membership growth and union influence. The experience of Silicon Valley may offer some insights. Based on his studies in information technology sites in Silicon Valley, Benner (2002) points to a growing blurring between services offered by professional bodies and those offered by unions. Clearly, software work represents an occupation which possesses the principal criteria associated with professionalism, that is, discipline mastery, advanced learning, high-level intellectual skills; and autonomy and discretion for practitioners (Middlehurst and Kennie 1997). Unions in Silicon Valley have been taking steps to enhance the overall labour market standing and career trajectories of their members by drawing upon both professional and union-focused initiatives. These include: provision of regional labour market information and developing local occupational and sectoral networks; assisting in career development through providing access to employment linkages, skills enhancement and training opportunities; and treating service provision and collective organisation as mutually reinforcing rather than distinctive or competing union strategies. According to Benner these initiatives, 'are helping members build success careers. By strengthening networks among people in similar occupational communities, they are helping to mitigate the risk of the high turnover and volatility inherent in information technology industries. In the process, rather than building careers based in a single firm, members are building careers through their occupationally based community networks' (2002: 175–6).

Similar approaches can be seen in the early initiatives being developed by Connect, the 'union for professionals in communications'. Recognising the volatility of employment and continuous change inherent in the communications industry, the union offers an employment exchange service, career counselling, advice over employment contracts and advice on employment matters as well as provision of other services. Where 'Connect works in partnership with your employer' the union even offers 'to negotiate on your behalf' (Connect advertising leaflet 2002). Whether this shift to a professionalised service model will be effective in gaining recruits is perhaps too early to say, though signs given by employees and employers in the reported study are not promising.

Acknowledgements

This chapter is based on data collected as part of an ESRC project funded under the Future of Work Initiative (award number L212252006) – 'Employment and Working Life Beyond the Year 2000: Two Emerging Employment Sectors' (1999–2001). The full research team at Strathclyde, Stirling, Aberdeen and Heriot-Watt Universities is as follows: Peter Bain, Chris Baldry, Nicholas Bozionelos, Dirk Bunzel, Gregor Gall, Kay Gilbert, Jeff Hyman, Cliff Lockyer, Abigail Marks, Gareth Mulvey, Harvie Ramsay, Dora Scholarios, Philip Taylor and Aileen Watson.

3
Failing to Organise – or Organising to Fail? Challenge, Opportunity and the Limitations of Union Policy in Four Call Centres

Peter Bain, Phil Taylor, Kay Gilbert and Gregor Gall

Introduction

The sustained growth of call centres since the early 1990s has been one of the most significant developments in the changing structure of employment in North America and Western Europe (Deery and Kinnie 2002). Transforming the processes and loci of customer servicing, call (or contact) centres have extended to virtually every economic sector. The integration of computer and telephonic technologies characterises the call centre and produces its distinctive form of job design and work organisation (Taylor and Bain 1999). Applying this definition, at least 500,000 people are employed in UK call centres (IDS 2003: 13–15). While growth rates have slowed since the late 1990s, these jobs remain disproportionately important in particular regions (Bristow *et al.* 2000). In Scotland, for example, 46,000 were employed in call centres in 2000, rising to 56,000 by 2003 (Taylor and Bain 2003a). The financial sector and media/telecoms each account for about one-third of all jobs, and a quarter are outsourced. Constituting 1 in 43 of the working population, the size of this workforce poses significant representational and organising challenges to trade unions.

To date, our understanding of the role of unions in call centres has been limited by the fact that most published research has focused on issues of work organisation and management control. Although there is an emerging literature on industrial relations developments (Taylor and Bain 2003b; 2001b; Bain and Taylor 2002; 2000; Rose 2002) and Human Resource Management (HRM) practices (Kinnie *et al.* 2000), union representation remains relatively under-researched.

Recognition is widespread in particular sectors, and there are similarities in the ways in which union organisation was established and developed in telecommunications, utilities, and in the finance, travel and public sectors, through the extension of long-standing national agreements to new call centre operations (Bain and Taylor 2001: 108). In some cases, unions were able to get in 'on the ground floor', by using their influence in existing bargaining arrangements with the parent company to negotiate terms and conditions prior to the establishment of their call centres (e.g. banking unions at First Direct and TSB). Agreements were also signed in anticipation of, or consequent upon, Employment Relations Act provisions (2000), such as those between Barclaycall and UNIFI, Vertex (ex-Excell) Glasgow and the Communication Workers' Union (CWU), and Vertex and UNISON in Bolton. There are also many non-union call centres, including large employers such as BSkyB, Direct Line, Kwik-Fit, NTL and Telecom Services Centres and, significantly, non-recognition is extensive in outsourcing. Within recognised locations, densities vary considerably (Bain and Taylor 2002: 250; Taylor and Bain 2001b: 55), as does the effectiveness of workplace organisation. Recognising significant recruitment and organising opportunities, both the British and Scottish Trades Union Congress (TUC) have sought to avert inter-union competition (STUC 2000; TUC 2000a).

Aims

The chapter is concerned with three related issues – worker attitudes to independent employee representation, employee propensity to unionise and membership propensity to embrace 'unionateness' (Blackburn and Prandy 1965). The purpose is to investigate these in two contexts; workplaces with existing recognition and representation agreements, and those with negligible union presence and no agreements. In the former, the challenge for unions is to reinvigorate existing, and further develop, presence, organisation and bargaining power. In the latter, the challenge is to establish and develop these from virtually no base. Broadly speaking, the *modus operandi* available to unions are 'organising' or 'servicing', and 'oppositionalism' or 'partnership' (Heery 2002; Bronfenbrenner and Juravitch 1998). Workers' desire for independent employee representation, and their ability to achieve this, is closely related to the availability of the union resource and to employers' strategies.

In exploring these issues, the chapter develops the concept of the 'representation gap' (Towers 1997). This can be defined as the void between the number of workers employed, and those covered by union recognition and collective bargaining. Here, we widen the concept to include the void between the number employed, and the number covered by any form, or manifestation, of worker representation. Within this framework, we refer to three axes of the 'representation gap', where workers are discontented and have grievances, but (a) have no recourse to institutional means of redress; (b) have no recourse to independent and collective means of redress; and (c) where unions have attempted to organise but without connecting with the workforce.

We first summarise the salient features of call centre work *per se*, before describing our case study locations and the methodology adopted. We then discuss questionnaire findings related to the workforce's attitudes to the broad employment relationship, and report employees' experience and perceptions of union recruitment and organisation activity in each call centre. We conclude by summarising the nature of the challenges unions face in call centres, and suggest that the role of workplace leaders is a key factor in the process of recruitment and organisation.

'A unique working environment' and its discontents

It has been argued that the call centre, generically, constitutes a 'unique working environment' (HELA 2001), in which the distinctive form of work organisation contributes to an experience of task performance that is intensive, pressurised and frequently stressful. Contrary to optimistic depictions which have emphasised the potentially creative aspects of the customer–agent interaction (Alferoff and Knights 2002; Kinnie *et al.* 2000; Frenkel *et al.* 1999), labour process critiques have focused on questions of control. Call centres have been seen as representing new developments within Taylorism (Bain *et al.* 2002; Callaghan and Thompson 2001; Rose 2002; Taylor and Bain 1999). Although call centres are not homogeneous and vary according to quantitative and qualitative characteristics (Taylor and Bain 2001b; Batt 2000), the balance of evidence confirms that most call centre work is repetitive, volume-driven and may lead to stress, emotional exhaustion and burnout (Deery *et al.* 2002). Significantly, the performance of 'emotional labour' may be seen to lie within these new boundaries of management control (Taylor, S. 1998).

Studies examining employees' perceptions have focused on discontents resulting from the relentless flow of calls, the lack of time between calls, the repetition and monotony of tasks, and the infrequency and brevity of breaks (D'Alessio and Oberbeck 2002; Taylor and Bain 2001b). However, the prevalence of quantitative and qualitative targets, entailing the most detailed statistical measurement of employee performance and subjecting the speech of agents to continuous evaluation, appears as a principal dissatisfaction amongst call-handlers (Bain *et al.* 2002; Taylor *et al.* 2002). Indeed, the pressures associated with target fulfilment have been identified as the single most important cause of ill-health and absence (Taylor *et al.* 2003).

The tight matching of staffing levels to actual, or anticipated, customer demand has led to an unprecedented extension of working time in clerical/service work (Arzbacher *et al.* 2002; Bain and Mulvey 2002). The complex mosaic of shifts, driven by considerations of 'temporal flexibility', has generated new sources of employee discontent, and shift changes imposed at short notice may disrupt carefully constructed childcare arrangements, a particular concern amongst predominantly female workforces (Belt 2002).

Survey evidence confirms the existence of additional dissatisfactions, such as flat structures which militate against promotion and career prospects (Lockyer *et al.* 2002), and the inability to deliver quality customer service as sales revenue generation takes precedence (Callaghan and Thompson 2001).

The call-centre workplaces

As Table 3.1 shows, the four call centres were identified by the nomenclature of 'H' (travel), 'M' (financial services), 'E' (entertainment/communications) and 'T' (outsourcing). All were owned by large public limited companies, each with several UK sites. Two (M, T) were situated in a city, at the centre of a large conurbation. 'H' and 'E' were located in small towns, one within and one outwith this conurbation. The workforce was predominantly female (70 per cent), relatively youthful (59 per cent under 30) and largely employed as call-handlers (81 per cent) on full-time contracts (86 per cent).

One centre (H) had a recognised union ('Transunion') but relatively low membership and weak organisation, and one (M) a staff association ('MSA') with low membership. Both 'T' and 'E' had few union members despite limited recognition in other parts of their operations – in effect, these two workplaces were non-union. The four call centres present an ostensible mixture of differing union strengths/weaknesses, forms of worker representation, and managerial approaches to trade unionism and employment relations.

Table 3.1 Some characteristics of the case study organisations

Call centre	Sector	Union presence	Workforce numbers	Respondents workforce %
H	Travel	Transunion	440	58
M	Finance	MSA	128	85
E	Entertainment and communications	None	540	47
T	Outsourcing	None	368	63

Methodology

The findings discussed here are drawn from extensive fieldwork conducted as part of a wider three-year study of call centre and software development companies carried out under the Economic and Social Research Council (ESRC) 'Future of Work' programme. The broad aims were to examine the content and organisation of work, employment relations, and the links between workplace, community and household which influence employee attitudes and capabilities. Periods of six to eight months were spent in each workplace by a team of four to five researchers. Detailed non-participant observation and informal, unstructured 'on-the-job' interviews were conducted with employees, initially for periods of four months. In this way, knowledge of work processes and social relationships was gained, as well as establishing the credibility and familiarity of the research team amongst staff, prior to conducting structured interviews and distributing a questionnaire to all employees. Consequently, formal employee interviews were both detailed and extensive (19 in H, 20 in M, 25 in E and 15 in T) and 855 useable questionnaires were returned (58 per cent). Structured interviews were also conducted with supervisors, managers, Human Resource (HR) staff and union/staff association representatives. Finally, documentation and information was gathered directly from companies and from staff.

The case studies: worker attitudes

The workplace survey included standard questions aimed at investigating employee attitudes to aspects of the employment relationship both in general, and in terms of their own workplaces. Some of the more pertinent findings are presented here (see Table 3.2).

Almost three in five respondents stated that independent employee representation was important to them, with three in ten saying it was either very important or absolutely critical. While the pro-representation response in the two formally 'unionised' centres (H and M) was higher than in the two non-union establishments (E and T), as might be anticipated, even in T a majority of respondents indicated that independent representation was important to them. In terms of union recruitment and organising potential, the greatest encouragement is perhaps to be found in the proportion in each centre who considered representation to be very important or absolutely critical. While the proportion in the unionised centres was just under 30 per cent, in non-union E it was almost one-third and more than a quarter in T.

Table 3.2   In any job – how important to you is independent employee representation? (percentages)

	H $n = 241$	M $n = 105$	E $n = 247$	T $n = 222$	All $n = 815$
Quite/very important/ absolutely critical	61.4	71.4	59.9	52.8	59.1
Very important/ absolutely critical	29.9	28.6	32.4	26.2	29.5
Not very/not at all important	38.6	28.6	40.1	47.2	40.9

The most noteworthy finding from Table 3.3 is the fact that less than 10 per cent agreed or strongly agreed with the proposition that unions have too much power. The salient point here may be that, in the past, the perception that unions wielded too much power was seen by some as negatively

Table 3.3 In Britain generally trade unions have too much power

	H *n* = 245	M *n* = 107	E *n* = 250	T *n* = 225	All *n* = 827
Disagree/strongly disagree	32.7	41.1	46.0	39.1	39.5
Agree/strongly agree	8.1	9.4	6.0	10.2	8.2

influencing public opinion and deterring potential members (Hyman 2003: 50). It could also be argued that some of the two in five respondents who disagreed with the proposition were expressing pro-union sentiments and/or a wish that unions were more powerful. From this perspective, the fact that the proportion of those who disagreed was highest in E, while that in T was only marginally below M, but above H, could again be interpreted as indicating recruitment potential in non-union environments.

Table 3.4 In Britain generally people should always have the right to take industrial action in order to get a fair deal

	H *n* = 246	M *n* = 107	E *n* = 250	T *n* = 225	All *n* = 828
Agree/strongly agree	64.3	72.9	67.2	72.4	68.4
Disagree/strongly disagree	10.9	7.5	9.6	6.2	8.8

Two-thirds of respondents agreed with the proposition that people should always have the right to take industrial action to get a fair deal, while fewer than 10 per cent disagreed (Table 3.4). These findings clearly demonstrate a widely held conviction that workers must be able to counter perceived injustice with collective action. While respondents in M expressed this view most strongly, they were followed closely by those in non-union T and E, and then those in unionised H. This indicates further the existence of a deep well of 'unionate' attitudes in both unionised and non-union call centres.

Examining attitudes to management at the level of respondents' own workplaces, provides evidence of the persistence of 'them and us' attitudes (Kelly 1998: 30–1) and confirms the distance between management and workers identified also in the qualitative research (see below).

Concerning their own workplaces, one in two agreed that management was only interested in profits and efficiency, and slightly fewer believed day-to-day policy-making to be too remote (Table 3.5). The less critical responses in H and M to the latter question may reflect the existence of union 'voice' and presence, although relatively weak. In Table 3.6, large numbers expressed deep dissatisfaction with, and suspicion of, management attitudes, which could serve to assist union recruitment and organising initiatives.

Table 3.5 Attitudes to management in call centres

	H	M	E	T	All
In your call centre, management are only interested in profits and efficiency	n = 240	n = 109	n = 254	n = 225	n = 830
Agree/strongly agree	51.3	42.2	52.3	49.0	50.0
Disagree/strongly disagree	20.8	22.9	18.1	18.1	19.6
In your call centre, policy-making is too remote from day-to-day activity	n = 237	n = 109	n = 251	n = 225	n = 822
Agree/strongly agree	34.6	44.9	52.9	52.6	46.0
Disagree/strongly disagree	15.6	12.8	13.5	11.6	13.5

Table 3.6 Attitudes to management in Britain

	H	M	E	T	All
In Britain generally management have the welfare of employees at heart	n = 246	n = 107	n = 250	n = 226	n = 829
Agree/strongly agree	18.3	15.0	16.0	15.5	16.4
Disagree/strongly disagree	50.8	60.7	57.2	56.9	55.7
In Britain generally management are only interested in profits and efficiency	n = 246	n = 107	n = 249	n = 226	n = 828
Agree/strongly agree	60.1	65.4	65.0	58.2	51.7
Disagree/strongly disagree	11.4	11.2	8.8	13.8	11.4
... should have the right to manage their organisations without interference	n = 244	n = 107	n = 250	n = 225	n = 826
Agree/strongly agree	25.0	16.8	13.2	18.3	18.6
Disagree/strongly disagree	40.2	57.0	52.8	50.0	48.9
In Britain management generally will always try to get the better of employees given the chance	n = 246	n = 107	n = 250	n = 223	n = 826
Agree/strongly agree	41.9	39.3	40.0	36.5	39.4
Disagree/strongly disagree	22.4	26.2	26.8	24.3	24.8

Yet despite these findings, the standing of the existing unions in the two relevant case studies was not high. For example, only 17 per cent at H, and 20 per cent at M, believed their representative organisations were effective in negotiations over pay. At the same time, the union and staff association were regarded more positively in representing members over health and safety issues. Save in relation to recruitment activities, there is no quantitative evidence that Transunion is seen by the workforce it represents to be more effective than the MSA in relation to M employees. The most striking findings are that, in H and M alike, more than 60 per cent reported that they were 'unsure' whether Transunion and MSA were effective or ineffective over pay negotiations, health and safety or in pursuing member grievances. The overriding conclusion is that the activities and influence of Transunion and the MSA respectively do not impact on the consciousness of the majority of employees they aspire to represent.

The case studies: the workforce, union organisation and activity

In discussing these findings we focus upon union recruitment, organisation and recognition efforts, and set out employee attitudes to unionisation. Sources of employee discontent and existing 'voice' policies will also be identified. First, the two call centres in which unions were recognised (H and M) will be considered, followed by the non-union workplaces (E and T).

Case study H

Transunion had been recognised by H, a long-established holiday and travel firm, since the 1920s. Recognition and full bargaining rights were extended to the company's new call centres, including the HDirect facility opened in central Scotland in late 1997. Although this history suggests a stable and secure position for Transunion at HDirect, the reality was more complex, with the character of workplace unionism shaped by the interplay of contradictory factors. These included the company's formal acceptance of Transunion, vis-à-vis the antipathy exhibited by local management; a position of relative strength, as evidenced by claimed 50–60 per cent membership density, contrasted with a low level of workplace union activity and representation; collective bargaining at national level, but a highly circumscribed agenda in the call centre.

Despite formal recognition, the union barely existed in the year following start-up and, even given the higher priority given to organising by Transunion (Heery *et al.* 2000) – one full-time officer and two 'recruiters' were committed to HDirect – growth was not automatic. According to the leading activist, 'a lot of people weren't joining because there was a fear factor involved ... vague threats were made that it would not bode well for people's careers if they associated with the union'. Recently demoted as Team Manager, Angus became the workplace rep and, through the commitment displayed in pursuing grievances, he proved to be the catalyst in establishing a significant membership base. The evidence supports the importance accorded to leadership by mobilisation theory (Kelly 1998; McAdam 1988), and the role of key individuals or groups in the union building process

(Taylor and Bain 2003b; Darlington 1994). By the end of 1998, membership had risen to 50–60 per cent of the workforce.

Angus's departure in early 1999 to work for Transunion, prompted both by management 'making things really difficult' for him and the union's desire to utilise his talents, altered the dynamics of workplace unionism:

> At the point he left, that's when it seemed to just dissipate completely. He did seem to be recognisable, he had made himself known, that's what his role was. He was one of those people who was always walking about a lot ... anything that moved he was aware of. Whereas now it doesn't seem to be there. People who have joined Transunion, have found that it can't really negotiate on their behalf because there is no individual who can.

Increasingly, Transunion came to substitute periodic recruitment activities, conducted by external officers, for developing workplace representation and organisation. HDirect's attrition rate (37 per cent for 2000–01) meant that, as in many call centres, continual recruitment was necessary in order merely to maintain membership at existing levels (Bain and Taylor 2002). However, the success of these activities provoked local management, particularly the openly hostile HR manager, into prohibiting union access to the unobserved canteen and smoking areas, where the greatest gains had been made. Transunion's right to address new starts at induction was also withdrawn, but this did not amount to union exclusion. In allowing the union to set up stalls every 4–6 weeks in the open-plan workspace, thereby formally complying with the terms of the national agreement, management subtly curtailed the free circulation of recruiters amongst the workforce. The onus was now on workers to openly make themselves known to Transunion (and to a watchful management), rather than on the union approaching potential recruits.

Although permitted 3 union representatives – few anyway for a 400-strong workforce – the combined effects of maternity leave, individual exit and reluctance to assume responsibility, meant that, in practice, only one rep was in place for much of the research period. With management preventing sickness absence, and even health and safety issues, from being negotiated locally, the ability to progress members' grievances was further restricted. Symptomatic of Transunion's circumscribed role was the fact that there were no regular meetings between reps and the HR manager. The union's low profile was compounded by a failure either to establish a functioning branch or to hold workplace meetings, and by the lack of contact between recruiters and reps.

Yet, despite these palpable weaknesses, the successful defence of individual workers in disciplinaries, a recognised source of new recruits in call centres (Taylor and Bain 2001b), enhanced Transunion's standing. Further, new workers continued to join for a variety of reasons, including the pressure of targets and, 'The absentee procedures, the shifts, flexibility for management but non-flexibility for staff, issues relating to women – time off, maternity allowances'. The apparent strength of Transunion, in terms of formal membership and the maintenance of collective bargaining, was undermined by the relative weakness of organisation and absence of representational structures at workplace level. The opposition of management, who tolerated union presence insofar as it did not encroach on their definition of their prerogatives, was clearly important. Further insight into the contradictory nature of trade unionism at HDirect is provided by workers' own testimony.

The reasons given by many agents for joining Transunion echo those found in other studies (Waddington and Whitston 1997). In particular, the need for protection, 'insurance against the unknown' – in the words of one employee who joined Transunion on the day her probation ended – was a common refrain. Others joined for the simple and obvious reason that their workmates were doing likewise. Statements such as, 'I just joined for the sake that everybody else was joining', and 'the wee wifie came round and ... explained if you had any grievances, any bother, it's only £10 a month kind of thing' are evidence of the effectiveness of the recruiters' approach, tapping into an underlying sense of self-defence through collectivism.

Some questioned the union's effectiveness after joining. Sally, an ex-member, expressed reservations shared by several colleagues, 'They don't seem to be much good. I don't understand what their job is. What are they doing? Why are they relevant to me? What are they doing for my money?' A symptom of Transunion's perceived lack of impact was the fact that many non-members and members believed membership to be lower than it was. Several members indicated that they were vaguely aware of who their reps were 'There was a ballot for a union rep last week but I didn't know who any of them were or what they were about'. With pay negotiations occurring at some remove from the workplace, Transunion often appeared distant and remote, with members having 'no feeling either in terms of a national picture or what it is doing'.

A 'representation gap' can be said to exist in several senses. First, many did not see Transunion as an appropriate body to pursue grievances on their behalf. Instead, raising issues with managers was perceived to be the appropriate course of action. Of course, this attitude was not universal as longer serving workers tended to see managers' willingness to listen as liberal veneer on an authoritarian style. Second, of greater concern, from Transunion's perspective, was the fact that even if workers did experience problems they did not see the union being able to secure redress. While there was no shortage of grievances, it was 'very difficult to get a resolution', partly because of the individualising experience of call-centre working conditions, and partly through union weakness:

It's so difficult and so staggered and split up and there is only 15 minutes break. By the time you have walked outside, lit a cigarette, got into conversation, it's time to go back in. There's no resolution. And people are dissatisfied. And they do express it. But there isn't a way of getting that information together or somehow working on it. The union is just not there.

In these circumstances, it is not surprising that exit became the preferred option for many, a response which, in turn, exacerbated the difficulty of forging meaningful collectivity. However, the readiness with which workers joined Transunion and the plentiful grievances arising from the experience of call-centre work, suggest union potential failing to be realised.

Case study M

For many years, the company had recognised the MSA for representational and collective bargaining purposes. All employees below the Senior and Executive Management Group, whether working in a 'high street' branch, call centre or in the company's national office, were eligible for MSA membership. Almost 80 per cent of the national membership (TUC 2001e) and of the MDirect call centre workforce was female. Reflecting a general trend in finance sector employment relations throughout the 1980s and 1990s (Morris *et al.* 2001; Gall 1997), the MSA had evolved from the narrow 'company staff association' ideology which it embodied when founded in 1978, to 'independent union' status in 1984, and then to TUC affiliation in 1998. In the latter year, and motivated by related concerns, the election of a new slate of national officials (General Secretary, Chairperson and Vice-chair) was interpreted as reflecting a widespread feeling that the MSA had not been 'fighting enough for people'.[1]

The MSA had a tightly structured formal relationship with the company, and they had discussed signing a 'partnership' agreement. National officials met management quarterly at the Joint Consultative Negotiating Committee (JCNC), chaired by the HR Director, to discuss company-wide employment relations issues. The JCNC was also the forum for annual pay negotiations, and MSA's lay National Executive Committee could accept or reject the outcome of these deliberations. Quarterly meetings of bipartite Job Security and Health and Safety committees took place at national and regional levels.

Although M operated a 'check-off' scheme, and the MSA claimed 45 per cent density company-wide, membership in the MDirect case study call centre was only 6.4 per cent. This low membership level can be partly attributed to limitations imposed by the MSA's organisational approach to the company structure. M employed almost 2000 people in the office building in which the call centre was located, but the yawning representation gap indicated above was both evident and unaddressed by the MSA.

In the same building, there was another call centre, part of the company's insurance subsidiary, MFIS. The MSA had 200 members in the MFIS offices, and 6 workplace representatives who functioned as a committee. The reps met weekly, combining committee meetings with surgeries for members seeking advice or assistance. The reps also attended MSA area committee meetings, met management at monthly Local Consultative Committees and the HR Director every quarter. The MSA General Secretary stated that the MFIS area committee was 'the most active it's ever been'. However, as MFIS fell under different management, the MSA reps accepted that they could only advise, but not represent, actual or potential members employed in the MDirect call centre.[2]

Accordingly, any issue which MDirect members wished the MSA to raise with management had to be referred to a union rep employed in another MDirect call centre, 600 yards away. Understandably, the MSA rep here had concentrated on building and consolidating membership in her own workplace, and did not even know the number of union members in the sister call centre. Furthermore, while the MSA had the right to a 30-minute slot during employees' induction – an opportunity taken up in MFIS and elsewhere – they made no such intervention in the MDirect call centre.

Thus, there was little organised effort to bridge the representation gap evident in the case study MDirect call centre, despite the presence of active MSA reps in another (MFIS) call centre in the same building, and rising membership and activity in a nearby sister MDirect operation.

Generally, the MSA faced hardening attitudes from call centre management. In 1997, against a background of rapid growth in the size and range of their business activities, and concurrent re-structuring of their operations internationally, M announced 'a major change' in their approach to HRM. The 'old ways of managing people' were too restrictive, and managers needed 'the flexibility to respond to changing business requirements and a better system for rewarding staff achievement'. The implicit message was delivered by the HR Director, who underlined 'the primary relationship between an employee and their line manager, and the role of managers as first point of contact'. This approach was re-affirmed in advice to employees that, 'prior to raising a concern with your manager ... in the majority of cases the best person to help you', staff could use the company's Employee Assistance Line (EAL) to obtain 'information and personal support, including confidential advice on work-related problems'. Although claimed that the EAL 'has been developed in conjunction with MSA', the latter's role was marginal.

Consequently, and notwithstanding national agreements, MSA workplace reps complained bitterly about the attitude of a new breed of 'very very young managers'. As has been the experience elsewhere in the finance sector (Bain and Taylor 2002), these managers clearly resented the MSA's presence and were perceived to be continuously inventing 'rules' or claiming practices were not covered by formal agreement. Within the company generally, but particularly in areas of low unionisation and organisation such as our

MDirect call centre, M's policy of emphasising line managers' responsibility for human resource practices clearly undermined, or marginalised, the MSA in communicating with, and representing, potential and actual members.

Unsurprisingly, some employees, while conscious of the need to defend and improve working conditions, expressed doubts about the MSA's capabilities,

> ... there's a lot of moaning and bitching in the canteen ... I know some colleagues are union members and they've tried to get me to join, but I'll fight my own battles.
>
> Things are changing for the worse and are a lot more pressurised now. I'm a union member and I'm thinking of going to see the MSA rep ... think there is only myself in here – most people have an attitude of 'I won't be here long'.

However, overall, employee responses indicated the presence of a consistent bloc of support for the MSA (from a quarter to a third of our respondents) in an environment where only 6.4 per cent said they were union members. In addition, it is not inconceivable that some MSA members were amongst those critical of its effectiveness.

Case study E

For three years, E had been a recruitment and recognition 'target' of two trade unions, the Broadcasting, Entertainment, Cinematograph and Theatre Union (BECTU) and the CWU. The rationale was to obtain presence and influence in a major communication and entertainment company from a very small combined membership base (1.2 per cent from our questionnaire returns). Since both unions' (national) membership and strength had been under challenge for some time, they wished to establish a presence in the growing 'new economy'. The imminence and implementation of the Employment Relations Act (ERA), 1999 stimulated these campaigns by providing a route by which to obtain (individual) representation and (collective) union recognition. More specifically, BECTU had a foothold in the form of a recognition agreement with E for a small number of technicians, originating from a predecessor company acquired in E's evolution.

In practice, neither union translated these aspirations into significant activities. Both organised campaigns where full-time officers distributed leaflets at the workplace entrances, with the immediate objectives of recruiting members directly, and identifying those sympathetic to unionisation. In the longer term, the purpose was to build up knowledge of workplace grievances and provide support to existing members, with a view to reaching a critical mass of membership enabling a campaign for recognition. Other than BECTU technicians covered by recognition, the existing trade unionists at E were workers who had either maintained previous membership or joined for individual protection. But the externally organised union activity had been infrequent and sporadic, without discernible positive impact on membership. In explaining this, inter-union competition was not a significant consideration. Rather, meagre efforts, resulting in meagre returns, appeared to have disinclined the unions from undertaking further serious work, particularly where both had other, more promising targets requiring the commitment of substantial resources for realisation. The comment by one worker that, 'The [Communication Workers] Union had attempted to hand out leaflets but had been bombed out' gives a flavour of the discouraging response to these efforts. Union efforts at outside recruitment can be met with such indifference, based on unfamiliarity of one party with another, and reluctance to be seen speaking to union organisers.

The salience of this is twofold. First, the forces inside E which were sympathetic – for instrumental or ideological ends – were as yet unidentified by the unions, acting externally. However, in E, there was ample evidence of *weltanschauung* favourable to union building, with over half of the workforce agreeing that management was too remote and only interested in profits and efficiency. Second, those workers who were, or might become, pro-union, existed without access and recourse to the resources for advancement and protection of their interests through unionisation. Thus, while any worker can contact a union externally with a view to organising, this task is more onerous and risk-laden than becoming involved in existing activity. Furthermore, workers lacked the personally internalised resource of positive knowledge and experience of trade unionism. In effect, most workers, in most cases like these, are disenfranchised by the situation where they are denied access to organs and resources for collective representation – as one worker put it:

> There's nobody really [to go to for resolving grievances], we don't have a union here or anything. I'd heard rumours of a union coming in but nothing has happened yet. I tell you what is needed is one union for all call centre workers.

Evidence of dissatisfaction undoubtedly existed amongst E's workforce; *inter alia* only 22 per cent reported feeling never or rarely stressed, 41 per cent never or rarely valued, and 86 per cent never or rarely relaxed. Other important issues of contention included shift patterns, targets and the operation of the sick/absence scheme leading to disciplinaries. Alongside this, a fault-line running through the workforce was differing terms of employment arising from earlier mergers and acquisitions.

Thus, although significant sections of the workforce had grievances, a major reason why underlying discontent had not manifested itself in collective efforts to seek redress was the lack of access to the necessary resources. In terms of mobilisation theory, worker dissatisfaction had not resulted in the collective response necessary to transform it into a widely held sense of injustice (Kelly 1998: 27–9). Without company-organised structures *per se* (let alone credible or effective ones), to articulate employee *voice* and establish employee representative *mandate*, we can identify a significant 'representation gap'. The gap was as broad as it was deep, and workers spoke of this in terms of:

> Everybody knows there is no point [in complaining] because the team leader doesn't want to take it higher up, because it's not even the customer service managers' fault, it's coming from higher up than them.

A key factor influencing workers' orientations was the stance of E. Directly and indirectly, consciously or unconsciously, the company's actions were not conducive to the process of collectivisation or unionisation. Although not overtly anti-union, either through policy or by reactive practice, E had in place arrangements associated with non-unionism, such as workforce communication through teams, focus groups, personal performance plans, free employee share scheme, a 'fun' workplace culture and a strong internal labour market. Whilst these measures did not create a contented workforce, the practices associated with non-unionism contributed to a situation where a critical mass of dissatisfaction, leading to collectivisation, had not emerged. In the meantime, and to the extent that workers sought *voice*, this was through the company communication system which operated primarily through team leaders, minor and individualised acts of resistance (absence was running at 13 per cent), and exit strategies, with annual turnover at 37 per cent in 2001.

Case study T

Originally a spin-off from a unionised company, T was formed as a new outsourcing organisation, with little union involvement (our questionnaire showed only 3.1 per cent were union members). On the surface, T did not appear hostile to trade unions, with recognition for 30 members in more traditional areas of employment. The HR manager argued that the legal right to be accompanied at a disciplinary hearing would have no effect on the company, since people could already request this. Generally, employment policies followed those of the founder company, based on collective bargaining agreements. It was made clear that T's success as an outsourced call centre was because they offered lower (particularly labour) costs.

Unsuccessful attempts had been made by unions to recruit with the longer term objective of recognition. Some employees expressed positive attitudes, with one agreeing that a union was needed to enforce rights. This theme was reiterated by others:

> The call centre problem is a problem that is in most workplaces. Under Thatcher the unions were broken. Don't get me wrong they had to

change, but … management ended up being able to do much what they wanted. They can change your shifts when they want. It's the same in most workplaces, sometimes they call it flexibility. It's swung too far away from the unions now.

Equally, however, employee interviews revealed a problem of perception, with many having little understanding of the role of unions, exemplified by mockery of a leaflet which was brought in and circulated. During induction, one employee spoke of the lack of rights for temps, while he was not sure whether there was a union. Speaking of an offer made by T's parent company to their unions, one agent said it was a good deal and, if she were a union member she would sign up to it. She continued, 'there's no union in here right enough', indicating a lack of awareness that employees could become individual members. Another compared T unfavourably with his previous employment:

It was highly unionised and after going from working for a progressive Japanese company to working for a very depressive British one, it was not something I was happy about.

At times, frustration towards management was apparent.

There are tensions here. They'll still ask questions like, 'Why did you log on late, why were you five minutes late logging on?' All they are interested in is stats, which has nothing to do with the job we do.

Pay appeared to be loosely regulated. There were differences within the same section, while disquiet was expressed over the basic rate being paid for working between Christmas and New Year:

They always test the water. They get one or two guys like you to sign up and they think they've got away with it, paying people buttons.

Instances of resistance were also manifest, and employees' use of humour and joking practices had a satirical content, subversive of managerial authority (Taylor and Bain 2003c). Some employees resented their lack of influence over monitoring practices:

There's nothing I can do about it. What I will say is that this stuff about it being to improve your performance and for coaching is a lot of … It's just big brother as far as I'm concerned.

However, this feeling of impotence was not universally shared. One agent stated,

I hope that if anybody did have any problems with another supervisor, they could go to somebody that they do like, because there's a lot of team managers that are really nice and really friendly and my team manager is superb.

Notable was a lack of reference to procedures. It could be argued that the company's *laissez-faire* attitude in individual circumstances contrasted with a *dual* approach to consultation on collective issues. The HR manager claimed that, when developing a new policy, the company liked to have 'good consultation' with both the relevant unions and the employee representative forum, 'VOICEBOX'. There may have been a lack of confidence in this process, since the manager also stated that if policy change were more fundamental affecting, for example, employee contracts, then they would have a much wider consultation, using the training department. This suggests an information provision, rather than consultative, approach.

In T, HRM played a central role, with each section having a dedicated HR manager, but these policies and practices did not seem to be consciously used as anti-union devices. Not only did it appear that communications were generally unreliable, and team meetings irregular, but there was periodic antagonism between the HR team and general management. For example, at an HR managers' meeting focusing on absence, while the target was 3 per cent, actual rates of 13 per cent and 7 per cent were reported. These relatively high rates were related to management style, because 'many are inexperienced', and too much 'maverick management has been allowed' while 'some are kept on a very tight leash'.

Case studies: summary

In terms of workplace composition and operational characteristics, our four case studies are quite representative of the call centre sector as a whole. Further, in broad terms, the findings from the locations conform to the wider understanding of the sources of employee discontent found in the literature. All of the widely acknowledged dissatisfactions described revealed in the survey research, are manifest in our case studies. Previously, we have identified a lack of control amongst call-handlers (Taylor *et al.* 2002) and increased demands for target fulfilment which amount to an intensification of effort (Bain *et al.* 2002). These pressures on call handlers are inexplicable without reference to the economic contexts in which call centres operate and which have recently witnessed sharpened competition, widespread benchmarking, continual internal restructuring and the imposition of increasingly demanding performance criteria (Gall *et al.* 2004).

Yet employee concerns are not related solely to the distinctive character of work organisation. The call handlers in our case studies are no different from those throughout the industry when they express dissatisfaction with pay and bonuses, holiday entitlements, changes to employment contracts, managerial styles, and the unfairness of disciplinary measures. We have neither the space, nor is it appropriate, to construct a detailed, case-by-case profile of employee discontent, since our purpose here has been to demonstrate the widespread nature of dissatisfactions amongst call-centre workers, and to suggest that their existence is (or should be) a matter of crucial importance to unions as they aspire to bridge the representation gap. However, of themselves, discontents do not necessarily result in, far less guarantee, unionisation.

Conclusion

Trade unions face a Sisyphean task in having continuously to recruit members in order to retain power and influence. While potential models and strategies abound, individual unions' organisational practice will be strongly influenced by their ideological stance. If the union aspires to a relationship with the employer which is essentially consensual, then examples of 'sweetheart' deals may result (Findlay and McKinlay 2003), while the concept of formal 'partnership' agreements has gained wide acceptance in recent years (Heery 2002; Ackers and Payne 1998). Unions following such strategies might also be expected to place more emphasis on providing benefits and services to potential members, rather than on building collective organisation to combat the employer (TUC 1999; 1988b). Accordingly, consensual approaches attach great importance to winning employer support and approval both pre- and post-recognition. Conversely, unions who view employment relations as fundamentally adversarial are more likely to display features of 'unionateness', and to stress the need to develop and sustain policies and structures which are independent of the employer (Kelly 1998). In the actual process of building union membership and organisation, the bottom-up, workplace-focused approaches intrinsic to 'mobilisation theory' (Kelly 1998) and the 'organising model' (Bronfenbrenner and Juravich 1998; Carter 2000) are consistent with an adversarial perspective.

However, our main objective here is not to dissect the range of models and approaches (cf. Taylor and Bain 2003b; 2001b; Gall 2003; Bain and Taylor 2002; 2001), nor to focus in detail on our broad aims (i.e. to examine worker attitudes to independent representation, their propensity to unionise and become 'unionate'). Rather, in the light of evidence from the four call centres, we will summarise the nature of the challenges and opportunities before the unions, and posit a fitting strategic response. First, we will consider the challenges posed by the *substantive* call-centre issues already identified; second, the *organisational* barriers confronting unions; and third, the significance of possible *ideological* constraints on union objectives. Finally, we will postulate that the 'organising model' might provide a useful approach to building union strength in call centres.

First, there is now strong evidence that the 'unique working environment' of the call centre frequently generates conditions that result in large numbers of employees experiencing their daily tasks as intensive, stressful and routinised, which contributes to high levels of 'burnout' and 'churn'. These stereotypically call centre 'point of production' issues also feed into employee discontents over target and output driven managerial approaches to 'traditional' employment issues, such as pay, working hours, disciplinary action and health and safety. In our four call centres, widespread worker unease was manifest, and showed few signs of abating, while there was growing evidence of emerging grievance formation and attribution – over shifts and time off in H; targets and management style in M; targets, shifts and absence procedures in E; and pay and communications in T. Thus, the challenge for unions is to develop bargaining agendas which identify, address and prioritise the substantive issues of greatest concern to call-centre workers.

Second, certain operational features, associated with the call centre, present organisational barriers to union recruitment. These include constraints, imposed by the intensive and individualistic nature of work, on employees' ability to interact with colleagues or to leave workstations. Complex and variable shift patterns, and high levels of employee turnover, also present difficulties in maintaining contact with potential or actual union members, and in developing collective consciousness. The nature of these challenges suggests that the medium/long-term aim of building self-sustaining, workplace-based organisations perhaps offers the best prospect of establishing and consolidating union presence, not only in non-union call centres such as T and E, but also in the formally, but weakly, unionised environments of H and M.

Third, it is sometimes argued that the relatively youthful call-centre workforce is the epitome of 'Thatcher's children' and deeply imbued with anti-union and/or 'individualistic' attitudes. This antipathy to unionism might be facilitated by the high proportion of what are seen to be less 'unionate' women workers and by the relatively large number of part-time employees. Yet, to all the key questions outlined above there are no statistical differences in responses according to age, gender and contract. Therefore, large percentages of respondents, irrespective of these characteristics, are broadly sympathetic to union representation and the right to take industrial action, they think management are only interested in profits and efficiency, and do not accept managerial claims to have the interests of employees at heart. Generally, these views were held as strongly in non-union T and E, as in H and M. These are patently not the views of anti-union individualists but, on the contrary, suggest that there is already widespread identification with and receptiveness to, unionate attitudes.

Having summarised the nature of the challenges to call-centre unionisation, we will briefly consider the applicability of one possible response, namely the 'organising model'. What is discussed is, of course, an 'ideal type', but the model's significance is twofold. First, it reflects the fact that 'the labor movement has begun to focus its energy on the one element of the organizing process that it controls – union strategies and tactics' (Bronfenbrenner and Juravitch 1998: 19). Second, it proposes continuity of method, and a means of integrating pre-recognition organising campaigns with building post-recognition workplace structures. At the model's core is an emphasis on the union's relationship with rank-and-file activists – initially contacting them (a small minority of the workforce) and seeking to build a workplace-based organising committee. The committee, in turn, bases its recruitment material on employee perceptions of the key issues the union needs to address and, post-recognition, assumes the lead role in negotiations with management. The role of union full-timers and 'official' bodies is to offer organisational and ideological support and training to the rank-and-file activists, while consciously seeking to avoid substituting for them. The 'organising model' strategy requires careful planning, and an acceptance that union resources will be committed over a period of time. However, while the model cannot be crudely transplanted, its emphasis upon workplace-based, 'bottom-up' organising may seem particularly applicable in the context of the call-centre environment.

The conclusion is that while these call-centre workers may portray a range of *attitudinal* and *ideological* characteristics that are necessary for, or at least compatible with, collectivisation and unionisation, on their own these are insufficient to set either in train. The missing components are *behavioural* and *institutional* constructs, albeit not in the sense that merely adding these to the *attitudinal* and *ideological* characteristics would necessarily result in either collectivisation or unionisation. Rather to utilise these existing *attitudinal* and *ideological* characteristics (and develop them further), supportive *behavioural*, *ideological* and *institutional* constructs are needed, be they the actions of other workplace colleagues acting as opinion formers, articulators of discontent and shadow stewards, or unions deploying sufficient resources (ideological and organisational) over time to establish their credibility. The emergence – and cultivation by their union – of workplace leaders would seem to hold the key to call-centre unionisation.

Notes

1. Soon after our research was completed, the MSA changed its name to include the word 'union'.
2. This was before implementation of the clauses in ERA 1999, concerning the right of individuals to union representation, which came into force in June 2000. The MSA had informed the company they intended taking up this issue when the legislation was implemented.

4
Worker Representation within and across Organisational Boundaries: A Case Study of Worker Voice in a Multi-agency Environment

Mick Marchington, Jill Rubery and Fang Lee Cooke

Introduction

During the last decade, there has been an emerging interest in what have been termed network firms (Birkinshaw and Hagstrom 2000; Castells 1996), new organisational forms (Lewin *et al.* 1999; Daft and Lewin 1993) or 'extended' organisations (Colling 2000). Given the growth of sub-contracting arrangements, supply chain networks and joint ventures, this interest is hardly surprising. These forms of organisation are apparent not just in the private sector but are also emerging in the public sector through public–private partnerships (PPPs), seen by some as a mechanism for improving the efficiency of the public sector. Most of the attention has been focused on how these 'new' organisations are more suited, due to their supposed flexibility, to the increasing challenges of a competitive world and national economy. The role that workers might play within this type of organisation has been restricted to how they might contribute to improved levels of performance through increased opportunities for learning (Bartlett *et al.* 1999; Child and Faulkner 1998).

Much of this literature tends to be upbeat and positive, implying that flexible organisational forms are beneficial for all stakeholders. However, this often rests on claims made by the proponents of such initiatives and by the senior managers who are responsible for making such systems work. There are growing doubts about whether performance is enhanced in these circumstances, in particular given the increased costs required to oversee contracts that are no longer under the direct control of managers within the client organisation (Marchington *et al.* 2003; Rubery *et al.* 2002). Questions are also raised about whether the outcomes are mutually beneficial to all stakeholders or whether workers bear the principal risk in these situations by suffering worsening terms and conditions in relation to pay, training, career development and promotion opportunities (Cooke *et al.* 2004).

Moreover, as Rubery *et al.* (2003) argue, employment relations in these kinds of network are more complex than those that occur within the confines of the single enterprise. Individual workers are influenced not only by the actions of their own managers but also by those employed by clients who intervene (either explicitly or implicitly) in the management of the employment contract. These cross-border relations are both horizontal and vertical, involving, for example, co-operation between similar grades of staff as well as attempts by managers in one organisation to direct and control employees in another. The direct and indirect influences of customers on the human resource (HR) policies of suppliers are also noted in the study by Hunter *et al.* (1996). The intervention of 'non-employers' can result in workers being subject to multiple sources of control and evaluation, so highlighting tensions and conflict at work as well as issues of fairness and equity in the employment relationship.

Rather than examine all elements of the employment relationship in this chapter, we focus on how inter-organisational relationships influence the opportunities for workers to exercise their voice, in particular through trade unions. It is widely accepted that the role and influence of trade unions has been reduced due to a mixture of more assertive management styles, a shift to individualism and a lessening of worker interest in trade unions (see e.g. Cully *et al.* 1999). This has affected continuing organisations, that is, those that have remained in business and continue to employ workers on similar kinds of tasks, where the opportunities for worker representation would seem to be greatest. More seriously, given the shift in employment from areas where unions were traditionally strong to those where they have less prominence, the decline of trade union membership and influence has been even more marked, particularly at workplaces that have been established over the last 20 years (Machin 2000: 642). Yet more problematic, the increased tendency for organisations to sub-contract tasks that used to be undertaken in-house – typically to smaller firms – has meant that the workplaces in which these tasks are now located have also changed; in other words, worker voice has been externalised.

With the exception of work by Heery *et al.* (2002; 2000) on agency workers and Erickson *et al.*'s (2002) study of janitors in Los Angeles, there has been hardly any analysis of worker voice and representation across organisational boundaries, except where that representation is organised on a single industry or occupational basis. In this situation, workers are in a double bind. Not only are these workplaces predominantly less unionised than the sites where the work used to be undertaken, the workers involved are under the direct control of different employers or belong to agencies. Even if these workers decide to take up union membership or retain it in the case of transferred staff, the opportunity to express their views to the client organisation is almost non-existent. Moreover, they may be physically separated from workers doing similar tasks but employed on different business contracts or indeed from those who remain working for the client firm. In short, serious though the problem is for workers who remain employed by continuing organisations, the position of workers who are employed by suppliers or by agencies is much more uncertain and atomised. For these workers, such fragmented workplaces make them increasingly dependent on employers opting for supportive management styles or high commitment Human Resource Management (HRM) to deliver decent employment conditions, rather than having an independent – and arguably more effective – voice through trade unions. As Erickson *et al.* (2002: 544) note, it is difficult trying to organise workers 'where the employer is elusive and where layers of subcontracting diffuse responsibility across multiple actors'. For those who are concerned about issues of equity and justice, rather than just organisational performance and efficiency, these are serious matters.

In this chapter, we analyse worker representation at a relatively new company (TCS) that specialises in customer relationship management. It is typical of a new breed of organisation operating in the service sector, which engages in multiple contracts with a wide range of other organisations. The fact that it deals with client organisations both in the public and the private sectors increases this complexity yet further, as does the degree of autonomy allowed to different sites in the group. Although the company is proud to publicise its partnership agreement with UNISON at one of the sites, the environment in which it operates is hardly conducive to the establishment of stable, long-term and extensive relations with trade unions across the board. The complex web of relations existing in the TCS network comprises several sites operating with a range of different types of business contracts, utilising a mix of direct employees and agency workers, and with quite varied sets of HR practices and representative machinery. We specifically examine worker representation at two quite different sites, as well as analyse briefly corporate-level initiatives and their implementation at a third – well established and older – site. We argue that, given the growth of inter-organisational contracting, the future for worker voice and representation is bleaker than extrapolations based on traditional workplaces would suggest. Whilst trade unions can take action to revitalise membership within individual organisations, policies that operate across workplaces – and in particular along the supply chain (Earnshaw *et al.* 2002) – are also required to protect and enhance workers' rights.

Worker representation across organisational networks

The issue of how to renew and revitalise unions at the workplace has been a source of concern and interest to practitioners and academics alike for a number of years (see e.g. Waddington 2003; Terry 2003b; Heery *et al.* 2000; TUC 1999; Kelly 1998). Broadly, two different and potentially contradictory strategies have been proposed for how this might be achieved – partnership and organising – though some argue the two strategies could be used in conjunction or in sequence (Heery 2002). We return to this later.

The partnership approach rests on the assumption that the best way for trade unions to protect and enhance their members' interests is to co-operate with employers in order to achieve mutual gains. It is argued that employers are in a better position to offer good wages and conditions, employment security and training if workers are prepared to operate flexibly, contribute to improved decision-making through involvement and participation, and show commitment to organisational goals. The pay-off for trade unions under this scenario is that they are offered recognition, allowed access to new recruits and given time for meetings during working time, as well as being provided with information and guaranteed access to senior managers to discuss issues in a climate of trust. The Trades Union Congress (TUC) has lent support for this approach through its Partnership Institute and its collaboration with the Involvement and Participation Association (IPA) (Coupar and Stevens 1998). Despite the fact that there are not that many quoted examples of partnership, it is still seen as one viable way forward for unions (Guest and Peccei 2001). However, questions have been raised about whether or not partnership can exist without a trade union presence (Ackers *et al.* 2004), and more seriously about whether it is likely to deliver gains for trade unions and their members (Kelly 1998). Indeed, even those that are supportive of the partnership notion, such as Guest and Peccei (2001), acknowledge that the balance of advantage probably lies with management, more than it does with workers and trade unions.

Most of the quoted studies of partnership are drawn from simple organisational forms, often in a single industry (say, finance or food retailing) or a single workplace (say, in manufacturing). In these circumstances it is relatively easy to see the types of benefits that might flow from having an agreement covering the entire workforce because of its similarity, or the value in uniting to defeat a common enemy – in terms of a supplier or customer. The likelihood that the partnership approach can also secure advantages for unions in a multi-agency context is less apparent, and it is clear that an additional set of challenges is posed where there are links across organisational boundaries, as Table 4.1 illustrates.

The partnership notion rests on the assumption that common interests exist not just between management and unions, but also between different groups of workers. Whilst this may well be achievable in a single organisation that is facing what can be characterised as a common threat, there are always likely to be tensions across the network because competing firms have different interests and requirements from the business contract. This can also spill over into relations between workers on different contracts, either through pressures on terms and conditions of employment or through the allocation of blame for failure to other actors in the network. This is exacerbated if penalties are invoked for poor performance or there is a strong likelihood that business contracts will be cancelled.

Table 4.1   Applying the partnership model to a multi-agency network

Claimed benefits to unions and workers from developing partnership with a single employer.	Likelihood of these benefits being achieved through management–union partnership in a multi-agency network.
A single union deal covering all workers in the organisation might help to mobilise common worker interests.	Workers in different organisations likely to have competing interests, so making representation by a single union (or branch) hard to achieve.
Agreement from senior management in one organisation to recognise unions can boost membership.	Range of occupational groups, types of employment contract and management styles in a multi-employer network makes commitment to unions more difficult.
Employment security offered by single organisation in return for willingness to offer flexibility.	Short-term contracts and use of agency workers makes this unlikely to be a goal across the network.
Possibility that union–management co-operation could increase organisational competitiveness and provide additional benefits for 'insiders'.	As cost savings often depend on cheaper forms of labour (e.g. agency workers) and work intensification at suppliers, benefits not shared equally across all workers.

If suppliers work for a large number of clients on contracts of varying lengths and complexity, they are unlikely to want to be tied into a partnership agreement across the board for fear that this will remove any flexibility. Moreover, if these business contracts are for quite different types of service and require workers with specific technical skills, the opportunity for transferring workers from one contract to another is minimal. In this situation, the prospect of being tied into a long-term partnership deal, which promises employment security for staff, hardly makes any sense for an employer. If the problem is severe enough for staff working for the same employer, this is exacerbated when agency workers are involved or when people working for another organisation are employed on the same sets of tasks. It may be that some employers see advantages in providing additional benefits for agency staff that perform to a high level because this form of labour is used as a filter for hiring good workers without any obligation at the outset. But most employers are likely to view agency staff as a cost rather than as a resource, so there is little prospect they would receive any of the advantages flowing from partnership. 'Permanent' staff might also have negative views about agency workers, partly because they are seen as a threat to their own continued employment but also because some agency workers in areas of skill shortage are able to earn premium rates without necessarily having equivalent skills. In short, it is unlikely that partnership arrangements can work effectively right across a diverse organisation, and there is even less chance that they will operate across organisational boundaries.

If the partnership approach looks set to encounter difficulties in this situation, how is the organising approach likely to fare? The organising approach, like partnership, is not always clear but it puts a primacy on recruiting new members rather than servicing existing ones, and in attempting to develop workers (and worker representatives) so that they can deal directly with their own problems rather than having to rely on paid officials. This works on the principle that grassroots activism is the best way to mobilise and sustain union renewal because it is embedded within the workplace. As with partnership, the organising model has been supported by the TUC through the Organising Academy (Heery *et al.* 2000).

Similar conceptual problems arise in relation to the organising model when it is applied across organisational boundaries, especially if networks do not have the benefit of long-standing and well-developed union agreements. Any attempt to organise across business contracts would not only be difficult but, as trade union recognition procedures are based on the presumption of single employer workplaces, would not provide leverage for new recognition or bargaining agreements. In Table 4.2 below, the proposed benefits and limitations of the organising model are applied to the multi-agency situation.

Table 4.2 Applying the organising model to a multi-agency network

Claimed benefits to unions and workers from applying the organising model to a single employer.	Likelihood of these benefits being achieved through organising approach in a multi-agency network.
Workers can be mobilised into action due to dissatisfaction with terms and conditions of employment, work intensification and so on.	Workers lack a common goal and tend to be fragmented within and between organisations, thus putting employers in a more influential position.
Worker representatives can be trained up to frame issues in a collective way and unite different groups.	Workers who are dependent on clients or agencies for continued employment are often reticent to raise concerns and lack the time, the resources or the support to develop these skills.
Terms and conditions of workers can be improved across the board through support from colleagues in stronger positions.	Clients may not continue with existing business contracts or award new ones if unions are seen as having too much influence with suppliers or across network.
Opportunity to engineer pacts with other workers in similar occupations/locations to produce solid front.	Limited opportunities to interact with colleagues elsewhere due to nature of work or different managerial stances regarding unions and time off to attend meetings.

Some of the same problems arise in relation to the organising approach as did with the partnership model. Broadly, the difficulty of mobilising workers in a non-union environment, be it through a partnership or an organising approach, are well documented (Terry 2003b), especially if management takes a negative stance towards unions. This is made even more difficult if work is fragmented and undertaken by workers who have little opportunity to compare notes with one another about their employment conditions. Moreover, it requires remarkable resilience for agency staff openly to declare themselves as willing to be a union representative in an environment where it is known that unions are not welcomed. The possibility is that they will not have completed their training, let alone started to mobilise other workers, before the contract comes to an end. Furthermore, it is unlikely that unions would see immediate benefits from trying to organise groups of workers in small workplaces, especially if they are on short-term contracts or do agency work.

Rather than trying to create closer relations with other staff working for the same organisation but employed on very different types of work, an alternative approach might be to secure pacts or develop relations with similar workers employed by a different organisation at the same workplace. Potentially, this could be a source of strength in PPPs where workers have been transferred from the public sector under Transfer of Undertakings (Protection of Employment) Regulations (TUPE) arrangements and retain their union membership and connections with other members of the same union branch. However, at a minimum, this depends on the new employer continuing to allow time off for union meetings and on a core of the workers who were transferred remaining at the same workplace and doing the same kind of work.

Having reviewed at a theoretical level the potential problems that may arise with attempting to apply either the partnership or the organising approach to retaining and revitalising union membership, we can now turn to examine the data from the case study. Before dealing with the specific issue of worker representation, some brief details are presented about the organisations and business contracts involved in the network.

Worker representation in the TCS network

TCS was formed in the mid-1990s as a spin-off company, following the merger of two large firms, with a brief to provide business process outsourcing services to organisations in the utilities, private services and public sectors. It specialises in customer relationship management, principally through the use of call centres and an information technology infrastructure to achieve benefits for its clients. The company grew dramatically during the latter part of the 1990s, and in 2001 more than 8000 people were employed by TCS. In addition, large numbers of staff working on TCS contracts are

Table 4.3 TCS company culture

1. Our customers are our business
2. We will respect every individual in our company
3. We will adopt a performance-based approach
4. We will be flexible and decisive
5. Quality is a way of life

supplied by agencies. From an early reliance on contracts with firms in the utilities sector, the company has shifted its base and expertise to offer services across the board, including a growing number of contracts with the public sector. TCS was set up specifically to find new business and operate as flexibly as possible, and its mission statement reflects this entrepreneurial philosophy. There are five key points in the publicised company culture as Table 4.3 illustrates.

Each part of the business is allowed considerable autonomy in how it manages employment relations, and there is a minimum of (overt) co-ordination of activities from the centre. One of the company's senior managers told us that TCS wanted to portray an employment model of flexibility, employability and risk-taking rather than relying on 'old' cultures based upon permanence and long-term careers. In its early days, the company was known to be anti-union and keen to break away from what were seen by management as traditional bureaucratic values, and under the direction of the first managing director this approach was pursued with vigour. UNISON was derecognised across the company and, whilst membership levels held up reasonably well at one of the sites (approximately 40 per cent), at others it plummeted.

The role of partnership and union membership across the sites

Towards the end of the 1990s, however, there was a series of changes in the senior management team that included the departure of the most active anti-union hawks, and the new team became aware that, given its majority in the 1997 general election, Labour was likely to be in power until at least 2005. Two specific factors prompted the re-opening of discussions between the company and UNISON. First, the new legislation on union recognition provided UNISON with a chance to re-establish its presence at the company, and – according to two of the union representatives we interviewed – this persuaded management to start talking again. Second, both sides were attracted to the new emphasis on partnership and the possibility of a different kind of deal. They called in an external facilitator from a trade union college to help change the relationship from one that was characterised as being like 'a boxing ring' to be more akin to 'a dance floor'. This led to a shift in management attitudes and a pragmatic acceptance that there was little to be gained from opposing them as a matter of principle. The employee handbook states that the company 'recognises the fundamental right of individuals to join, or not to join, a trade union' and to engage in collective bargaining where 'the culture of the particular business determines that (it) is appropriate'. This final clause is critical to our understanding of whether or not unions have much chance of being revitalised under the current structures at TCS. The convenor responsible for developing partnership also acknowledges that the chance of extending union membership across all sites is limited. To some extent, this is a matter of union priorities and it is felt that the need to service existing members and recruit new members at sites where there is already recognition is a more valuable use of their resources. The union is also aware that TCS does not want to upset clients:

> They are comfortable with the public sector because they are pro-union and to some extent so are some of the private sector employers, but there is a sort of wariness amongst what can be described as the enterprise companies. So that is where the difficulty lies.

Following the creation of the new management team, UNISON was re-recognised at the 'oldest' and most unionised site, and a partnership deal was accepted after a majority of the staff voted in favour. Moreover, a series of membership drives at other TCS sites, mostly call centres, has led to other unions being recognised, especially in Scotland (Bain and Taylor 2001). At those sites where UNISON has a presence, the union has worked closely with TCS to publicise partnership. For example, the TCS employee relations manager and a senior union representative made a presentation to the Board about the value of partnership to the company and its staff. It was also recognised that, should TCS wish to tender for more contracts in the public sector, a more benign stance towards unions could well be helpful in negotiations whereas outright opposition could lead to major difficulties in gaining approval for and operating these contracts. Partnership has developed in a very patchy and uneven manner across the sites, ranging from its systematic implementation at this site through to a non-union variant at another and lack of prominence at a third. This is examined more fully below.

The partnership philosophy is similar to that espoused by the IPA (see Guest and Peccei 2001; Coupar and Stevens 1998) in articulating the notion of mutuality. The guiding principles behind the original partnership agreement between TCS and UNISON were:

1. The business and the trade unions share a commitment to achieve and maintain an industrial relations climate of mutual trust and co-operation.
2. We also share a common interest in the success of the business.
3. We all recognise the need for both managers and staff to be flexible in their outlook and receptive to change.

4. The business recognises the right of staff to belong to a trade union and the right of the unions to represent their members.
5. The unions recognise the right of management to manage the business in an effective and efficient manner.
6. Representatives within the employee relations structure recognise their responsibility to reflect the views of all staff, not just trade union members, or a particular group of interests.
7. There is a common understanding that the objective of this agreement is to look forward not backwards. We start from where we are and aim to improve.
8. It is jointly recognised that there is a place for both a consultative and a negotiating framework. The business recognises the need to strengthen the existing consultative framework to ensure both forums are fully effective.

It states clearly in the agreement that forums should be set up to cover both consultative and negotiating issues, but these should include only TCS employees. Therefore, the forums are not explicitly intended to include agency staff or any other non-TCS workers – but see below for how this operates in practice – nor are managers or team leaders allowed to elect representatives to the forums. The consultative forums operate at site level. Within their remit is a range of issues including: business performance and opportunities; local application of the performance and development scheme process; issues affecting staff; sounding board for the negotiating forum. The constitution allows 1 elected representative for every 50 staff, and these people are provided with time off to fulfil their roles, as well as access to telephones and training as appropriate. It is expected the meetings will take place every three months, with additional meetings as required.

Although the principles of partnership are meant to apply across the entire company, in practice this has developed most systematically at one of the sites that was not among those examined in depth for this project. Not surprisingly, this is in an area of the business that has the strongest and most historically embedded systems for employee representation as well as the longest standing relationships between UNISON and TCS. Both parties seem extremely committed to the concept of partnership and UNISON representatives have been active in pushing the benefits to a wider audience through presentations at conferences as well as through published literature. Moreover, there have been joint union–management presentations to staff at other sites around the company extolling the virtues of partnership. The senior UNISON representative who leads on partnership throughout the company was convinced this had helped TCS gain more contracts. He said:

From a TCS point of view they see partnership as a business plus. They took the view because it worked well they can go into bids for contracts and say 'look, we are successful at working with our staff and our trade unions, look at this wonderful partnership', and they can go confidently and bid for contracts and say 'compare us with other contractors'.

Partnership in a non-union, multi-agency environment

At its north-west call centre set up as a greenfield site in the very late 1990s, TCS operates contracts with a number of customers for the provision of different sorts of services, each of which varies in terms of the proportion of permanent to agency staff. At the time of our interviews, the clients included a utility, a bookmaker, a mail-order company, a firm dealing with vehicle rentals and breakdowns and a mobile-phone service provider. Just two years later several of these contracts had come to an end and some new contracts introduced instead, demonstrating clearly the insecure and temporary nature of work in this sector. Of the 950 people working across the site as a whole, about 60 per cent were supplied by agencies whilst the remainder were on permanent or temporary employment contracts with TCS. Shiftworking was the norm on these contracts with operating hours varying – depending on the client – between 15 hours each day to all round the clock. Recruitment was outsourced to an agency that had an office on site and placed adverts in the local paper each week for staff. Successful applicants were given a six-month contract with the possibility they might be recruited onto a permanent contract with TCS at the end of the period. All staff worked in teams, usually containing both permanent and agency staff alongside one another. In addition, all staff – including agency workers – were included in principle within the TCS performance and development process, which involved a formal appraisal every six months and more regular informal meetings with their supervisor to assess progress against targets. In reality, of course, this did not always happen as the responsibility for undertaking appraisals rested with the relevant line manager.

Most of the clients at the time of our research were from the private service sector. Some had no tradition of unionisation while others were unionised at their main site but may have viewed TCS as an opportunity to evade union controls on in-house operations.[1] The clients did not exert any pressure on TCS to deal with unions and the company was therefore able to block any approach by referring to its 'culture' (see above extract from the handbook regarding union recognition). Given there was no great union consciousness on the part of workers either, it was hardly surprising that no recognition agreement was in place with UNISON for the call centre. The general manager was aware that there had been attempts by the GMB to get access to staff and it was also clear from other discussions with UNISON representatives that it was keen to recruit members. It was understood that TCS was wary of setting up discussions with the unions to represent staff working on certain private sector contracts for fear of upsetting customers, even though the company did deal with unions on other sites. The regional

HR manager who covered the site felt that union recognition would come eventually. Moreover UNISON had started making presentations to agency staff during their induction course at some other sites, and whilst the union did not yet have any recognition deals with any agencies, it had 'come close' to achieving one with a major company according to one of the union representatives we interviewed.

During interviews with customer representatives at the site, there was no mention of unions, but there was some awareness of the staff forums that were supposed to be the major channel for worker representation at TCS-NW – both for TCS employees and for agency staff. There had been problems maintaining interest at times and there had been periods when meetings had been cancelled or only run intermittently. However, by the end of the research period the forums were still in operation and the new regional HR manager was seeking to 're-energise' them. According to her, the forums were 'part business, part local driven', and each meeting included a business update from one of the management team, as well as discussions about canteen facilities that were available to all customer service representatives (CSRs) across all the contracts, including agency workers. The forums could be attended by up to seven managers – the regional manager, different customer service managers and the communications manager, as well as the HR function. On the staff side, a total of 12 representatives had been elected by customer service personnel – drawn from the range of business contracts – roughly on a ratio of 1 : 50 as specified in the agreement. In principle the forums did not deal with issues related to agency staff but at the time we undertook the main interviews, one interviewee – a permanent customer service agent – suggested that issues of pay differentials between permanent and temporary staff was a source of concern to staff and had been taken up in the forum. At the time we returned to undertake some more research on the forum arrangements we found that, on the one hand, although there was no specific requirement for this, two agency workers attended the forum because many of the issues related to the site as a whole and facilities were shared by workers on the different contracts, irrespective of whom they worked for. However, the agenda for the forum did not include any issues specifically relating to the agency.

Awareness of the staff forums and their operation varied across the sample of customer service representatives that were interviewed. About half demonstrated a sound understanding of the role and regularity of meetings and a quarter displayed virtually no knowledge of their existence. Of those that were fully aware of how the forums worked, one explained in very positive terms that:

> If there are any problems there is a meeting very regularly, and its voiced there and discussed. Any solutions are made there and we get feedback from that. So, if you've got a problem, it does get sorted (Truckco CSR).

None of the interviewees who had knowledge of their operation voiced any negative views about the forums, and some pinpointed gains that had accrued from the forums, such as the location of a new canteen at the centre of the building. Though issues such as this are often regarded as trivial – and indeed they are in relation to wider business decisions about the future of contracts – for those who were working on shifts, this was an important factor. Despite this, it was also acknowledged (Phoneco CSR) that there was very little contact between staff on different contracts unless they already knew someone working elsewhere. In other words, there was little common identity across the contracts even for people employed by TCS. Three agency workers were interviewed, two of which knew all about the forums. The other was less aware: 'I think there's one girl who deals with complaints but I'm not sure' (Utilityco CSR). In other words, there is a suggestion from the small number of interviews with agency workers that, despite not being employed by TCS, they did at least have some recognition of the employee forums. Moreover, their level of awareness was on a par with those employed directly by TCS.

Nevertheless, high levels of labour turnover and a range of different working hours and contracts all limited the extent to which workers – or their representatives on the forums – were able to build up expertise or any embedded collective awareness of issues. Even though they worked in the same building and shared a canteen, factors that may have facilitated some degree of collective identity, this did not seem to have materialised. One of the CSRs, employed by TCS on the Phoneco contract, explained that:

> We don't necessarily mix. Even though they are just down there, there's not really much mixing, only if you've got a friend (on one of the other contracts). We don't really get to know the people who work on them.

Working time arrangements varied across contracts whilst terms and conditions differed between permanent and agency staff, both of which could have led to unrest had there been a union presence at the site. In addition, pay rates were lower here than at the other two sites we examined. The complexities of representation in a multi-employer environment and having to go through multiple channels, however, was also very apparent for the agency staff as shown by the following quote from a member of the forum:

> The issues raised in Gambleco are seen to by our managers and then they're raised with us as representatives. We take it to the TCS people; it goes through the forum. (Gambleco CSR)

In summary, although TCS had publicised its commitment to partnership through employee forums, these were hardly central to employee experiences or to management strategy at the north-west site. In the absence of union recognition, the forum represented the sole opportunity for workers – both those employed by TCS on different contracts and the agency staff – to express their views to management. Although it was patchy, the forums continued to function, and it also appeared that a majority of the CSRs that were interviewed knew something about them. Given some of the problems outlined above, whether they actually led to much influence over issues other than 'hygiene' factors is less obvious, and it would be hard to claim that they filled a 'representation gap'.

Union activity and representation at the London site

This was the first venture by TCS into the local authority market, and it followed a decision by Council X to outsource its housing benefits admin-istration due to continuing poor performance. This was in line with the action taken by quite a number of councils in the London area during the latter part of the 1990s, although since then some authorities have taken the service back in-house, whilst others have re-tendered and found new providers. The council services a population that is multi-racial and multi-lingual, thus requiring a specific range of skills to deal with such a popula-tion, and in the last few years there has also been an increasing number of asylum seekers. Claimants come from amongst the poorest backgrounds in the area, and many of them have difficulty completing forms. At the same time, there have been many changes to the legislation, the introduction of a tougher stance in relation to fraud and an increasing degree of quality con-trol and double-checking of payments. In short, dealing with 'customers' in this environment is markedly different from that in most other areas of the business (e.g. betting, van hire, mobile-phone sales) where contact is with people who have money to spend.

TCS won the contract with Council X after beating off competition from three other outsourcing companies. According to senior managers on the council side of the contract, whilst it was recognised that TCS lacked knowl-edge of how to operate a housing benefits service, it was nevertheless felt that the company's experience in customer service management and its pre-paredness to invest in Information Technology (IT) so as to establish a call centre was precisely what was needed. The senior union representative at the London site attended the presentation by each of the companies and was impressed by the willingness of TCS to work with the union. This led him to believe that this was likely to be the most beneficial bid for their members and the future of the service. However, this was tempered by a view that the others were more authoritarian. As one of the union representatives put it:

At the end of the day, we decided they were the least-worst option of the four because we got a recognition deal out of them. We got guarantees about terms and conditions, guarantees as far as we could about avoiding compulsory redundancies, and as its panned out we've had none.

About 70 workers were transferred across from the council to TCS, about 30 left under a voluntary redundancy deal whilst the remainder decided to stay with the council. Given the TUPE regulations, the staff that transferred was able to retain their existing terms and conditions, including membership of UNISON. TCS also agreed to continue with collective negotiations for these staff, the vast majority of whom were union members, although the bargaining unit was now different – comprising just TCS staff rather than all council employees. The *Staff Handbook*, which was given to all new recruits, referred to a recognition agreement between TCS and UNISON, and union representatives were given access to new recruits. During the first few years of the contract further recruitment took numbers employed up to about 120, about 20 of which were agency workers. Despite some of the original staff leaving, union density dropped only slightly to about 80 per cent of permanent staff, but agency workers were not covered by collective bargaining – and were also unlikely to be union members. Interestingly, according to the TCS HR Manager at the site, a high proportion of the new recruits going through the training programme have actually joined UNISON, something he attributed to the continuing strong local government ethos amongst housing benefit officers.

The type of workers employed in housing benefits is also rather different from those employed in the TCS call centre in the north-west. They need specific technical expertise that is gained through regular attendance on courses, many of them worked in local government – and particularly in housing benefit – for years, and they had expectations of a career in the field. The contract between TCS and Council X is also complicated by the fact that staff working for TCS communicate with the claimants and prepare cases for payment, but then have to send their estimates and draft letters for approval by a team of housing benefit officers employed by the council. Many of the people who are now employed by TCS used to work for the council before they were transferred, and indeed they were workmates of the people now employed to check they have estimated benefits correctly. Whilst at one level this might be expected to encourage a shared identity across organisational boundaries and thus make it easier for a collective ethos to be maintained (Hebson *et al.* 2003), in reality this has proved difficult due to tensions about performance on the business contract. For example, several of the housing-benefit officers we interviewed who now worked for TCS regarded their former colleagues in a very negative light.

Although the number of workers remaining in the union following the transfer was high, the role of union representatives and the experience of union membership had changed significantly. Housing-benefits staff had a history of militancy prior to the PPP and they played a particularly active part in the UNISON branch according to the Council X Branch Secretary, but following the transfer it became much more difficult to maintain links. None of the branch officials came from those employed by TCS, which is hardly surprising given that the branch as a whole had over 2000 members, and indeed it became increasingly difficult for the shop stewards representing TCS workers to take time off to attend these meetings. Indeed, one of the Council X managers felt the branch was no longer interested in its members in TCS:

> You have seen a weakening of their position. Union representatives used to have the support of local branch officers but they no longer have that as they work in a private industry. The branch officer is the branch officer for Council X members and has nothing to do with TCS.

This situation is further complicated because UNISON has ambivalent views about how to cope with work being transferred to the private sector. One of the caseworkers felt that given their isolation from the rest of the union membership in the council and in TCS more broadly, the local shop stewards had done a good job in representing them to TCS management. The primary concerns of union members at TCS were also rather different from those working for the council, and branch meetings were arranged at times when it was hard for staff working for the private sector to attend. Indeed, despite offering support for the union in principle, unlike other parts of the council, TCS management did not specifically allow time off to attend branch meetings. Another of the caseworkers said:

> Before (the PPP) I would be at every single meeting. Now I pick and choose. I look at the staffing situation and if there is not enough staff I won't go to the meeting.

This lessening of collective identity with other council staff was probably inevitable after they moved employment from the local authority to TCS, and a growing recognition that their futures were more intimately tied into the success of the contract, and perhaps more broadly the fortunes of TCS. Moreover, management at the site was very keen to move away from a total reliance on collective channels and involve individual workers instead. Indeed, one of the shop stewards who had been highly critical of outsourcing and of TCS at the time of the transfer felt that managers were much more open than the council had ever been, and regular meetings had helped to transform her views. She has since been promoted into a supervisory position. The TCS HR manager also laid great emphasis on the importance of having frequent meetings with all workers, not just union representatives, and he also stressed that all workers had equal access to management and that the union had not been granted special favours in this regard:

> We try to be inclusive with the trade union but we also try to be inclusive with all staff. We've opened it wider and I will happily discuss issues with staff without any trade unions being around.

Despite trying to encourage worker commitment to TCS (rather than the union) by publicising its core values and conducting organisation-wide attitude surveys, the company dealt with most employment issues at the local level. There had been some discussion amongst senior UNISON representatives about the possibility of a TCS branch of the union – representing workers across all TCS sites – but that had not been developed, partly because of the geographical spread of the company but also because of the widely differing levels of union membership and representation. Senior union representatives within the company felt the best approach was to develop membership at specific sites, and use the provisions of the Employment Relations Act on recognition, rather than try for a blanket recognition agreement across the company as a whole. This probably also suited TCS because of its preference to deal with industrial relations at site level, so keeping discussions about employment issues divorced from wider business decisions. Whilst managers were increasingly expected, and indeed encouraged, to move around the organisation, other groups of workers were not. Perhaps senior managers were aware of their vulnerability to concerted industrial action. One of the union representatives at TCS-L certainly felt that local management had backed down because of concerns about poor publicity at a time the company were looking to gain other contracts. Union representatives as a whole felt that TCS at the site had refrained from making changes because they were fearful of any backlash and its impact on the company more generally. For example, the convenor at TCS-L spoke of one example where Council X had attempted to introduce amendments to working hours, which led to a dispute with UNISON members working for the council. The union at TCS-L was asked if it would support the council workers on this issue. Following a written assurance from TCS that it would not seek to replicate the council's stance, union members at TCS decided not to join in the industrial action. This shows, yet again, the complexity of employment relations in a multi-agency environment, as well as the tensions and contradictions that characterise relationships between different groups across the network.

The London site had strong traditions of trade unionism, also in UNISON but in a different section from those in the rest of TCS, and perhaps because of this the partnership forums had not developed there. There had been some efforts soon after the PPP was established to instigate forums but the union representatives had been suspicious of the company's intentions and made sure they filled all the seats on the forum in the first instance. The UNISON convenor at TCS-L explained that the draft agreement originally included a clause allowing for a staff forum:

> As far as we were concerned this was an attempt to undermine collective bargaining. The way we countered that was by making sure that all the reps were from UNISON, so effectively we had two opportunities to discuss

things with them rather than one. And actually the staff forum's been defunct now for about nine months, although one is scheduled for Thursday. I think probably because they've been told to by head office, but our approach will still be to say that as the vast majority of staff are in UNISON, the representatives are accountable.

This was reinforced during interviews with individual workers – both from TCS and the agency – as nobody mentioned the forum when we asked questions about meetings with management. In short, the union occupied a rather complicated role at this site. On the one hand, it remained powerful due to its historical strength and high levels of union membership, but it had been unable to resist the introduction of agency workers onto the site and it no longer felt part of the wider UNISON branch at the London council. Moreover, management at the site had been attempting to communicate with staff more directly, rather than just through the union, and as the critical mass of new workers – either into TCS or via the agencies – grew, their collective identity and links with the council became even more distant.

Conclusion

The unions are putting a lot of emphasis on opportunities for revitalisation through the partnership and organising approaches. But both approaches are predicated on a notion of the single employer, or if extended to multi-employers, confined to a single industry or occupation. Applying the approaches within a context of inter-organisational relations that extend across traditional industrial borders raises a number of issues which cast doubt on the likelihood of effective renewal solely through these methods. New approaches to union organisation and to union engagement with management may be required to provide effective voice mechanisms in a changing system of production and employment relations.

The partnership approach relies heavily on reaching accommodations with management, on the basis that co-operative relationships will provide a route to achieve mutual benefits. Some commentators are not convinced that this approach will work even in the single employer context, but our study suggests that the concept becomes more complex and problematic in a context of multi-employers operating across organisational boundaries. While the challenge to find common ground between management and workers and between all subgroups of workers and management is difficult enough within a single bounded organisation, the challenge increases considerably when more than one employing organisation is involved. Where the employing organisation is embedded in a range of inter-organisational relations, the employer does not necessarily have the freedom or discretion to deliver the benefits to the workforce that a partnership relationship is dependent upon. If business to business contracting is establishing many of the parameters to the organisation of work and employment – by shaping price, quality, timing and other standards – then to form partnerships that do not engage with the terms of such contracting clearly severely limits the scope for gains to one side of the partnership – the workforce. Yet extending the partnership concept to the network or set of inter-organisational relations raises new problems. Not only are there increased opportunities for diversity of interests among workers drawn from different employing organisations and among management servicing organisations with potentially different short- and long-term goals but the diversity of interests may emerge out of the nature of the inter-organisational relations. For example, much of the perceived advantages from contracting come from lower cost operations and shifting the risk from clients to suppliers. To the extent that inter-organisational relations are formed with such objectives in mind, there are strong grounds for anticipating that the interests of workers and management across the organisational divides can be characterised as more competing than complementary. Some of the literature on supply chains and network firms has focused on the mutual benefits, based on high trust relations, to be gained from inter-organisational relations aimed at sharing expertise. Dyer and Singh (1998) have suggested that the notion of social capital – that could be considered the basis for generating gains from partnership – should be conceptualised as embedded in the network rather than in the individual organisation. Under these conditions a partnership model could be regarded as still appropriate. However, such ideal type examples of relational contracting are likely to be relatively rare in practice, particularly within a low trust environment as in the UK. Moreover, the partnership now has to deliver not only a means whereby mutual benefits emerge out of the internal employment relationship but also from inter-organisational contractual arrangements. The term partnership has been in vogue to describe not only new agreements between management and workers (or trade unions) as discussed here, but also new inter-organisational relationships between the public sector and private sector service providers. However these two uses of the term have not normally been taken together. The possibility of partnership delivering simultaneous mutual gains from both inter-organisational relations and management–employee relations is perhaps just a little too Panglossian, even for public rhetoric.

Comparable problems arise when applying the organising approach in a context of fragmenting organisations and complex inter-organisational relationships. This approach depends on unions (and in particular worker representatives) being able to mobilise common interest among workers at the workplace, and on sufficiently strong local organisation to put pressure on management. Unions have had some successes in mobilising workers at call centres (Bain and Taylor 2001), but the trend towards subcontracting and fragmentation make this more difficult to realise. Where workers are engaged on relatively short-term contract work or employed through agencies, there are difficulties in building up areas of local union strength and in finding workers able and willing to take on representative roles within individual organisations. It is difficult to generate real shared interests among workers who are employed by different firms and on different types of contract, across different parts of the production or service delivery process. The traditional organising approach in a context of fragmentation is to establish common communities of interest at the industry or occupational level. While there may be scope for some renewal of the organising approach around the development particularly of new occupational and professional categories, the workplace-based recognition legislation does not foster such an approach. Moreover for many groups of workers, such an approach does not address the issue of where the real power in their employment relationship actually lies – that is within the supply chain relationship or within business-to-business contracting (Dean 2002; Erickson *et al.* 2002; Johnston 1994). Decisions over whether to recognise trade unions within the workplace are not based solely on the relative merits of providing employee voice over limiting internal management discretion; they may also depend on management's expectations of both current clients' and future clients' attitudes towards subcontracting to a unionised or a non-unionised supplier organisation. The dynamics of trade union organisation and renewal are therefore also closely tied in to the dynamics of inter-organisational relations and contracting.

If there is to be trade union renewal through either new relationships with management or through new ways of organising, there is need for trade unions to take on board the changing nature of economic organisation and to recognise the need to develop new communities of interests and contours of both organisation and bargaining. However, trade unions also need to be supported by public policies that facilitate rather than hinder the adaptation of collective mechanisms to new arrangements. Trade unions have been particularly restricted in developing new communities of interests by the very restrictive interpretation of their legitimate sphere of interests – to the immediate workplace – as found in both the collective labour law of the 1980s and 1990s and indeed in New Labour's legislation on trade union recognition. The treatment of industrial relations issues as ones to be resolved at the single workplace has been in contrast to the increasing inter-dependency between organisations in the production process that may influence both management attitudes towards recognition and the possibilities of developing strong systems of worker organisation. The need for a broader approach to collective organisation has only recently come back on the agenda through the debate over the impact of public sector contracting on the creation of a two-tier workforce (Earnshaw *et al.* 2002). For the first time since the 1980s there is active talk of taking into account the industrial relations record – including the equal opportunities policies – of potential supplier companies in decisions over business-to-business contracting. Such developments in public policy could help to swing the balance of employer opinion, from assuming that the development of union recognition agreements and partnership agreements creates risks of client disapproval to a situation where, given the importance of the public sector, that evidence of active engagement with unions could be a point of advantage in the competitive bidding process. The case study of TCS exemplifies both these tendencies – it has a well publicised partnership agreement that it uses to demonstrate its good faith in public sector bidding, while for its private sector clients it has been happy to retain a non-union environment in its multi-client call-centre sites. Facing both ways, as TCS itself acknowledges, will not necessarily be a viable long-term strategy and there is a need for a new policy environment that require the organisation's full record on employment relations to be taken into account in public procurement, not simply its policies at selected sites. Trade union renewal cannot necessarily be achieved simply through the initiatives of unions and the pursuit of mutual gains – even if accepted as a viable strategy – needs to be pursued at a wider level than the individual workplace. Unions need to start thinking outside the traditional box of single employer workplace organisation and partnership and establish new alliances up and down supply chains But their efforts in this regard need to be supported by public policy that promotes the legitimacy of these new communities of interest and contours of collective bargaining and partnership.

Note

1. For example the bookmaker had a partnership agreement with unions at its in-house operations, while the mobile-phone company had no union recognition at its main site operations.

5
Inspiring Activists: The Experience of Minority Ethnic Women in Trade Unions

Geraldine Healy, Harriet Bradley and Nupur Mukherjee

Introduction

Renewal or revitalisation has been a major concern for unions internationally. The debates have raged from the contentious service model to the focus on protection in the workplace (following Waddington and Whitston 1997) to the more activist emphasis in the literature on union renewal (see Calveley and Healy 2003; Fairbrother 2000; Fosh 1993) or mobilisation theory (Kelly 1998). The need to address a more diverse membership base has been crucial to the strategies adopted by the Organising Academy (see Heery *et al.* 2002), which has promoted the view that recruitment will be more successful if union organisers and potential members have similar personal attributes, a like-with-like model. For example, young organisers are considered more effective recruiters of young people than are older organisers. Women, too, are part of the debate as unions have come to realise that women are an increasingly important part of their membership base and the importance of women organisers in organising women and bringing equality issues to the bargaining agenda is affirmed in the literature (Bradley 1999; Kirton and Healy 1999; Colgan and Ledwith 1996). Union attention to black and minority ethnic (BME) groups has also grown in significance. Traditionally, black and minority ethnic workers were more likely to become union members, particularly African Caribbean workers (Modood *et al.* 1994) although recent Labour Force Survey data suggest that this has been sustained for women but not for men.[1]

Little research attention has been paid to the experience of black and minority ethnic women trade union activists and this chapter aims to address this deficit. Against the contemporary background of race relations in Britain, the chapter explores why and how black women become active in their unions. In doing so, the chapter seeks to place black and minority ethnic women in the debates about union revitalisation and renewal. It examines the role that trade unions play in involving and representing black workers and brings the cross-cutting nature of gender and ethnicity into the literature on union activism. This is important as traditionally industrial relations researchers adopt a gender-blind approach to their work (see Wacjman 2000). Whilst there is an increasing awareness of the importance of gender to industrial relations analyses, only a few studies consider the interrelationship between gender and race (e.g. Kirton and Greene 2002; Munro 2001; Colgan and Ledwith 2000).

The context

Black and minority ethnic workers are an important group in the British labour market and therefore for unions to organise. Whilst the 2001 Census data reveals that 9.9 per cent of the population of England and Wales in April 2001 identified itself as being from an ethnic minority (including 1.2 per cent Irish), there are wide differences across the country and between sectors. London, for example, is the region with the highest proportion of people from an ethnic minority (32.1 per cent) (Census 2001). Sectoral differences show that women are more likely than men to work in the public sector and this tendency is greater for black women and those from other ethnic groups (except Indian women) (Hibbett 2002). The public sector is the new heartland of trade unions, which further strengthens the incentive of trade unions to take the organisation of black and minority ethnic workers seriously. Thus a combination of social justice and pragmatism puts ethnic minority workers' concerns on the trade union agenda.

The profile of such concerns has been raised in recent years in Britain. The racially motivated murder of Stephen Lawrence and the extraordinarily tenacious fight for justice by his parents has had far-reaching effects on organisations in Britain.[2] The Inquiry into the death of Stephen Lawrence stated unequivocally that 'It is incumbent upon every institution to examine their policies and the outcome of their policies and practices to guard against disadvantaging any section of our communities' (MacPherson 1999). The impact of this Inquiry has been significant, not least upon the Trades Union Congress (TUC) and its constituent unions. The TUC subsequently set up the Stephen Lawrence Task Group (SLTG) to consider institutional racism in trade unions. It is significant that the unions who participated in our study all had a member on the Task Force committee and its impact was resonating during the course of our research. A legal response to the Stephen Lawrence Report was the passing of the Race Relations (Amendment) Act 2002, an Act, which whilst welcome, is restricted in its effect by its limitation to the public sector. The push for change in national policy-making in trade unions forms the backcloth that shapes the central issue of the chapter, union activism and participation.

Debates about activism tend to be linked with possibilities for union renewal and revitalisation (Fairbrother 2000; 1996; Fosh 1993). Fairbrother's work has formed the base of the renewal debate which is seen as comprising a set of processes concerned with union survival and development within the workplace; these include, the recruitment and replenishment of new generations of activists, the building of workplace activity in the context of restructuring and the development and promotion of mutual support between local union members and leaders (Fairbrother 2000, 47–78). Indeed the importance of local union activism is widely acknowledged (e.g. Calveley and Healy 2003; Greene *et al.* 2000; Darlington 1994; Fosh 1993). According to Fosh 1993: 577), 'the possibility for union renewal comes through building up the base level of participation by careful local leadership so that members can more easily be encouraged to take part in collective activities in times of necessity'. Fairbrother's argument, set against a public sector context, is that with the development of a more decentralised and devolved form of management, albeit within the confines of centralised government controls, comes a corresponding devolvement of industrial relations issues. Consequently workers have turned to their immediate trade union representatives for assistance thereby increasing local union activity, which in turn encourages union renewal in the workplace (Fairbrother 1994; 1996). The literature both supports and contradicts Fairbrother's view. For example, Bradley found conditions of renewal, such as the challenge to market testing and opposition to appraisal, that led to an increased and explicit collectivism (1999: 200–1), whereas Fitzgerald and Stirling, argue that 'resilience' is more apposite than 'renewal' (1999: 47).

Such findings indicate that the conditions for renewal are complex and in no way deterministic. Calveley and Healy (2003) argue that there will be circumstances where workers may experience heightened activism but meet conditions that negate the transformation of this activity to renewal (through the processes identified by Fairbrother 2000), and that could arguably lead to retreat in a particular workplace. Nevertheless, this process should not be viewed in a static way; the authors go on to remind us that workers and union members bring their experiences and politics with them into the workplace, and these will influence current and future interpretations of management actions, union responses and their preparedness to take action. Their study shows that the dynamic nature of workplace industrial relations indicates the constant and complex interrelationship of the renewal process with both resilience and retreat (Calveley and Healy 2003: 110).

The union renewal thesis mirrors much industrial relations research in being blind to issues of gender and ethnicity. When gender and race are brought into the debate, it is enriched. The diversity of union membership and the role that diverse groups might play in contributing to union renewal or revitalisation is rarely if ever to the fore in renewal debates. There are, nevertheless, important studies on black workers and trade unions (e.g. Virdee and Grint 1994; Lee and Loveridge 1987). Virdee and Grint (1994) argue that a self-organising strategy may be a viable addition if not necessarily an alternative to conventional organising. In their study of self-organising groups in 1989/90, they found that self-organisation was especially important, 'where general representatives are not regarded as adequate to the task of articulating and resolving the grievances of particular interests' (1994: 222). They go on to contend that 'the more black and minority representatives there are at the superordinate and subordinate levels the more likely it will be that policies are enacted' (1994: 223). For Virdee and Grint, trade unions are not simply class-oriented organisations, but nor are they essentially exclusivist or inherently racist; they see trade unions as neither unambiguously advantageous nor disadvantageous for black members. We would argue that it is the interrelationship between union structures, officers and active members that create the conditions of advantage or disadvantage for particular groups.

This is evidenced in the increasing body of literature on women's self-organisation (Colgan and Ledwith 1996; 2002; McBride 2001; Munro 2001) which also highlights the way that women's factions challenge union oligarchy (Healy and Kirton 2000), and in the work on black self-organisation (McKenzie 2003; Virdee and Grint 1994; Lee and Loveridge 1987). In some circumstances unions can and do enable; in the context of sustained union membership, Briskin (1999) asserts that 'the Canadian experience has demonstrated that unions can help to reconcile the competing interests of diverse groups of workers and build a stronger labour movement'. The development of black and women's separate organising has been a feature of modern trade unionism and reflects a challenge to the dominant order of trade unions. Further it implicitly reflects on the relevance of different levels of analysis, in particular the interrelationship between the macro context (which sets the dominant gendered and ethnicised orders) with the micro context of the workplace.

The research

Our work was undertaken some ten years after that of Virdee and Grint (1994) and focused on black and minority ethnic women. The data are drawn from a study of minority ethnic women activists within trade unions. The study aims to render visible aspects of the experiences of this under-researched group.

The research draws on case studies of four unions, the CWU, NATFHE, UNISON and USDAW. The four unions represent a range of occupational groupings from professionals to clerical workers to manual workers and have different gender compositions. The aim was to reflect the diversity of minority ethnic women's employment experience in unions. It was particularly important to include UNISON as, whilst already well researched (see e.g. McBride 2001; Munro 2001; Colgan and Ledwith 2000; 1996), it represents a benchmark for democratisation. UNISON has introduced the most far-reaching structural changes designed explicitly to include the interests of women, black and minority ethnic, disabled and lesbian and gay members' self-organising groups (SOGs).

Phase One of the project began in late 2000 and involved (a) discussions with ten national union officers about policies on ethnicity and gender and union initiatives to improve representation and participation and (b) documentary data collection. Phase Two involved 55 in-depth interviews with minority women activists mainly located in London and Bristol, undertaken in 2001–02. These give insight into the experience of a potential 'double disadvantage' of ethnicity and gender in their workplaces. Our sample was identified in a number of ways: (a) by the case study unions (b) by women who had already been interviewed (a snowballing effect) and (c) by approaching women at conferences. We also actively sought to achieve a reasonable balance by ethnicity, particularly with respect to African-Caribbean and Asian members. In fact despite our best efforts, the sample was skewed to African-Caribbean women.[3] Although the women portrayed their own ethnicity in a range of ways, we use a narrow categorisation which follows common sociological terminology (see Table 5.1).

The methodological approach was primarily qualitative. The interviews were in-depth and semi-structured with the intention of allowing the interviewees to give their views and stories in a minimally directed context. We defined 'activist' in an open way. We wanted to allow for different degrees of activism and to recognise that people may come in and out of activist roles, a point that may be more apposite to women, who tend to have different working patterns over the life cycle (see Bradley *et al.* 2004). Thus, we sought to interview women who could be described as 'formal activists' and 'informal activists' (Fosh 1993), that is, women who had a formal lay union role at the time of the study, those who previously held such roles, and women who were less formally active (they attended union meetings, spoke up on issues, would stand on a picket line and so on). We therefore interviewed women who were full-time lay officials, including those seconded to the union, women who were shop stewards and women who participated in the union activities but held no formal roles.

Table 5.1 Ethnic origin of respondents

	CWU	NATFHE	USDAW	UNISON	PILOT	Total
African	2	2	4	1	1	10
African-Caribbean	5	4	8	13	2	32
Asian	4	5	2	1	—	12
American	—	—	1	—	—	1
Total	11	11	15	15	3	55

Attendance by the researchers at a number of women's and black workers' events (conferences, workshops and SOGs) helped inform an understanding of the specific issues and problems that concern women and black and other ethnic minority workers.

Policies and practices for inclusion

The inclusion of women and black workers in trade unions has been characterised by structures, strategies and edicts to recruit and involve a more diverse membership. These approaches have been uneven in their effect across the trade union movement and their prioritisation over time. This section aims to provide a picture of the range of equality structures in the four case study unions (CWU, NATFHE, UNISON and USDAW) and their links to TUC initiatives. The section is informed by interviews with equality officials in the TUC and the case-study unions and by documentary sources.

All four unions are affiliated to the TUC and send delegates to both the TUC Women's and Black Workers' Conference. This is one means of women and black workers finding voice in the wider trade union movement. Women and black workers have pressed over time to ensure that the union movement gives importance to their respective concerns. It was in 1979 that the TUC produced the Equality Charter for Women and since then a range of initiatives have been introduced to ensure women's wider participation in the union and to get equality issues on the bargaining agenda in Britain and in the European Union (EU) (Dickens 1998). Women's progress in union government over time was demonstrated by Healy and Kirton (2000). Similarly, the importance of black workers to the TUC and its affiliated unions is not a new issue. In 1981, the TUC launched the *Black Workers' Charter*. In 1990 it commissioned a research report on the involvement of black workers in trade unions. In 1993 the TUC Black Workers' Conference asked the TUC to review the progress of unions in implementing the recommendations of this report and also sought information on action with respect to black women (TUC 1994: 2). The push from women and black workers' delegates ensured women's and black members' issues remained on the union agenda and this push is a recurrent theme today.

The SLTG set in train a new era for race initiatives in unions and its composition[4] reflected the need to give a high profile to race and racism. The broad aim of the Task Group was to tackle institutional racism both in the workplace and the union. The range of reports, conferences and educational initiatives that has emerged from the work of the Task Group is impressive as are the initiatives to embed race equality issues into union policy, for example, in partnership and organising. The TUC is committed to a 'serious shift of resources to tackling racism in the workplace'. At the same time, public and union awareness of key areas of disadvantage have been highlighted through for example, the freephone 'root out racism' hotline, the SLTG Web Site,[5] TUC and other union publications.

Against the background of the SLTG and the push for separate organising, the relationship between inclusion and separatism comes to the fore. Each union and the TUC have separate conferences for black workers and women, which submit motions to the union annual conferences and the annual TUC respectively. The four unions have a range of equality initiatives, many of which involve separate structures such as informal networks, training for black members, SOGs and others which involve explicit inclusion, such as additional seats and reserved seats. Importantly, strategies of separateness aim to ensure inclusionary outcomes. National conference debates reflected concern for injustice and ranged from workplace to sectoral to societal (national and international) level[6] and served to inform and raise consciousness about gendered or ethnicised issues.

Turning to the four case-study unions, Table 5.2 indicates the proportion of women and black members, women in conference and the executive in each union. It is evident that women are not represented proportionally in any of the case study unions.

The CWU is a male-dominated union, which recruits members from the Post Office, BT and other telephone companies, cable TV, the Alliance and Leicester and Girobank, although in practice BT and the Post Office are the dominant employers. Occupational groups represented include: engineering, computing, clerical, mechanical, driving, retail, financial and manual skills. The CWU Equal Opportunities Department was formed at the inception of the union.[7] There are four Advisory Committees established, dealing with areas of potential discrimination. These are: the Women's Advisory Committee (WAC); the Ethnic Minorities' Advisory Committee (EMAC); the Lesbian and Gay Advisory Committee (LGAC) and the Disability and Special Needs Advisory Committee (DSNAC).[8] There are no reserved seats.

The CWU mainly operates through two contrasting cultures. Harassment and bullying on both sexist and racist dimensions were reported in the Post Office through, for example, pornography, indecent postcards, and racist

Table 5.2 Representation in the union

	Total membership	Female membership (%)	Black membership (%)	Women at conference (%)	Women in executive (%)
CWU	300 000	21	7	na	6
NATFHE	65 000	47	4	na	25*
UNISON	1 300 000	72	10	58	62
USDAW	310 000	60	5	44	53

Note: * at least 25 per cent.

Source: SERTUC, March 2000.

comments on frames and walls. Cases were reported but not dealt with due to management and union collusion. BT was a different scenario. In 2001, BT was cited as the number one-rated company for promoting racial equality in the business environment by Business in the Community's Race for Opportunity (RfO) campaign.[9] Nevertheless, the gap between rhetoric and reality in human resource management in BT was evident in the CWU experience. Following the Stephen Lawrence Report, the CWU commissioned an independent audit to investigate the state of race equality in the union. The report was an important milestone in the union's approach to equality because of its transparently critical nature.

NATFHE recruits academic and academic-related staff in a range of educational institutions. NATFHE describes itself as a professional association but this 'professional' role is interrelated with its key trade union role. As part of its inclusionary strategies, the (elected) National Executive Council (NEC) has two black representatives, one lesbian and gay representative, and one disabled representative. At least 25 per cent of the NEC must be women. NATFHE is the only union to have had a black president. NATFHE has a range of member networks and aims to use its website to enhance links within and between networks. Of interest to this project was the view among NATFHE officers interviewed that 'black women tend to go into black members' groups rather than the women's group ... they identify a felt oppression based on race not gender'. Indeed it was felt that 'white women collude with structures which are disadvantageous to black women'. In NATFHE, the prioritising of identities is brought to the fore, since unlike some other unions members have to choose only one group to join. The collective sense of oppression identified is translated into a more closed approach to black networks in NATFHE. For example, unlike the CWU, only black members are allowed to attend the Black Members' Conference.

Following the SLTG, NATFHE appointed an officer to co-ordinate the Stephen Lawrence project. We were told 'we are pushing at an open door'. This led to plans to tackle issues of racism in every department in the union organisation and to initiatives to reactivate black networks that were established in the early 1990s. Other important initiatives emerged including the initiation of the Commission for Black Staff in Further Education with the Further Education Funding Council, UNISON, and the Association of Colleges about taking a joint approach. In 2000, an Equality Unit was created. Joint union initiatives with the Association of University Teachers (AUT) also pushed to get tangible agreements through Universities UK to get an Equal Opportunities framework agreement. The equality official works with/sits on a range of bodies dealing with race equality issues, e.g. Qualifications and Curriculum Authority Equal Opportunities Forum, Equality Challenge HE Steering Group, CRE Education Strategy Group.

It was reported to us that black members in NATFHE face subtle forms of discrimination in colleges and universities, where they are often in a tiny minority; at about 4 per cent of the teaching force, black academics are under-represented in both further and higher education. The gendered pay gap identified by the Bett Report (1999) and the increasing use of agency staff and part-time staff create negative conditions for women in the education sector, which are disproportionately experienced by black and Asian women, who make up a high percentage of part-time or casualised staff.

UNISON is the largest trade union in the UK with a recorded membership of 1.3 million, 72 per cent of whom are women, with an estimated 10 per cent being black (SERTUC 2000). UNISON is the result of a merger of three public sector unions, COHSE, NALGO and NUPE. UNISON members work in the public services, utilities and for private contractors providing public services. They include manual and white-collar staff working full or part time in local authorities, the health services, colleges and schools, the electricity, gas and water industries, transport and the voluntary sector.

UNISON's approach to equality is enshrined in its constitution. The mechanism for achieving gender equality was threefold: proportionality, fair representation and self-organisation (Colgan and Ledwith 2000: 246), a combination of inclusion and separateness. The NEC has 70 seats plus four additional seats for each SOG. SOGs for women, lesbians and gay men, black members and members with disabilities exist at national, regional and branch levels and are supported by officers at national and regional level. Election mechanisms ensure that at least 60 per cent of the executive are women, including 14 reserved seats for low-paid women. The complexity of UNISON is all the more evident with the recognition that there are 2000 branches, each of which is encouraged to have a lay equalities officer. Issues relating to black and women members feed through to the Black Members' or the Women's National Conference or via regional structures which feed into the NEC and the annual conference. There is a Black Women's Caucus at UNISON, which is not policy-making but offers support, advice and an open network for black women within the union. In mid-2001, there were two black women on the NEC. At every level of the union, when people are elected to committees or delegations, women must be elected in fair proportion to their membership. For example the NEC has to elect 44 women out of its 67 seats and low-paid women hold 13 seats. An equality officer focuses on NEC race policy and the membership of black members, advises and services the SOGs and was on the TUC's SLTG and its Race Committee. At the time of the fieldwork there were 15 people with equalities responsibilities in UNISON, although it was made clear that all organisers should also deal with equalities.

In response to the SLTG, UNISON has developed an action plan that covers bargaining, organising, training and learning and the role of UNISON as an employer. UNISON reported that black and women's issues are high on the agenda. Indeed it was said that 'it's a women's union'. Issues that specifically concern black members are redundancies, fixed term contracts and disciplinaries. The context within which UNISON members work provides the backdrop to this picture. The public sector has gone through dramatic and seemingly perpetual change with increasing managerialism, devolvement and increasing measurement of services and workers. This is coupled with increasing insecurity and in some sectors major labour shortage and turnover. Such a context provides a fertile environment for discrimination, harassment and bullying.

USDAW has about 310 000 members: 60 per cent are women and an estimated 5 per cent are black members. Union of Shop, Distributive and Allied Workers (USDAW) members work in a variety of occupations and industries, which include retail, distribution and manufacturing. USDAW, a union with high turnover, has also increased its membership by nearly 7 per cent since 1997. Its major remit is recruitment and membership of the TUC's Organising Academy is important to a union that has to recruit a significant proportion of its membership each year in order to stand still.

Whilst USDAW has had equality officers since 1985 and a National Race a National Race Relations Committee since 1991, equality policies and practice were uneven in their effect due to changes in personnel and structures. The appointment of a Women and Equalities Officer in 1999, with a remit for women, black, disabled and gay and lesbian members' interests, led to a more consistent approach. The Women and Equalities Officer acts as Secretary to the National Women's Committee and the National Race Committee. Her job is to implement the wishes of the committees but also 'give them a bit of a steer'. The interrelationship between an official with expert knowledge and members with direct experience of discrimination forms part of the inclusionary process of representation between officials and members.

The uneven development of equalities structures across unions is evident in USDAW, but the SLTG has raised their profile. The focus has previously tended to be 'out there' but USDAW members are now looking inward and 'are pushing on reserved seats'. This would clearly be a departure for the Union and its culture in that we were told that the idea of reserved seats 'is quite new and it's very difficult to use that language here'. Clearly such discussions promoted nervousness. There has been a positive change in gender composition with the EC now having nine women but at the time of the interview there were no black members and in memory only one black person had been on the EC. In recognition of the need to provide structures to encourage black members' activism, there are black members' and black women's get-togethers and 'tackling racism' training courses to challenge racism in the workplace.

USDAW representatives work in a highly competitive business environment. Bullying has increased as a problem for USDAW members directly resulting from competitive pressures on managers who have to deliver targets. The push for customer loyalty compounds the problem of bullying around working time arrangements. Black and white women suffer from the unfriendly working practices. In theory, because of the availability of part-time work, the problem should be less for part-time workers. In practice, part-timers' needs are not prioritised. Part-timers are often employed on low hours' contracts with a 16 hours' base that requires them to be flexible, 'to flex up'.

Whilst each of the case study unions had adopted positive action strategies, these were of different degrees of breadth and depth ranging from the liberal (CWU and USDAW) to the more radical (NATFHE and UNISON). We also noted some institutional efforts to reconcile black women's multiple identities as both black and female. Taking two of the processes identified by Fairbrother (2000), we have identified the particular conditions relevant to women and black workers of 'mutual support between levels of union members and leaders'; we shall now see the impact these have on 'the recruitment and replenishment of new generations of activists'.

Activism

We sought to interview 'activist' women. The term 'activist' is often used in a taken for granted way and it is important to make the case for widening the definition of activism to consider not only the credentialised steward, but other key union actors in the workplace. When asked what meanings the interviewees attributed to the term union 'activist', their replies reflected a range of meanings and a perspective over time, alongside their own specific experiences. Women's definitions of 'activism' varied. For some it was about fighting for social justice but racism and discrimination were often to the fore in activists' self-identification. The following woman personifies the total commitment often associated with activism.

> I would define myself, first and foremost as somebody who is here to break down every barrier that constitutes discrimination, or racism, or unfairness on my colleagues or on myself. I would describe myself as somebody who fights for, and will continue to fight for equality in your day-to-day work, Monday to Friday, to whatever hours you do. And if that makes me an activist then I'm an activist.

This total commitment to the union was also expressed by another woman, who stated that for her an activist was:

> Somebody that will give their all to the union basically, somebody that will try and help anybody within their branch as well as their members, and outside which I do.

Whereas another demonstrates a reluctant activism, because she does not fit her own image of an activist:

> I'm probably reluctant to say yes but in the sense that um, if there's an issue on the board I will argue it, I will argue it to other people, in the sense that

I will take a position or line on it...And as I said I will go out with the action and you know, suffer the consequences. You know, so in that sense yes. But if I was arguing that I am a political activist then I would say no. You with me? It's probably because I am not consumed by it, and that's probably how I would evaluate it...I try and get a life outside of work.

A sense of the 'typical' union activist as a 'banner-waving militant' was expressed and again this may put women off union engagement, a finding that also emerged in Bradley's North East study (1999). Indeed it also emerged that the dichotomy between 'activist' and 'member' was alienating to some 'informal activists'. It may also deter women from volunteering themselves for union roles, since they see themselves as unable to fulfill the impossible ideal of 'giving their all'. The disapproval of the 'activist/member' distinction sometimes made on training courses is illustrated in the following comment:

She (the trainer) drew a distinction between activists and members, so when she put it across to us I said I felt, that I would feel really devalued because she more or less inferred that as a member even attending the training that you were not in the same league as an activist. Does that make sense? And what we were told by the tutor for this weekend, well actually (the union) has been looking at the use of this term, so you have touched in a sense on a subject that we have been looking more closely at, as to how people are perceiving these terms, and they said that we are looking to gain, towards a new term called active members, as opposed to activist or member.

This woman described her own activities in the union but she also identified the limitations she put on her commitment:

what I am in a sense saying as a committee member, there is certain things on the work programme that I then have committed or am committing myself to doing or helping. A bit like this women's caucus, where, you know, I have committed myself to taking and giving information and making contact with people, but I wasn't taking, you know, the whole responsibility.

This example is important as it points to the benefits of wider collective involvement in union activities. To some extent this is becoming increasingly formalised with the greater number of union roles, such as safety representatives, learning representatives and equality representatives, thus providing an incremental route to activism. For the following woman, the safety representative role was a milestone for further activism.

Because of my union activities I became a safety rep a few years back, which then I ended up getting more involved with the union.

Whilst the widening of formal union roles is important, greater explicit acknowledgement and encouragement of informal activists' participation is needed. Here the development of the category of 'active member'; as part of union discourse may be a helpful way to enable unions to become more inclusive. This may also be a means of overcoming women's reluctance to take on tasks unless they feel they have the time and resources to 'do the job properly':

> Because there's so much going on that you need to be spot on with everything. And I'm a bit of a person if I can't do it the whole way, I don't do it at all.

Understandings of the term activism are informed by perceptions of political activism and the more pragmatic evaluation of different degrees of commitment.

Reasons for becoming active

For most activists, activism will be an emergent process stemming from factors that identified in the threefold theoretical model presented by Klandermans (1986): frustration–aggression, rational choice and social interactionist. In our research, the women's accounts displayed elements that would fit all three strands of this theory at different times. We shall use this as an organising device but recognise their interrelationship and the importance of time and change.

Frustration–aggression. These approaches see trade union participation as a reaction to frustration, dissatisfaction or alienation in the work situation (Klandermans 1986: 190). Amongst the women interviewed this reaction often emerged from an enduring sense of injustice. Sometimes, too it was informed by their home background and upbringing. In many cases, it emerged from a case of harassment or discrimination involving themselves or their co-workers. Racist and sexist treatment creates frustration–aggression in the workforce and may be a spur to union participation.

The following woman has been quoted at length; her account illustrates her experience of injustice and frustration and the way she decided to become a union representative. This suggests that frustration/aggression may be part of the explanation, but not sufficient. The family context was also taken into account in her decision to become active. This woman is all the more interesting as she is a part-time worker.

> Well, as I said I am a very vocal person basically, getting constantly into trouble, because I would be like, calling up managers and saying that this isn't in the handbook, that's not in the handbook and I was getting more

and more frustrated that my voice wasn't being heard and you know I got tired of talking to people, but they were being picked on, they weren't doing anything to like protect themselves. So I thought, I have had enough of this, and then I said um, I'm not going to stand for this and I went home and talked to my partner about it, and he said why don't you get more active in the union, because these people they need a voice and that's why they are asking you to help them. You know through the union you can basically help them. So I thought I'd do it and I applied to be a trade union rep and got accepted and have been one ever since.

Just as an effective union challenge to injustice may lead to greater union participation, paradoxically an ineffectual, or indeed racist, response may have the same outcome. The women in our study tended to face an existing gendered representation structure: 'The union is white male dominated; it's a man's domain'. As is well documented elsewhere (e.g. Healy and Kirton 2000; Bradley 1999; Colgan and Ledwith 1996), white men tend to dominate trade unions. This may not be sufficient to galvanise women to action; however where such representatives did not take equality issues seriously, the resulting frustration led to challenges within the branches and examples of black women standing against white men:

If there is any problem and you told him about it, he would say, 'Okay, I'll get back to you , I will let you know what I'm doing about it', and he'll forget about it, so we didn't know that he was trying to play a safe game with the managers.

In our research, the women union members who worked in particularly male-dominated workplaces found themselves in an environment where there were strong traditional and gendered union values and practices. A work culture of bullying and harassment was supported by a hard-nosed management approach. In this environment, sexism was as strong as racism. We were told of male arrogance and a dislike of 'noisy women'. There is little doubt that this culture spurred some of the black women in our study to get involved in the union.

By contrast, frustration emerging from racism may also drive people out of the union and their employing organisation:

Why am I not staying and fighting, when you see that there's no support at all? And my colleagues are supportive but they're not members of the union because they've withdrawn from the union ... You can't fight this sort of thing anymore. If there were one or two other black women, I would've felt comfortable.

Here was a woman, who was planning to retire early. There was a sense that she was driven out by the treatment she received. She was someone who had real potential to contribute to union revitalisation in her organisation, but felt too isolated to take on the challenge. This raises important issues about the limitations of union activities. This woman was well informed and knew how to get support, but:

> Because if there's no network, there's no support, you can't run to the equality conference delegates every time something (happens). And it's just an isolating experience. And I would say that (the union) should actually deal with their branch members and officers and explain to them how to deal with people who are isolated in their organisations.

In her workplace, it was the case that, 'There's no support. Nobody even understands the issues'. In this example there is clearly a management responsibility, but the union's task is to ensure their representatives are fully informed and sensitive to race and sex grievances. In itself this is a difficult task, since we know those whom the unions need to target most will be most resistant.

Rational choice theory. This accounts for participation from consideration of the individual costs and benefits of participation (Klandermans 1986: 190). Members make an instrumental calculation, in which the interest, support and ability to make changes through union activity are balanced against the time and effort involved and any attendant risks of participation. There are gendered aspects to this:

> ... women don't get involved in it. I can understand the reasons behind it because being like a rep, you're being asked to use a lot of time that isn't your own. You know... even though you're supposed to do everything within work time... You are using your own time. So the fact that you've got to go to work, come home, look after your family, children and everything else, you haven't got time to be a rep.

Many women became active when their children had left home and they had more time to get involved. The costs may also be in the workplace. There are risk factors for those who are prepared to challenge management through union activism (see Calveley and Healy 2003) or simply through becoming a union member.

> They (activists) will question not in a rude way and they'll just be told stop whinging, stop whining, I've seen it performing appraisals for them, and its sort of oh you'll be targeted and they are feeling targeted... I mean I'm not saying that everyone wants promotion or something but just to get on with their job. I feel (it) would be a mark against them if it's

known that they are members, some people don't care or it doesn't matter or they'll deal with it but most of the people don't want managers to know or their colleagues or team leaders to know, because you never know who gets promoted in the future and they'll remember it.

The calculation of risks may act against a propensity to participate, and as was evident here, to join.

It is also the case that a *post hoc* rationalisation may come into play. In some cases this emerged in very simple forms. One woman was extremely active in the union, but did not have a 'role'. By taking on the role of the safety representative, she was entitled to 'paid time off for union duties'. Her commitment to the union was no greater in time or energy, but her response was instrumental in the direction she chose. This example demonstrates both a prior union orientation and structural influences on the chosen form of participation. This is not however to suggest, that participation itself emerged from a purely instrumental (rational choice) perspective but that instrumentalism may be part of the equation.

Interactionist theories. These theories relate union participation to the networks and groups inside and/or outside the company in which employees work, that is, participation is inextricably bound up with group culture (Klandermans 1986: 190). In many ways this can be equated with solidaristic approaches to collectivism (see Healy 1997). The following woman illustrates the incremental nature of the development of a solidaristic approach:

> I've always taken full interest in the student union. I was involved in – sort of never actively involved in setting up particular groups. But I always used union facilities, always voted, was always interested in what the union was putting on and the issues they were dealing with. And naturally, when I went into the workplace I joined. I used to be part of the black caucus and was quite active in that. So I always turned up to my union meetings. I always contributed. So when I became part of (the union), we were very fortunate ... we had a small branch where it was ... And we all turned up and we didn't need meetings upon meetings to communicate. We'd get in there and sit and talk. It was like a big family, a happy occasion.

A number of women were pressed by their work colleagues to become representatives, particularly because they were outspoken, known as 'strong women'.

Collective motives deriving either from forms of class identification or from loyalty to the 'primary group' of co-workers are commonly cited reasons for getting involved. However, there is an additional element relating to ethnicity and commitment to anti-racism, which differentiates the experience of these ethnic minority women. In this case their primary identification is not with class or workgroup but with their ethnic community(ies).

Thus, black members' networks were crucial to the involvement of many women. These particularly took the form of SOGs in UNISON, but also gatherings and networks in other unions. Critically, this was a form of separatism, of faction. Studies of UNISON have demonstrated the value of SOGs in relation to the development and involvement of women and black members, lesbian and gay members and members with disabilities (see e.g. Colgan and Ledwith 2002; McBride 2001; Munro 2001).

Women in our study were inspired by attending SOGs and felt empowered by this involvement. We were told that whilst there might be a 'lukewarm' response to a notice publicising a union meeting, if there was a notice for a black SOG, it prompted more interest; as one woman said 'that was it for me. I was in there'. SOGs also widened members' horizons. Through these events they became enthusiastic attendees at courses and conferences. As one woman said:

> I enjoy every minute of it. I enjoy going to meetings, I enjoy going to my courses and finding out from my members what their problems are. So I take all the learning I can get ... It's my way of getting further education ... I feel much better, I feel like I've grown, I've really grown, it's amazing.

These groups are extremely important in the members' union lives, but also in terms of their personal development. We would argue that 'black' is an important organising rallying call within the union movement. We were told black networks promote curiosity which leads to attendance and then in many cases involvement:

> I mean everyone wants to know. (They think) 'OK, this is a black workers' conference. I'm a worker, I'm black, let's go and see what it's about.' So out of curiosity probably they will tend to come, turn up and then if they like what they see they will probably come again and tell their friends.

At the same time, we detected among the black women in our study an enthusiasm, energy and passion for union activity 'I love my union'. When we asked what could be done for black women, the following response was not untypical:

> I would say for black women, the first priority would be to get together and establish proper networks. Once you have established networks then you can plan various things with the union ... So I would say networking, then getting involved in the local committees etc. And the union should fight to get time for that.

In this way an initial interest in furthering racial justice and promoting equal opportunities can lead in to a much more generalised commitment to and belief in unions. A good few of our respondents now wished to 'give their all' to the union by moving one step further and working for their unions as paid officials. If unions are serious about their commitment to 'diversity' they should recognise this specific route into union work and promote and capitalise on it.

Making a difference?

We would argue that the women in different ways contributed to the recruitment and replenishment of a new generation of activists (see Fairbrother 2000). The interviews indicated the high level of enthusiasm and apparently boundless energy that the women had. This impacted on renewal through the recruitment of new members. For example, two of the women had set up branches in non-unionised firms. One reported winning a prize as the best recruiter of new members and another had joined up to 60 people in the previous year. Many also told of how they encouraged family members and friends out in their communities to join the relevant union in their job. The effect of these activists' participation in building unionism and challenging injustice has been inspiring.

We quote the following woman at length to indicate the different approaches used to promote activism:

Yeah, I tend to focus on black people, maybe I shouldn't, I mean where I work, there's only one black member of staff there and I made sure she joined UNISON, but even my white colleagues, I say look, you better join UNISON. But at the black workers' forum, I promote UNISON every time there's a meeting, I talk about them becoming stewards, there's not enough black stewards in this area, and they say 'oh UNISON don't do this, they don't do that ... ', I say, 'look it does as much as it can do, if there were more of you joining it, then we've got a voice, and our voice will be heard, but I can't do everything alone, you need to join'. And I try and give the positive things like, they do training courses, you can come on weekends, we do lots of workshops and anybody can come along as long as you let your branch know and they'll pay for it, they pay for childcare. I give them all the positive bits of UNISON, especially, those people, the staff who work in direct service delivery, social workers, those who are in residential, I said, 'look you may not like unions, but cover your backs, join a union and it may be hard, but if anything happens you need support here, join the union. And the majority of, I think you will find that most of um, black staff in our department, they may moan about the unions, and most of them have joined the union ... They pay their dues.

This woman is bringing together the complex set of interrelated motives identified by Klandermans (1986) by using the black workers' forum as a collectivity through which to encourage union recruitment and activism.

The impact of union initiatives emerging from the SLTG were important in building collectivism at the workplace and indeed in a wider context, for example:

> At the time of the MacPherson Report, it was like our branch that started off the training and stuff. Because it was meant to be just training within the branch, and it got into our local paper, *The Voice*, and then other people heard about it and we started getting calls like, 'Can we come on the course?'

The women in our study recognised that they faced multiple discriminations but acknowledged that their involvement in the union had helped themselves and others to challenge the combined impact of racist and sexist injustice:

> I am fortunate enough that I have the skills to challenge things that I think are not right but other people don't have those skills. For example, I have a few black colleagues here who don't have those kinds of skills (and just keep quiet).

The women challenged racism and sexism in both union officers and management. In the unions some older white male, long-term activists were reported as finding it hard to adapt to a more egalitarian climate. They were described as patronising and insulting to women, for example:

> And sometimes, when a member has gone, I says 'Why did you have that attitude towards her?' 'Oh she don't understand'. 'Then why didn't you try to make her understand?' Because I don't think he should be doing a lot of the cases he's dealing with because he has this thing, 'I am the man … and you are the woman, know your place'.

And

> (The men) they don't want to change. They're there; they get nominated, elected time after time after time.

The perception of women as passive trade union members was refuted many years ago, but the belief still lingers in male-dominated union contexts.

> They've got their ideal of what is best, and unfortunately it's a male dominated environment and they sort of feel that the little woman don't

help. You know, or the little women are the ones that are gonna break the strike. But in fact, it's the women that are saying, we've had enough of this crap and we need to go forward. And it does feel like we're taking it day in day out and we will strike because it's us who are suffering. And I think it was a real shock to them when they realised that these people were gonna stand up and be counted.

Exclusion may well lead to a more critical reflection. Those who may be marginalised in the workplace union may well find that they are freer to interpret events and propose solutions that are not hidebound by old traditions, customs and routines. As one woman said:

I think it's like a self-fulfilling thing. If you keep thinking that the members are like babies and you treat them like babies, then they'll act like babies. And that's what's happening.

After years of low degrees of participation in her union, becoming involved in a black workers' group led the following woman to initiate a major campaigning effort:

I was voted as the convener or something, and then I went out there on a campaign, I got everybody, every black person I knew in college and told them to tell friends and all that, so we had our first meeting and, it became quite big the group.

It is not easy to unpick the interrelated aspects of gender and race. As the following woman said:

If you just deal with the racism, it's not going to stop black women being harassed because of their gender. Sometimes obviously it's difficult to tell if a white person is harassing a black woman, is it because she's black or is it because she is a woman?

Her response, with others, was to form a women's group:

So we actually developed um, a women's support group. Which was mainly for political change but it was also to support each other as well. You know because things like harassment wasn't recognised as a trade union issue at all. There was still wolf whistles at women who went up to the rostrum at conferences and things like that.

In the context of a male-dominated environment, she was giving primacy to gender issues. However, this woman was also active in the black workers' collectivities in her union. She was in effect acknowledging the need to draw on multiple structures to combat injustice.

Conclusion

The cross-cutting aspects of ethnicity and gender are often neglected in studies on union revitalisation and renewal. In bringing these together, our analysis has focused on two levels, national union policy and the experience of activists in the union and in the workplace. In doing this we are not offering a dichotomous approach, which postulates the primacy of either a union-led or of a workplace activist-led explanation. Instead, we have emphasised the importance of the interrelationship between these two levels in understanding the current and dynamic reality of gender and ethnicity in trade unions.

Unions provide the means to recognise and challenge injustice. In the case of gender and ethnicity, they also contain the conditions which both enable or constrain the challenge to injustice. Structural reform in trade unions is mainly the response to the mobilisation of committed activists who seek to transform their unions to take account of gendered and ethnicised injustices. At the same time there may be movements in society which facilitate such activism; for example, the effects of the Stephen Lawrence Report and, in the public sector, the impact of the Race Relations (Amendment) Act. We also recognise that there may be potential collectivist costs for giving primacy to equality issues (see Bradley 1999: 205) and it is incumbent on unions to enable members to understand that injustice on a wide, rather than a traditional economistic, agenda is equally unacceptable.

The mobilisation of the women in this study increases the likelihood of enabling conditions. We would suggest that union renewal may also emerge from the gendered and ethnicised manifestations of injustice in the workplace. Our findings concur with those who argue for the importance of workplace leadership (Calveley and Healy 2003; Fairbrother 2000; Darlington 1994; Fosh 1993). However such leadership does not fall easily into Batstone *et al.*'s (1977) representative/delegate dichotomy; rather its form is dynamic and time specific. Batstone *et al.*'s model is too static to capture the complex lives and union activities of the women in our study. Indeed Darlington makes the obvious point that 'stewards may behave differently in varying situations and circumstances, depending on the issue and the work group involved' (1994: 20). What makes this particular group of women special is that they experience at first hand the gender and ethnicised order in all its harsh manifestations, both inside and outside the work environment. The women in this study challenged the injustices they saw flowing from this. Dedicated SOGs became the means both to recruit members and nourish activists.

This process is not unproblematic given the different meanings of 'activism' and 'activist'. For unions this raises important policy issues about formal and informal roles. Our study indicates that the increasing number of formal roles (e.g. safety representatives, learning representatives, equality representatives) should lead to a wider and stronger workplace union base. What is also important is the strengthening and acknowledgement of informal activities undertaken by committed union 'activists' and to promote a new category of 'active member', which might encourage the fainter-hearted to greater participation. We have drawn on Klanderman's (1986) conceptual framework, but stressed the interplay between the elements of his threefold model of union participation. The women in our study reported not only experiences of racism and sexism but also problems of resolving these through management or their trade union. This became a stimulus to activism, and a challenge to existing union structures. However, in some cases where there were no established networks, this had the reverse effect. In other words, the alienating effect of racism and sexism may on the one hand encourage union participation, but may also lead to union resignations. We have shown how women may calculate the costs of their involvement in trade union activism and reject this due to lack of time or the risk incurred in standing out against management. We suggest that this perspective may come into play at different points in decision-making and be manifested in different forms. We also found evidence of activism being facilitated by instrumental strategies to access, for example, time off for union duties.

An essential attribute of Kelly's (1998: 45) approach to mobilisation is attribution of blame for injustice to management; we would suggest that such attribution of blame may be also directed at unions. The evidence in our study is that, under certain conditions, women may attribute blame to their unions for (in)action in challenging injustice, which in turn may lead to union activism. Mobilisation and transformation of unions may go hand in hand; thus, the importance of local organisation and its sensitivity to race and gender issues is paramount. We would argue that the importance of separate organising is of particular significance to union revitalisation. The unions in our study are at different stages of development with respect to separate organisation, but our work indicates that this is a development that will motivate and collectivise workers who may hitherto have felt alienated. As we have argued elsewhere (Bradley *et al.* 2002); separate organisation may paradoxically lead to inclusion and collectivism in the union.

Whilst the path to inclusion and collectivism may be fraught with difficulties, our study indicates that black and minority ethnic women have an important part to play in the revitalisation of unions. Their experience suggests that in the future, the structuring of union representation needs to be sensitive to issues around social justice, ethnicity and gender. The women in our study were inspiring and as such they inspired others to participate in trade unionism; unions will be wise to take heed of their voices.

Acknowledgement

This research was funded by the ESRC Future of Work Programme: Project number: L212 25 2061, Handling Double Disadvantage: Minority Ethnic Women and Trade Unions. We are indebted to the women and the trade unions who took part in this study. We are also grateful to Edmund Heery for helpful comments on an earlier draft.

Notes

1. Holgate's analysis of union decline between 1993–2000 shows that despite a slow down in the fall in membership post-1997, the decline appears to have affected BME workers more than white workers. BME men have experienced the largest decline in density with an 11 per cent fall, compared to white women who experienced the lowest decline at 3 per cent. Of interest to this chapter is that BME women had the highest density in 1993 and, despite a decline of 8 per cent, they still have a union density, which is 5 per cent higher than any other group (Holgate 2003: 15–16).
2. Stephen Lawrence was murdered on 22 April 1993; his alleged killers, five white men, were never brought to justice. The lobbying for justice of Stephen Lawrence's parents led to the setting up in July 1997 of a Committee of Inquiry into his death. Chaired by Sir William Macpherson. MacPherson was charged with inquiring into the matters arising from the death of Stephen Lawrence in order particularly to identify the lessons to be learned for the investigation and prosecution of racially motivated crimes. The Inquiry found that the investigation was marred by a combination of professional incompetence, institutional racism and a failure of leadership by senior officers. Crucially, the Inquiry recognised the pervasiveness and complexity of racism by drawing attention to the discriminatory impact of institutional racism, defined as:

   > The collective failure of an organisation to provide an appropriate and professional service to people because of their colour, culture or ethnic origin which can be seen or detected in processes, attitudes and behaviour which amount to discrimination through unwitting prejudice, ignorance, thoughtlessness and racist stereotyping which disadvantages minority ethnic people. (MacPherson 1999)

3. The skewing may be partly the result of (b) above. The view of the key gatekeepers in our unions was that African-Caribbean women were more likely to be activists than were Asian women.
4. It was chaired by John Monks (the TUC General Secretary) and its membership reflected senior trade unionists including, from our case study unions, the General Secretaries of NATFHE, USDAW and UNISON and a Deputy General Secretary of CWU.
5. This includes hotline data, hotline stories and advice on tackling racism at work and examples of union best practice.
6. For example, the 2001 Black Workers' Conference reflects the diversity of themes of motions and composites including: development and training, Stephen Lawrence Task Force, action against institutional racism in the workplace, tackling racism through partnership, racist banter at work, trade union action on institutional

racism, psychometric testing, black workers and discrimination in appraisal and pay systems, equal opportunities monitoring, monitoring of employment tribunals applications, bereavement leave, anti-discrimination legislation, European race directive, religious discrimination, The Criminal Justice System, public inquiry – Zahid Mubarek, the Roger Sylvester case, deaths in custody, zero tolerance, representation of minority ethnic staff in the public sector, equality in performance management, recruitment of NHS staff, Civil Service Diversity Programme, education and MacPherson recommendations, refugees and asylum seekers, exploitation of developing countries' workforces, confronting hate crimes, HIV/AIDS in Africa, under-representation of black staff in Further and Higher Education.

7. The CWU is the result of a merger between the UCW (a mostly postal union with some telecommunications members) and the NCU (a mainly telecommunications union with some postal members).

8. Each of these committees is elected at Conference from among the membership and any members who are interested and are nominated by their Branch are able to apply. The four Advisory Committees feed into the Equal Opportunities Sub-Committee of the National Executive Council, which is the focus at national level for progressing equality issues. The Equal Opportunities Committee is also responsible for ensuring that the Union's policies on equal opportunities issues are implemented. The Advisory Committees, together with the Equal Opportunities Committee are responsible for making recommendations to the National Executive and also for campaigning on issues within their remit. The Equal Opportunities Department, as well as dealing with the work of these Committees and being involved in campaigning issues, gives advice to Branches on equal opportunities issues and through the hotline number provides assistance to members in respect of harassment and discrimination. In conjunction with the Branches and with the Union's Legal Department, the Equal Opportunities Department also pursues equality cases.

9. Research for the report was conducted over a three-month period against ten key indicators of organisational performance, spanning leadership and vision, investment, policy and planning, communication, marketing, ownership, employment (selection and retention, development and training), community involvement, supplier development and results/impact.

6
Trade Union Responses to Non-standard Work

Edmund Heery, Hazel Conley, Rick Delbridge,
Melanie Simms and Paul Stewart

Introduction

Throughout its history the trade union movement has had to adapt to changes in workforce composition. In recent decades, however, the rise and fall of industries and occupations has been overlain by another insistent pressure; the growth of forms of employment that diverge from the (male) norm of a full-time, open-ended contract. Across much of the developed world, there has been a growth of both temporary and part-time work (Booth *et al.* 2002; Smith *et al.* 1998), the latter being associated particularly with the feminisation of the workforce. The composition of jobs has altered, albeit with substantial variation between countries and across industries, with full-time and permanent jobs giving way to those with reduced hours or of limited duration. There has also been a shift away from direct employment towards self-employment and the supply and management of workers by labour market intermediaries (Phan 1999: 79).

In this chapter, we are concerned with the response of trade unions to these growing forms of 'non-standard' work. Non-standard work presents trade unions with a potent challenge. On the one hand, workers in non-standard jobs may have an acute need for union representation. Part-time and short-term temporary workers are more likely to be low paid, to be excluded from training and workplace benefits and to experience low job quality (Booth *et al.* 2002; Gallie *et al.* 1998: 154–84). Even well-paid freelance workers can face the problem of insecurity and find it difficult to maintain skills and access to paid work without the shelter of a conventional employment relationship (Dex *et al.* 2000; Kunda *et al.* 2002). On the other hand, the presence of non-standard workers may threaten the interests of existing union members through the undercutting of negotiated terms of employment (Heery and Abbott 2000: 158). The challenge for unions therefore is to weigh these competing pressures and decide whether or not to accept non-standard workers as part of their legitimate constituency: should trade unions seek to regulate and improve non-standard work or should they try and exclude non-standard jobs from the labour market?

In what follows, we examine how and why British unions have responded to the challenge of non-standard work for four separate categories, all of which have grown appreciably since the 1960s. The first and largest group are part-time workers, who have grown from 9 per cent of employees in 1961 to 16 per cent in 1971 to 21 per cent in 1981 before stabilising at a quarter of the workforce in the 1990s. Although the last decade has seen a sharp growth in the number of men working part-time, it remains a form of employment that is heavily gendered: in 2001 43 per cent of women were in part-time employment compared with only 8 per cent of men (Twomey 2002). The second group is made up of workers on fixed-term contracts (FTCs). FTC workers form a large component of Britain's temporary workforce, which grew rapidly in the early 1990s before tailing off at the end of the decade at about 6 per cent of total employment (Nolan and Slater 2003: 62–3). The public services, such as health and education, have been particularly heavy users of FTC labour though the incidence of temporary work has risen across much of the UK economy (Casey *et al.* 1997). The third group also forms part of the temporary workforce and consists of workers supplied to clients by private employment agencies. It has been estimated that about one million workers are engaged on agency placements at any one time, about 4 per cent of the workforce (Sisson and Marginson 2003: 167). There was strong growth in the scale and value of the private recruitment industry in the 1990s, coupled with an increase in the proportion of employers making use of agency labour (Millward *et al.* 2000: 47; Druker and Stanworth 2001: 74). The final group consists of self-employed freelancers, involved in selling labour services to employers. These are an important component of the self-employed, a group which expanded markedly in the 1980s from 7 per cent of total employment to a peak of 13 per cent before falling back to its present figure of 11 per cent (Nolan and Slater 2003: 63). As with agency work, there is evidence from the Workplace Employee Relations Survey of an increase in the proportion of employers using freelancers (Millward *et al.* 2000: 48), with industries such as television and publishing registering particularly strong growth (Dex *et al.* 2000; Saundry 1998; Stanworth and Stanworth 1997).

In examining trade union responses to these four types of labour, we have pursued a series of objectives. In the first place, we have used qualitative and archival research to identify the range of union responses to non-standard work that have emerged from the 1960s onwards. The aim here is to map the depth of union engagement by examining the form and rationale for policies that go beyond attempts at exclusion. Second, we have used a survey of trade union paid officers to identify the frequency of different responses across the trade union movement as a whole, to measure the breadth of engagement. This survey has also been used to identify the correlates of positive union responses to non-standard work and to test formally a series of explanations of union behaviour. Finally, we have used another survey, this time of trade unions, to identify the range of methods that are employed to represent the non-standard workforce. A core objective here has been to test claims that, for workers of these kinds, unions rely primarily on the provision of individual services (the method of 'mutual insurance') and on the provision of protective law (the method of 'legal regulation').

The qualitative research focused on trade unions that were known to have developed policy on one or more of the categories of non-standard work. The research included more than 100 interviews with paid and lay union representatives at different levels of union organisation and employers' representatives and analysis of union archives. We examined union annual reports, journals and the verbatim records of union conferences back to the late 1960s. The unions that were selected for this focused research were NATFHE, TGWU, UNIFI and USDAW for part-timers, AUT for FTC workers, ATL, NATFHE and TGWU for agency workers and BECTU, Equity and NUJ for freelancers. In addition, we used interviews and archives to trace the evolution of TUC policy on all four types of non-standard work from the 1960s to the present day. We also researched the cuttings archive of the pay research organisation, Incomes Data Services (IDS), for the period 1971–2002 to follow the evolution of collective bargaining and union legal activity on part-time work.

The two questionnaire surveys were administered to provide more systematic and broadly representative data. In 2001, all TUC-affiliated unions and all independent unions with at least 3000 members were surveyed on aspects of their formal policy on non-standard work. Questionnaires were completed by a senior national officer of each union (in most cases the general secretary) and a total of 56 completed returns were received (60 per cent), including 10 responses from the 15 largest trade unions in Britain. In 2002, a second survey was carried out of union paid officers working for 19 TUC-affiliated unions. The sample included large general unions like the GMB, Transport and General Workers' Union (TGWU) and UNISON and specialist unions with a tradition of representing workers on non-standard contracts, such as AUT, BECTU, CSP, Equity, NATFHE, NUJ, UCATT and USDAW. This questionnaire was sent to 1600 officers and gathered information on their involvement in recruiting and negotiating on behalf of part-time, FTC, agency and freelance workers. A total of 585 responses were received (42 per cent). The research as a whole was designed to combine the insight generated by case studies of innovation with the capacity to generalise, afforded by representative survey data.

Types of union response

The qualitative research identified four discrete union responses to non-standard work, each of which is characterised by a greater degree of acceptance of the specific needs of these workers. The four responses are set out schematically in Table 6.1 and range from exclusion, through acceptance but in a subordinate position, acceptance on the basis of equal treatment with workers in 'standard' employment to 'engagement', characterised by union attempts to represent the specific and differentiated needs of the non-standard workforce. Underlying each of the responses is the degree of legitimacy accorded to the interests of non-standard workers; each rests on a particular conception and evaluation of the interests of these workers. The responses have found expression in the set of 'internal' and 'external' policies unions develop on behalf of the non-standard workforce. The former consist of membership rules and arrangements for participation in union government, while the latter consist of bargaining and other policies to secure concessions from employers and the state.

Exclusion from membership and employment is a common initial response of unions to the emergence of new categories of labour within their job territories, which has been observed in the cases of both women and black workers (cf. Virdee 2000: 209; Cockburn 1983: 152–9). We identified cases of unions responding in like fashion to all types of non-standard work but the strongest attempts were directed against agency workers. The official

Table 6.1 The logic of interest representation

Union response	Legitimacy	Internal policy	External policy
Exclusion	Low: interest of non-standard workers non-legitimate	Exclusion from membership	Exclusion from employment
Subordination	Low: interests of non-standard workers secondary to those in standard work	Secondary membership status: reduced rights to participation and servicing	Secondary status in collective agreements: less favourable terms and conditions
Inclusion	High: interests of non-standard workers equivalent to others; equal treatment	Equal status in union government; participation through 'liberal' equality policy	Equal status in collective agreements: pro rata terms and conditions
Engagement	High: recognition of specific and differentiated interests of non-standard workers; diverse treatment	Tailoring of union government to reflect specific needs; participation through 'radical' equality policy	Tailoring of collective agreements to reflect specific needs: distinct and differentiated terms and conditions

policy of the TUC for much of the twentieth century was one of opposition to agency work, which intensified with the growth of private recruitment bureaux from the 1960s onwards. In the 1970s, the TUC twice declined invitations from government to consult on the closer regulation of agencies, on the grounds that to do so would only confer legitimacy, and advised its affiliates to withdraw from all collective agreements with agency suppliers. Individual unions followed suit. In 1985, the TGWU's Biennial Delegate Conference (BDC) adopted a strong resolution against agency work and instructed the union's leadership to withdraw from its long-term relationship with Manpower, one of the UK's major labour suppliers. This resolution was subsequently rescinded but opposition to agency work remained strong within the union's road transport group, whose lorry-driver membership was threatened most acutely by agency-labour (Smith 2001: 177).

The primary target of this policy was the employment agencies, which were regarded as essentially parasitic. However, the policy also rested on the denigration of agency workers. 'Who are the agency drivers?' a TGWU delegate asked at the 1985 conference and replied that they are 'firemen, shift workers, taxi drivers, people who come in who already have a job'. Agency workers are depicted here as moonlighters who are 'driving wagons just to make the extra money, not because they need it'. As such, their interests are not legitimate. They are also condemned for lacking solidarity and conspiring with agencies to undermine trade union organisation: essentially for spurning the obligation on all workers to act collectively and maintain hard-won employment standards. 'They are not interested in the future of their job', a delegate observed at the 1974 TUC conference, 'Because their employers are the agencies they are not concerned with the improvement of wages and conditions of service and certainly not concerned with trade unionism'. Agency workers are here presented as an out-group which poses a threat to unionised workers and significantly both the TGWU decision on Manpower and the TUC's earlier advice to affiliates was aimed at stopping the recruitment of agency workers into trade unions. 'The only way to organise them', a TGWU delegate declared, 'is to kick them out'.[1]

A low evaluation of the interests of workers on non-standard contracts also lies beneath the second union response, subordination. In this case, non-standard workers are accepted, perhaps grudgingly, into the union-fold but they occupy a secondary position, reflecting the fact that their interests are regarded as less vital than those of workers in conventional employment (cf. Ledwith and Colgan 2002: 11–12). This response was the dominant, initial reaction of unions to the growth of part-time work in the 1960s and 1970s. With regard to internal policies, many unions created separate membership categories for part-timers with full or partial exclusion from individual member benefits. In 1976, for instance, NATFHE denied part-timers legal assistance and USDAW (Union of Shop, Distributive and Allied Workers) excluded them from provident benefits (IDS 1976: 5). It was also practice in some unions to deny part-timers the right to serve as shop stewards (Knox and McKinlay 2003: 34). With regard to external policy, part-timers were often excluded from collective agreements or clauses of agreements that provided benefits to full-time workers. Records of agreements published by IDS in the 1970s indicate that although part-timers were generally guaranteed equal pay and paid holidays on a pro rata basis they were frequently excluded from negotiated sick pay, maternity leave and occupational pension schemes. Moreover, where there was provision, this was frequently denied to part-timers working below a set number of hours or was dependent on a longer period of service than was required of full-time employees (IDS 1973, 1976). It was also common for agreements to specify less favourable treatment of part-timers. Until the 1980s, it was usually accepted that part-timers should be first on the list of priority dismissals within redundancy agreements: 'When it's inevitable, first it is voluntary redundancies, then after that it's early retirement and then it's the part-timers' (union officer quoted in *The Guardian* 5 March 1982). Even when the union movement lent its weight on behalf of part-time workers in the 1970s, their subordinate status was maintained. The TUC pressed successfully for part-timers to be covered by the individual rights introduced through the Employment Protection Act 1976. But coverage was conditional on a five-year service requirement for part-timers working between 8 and 16 hours (as against 26 weeks for full-time employees) and those working fewer hours were excluded altogether.

These regulations were presented initially as a union triumph but rapidly became the target of reform. During the 1980s securing equal treatment for part-timers became a central plank of the TUC's renewed commitment to advancing individual employment rights (Howell 1999: 46–50), which eventually bore fruit in the recent European directive on part-time work. The TUC, along with other European trade unions, has pressed successfully for parallel legislation on FTCs and agency workers. Individual unions have also pressed for equal rights for non-standard workers both through lobbying and by sponsoring test cases. Thus, the AUT (Association of University Teachers) secured the full extension of protection from unfair dismissal to FTC workers in the Employment Relations Act 1999 and lobbied hard for a more effective transposition of the fixed-term worker directive into UK law. Changes in law have served as a lever for collective bargaining. The AUT has begun to negotiate improvements for FTC workers under the shadow of the FTC regulations, while the Broadcasting, Entertainment, Cinematograph and Theatre Union (BECTU) has used the regulations on working time to negotiate enhanced entitlements for freelancers. For part-timers, there has been a continuing revision of collective agreements on pensions, sick pay, maternity leave, holidays and other benefits as test cases and new regulations have clarified their entitlement to equal treatment. Developments in internal policy have been less widely noted but in many unions, discriminatory rules of membership, participation and entitlement to union services have been abolished. Some unions have also tried to remove barriers to the active participation of workers with non-standard contracts. This is most apparent for part-timers, where experiment with the scheduling and location of meetings and the provision of childcare have become more common. In some cases, unions have introduced job-sharing arrangements for lay representatives to make it easier for part-timers to play a part in union government (TUC 1996).

Underpinning these movements towards inclusion has been a number of developments within union discourse that have served to legitimate the representation of non-standard workers. At the most basic level, there has been recognition that opposition to non-standard work is self-defeating: 'You have to be realistic', a delegate told the TGWU's 1985 debate on agency labour, 'You have to go along the path for the future'. The same point, that the growth of non-standard work necessitates attempts at unionisation, occurs repeatedly in the records of other unions and with regard to other types of worker. At the 1995 TUC conference, Margaret Prosser of the TGWU told delegates that, 'Becoming the voice of part-time workers is key to the trade union movement's future'. However she added, 'That is not just because our survival and growth depends on it but because trade union principles of equality, justice and solidarity with the lowest paid demand it'.

This second set of claims, that non-standard workers fully deserve representation, has been critical and has assumed a number of forms. For part-timers, there has been a stress on the legitimacy of their role as workers and the fact that paid work meets a real need: 'I tell you. I never went to work for pin money. I went to work to go to work, to provide the basic necessities of life' (NUPE delegate, TUC conference, 1985). There has also been a stress on their role as trade unionists, pointing to the involvement of part-timers, for example, in key strikes against competitive tendering. The central argument, however, has been that workers in non-standard employment are frequently exploited and thereby need trade union representation. This claim moreover has frequently been reinforced by a second legitimating discourse grounded in gender and race:

> What we are seeing in this country is a disastrous development – the growth of a new class of worker, a new servant class; many, many, people; six million in the 1990s, mostly women, mostly part-time, many black, always exploited, treated frankly with as much consideration as a scullery maid in Victorian England. Do not talk to them about the wonders of collective bargaining. Most of them do not have agreements. They do not even have representatives. They have no ballots, no votes, precious little dignity; they have just the constant misery of short-term, badly paid work in lousy conditions. (John Edmonds, GMB, TUC conference 1986)

In the 1990s, the case for inclusion continued to be made though increasingly through the discourse of 'casualisation'. Non-standard workers, of all types, were presented as victims of the deliberate policies of employers and government to reduce employment standards and generate insecurity. On this basis, they should assume a central position within trade unionism (TUC 2001b).

The assumption about the interests of non-standard workers that has underlain the fourth response, engagement, has differed slightly. In this case, there is acknowledgement not just that these workers are legitimate but that the forms of employment in which they are engaged can have legitimacy as well. Thus, Margaret Prosser, this time addressing TGWU delegates on agency-labour, remarked that:

> It just has to be said that not everyone who works for an agency is doing so under duress. Many people work for agencies because that is what they want to do; many people work for agencies for many years going from different job to different job. Our arrangements, our approach, have to take account of both of these ways of looking at things. (TGWU BDC, 1999)

A similar view was expressed by a national officer of the NUJ (National Union of Journalists) who said that established freelance journalists do not define their status 'as a problem': 'It's not a victim culture; something which is done unwillingly.' Unions have also accepted, at least from the 1970s, that properly regulated part-time work is desirable because it allows those with caring responsibilities to engage in paid work, a theme that has been accentuated in the current emphasis on work–life balance (TUC 2001c). The only form where this argument has not been developed is FTC work. The AUT continues to regard FTCs as undesirable and seeks to restrict their use because to do so improves conditions for university staff.

The external policy that flows from acceptance of non-standard work has two aspects. On the one hand, unions have tried to ensure that work on a non-standard contract is freely chosen. This has resulted in attempts to bargain and secure a legal right to reduced or flexible hours, while ensuring that there is no penalty associated with non-standard work and that employment protection and other aspects of the relationship will rest on the principle of equal treatment (TUC 2001c). On the other hand, it has led to attempts to advance the specific interests of non-standard workers that arise from their employment status. Thus, the bargaining policy of the media and entertainment unions on behalf of freelancers has tried to secure relatively high rates of pay to compensate for periods without work. Similarly, their legal policy has defended the anomalous status of actors and entertainers, who are self-employed but who pay National Insurance Contributions and so are eligible for unemployment benefits. Union services have also been tailored to the requirements of non-standard workers. The AUT provides help for FTC workers to obtain mortgages, the Association of Teachers and Lecturers (ATL) provides its agency membership with public liability insurance (PLI) and BECTU and other media unions provide a range of advisory and labour market services for freelancers (Heery *et al.* 2004a).

The hallmark of 'engagement' with regard to internal policy is the differentiation of non-standard workers as a distinct category within the union's membership. In some unions they have a special class of membership. In BECTU, for instance, freelancers can opt for a higher level of subscription in order to secure PLI, which often is a condition of being hired. In other cases, they may have their own representatives or structures of government. NATFHE has specialist representatives for part-timers and AUT has specialist representatives for workers on FTCs. AUT also has a developed structure of representation for FTC workers, culminating in two national committees for contract research and contract lecturing staff. BECTU and NUJ have specialist structures for freelancers. Developments of this kind are least apparent for agency workers but they have begun to appear. The TGWU has recently established a geographical branch structure for agency workers and has used its recognition agreement with Manpower to create a new position of agency organiser. These are lay posts, funded by the employer, to provide recruitment, advisory and representation services to the union's membership within the company (Heery *et al.* 2004b).

In most of the case study unions and in the TUC it is possible to identify an upward movement in policy over time from exclusion, through subordination to inclusion and engagement. This suggests that a 'logic of interest representation' may be at work, in which unions develop more sophisticated, tailored policy as new groups become established in the labour market. The case study unions were chosen as innovators, however, and developments at the level of the TUC may not filter down to individual unions or individual union officers. It was for these reasons that a survey element was included in the research design, in order to obtain representative data at different levels of the trade union movement. It is to an analysis of the results that we now turn.

The extent of engagement

The survey of union officers focused on their involvement in collective bargaining on behalf of non-standard workers in the last three years, a period marked by considerable disquiet over job insecurity and by policy initiatives within trade unions and beyond to address the needs of these workers. Officers were asked if they had negotiated or revised a collective agreement to limit the numbers of workers engaged on each type of non-standard contract or to restrict the type of work that they could perform. These questions served as indicators of exclusion and subordination. Officers were also asked if they had negotiated to secure equal pay or equal treatment for non-standard workers, indicators of inclusion. Finally, they were asked if they had negotiated on three current issues for each type of non-standard worker, which together comprised an indicator of engagement.

The results are shown in Table 6.2. What they indicate is that it is not possible to generalise about patterns of union representation of the non-standard workforce *per se*. Rather, there are four distinct patterns of response for each of the four types of worker. For part-timers only a small minority of officers report attempts at exclusion, while between a quarter and a half report attempts at inclusion or engagement. Progress through the 'logic of interest representation' is most apparent for this group though it should be noted that for virtually every item a majority of officers do not report negotiation. This may be because all agreements for which they are responsible were amended before the three-year period covered by the survey. Given the evidence of continuing unfavourable treatment of part-time workers across much of the UK economy, however it suggests that their interests remain fairly marginal across much of the trade union movement.

There is even less evidence of recent negotiation on behalf of FTC workers and in this case the pattern is different. Reported attempts at exclusion were roughly as common as attempts to secure equal treatment and there was a positive correlation between the two types of response. This may reflect the kind of anti-casualisation stance adopted by the AUT: there is an attempt to secure equal treatment for those on FTCs while seeking to restrict the numbers of such contracts and maximise the proportion of members in secure, open-ended employment. The most frequently reported action is negotiation on a specific FTC agenda, to do with the removal of redundancy waiver clauses and the length and renewal of contracts. This undoubtedly reflects recent public policy. The outlawing of waiver clauses for unfair dismissal seems to have provided a lever for negotiations on redundancy, while the fixed-term directive and impending UK regulations (at the time of the survey) appear similarly to have provided a lever for negotiations on contracts.

A third pattern is apparent for agency workers. Here attempts at exclusion are more frequent than attempts to secure equal treatment and develop a specific, tailored agenda. The conception of agency work as a non-legitimate threat to the interests of core workers who are members of trade unions seems to continue and underlie this pattern of response.[2] Once again, attempts at exclusion and inclusion were correlated, suggesting that unions have developed a dual strategy in response to the perceived threat of agency work. This was apparent at some of the workplaces visited during the case study research. Where possible, restrictions on the numbers of agency workers were imposed while at the same time insisting that they receive equal pay and conditions: 'Our biggest concern was that they'd take over core jobs', a TGWU convenor explained, 'so we tried to make it expensive to use temporary labour'.

Table 6.2 Collective bargaining on behalf of non-standard workers (percentages)

Attempted bargaining in the past three years	Part-time	FTC	Agency	Freelance
Exclusion/subordination				
Limits to numbers employed	6	14	23	5
Restrictions on type of work that can be performed	2	5	12	3
Equal treatment				
Equal pay pro rata	39	17	10	3
Company pension scheme	31	10	2	2
Paid holidays	38	18	9	4
Sick pay	32	13	5	2
Access to training	33	13	4	2
Access to promotion opportunities	25	7	1	1
Access to bonus or profit-share	20	6	1	0
Maternity leave or pay	28	9	3	1
Entitlement to premium payments	26	8	5	1
Specific requirements for part-timers				
Overtime pay at end of contractual hours	36			
Regrading of jobs to raise pay	33			
Entitlement to bank/customary holidays	50			
Specific requirements for FTC workers				
Minimum length of FTC		25		
Limit on number of FTC renewals per worker		31		
Removal of redundancy waiver clauses from FTCs		26		
Specific requirements for agency workers				
Declaration that agency is 'employer' of agency workers			17	
Removal or reduction of temp-to-perm fees by employment agency			9	
Creation or improvement of pension scheme for agency workers			6	
Specific requirements for freelance workers				
Creation or improvement of pension scheme for freelance workers				4
Employer provision of indemnity insurance for freelance workers				3
Higher rate of pay for freelancers compared with direct workers				3

Note: $n = 515$–522: Officers with responsibility for collective bargaining.

A possible fourth pattern is seen in the case of freelance workers. As with workers on FTCs, there is a rough equivalence in the frequency of reported exclusion and inclusion, probably for the same reasons. What stands out from the freelance data, however, is the absence of any attempt to regulate contracts of this kind by the vast majority of officers: all but 6 per cent report no attempt whatsoever to secure equal treatment. Regulating freelance work is simply off the radar as far as most union officers are concerned and clearly dealing with workers on this kind of contract is a highly specialist activity concentrated in particular trade unions, such as BECTU, Equity, MU, NUJ and UCATT.

What is it that accounts for variation in union responses to different types of non-standard work? Arguably three factors are important. The first is the relative incidence of the different forms of non-standard work. Officers are most likely to report bargaining on behalf of part-timers, followed in sequence by FTC, agency and freelance workers. The same rank order is apparent in the composition of union officers' allocations (the workers for whom they have responsibility): 92 per cent reported responsibility for part-timers, 76 per cent did so for FTC workers, 65 per cent for agency workers and 31 per cent for freelancers.

However, the difference lies not just in the level of activity but in its form. Officers are most accepting of part-time and least accepting of agency work, with FTCs occupying a position between. What this suggests is that the degree of union engagement reflects the degree of contingency of non-standard work. Most part-time workers are engaged on permanent contracts, while FTC workers are directly employed, in many cases on contracts of 12 months or more (Gallie *et al.* 1998: 170, 173). It is likely that these features of their employment render part-time and FTC workers more amenable to unionisation and allow the identification of common interests with 'standard' workers, facilitating integration. Agency workers, in contrast, may be more likely to be engaged on short-term contracts and have an uncertain or self-employed status. The barriers to union representation and integration with existing union members, in their case may be higher. The same is probably true of freelancers and the absence of significant attempts at representation, the dominant pattern in their case, arguably reflects their status as the most contingent of the four groups.

A third possible explanation has to do with the differential impact of law. In the period covered by the survey European directives were adopted on part-time and fixed-term work, which in the first case had been transposed into UK regulations while in the other this was pending. Unions have been critical of the qualified rights to equal treatment enshrined in these new laws but it may be that they have boosted attempts to negotiate improved conditions for these two types of worker. It should also be noted that the differential impact of law probably accounts for some of the differences in reported levels of activity across the rows of the table. With regard to equal treatment, for instance, negotiation to secure paid holidays is the most frequently reported for all four types of worker, probably as a result of the Working Time Regulations, which have established a legal entitlement to paid leave.

Variable engagement

As well as showing differences between types of non-standard worker, Table 6.2 suggests that there are differences between officers. This is indeed the case. For part-timers, nearly half of the officers reported no recent negotiations on equal treatment, while a third reported that they had negotiated on four or more of the items listed. The equivalent figures for FTC, agency and free-lance workers were 74 and 14 per cent, 85 and 5 per cent and 94 and 2 per cent, respectively. This raises the question of why some union officers accord high priority to representing non-standard workers while others accord less. Theoretical accounts of union behaviour suggest a number of possible answers to this question. 'Evolutionary' models posit a selective pressure to respond to changing workforce composition and suggest that unions will be driven to represent non-standard workers when they are faced with growing demand (an increasing number of such workers in the union's job territory) and a growing incentive (declining membership amongst other groups) (Herzenberg *et al.* 1998; see also Heery 2003: 279–83). Writers in the Oxford School have also stressed external influences on union behaviour though in their case the critical variable has been employer policy (Bain 1970; Clegg 1976). Rather than decline pushing unions towards innovation, the empha-sis here is on opportunities afforded by employers pulling unions towards change. Union action on behalf of non-standard workers will be most preva-lent, according to this view, where employer policy provides a favourable context for union bargaining.

Other accounts of union behaviour have focused on internal stimuli to change. 'Renewal' models, for instance, have pointed to the structure of gov-ernment and the distribution of power between the various groups of mem-bers, representatives and officials who compose the union (Heery 2003: 285–9). In some versions of this argument, change is a product of democra-tisation, which may take the form of a change in union government to pro-vide voice to hitherto marginalised groups (McBride 2001) or the devolution of bargaining to make it more susceptible to member pressure (Fairbrother 2000). An alternative, 'managerial' version of renewal, however, has argued that extending organisation to new groups requires the transfer of resources from existing to potential members which, in turn, may require the strengthening of the union centre (Willman 2001). The emphasis here is on the effective co-ordination of union resources in response to change, which may require the bolstering of union internal management and be facilitated by multi-employer bargaining (Terry 2000). A final set of arguments can be found in 'agency' theories of trade union behaviour (Heery 2003: 290–5).

These arguments rest upon the belief that union representatives have scope to interpret their role and that their characteristics, values and experiences will be important in determining how they choose to behave (Kelly and Heery 1994). In this theoretical current, the gender, generation, experience and ideology of representatives are assumed to 'make a difference' and will underlie attempts to represent non-standard workers.

Analysis

To test the validity of these different arguments, we first devised a measure of officer representation of non-standard workers. This was the sum of the average response to the nine questions on bargaining to secure equal treatment and the three questions on negotiation on matters of current policy (see Table 6.2). This gave us four dependent variables, one for each type of non-standard work, with values ranging between zero and two. The distribution in each case was skewed towards zero, heavily skewed in the cases of agency and freelance workers. For this reason, the results of OLS regression tests, presented in Table 6.3, should be treated with some caution: they are suggestive but the nature of the test is not ideal.

A series of independent variables were identified to serve as indicators of each of the explanations of union behaviour listed above. Some of these were derived from the survey of union officers itself, while others came from the survey of trade unions and from official statistics. Selection was guided by a desire to avoid problems of collinearity and inter-correlation of all independent variables was at an acceptable level. The variables themselves were as follows:

Demand. Two estimates of the level of worker 'demand' for union representation were included in the analysis. The first was taken from the survey of unions and consisted of replies on a five-point scale to a question asking if each of the types of non-standard worker were increasing 'as a proportion of the workers among whom the union recruits'. The second, taken from the officers' survey, consisted of an estimate (again on a five-point scale) of the proportion of the officers' allocation made up by each of the four types of worker.

Incentive. The same distinction between pressure at the union-level and the level of the officers' allocation was present in the measures of union decline. Certification Office and TUC data were used to calculate change in union membership between 1997 and 2001, while at the lower level officers were asked if union membership was rising or declining for the groups for whom they were responsible. Replies were on a five-point scale, ranging from 'increased by at least 10 per cent' to 'decreased by 10 per cent or more'.

Opportunity. The primary measure of opportunity to represent non-standard workers afforded by management policy was indirect. Union officers were ranked according to the percentage of their membership within the public

Table 6.3 Factors associated with bargaining for non-standard workers

	Standardized Beta Coefficients			
	Part-timers $n = 385$	FTCs $n = 385$	Agency $n = 365$	Freelance $n = 292$
Demand				
NS workers growing in union job territory	0.188***	−0.202**	0.056	0.065
Percentage of NS workers in officer's allocation[1]	0.089	0.133***	0.087*	0.262***
Incentive				
Union decline 1997–2001	0.205***	0.126**	0.086	0.088
Decline in officer's allocation	0.023	−0.039	0.074	−0.068
Opportunity				
Percentage of allocation in public sector	0.167***	0.167***	−0.024	−0.017
Employer support for improvements for part-timers	0.073	N/A	N/A	N/A
Voice				
Representative structures for NS workers	0.028	0.204***	−0.050	0.112
Involvement in single-employer bargaining	0.041	0.042	−0.077	−0.184***
Co-ordination				
Bargaining objectives for officer	0.061	0.026	0.086*	0.100*
Estimate of officer bargaining autonomy	0.077	−0.013	0.085*	−0.074
Receipt of relevant training	0.107**	−0.077	0.042	0.045
Involvement in multi-employer bargaining	0.130***	0.042	0.082	0.057
Officer characteristics				
Sex (1= female)	−0.057	0.021	−0.061	−0.020
Seniority	0.063	0.025	−0.053	0.013
Level of formal education	−0.060	−0.020	−0.150***	−0.057
Experience of NS work	0.045	0.035	0.086*	0.071
Declared commitment to representing NS workers	0.116**	0.275***	0.215***	−0.017
Summary statistics	R Squ. 0.203 F 5.52***	R Squ. 0.210 F 6.116***	R Squ. 0.175 F 4.635***	R Squ. 0.217 F 4.780***

Notes: Base = Paid officers with bargaining responsibility.

Significance: *significant at 10%, ** significant at 5%, *** significant at 1%.

[1] Non-standard (NS) work variables change for each regression; for example, for regression 1, the proportion of part-timers in the officer's allocation is used while for regression 2, it is the proportion of FTC workers.

sector. While the 'good employer' tradition in public service may be rather threadbare, it remains that public service employers are much more likely to recognise trade unions, engage in bargaining and countenance more progressive equality policies (Morgan *et al.* 2000: 98–101; Corby 1999). It was considered on this basis that officers representing workers in the public sector would be faced with a more benign environment. The second measure used was direct but was only available for the test on part-time workers. Union officers were asked if individual employers and employers' organisations had helped them improve 'pay and conditions for part-timers', with the results being combined to form a three-point scale.

Voice. Two measures of voice for non-standard workers were included in the analysis. The first was indirect but served to test an aspect of the 'union renewal' thesis developed by Fairbrother (2000). Officers were asked to rate the depth of their involvement in single-employer bargaining on a three-point scale: the hypothesis being that those engaged in local bargaining would be most susceptible to member pressure. The other measure was direct. The union survey contained four questions on participation and representation of non-standard workers, relating to the presence of specialist officers and representatives, specialist branches and national committee structures. Replies to these questions were added to create four statistically reliable scales.

Co-ordination. The 'managerial' renewal thesis stresses the role of union leadership in co-ordinating and allocating union resources. The degree of direction of union officers was measured by questions in the officers' survey on training on the part-time regulations and employment contracts, the use of formal objectives to guide collective bargaining and the degree of autonomy reported in setting the agenda of bargaining and making collective agreements. It was assumed that where management direction was most apparent and autonomy curtailed, bargaining on behalf of non-standard workers would be most evident. Co-ordination is likely to be easier where bargaining is centralised. Accordingly, this set of items also included an estimate of officers' involvement in multi-employer bargaining.

Agency. The final set of variables measured the individual characteristics of officers from a belief that these may influence the interpretation of their representative role. Measures included sex, seniority and level of formal education and whether or not officers had themselves worked on each of the non-standard forms of contract. Finally, officers were asked to rate their own commitment to 'improving conditions' for part-time, FTC, agency and freelance workers on three-point scales, ranging from 'weak', 'moderate' to 'strong'.

Findings

Evolutionary accounts of trade unions are often prescriptive: the facts of union decline and changing workforce composition lead to a recommendation that unions should change course (Hyman 1999). Our test was meant to establish whether advice of this kind was being followed. The findings shown in Table 6.3 provide quite strong support for the belief that declining unions innovate and seek to represent non-standard workers. The association between union decline and bargaining was strongest for part-time and temporary workers but was also apparent (though not statistically significant) for agency workers and freelancers. Interestingly, it seems that the key pressure was exerted at union level rather than at the level of the individual officer's allocation. The reverse seems to be true for demand. Bargaining on behalf of part-time workers was more apparent in unions faced with an increase of part-timers in their job territory but this pattern was not strongly evident for agency staff and freelancers and was reversed in the case of FTCs. The officers of unions reporting a decline of FTCs were more, not less, likely to report bargaining, perhaps reflecting the success of the dual strategy of exclusion and inclusion, described above. However, for all four categories there was a positive association between bargaining for non-standard workers and their presence within an officer's allocation. Where officers are responsible for representing significant concentrations of workers on non-standard contracts they have tended to initiate bargaining. Union activity on behalf of non-standard workers is both driven by decline and demand-led, as evolutionary models suggest.

There is also evidence that officers respond to opportunities for bargaining. Other things being equal, negotiation is more common for part-timers and for workers on FTCs in public services, arguably reflecting the greater receptiveness of public sector employers to union influence. Further analysis indicated that this pattern was most marked in public administration (central and local government), followed by healthcare, with officers in education reporting least activity. The direct measure of employer support, available only for part-timers, indicated a positive association with bargaining but one that was just short of statistical significance. In combination, the results suggest that employer policy can be an important, though probably secondary factor in 'pulling' union activity towards engagement with the needs of non-standard workers.

The creation of structures through which non-standard workers can voice preferences also seems to play a role in supporting bargaining. For workers on FTCs and, to a lesser degree, for freelancers, bargaining is found more frequently in unions where formal representative structures exist. Moreover, if the dependent variable is changed then this association is also found for part-timers and agency workers. The survey gathered information on the recruitment priorities of union officers and, for these two categories, there was a strong positive association between the existence of representative structures and high commitment to recruiting non-standard workers.[3] The other, indirect measure of voice, involvement of officers in single-employer bargaining, showed no positive association with bargaining. Indeed, for freelancers, it was officers who were least likely to report local bargaining who reported most activity. There was no support in the survey analysis for the 'union renewal thesis' though admittedly the test performed was not a strong one.

There was greater evidence to support the notion of renewal through co-ordination. Involvement in multi-employer bargaining was associated with negotiation on behalf of part-timers and to a lesser degree agency staff and there was some evidence that receipt of relevant training and the set-ting of bargaining objectives had encouraged a greater level of bargaining activity. There was no strong evidence, however, that a reduced level of autonomy for negotiators was associated with bargaining on non-standard work. Indeed, for part-timers and agency workers, the reverse was true: it was officers who reported greater freedom to set the bargaining agenda and con-clude agreements who reported most negotiation.

Autonomy can be important in providing discretion for officers to inter-pret their role and act on behalf of non-standard workers when they are inclined to do so. The final set of associations suggests that the characteris-tics of officers are significant in shaping bargaining activity. Those who report a commitment to advancing the interests of part-time, FTC and agency workers report most bargaining and there is also evidence that expe-rience of non-standard work predisposes officers to include their interests on the bargaining agenda. Other individual characteristics of officers, such as sex and seniority, perhaps surprisingly show no association with bargaining on non-standard work. The exception is level of education, with officers with limited formal education reporting most negotiation. The explanation here is probably structural: many part-time, agency and freelance workers are concentrated in unions of manual workers, such as USDAW and UCATT, and the employees of these unions are less likely to have received formal, post-school education.

The pattern of findings presented in Table 6.3 does not allow of a parsi-monious explanation of union behaviour. The results indicate that each type of explanation has some validity. Union representation of non-standard workers, as measured by the bargaining activity of paid union officers, appears to be a combined function of six forces. It occurs where the external context is favourable: where there is an incentive for unions to embrace new groups, where demand is present and where employer policy provides opportunities for influence. It also occurs where internal conditions are favourable. The survey suggests that systems of union government are important in shaping bargaining activity, in that bargaining is more preva-lent where there is provision for member voice and internal management promotes co-ordination. These findings are important because earlier research has suggested a strong bifurcation of bargaining and non-bargaining channels within unions (Undy *et al.* 1981). Our results lend support for a contrary view: that the reform of union democracy and union management can both play a role in re-directing union behaviour within collective bargaining. The final force can be labelled 'union agency'. Within the structures of union government and within the constraints arising from bargaining context, there remains scope for representatives to make a difference and initiate bargaining in accordance with their own values and experiences. An important practical lesson flows from this finding. If unions are further to develop their role as representatives of non-standard workers, then they should take steps to increase the proportion of officers with experience of these types of work and who are committed to improving conditions for part-time, fixed-term, agency and freelance workers.

Methods of engagement

The analysis in the previous two sections has concentrated on unions' use of collective bargaining but there are other methods that can be used to represent non-standard workers. Indeed, it has been argued that unions are likely to adopt distinctive methods to represent workers of this kind: that the specific interests of non-standard workers generate particular forms of union representation, which rely less heavily on collective bargaining. Thus, it has been suggested that the mobility of many workers on non-standard contracts and their consequent exclusion from firm-specific systems of welfare, render them peculiarly reliant on union labour market and benefit services such as access to job opportunities and insurance (Osterman *et al.* 2001; Tilly 1996). It has also been argued that the difficulty non-standard workers experience in supporting collective organisation and bargaining means that they are likely to be dependent on legal action by unions (Gospel and Palmer 1993: 162). Reliance on the law, and partial exclusion from the prime method of collective bargaining, may also express the subordinate status of these workers within unions.

Table 6.4 shows findings gathered from the 2001 survey of unions on the methods used to represent the four types of non-standard worker. It indicates that, while some unions have developed tailor-made services and used legal and political action, neither of these is dominant and the most frequently reported method is collective bargaining. Only for freelancers, perhaps the most contingent group, is bargaining not cited as the most frequently used method of representation (see Heery *et al.* 2004a). The evidence suggests that union representation of non-standard workers is not distinctive in the sense of displaying a primary reliance on individual servicing or legal regulation.

Table 6.4   Methods of representation of non-standard workers

Methods reported by unions	Percentage of unions			
	Part-time	FTCs	Agency	Freelance
Specialist services				
Consumer services	5	13	5	9
Labour market services	2	4	5	9
Education and training	13	2	0	5
Union benefits	14	13	11	11
Mean score	4.75	4.25	3.0	4.75
Collective bargaining				
Audit of collective agreements	18	9	5	4
Commitment to pro rata terms	52	34	25	14
Training for negotiators	29	14	13	5
Tailored agreements	36	18	16	9
Mean score	18.75	10.5	8.3	4.5
Legal and political action				
Sponsorship of test case	25	11	4	4
Special legal advice	23	16	14	11
Response to govt. consultation	21	16	14	7
Lobbying UK government	25	21	16	9
Lobbying EU Commission	11	9	4	5
Mean score	11.8	8.2	5.8	4.0

Source: Survey of trade unions, 2001.

Table 6.5 shows the degree of inter-correlation between the three methods of representation, bargaining, servicing and legal and political activity, again for each of the four types of non-standard work. It demonstrates that uniformly there is a positive association between bargaining and the other methods used: it tends to be the same unions that employ bargaining, servicing and engage in legal and political activity on behalf of non-standard workers. What the patterns suggest is that, far from the representation of non-standard workers being distinguished by the neglect of bargaining, it is characterised by the integration of bargaining and other methods. The table points to a particularly strong association between bargaining and legal work. The same finding emerged strongly from the archival research and has been referred to above. It was particularly apparent for part-time workers. The IDS cuttings archive revealed a clear pattern of union-sponsored legal cases prompting a wave of bargaining, as collective agreements were strengthened in the light of favourable judgements.

We suspect that this pattern has a wider validity and encapsulates two features of what might be thought of as post-voluntarist union representation;

Table 6.5 Association between union bargaining, servicing and legal representation

	Bargaining	Servicing
Part-timers		
Servicing	0.369***	
Legal/Political	0.750***	0.373***
Fixed-term contracts		
Servicing	0.228*	
Legal/Political	0.617***	0.521***
Agency workers		
Servicing	0.314**	
Legal/Political	0.657***	0.368***
Freelancers		
Servicing	0.624***	
Legal/Political	0.551***	0.639***

Notes: * significant at 0.1; ** significant at 0.05; *** significant at 0.01.

that is representation in an increasingly juridified labour market (Dickens and Hall 2003). The first is the strategic use of the courts to challenge employer and government practice and effectively extend workers' rights in law. Recent examples include NATFHE's challenge to the unequal treatment of agency workers in the Allonby case and BECTU's successful challenge to the working time regulations, which ensured entitlement to paid holiday for its freelancers on short contracts. A third example that never reached court was the threat of legal action by NATFHE, GMB and UNISON, which ensured the extension of the regulations on part-time work to those without a formal employment relationship.

The second feature is the use of favourable judgements as a lever to effect a kind of 'pattern bargaining', in which successful or threatened legal action against a target company is used to open up negotiations with employers across a sector or even the wider economy. Pattern bargaining of this kind was seen in the extension of mortgage allowance schemes to part-timers in financial services in the 1980s following successful legal action against Norwich Union by the Association of Scientific, Technical and Managerial Staff (ASTMS). It was seen also in retail in the 1990s when a threatened equal pay case against Sainsbury's, sponsored by USDAW, led to the re-grading of checkout jobs across much of the industry. More recently, the favourable judgement in the Preston case, on the backdating of pension entitlements for part-timers to 1976, has led to the negotiation of compensation for workers who suffered discrimination in banking, building societies, healthcare and public administration.

Conclusion

This chapter has reviewed the response of trade unions to the growth of non-standard work, over time and across a broad cross-section of the British trade union movement. We believe that four general lessons can be taken from the research presented above. The first is that it is possible to identify a 'logic of interest representation' in union responses to non-standard work, which may have relevance to other groups of workers. The 'logic', we believe, rests upon changing union conceptions of the legitimacy of both non-standard workers and non-standard work and proceeds from exclusion, through subordination, to inclusion and engagement. There is no necessity for this movement, however, and while our cases showed policy evolving over time, our surveys indicated that many unions and union officers continue to neglect or actively exclude workers on non-standard contracts. They also indicate complexity of response and the fact that the different stages of representation run into one another and exist in parallel as well as sequence. Movement through the stages is not teleological but contingent, prompted by external conditions and internal changes that predispose unions to accept non-standard workers as part of their constituency.

Our second conclusion is derived from the observation of different union responses to different types of non-standard work. For part-timers, as far as collective bargaining by union officers is concerned, attempts at inclusion-engagement far outweighed attempts at exclusion-subordination. For FTC workers the two broad types of response were balanced, for agency workers exclusion-subordination was dominant, while for freelancers the absence of response was what was most apparent. These findings underline what has been noted by those researching non-standard work directly: that this is a residual category which contains a variety of essentially dissimilar forms (Gallie *et al.* 1998). Nevertheless, we believe it is still possible to make a generalisation about union responses to non-standard work, albeit of a tentative form. The greater receptiveness of unions to part-time and FTC work was explained in part by their greater incidence in job territories and the greater opportunities to offer representation presented by developments in employment law. But they also seem to reflect the fact that these are the least contingent of the four groups studied. Our tentative generalisation, therefore is that variable union responses to non-standard work reflect the degree of contingency of different forms and the consequent ease with which representation of non-standard workers can be integrated with that of workers in 'standard' employment.

The research revealed variation by union and by union officer, within each of the four categories of non-standard work. The analysis of variation indicated that a range of factors could incline representatives to try and bargain on behalf of non-standard workers. Some of these were external to unions and an active response was conditioned in large part by the opportunities and constraints that unions face within their operating environment. Other factors were internal to unions, however and the research indicated that, systems of union government and management and the characteristics and experiences of union representatives 'made a difference' to bargaining activity. The lesson that can be drawn from this pattern of findings is a voluntarist one. Clearly unions operate within a constraining environment but if the goal of improving conditions for non-standard workers is accepted then it can be promoted by internal union reform. Changes in government to endow non-standard workers with voice, changes in management to promote training and objective-setting and changes in recruitment to ensure committed officers are appointed, all emerge as practical reforms that can be pursued. We feel that the research points towards a plausible strategy of reform that unions can develop to help the more effective representation of diversity.

Our final conclusion relates to trends in trade union behaviour. For much of the past hundred years it has been assumed that collective bargaining would be the pre-eminent method of job regulation for British trade unions operating within a voluntarist system of industrial relations. Other methods would occupy only a secondary role or would be applied mainly to marginal groups of workers, incapable of sustaining collective bargaining. The research has produced two findings that contradict this stereotypical pattern, both of which may have a broader resonance. Unions continue to be irremediable bargainers and collective bargaining emerges as the main method used to advance the interests of non-standard workers, despite their lower levels of unionisation and secondary labour market position. Bargaining is not conducted in isolation, however, and what also emerges is the integration, particularly of bargaining and legal and political work. The research, we feel, points to the emergence of a post-voluntarist pattern of union representation in which bargaining and legal regulation interact through a form of pattern-following based on the sponsorship of strategic court cases.

Acknowledgements

The research was funded by the Economic and Social Research Council (Award No. L212252023), as part of the *Future of Work* programme. We would like to thank all those trade union representatives and managers who agreed to be interviewed, to complete our questionnaires and who otherwise helped with the research project. Thanks are also due to Mick Silver for advice (and reassurance) on statistical procedures and to Geradine Healy for helpful comments on an earlier draft. Any errors of fact or interpretation are ours alone.

Notes

1. We encountered derogatory descriptions of the other categories of non-standard worker in the course of the research, which similarly were used to de-legitimate their interests and support policies of exclusion or subordination. In BECTU it was

said that freelancers were traditionally known as 'stringers' who lacked the skills to hold down a directly employed job, while in the AUT members on fixed-term research contracts were dismissed in like fashion as 'wannabe academics'. In BIFU, a conference delegate in the early 1980s noted of part-timers that, 'We have been successful particularly in the computer area to ensure that the complement of full-time staff is not polluted. However, in the normal branch environment there is a substantial increase in the use of part-time and hourly paid staff.'

2. At the GMB conference in 1999, in an echo of earlier debates at the TGWU, agency workers were described as follows by a delegate from Panasonic:

> At the end of the year they flood the place with agency labour. The agency people working next to my members have far reduced rates of pay, no legal rights and no conditions of work. That is what is happening. Unless we are pre-pared to stop this situation, agency workers will take over the workforce. You will never reach your recruitment figures if this situation occurs.

3. The analysis of recruitment data used the same set of variables shown in Table 6.3 but the estimation procedure was ordered probit, reflecting the fact that the recruitment measure was a four-point ordinal scale. Officers' declared commit-ment to recruiting part-time and agency workers was associated with the existence of dedicated representative structures in their unions, at a high level of statistical significance.

7
The Workplace Learning Agenda – New Opportunities for Trade Unions?

Anne Munro and Helen Rainbird

Introduction

While increasing union participation may not have been the initial or prime objective for the involvement of trade unions in workplace learning initiatives, such initiatives may offer significant new opportunities to increase organisational capacity (Munro and Rainbird 2000). In Britain, trade union interest in training developed in a context in which employee interests had been progressively excluded from the institutions of vocational training, as the Conservative governments (1979–97) shifted the training system from a tripartite to a neo-liberal model (King 1993). A number of factors contributed to this. First, the absence of representation suggested that as a legitimate arena for trade union activity, members' interests in relation to training could be pursued through bargaining and campaigning channels. Second, many unions were concerned with their ability to recruit and retain members at a time of membership losses and, for some, training constituted a membership-good. Third, the development of the 'new bargaining agenda' (IRRR 1991) in the early 1990s suggested some issues, such as training, equal opportunities and environmental protection could be privileged in developing a less conflictive approach to relationships with employers. Finally, this was also the period in which British trade unions' awareness of European social models was growing and with it an appreciation of unions' engagement in social partnerships with employers on training as well as workers' more extensive rights in the rest of the European Union (EU). John Edmonds, General Secretary of the GMB, famously claimed that this new agenda was about 'moving into the European mainstream' (Storey *et al.* 1993: 67).

Trade unions have a long history of supporting the education of working-class men and women. Contemporary developments on workplace learning have been seen as part of a move towards membership servicing role (Heery 1996). Nevertheless, it would be erroneous to see them only as an individual service to members, comparable with access to financial service packages. Indeed, there have been long-standing debates about training as a collective good (see e.g. Streeck 1989) and recent research on workplace learning emphasises its social nature (see Rainbird *et al.* 2004). Whether learning opportunities are provided internally by the union or through a partnership with an employer, they are provided within a collective framework. Those taking the courses share their membership of the union and/or place of work. Provision is often targeted at groups of workers who have limited access to employer-provided training and represents a benefit of negotiations (with the employer or providers) taken on behalf of the collective. Union workplace learning initiatives challenge the notion that individual services to members necessarily indicate a shift away from a collectivist approach (cf. Williams 1997).

Training is often seen as an arena in which management and employees have common interests and in many EU states, there are joint institutions regulating different aspects of the training system. The UK training system has not been characterised by social partnership. The workplace is a problematic site of learning and employer prerogative is significant in training decisions. Rather than representing a neutral intervention, training must be viewed in the broader context of the employment relationship. It is therefore important to recognise that employer and employee interests in relation to workplace learning are not the same. Streeck argues that strategies towards skill formation and lifelong learning can provide trade unions with opportunities for the constructive rethinking of policies, but they need to do this from a strong independent power base if they are to impose rules and obligations on employers that they would not voluntarily accept (1994: 252).

Training and development can be seen as linked to workers' acquired rights and the quality of the work environment (Bruno Trentin, former General Secretary of the Confederazione Generale Italiana del Lavoro, quoted by Meghnagi 2004). Hyman argues that such demands allow unions to respond to the '"qualitative" dimensions of contemporary managerial discourse' through reconstructing the bargaining agenda (1994: 127). He argues that:

> Increasing union concern, across Europe, with the issue of initial and further education and training indicates an attempt to frame an agenda which can be legitimated in productivist terms while appealing to members' own interests. Another direction of agenda reconstruction is an emphasis on procedural demands – from new institutions of workplace consultation to European works councils – which have no necessary and direct cost implications for companies (though indeed challenging traditional 'employer prerogatives').

The questions we wish to address in this chapter concern the extent to which the new roles that are developing within British trade unions provide scope for engaging in both the substance and the procedural questions raised by the workplace learning agenda.

For many years, workplace learning was primarily the concern of trade union officers with specialist interests in education and training and much activity was initiated by national or regional officers. Initiatives which were already taking place within individual unions were given a boost by the Labour government's creation of the Union Learning Fund (ULF) in 1998, which supported trade union innovations in lifelong learning. This allowed a range of experimentation in new learning representative roles and learning provision. Positive evaluations of the ULF (York Consulting 2001; Cutter 2000; Shaw 1999) contributed to the government's decision to award statutory rights to trade union learning representatives (ULRs) from April 2003 under the provisions of the Employment Act 2002. With new rights to time off, trade unions are increasingly identifying learning activities as offering a route for expanding organisational capacity and for making workplace learning more central to their activities.

We explore these issues in a number of ways. We start by a short discussion of the concept of forms of employee voice in relation to training, which identifies a central role for trade unions in expressing employees' interests through collective voice. In the next section, we examine the development of new union roles linked to the statutory entitlements for union learning representatives. We do this by comparing this role to that of the shop steward and with the development of health and safety representatives in the 1970s, which had some similarities in extending both the substance and procedures of bargaining.

In the third section, we explore developments in relation to lifelong learning in the public sector union, UNISON. As the largest trade union, UNISON has developed its own membership development programmes, such as 'Return to Learn', provided by the Workers' Educational Association (WEA). These can be located within the WEA's tradition of providing liberal education for working-class adults and have formed the basis for its partnerships with employers. This approach is distinguishable from that of the Trades Union Congress (TUC), which is generally supportive of the achievement of government targets, for example, on persuading employers to take up the Investors in People award, on certifying workers' competence through National Vocational Qualifications (NVQs), the use of on-line learning through LearnDirect, on providing basic skills training and (until they were abolished) the take-up of Individual Learning Accounts. We explore the ways in which the role of lifelong learning advisor (LLA), a variation of the ULR role, was formulated within UNISON through two ULF projects. This was seen both as a means of capitalising on members' interest in learning by fostering new forms of activism and for extending the duties of shop stewards. As participants in these projects we were well-placed to observe the strategic thinking behind the development of these roles. We also draw on two research projects on workplace learning, which provide us with background on the public sector context and some limited evidence of how these roles were emerging in practice, as well as evaluations commissioned by the union as it has developed its approach to partnerships with employers.[1]

Based on our analysis of strategic developments in UNISON in relation to these new representative roles, in the penultimate section we argue that the workplace learning agenda may offer a route for expanding union organisation. It also has the potential for a qualitative change in union activities which might make them more attractive and accessible to a range of workers who normally demonstrate lower levels of union activism. Although this potential exists, such developments are by no way certain. They depend critically on the willingness of both lay and paid officials to capitalise on students' interest in learning and in becoming more active in the union. The development of partnerships with employers and the role of these new union representatives within them is emergent. In the conclusion we argue that it is not yet clear what the impact of these roles will be on branch organisation and activism, since there are a number of factors which may prevent the full potential of the workplace learning agenda from being realised.

Different forms of employee voice on workplace learning

Many workers have limited access to employer provided-training. The Workplace Employee Relations Survey (WERS) shows that low-paid workers and part-timers in particular have least access to training provided by their employer (Cully *et al.* 1999). Workers on the lowest salary grades are often in jobs where there are few possibilities for career progression and no access to broader development opportunities. The only training that is available to them may be limited to induction and statutory training. Management tools such as the development review which are used to assess employees' training needs are not always extended to all employees, especially those on lower salary grades. When managers do conduct development reviews to identify workers' training needs, the resulting training is likely to be restricted to the immediate needs of the job rather than meeting their broader needs for training and development. Individual forms of employee voice, such as the development review, are not effective forms of expression of workers' training needs. This is because, as a management tool, they are designed to meet organisational rather than individual needs and any tensions between them will be resolved in favour of the employer (Rainbird and Munro 2003).

Trade union presence in the workplace is positively associated with workers' access to training. WERS evidence shows that employees in unionised workplaces are more likely to receive training than those in non-unionised workplaces. This is because employers are more likely to develop a range of practices designed to develop skills and promote worker retention where unions are present. Green *et al.* (1996) refer to this positive association as representing an indirect form of employee voice on training. Nevertheless, case study evidence on different forms of collective employee voice on training demonstrates that there is an added effect where unions are not only present but adopt conscious strategies on workplace learning (Rainbird *et al.* 2003). It is only when trade unions take the initiative on workplace learning, providing a mechanism for the expression of collective voice, that some groups of workers gain access to broader development opportunities. This effect is also noticeable amongst more highly qualified workers who do tend to receive employer-provided training. Evidence from Heyes and Stuart's (1998: 462–5) survey of Manufacturing, Science and Finance (MSF) members showed that when a trade union participates actively in training decisions members are even more likely to receive training than where representatives are not actively involved. Moreover, active union participation was linked to members' perceptions that there was a more equal distribution of training across groups and individuals. In this arena, there is strong evidence that unions make a difference. There is more training and more equitable provision where trade unions pursue conscious strategies towards training and development by representing a channel for the expression of collective employee voice.

Nevertheless, it is important to make the distinction between training for employee need and training for employer or business need. Training for business need primarily benefits the organisation and there may be few or only indirect benefits to the employee. Organisations may develop effective training to meet business needs, but provide no channels for the expression of employee needs. In contrast, training for employee need contributes to the workers' broader development and employability and does not restrict training to the needs of the current job. This is most likely to be found where trade unions provide a channel of the expression of collective employee voice on training (Rainbird *et al.* 2003). The primary beneficiary is the employee, but the employer may obtain indirect benefits from the impact of this learning on individuals and workgroups, as well as from the joint structures which are set up to manage such programmes (the Ford Motor Company's Employee Development and Assistance Programme provides an example). In assessing the development of union learning representative roles and partnerships with employers, it is therefore important to ascertain whether the learning provided is part of a wider, more liberal adult education tradition that addresses personal development or is located within 'a very powerful vocationally centred "competitiveness agenda"' (Caldwell 2000: 261).

Union learning representatives and their relationship to other representative roles

Recognised trade unions were given the power to appoint learning representatives under the provisions of the Employment Act 2002. This new role provides a union job with none of the stereotypical images of the shop steward which some members may find off-putting. There have been two distinct models to the development of learning representative roles. One has been for existing shop stewards to become learning representatives, whilst some unions have seen it as a means of recruiting new activists into representative positions. Shop stewards may be more experienced in negotiating with management and in this respect activities such as negotiating over release for training represent a broadening of their agenda. In contrast, new activists recruited to ULR roles may be committed to learning as a workplace issue. This in turn may open up the possibility of creating new ways to operate relating to the process of union organisation, which may be more attractive to categories of workers who have been less active in unions in the past. This has certainly been the case in UNISON, where a new role of LLA position has been developed, which we discuss in more detail in the next section. Other TUC affiliates have also seen the potential for attracting new activists into these roles, in particular, women and younger workers, though these have tended to be a relatively small proportion of those undertaking ULR training (Calveley *et al.* 2003: 15).

The role of the ULR, especially one coming through the new activist route, might be contrasted with the role of the shop steward. Shop stewards are elected representatives, have a clearly defined role within the union branch and tend to have an oppositional role in relation to management. For the latter, they are trained in negotiating skills. Coates and Topham (1980: 157) outline a range of activities which form the main parts of the shop steward's role:

(1) spokesman for the workgroup, (2) disseminator of information between the organisation and the group, (3) minor bargaining over grievances, (4) monitoring of information, (5) liaison with other groups and with managers, (6) exercising leadership to strengthen the cohesion and therefore bargaining power of the group, (7) decision-making, (8) formal negotiation with senior management.

Both the strength and potential limitations of shop stewards have been seen to derive from their democratic link to a particular work group, the constituency from which they are elected. This means that shop stewards can claim to provide a direct 'voice' for their membership, but also run the risk of taking an economistic, short-term or sectional approach to issues (Terry 1995).

The precise role of the shop steward varies enormously from union to union, from industry to industry and from workplace to workplace (cf. Batstone *et al.* 1977). Even within branches it has long been recognised that stewards may take on widely varying roles (see Fryer *et al.* 1978). In the public sector, much collective bargaining remains at national level and local bargaining is conducted primarily by branch officers, so most ordinary shop stewards focus on individual or small work group representational work

(Munro 1999: 131). Some stewards merely act as channels of communication between the branch and members and few ever face a formal election. As a consequence the question of an unelected as opposed to an elected position is not the main axis of difference between the new activist ULR and more traditional shop steward roles.

There are, nevertheless, a number of ways in which the role of the ULR differs from that of the shop steward. The main point of difference lies in their relationship to other members (and potentially non-members as well) which is a servicing rather than representational role. A second point of difference lies in the scope of their activities: their focus is on workplace learning rather than the range of issues outlined by Coates and Topham above. Although learning representatives coming through the new activist route might be unlikely, initially, to have any dealings with managers, this is not the case with shop stewards taking on the ULR role. The latter might therefore be required to apply their traditional negotiating skills to a new arena of activity, for example, negotiating paid release from work with line managers. A third point, of difference concerns the nature of their insertion into the workplace and the branch structure, access to union channels of communication, further training and support.

In contrast, there are some parallels in the development of the ULR role and that of the health and safety representative following the Health and Safety at Work Act (1974). This came into force in October 1978 and required trade unions to appoint safety representatives who were to be recognised by the employer although there were no clearly defined standards for their education (Bennett 2000: 73). Bennett reports that in some unions, such as the Amalgamated Union of Engineering Workers (AUEW), existing shop stewards were appointed as safety representatives. Others, such as National and Local Government Officers' Association (NALGO) and Association of Scientific, Technical and Managerial Staff (ASTMS), left it up to branches to appoint them, or some combination of branch and local officials. He comments that:

> In well-organised workplaces, shop stewards in reality already possessed the powers conferred by the HASWA, though rarely the skills required to exercise them. In less well-organised firms, the powers were often conferred on workers who had little union experience as well as lack of relevant skills.

Bennett points out that, safety representatives' responsibilities relate to four main areas of activity: representing fellow workers in negotiations with the employer; representing their members in consultations with the Health and Safety Executive; inspecting the workplace regularly; and inspecting the scene of accidents.

There is a potential for role ambiguity or a conflict of interest between the shop steward and health and safety representative role. Terry (1995) points out that when confronted with a safety hazard or dirty working conditions the response of the shop steward would traditionally have been to bargain for 'danger money' or 'dirt money', whereas health and safety training would always emphasise the removal of conditions creating the hazard. Similarly, safety priorities may support restrictions on smoking, yet the majority of a steward's constituents may resist such restrictions. For these reasons there has been an ongoing debate within and between unions concerning the value of the shop steward experienced in negotiating and the separate health and safety representative trained to see the wider implications of safety issues. It is possible that similar concerns will emerge over the ULR role.

Compared to the statutory entitlements for health and safety representatives, the provisions for ULRs are weaker. Under the Employment Act 2002, ACAS has drafted amendments to the *Code of Practice on Time off for Union Duties and Activities*. The provisions cover:

1. Paid time off for duties which might include analysing learning and training needs, providing information and advice, arranging training and consulting the employer about such activities.
2. Paid time off for training for employees who are officials of a recognised trade union in order to perform the learning representative role. This might include activities such as: learning the methods for identifying and recording learning needs and drawing up a plan to meet them; learning where to access information and to provide advice and guidance; arranging local learning opportunities and working with employers to meet the learning and skill needs of individuals and the organisation.
3. Time off for union members to receive the services of union learning representatives, although there is no requirement on the employer to pay them for this.

Learning representatives will be allowed reasonable time off to perform their duties and should have access to facilities to allow them to perform their duties, taking into account the patterns of work and location of all workers. The revised ACAS Code also points to the positive benefits of having formal agreements on time off, to provide clear guidelines and contribute to effective planning (Clough 2002). Learning representatives, unlike the health and safety representatives of an earlier generation are required to have completed a course recognised by the TUC or their own trade union.

Unlike the health and safety representatives, ULRs do not represent members in negotiations. There is no requirement on employers to consult with them or other trade union representatives on training.[2] In other words, important questions concerning workplace procedures have not been addressed. Indeed, when David Blunkett announced the government's decision to award statutory rights to learning representatives, he referred to them as 'foot soldiers' and 'workplace experts on skills' (*The Guardian* 28 August 2000). The government's consultative paper on the proposals emphasised that this role would be separate from collective bargaining and would have an impact on 'increasing motivation and enthusiasm for learning among employees and employers' (DfEE 2001: 1). The Department of Trade and Industry's webpage states, 'Both employers and workers stand to benefit. ULRs are *an inexpensive source of expert advice for employers* (our emphasis) and the proposals will not place a high administrative burden on employers' (www.dti.gov.uk/employment). This is a rather different proposition to Hyman's agenda of reconstruction 'capable of challenging traditional employer prerogatives' (1994: 127).

The development of the ULR role to date suggests that a series of issues remain to be resolved. First, serious questions must be raised about the types of training-offer that ULRs promote. Whereas employee development and information technology programmes with broad educational objectives can be categorised as training for employee need, this is not the case for initiatives linked to the adoption of the Investors in People award and competence assessment through NVQs. These might be classified more properly as training and assessment for employer need or even 'government need', insofar as they contribute to the attainment of government targets. Moreover, the whole area of adult basic skills training in the workplace is highly problematic. The TUC has generally been supportive of workplace basic skills training and, in particular, the employer pilots of paid educational leave for basic skills training. In contrast, writers from an adult education perspective such as Caldwell (2000), Hoddinott (2000) and Jackson (2000) have warned against the dangers of exposing workers with low levels of formal qualification to the scrutiny of employers and workmates in ways which are highly visible in the workplace and to the expectation that relatively short courses can enhance productivity.

A second area of concern is that most of these initiatives have been supported by short-term, project-based funding through the ULF and there are significant issues about their sustainability and the potential for losing the expertise of project workers. The fact that these developments have often been initiated by national and regional officers means that mechanisms are needed to translate them into organisational capacity in branch structures. Finally, there are a number of questions about the blurring of roles and lines of accountability, which we explore in the section on developments in UNISON, below. In other cases, trainers who are also union members have taken on these roles and, as Calveley *et al.*, point out, this can lead to the conflation of union and 'management' roles (2003: 19).

UNISON: the development of the lifelong learning advisor role

Although particular attention is being given to the ULR in the light of new legislative rights to time off, the idea of a union role in learning is not new.

At the time of the creation of UNISON through the merger of COHSE, NALGO and NUPE in 1993, there was recognition of the possibility of supporting new forms of activism and active membership in the union. The R2L programme, was first developed by NUPE in conjunction with the WEA in the West Midlands region in 1989. It was aimed at union members who had been disadvantaged in the formal educational system and was designed around a combination of distance learning and small study groups. Participation in learning can have the effect of building workers' self-confidence in their own abilities, a key to union activity. As a result of taking part in a developmental learning opportunity, some workers not only see the union in a positive light but may be prepared to take a more active role in the union, particularly in relation to learning opportunities. Kennedy's (1995) evaluation of the R2L programme showed that many former students became more active in the union following their participation. These findings were used to support the expansion of R2L and other UNISON programmes, as a means of enhancing the activism and participation of low-paid women workers in the representative structures of the new union.

Following on from the success of R2L, a strategy was developed to explore the ways in which the enthusiasm generated by participation in learning could be used to develop a new union role, to encourage learning amongst co-workers. The role of LLA was based on the WEA model of lay activism, the Voluntary Education Adviser (VEA). A ULF project was set up to explore the potential of this role in 1998–99.

In exploring the potential role of the LLA under this ULF project, three different models were emerging.[3] The first, the VEA model, was rooted in adult education and already established in some WEA regions. Individuals who had had positive experiences of returning to learn frequently wanted to 'give something back' and the VEA offered a role in which to maintain a link with education and access to continuing development without incurring major costs. Where VEAs were recruited from the UNISON R2L Programme, they had important links with both the workplace and the union. The actual roles undertaken varied according to the students' confidence, ambitions and the time they had available. Some were simply involved in welcoming new students to classes. Others supported WEA tutors in the classroom, advised students by telephone, attended weekend schools and became involved in recruitment or arranging transport to courses. The training VEAs received was also found to be variable and support came primarily from the WEA or their own support groups.

In the workplace, the capacity of VEAs to carry out their role as adult education advisers depended on the nature of their job, the attitude of management and the time they could afford. The limitation of this model was lack of support in the workplace but, despite this, some VEAs had had significant successes. One VEA interviewed had set up two R2L classes at her NHS (National Health Service) hospital trust on her own initiative, without reference to higher levels of the union. She had negotiated access to a room for teaching purposes with her manager. In the workplace context, the VEA model also raised questions concerning the type of learning that should be promoted. In a group discussion with VEAs a distinction was made between R2L which was voluntary and NVQ assessment which was compulsory in some workplaces. Although the consensus of the group was that they would not want to be involved in promoting NVQs, one VEA was acting as a mentor for staff undertaking NVQ assessment in her job role. This raised the question of learning for whom: the individual or the organisation?

The second model was employer-sponsored and involved the employer supporting the adviser through discretionary time off. A number of early pilot examples from local government, the NHS and universities had already been set up and were examined as part of the project. Here the role of the LLA was focused on management objectives such as increasing take up of Individual Learning Accounts (ILAs) or NVQs, or as part of a bid to achieve the Investors in People award. Employers frequently worked alongside Training and Enterprise Councils or through partnerships with UNISON. Lines of support varied. In one local authority it was made clear that support was provided via the employer's departmental training office, while in another there was an expectation that if learning advisers encountered problems they would go to local shop stewards to resolve them. There was therefore scope for role ambiguity.

The third model was the union-sponsored model, still then in the development stage. Here learning advisers were not shop stewards but members with recent experience of learning. It was argued that such experience allowed for 'a more sympathetic and understanding approach to potential learners' (UNISON undated a: 20). One of the purposes of the project was to explore the nature of this role. Questions were raised about the relationship between the LLA and existing branch officers, who should be recruited and how they should be supported. The project identified that there was a need for former students to be trained in this role; for them to understand the different levels of activity they might engage in; and for UNISON to put support structures in place within the union and in the workplace (Munro and Rainbird 1999).

The development of new union roles requires their recognition in union structures. The 1999 UNISON National Delegate Conference passed a motion urging all branches and branch education co-ordinators to promote learning on behalf of members. This included: taking full advantage of UNISON learning programmes; developing partnerships with employers; developing a team approach to education in the branch with the branch education co-ordinator supporting the work of LLAs; and building lifelong learning objectives into the branch development plan (UNISON undated c).

The organisational structures needed to support LLAs were developed through a further ULF project in 2001–02.[4] Although the target groups were former R2L students, a course was also run for shop stewards, including two new stewards. Both groups needed to understand the LLA role and how to access information about learning resources but, in other respects, their needs were different. Whereas the first group needed more confidence-building and induction into union structures, the latter were more confident and knowledgeable about the union. A project worker was employed by the WEA for one year and located in a UNISON regional office.

A considerable amount of work went into briefing the branch on the project. Despite the involvement of the employer and the national union in the project, there was a problem with the lack of continuity in management representation on the steering group. This may have been partly due to changes in personnel, but also raised questions about how trade unions relate to managers at different levels and in different roles within large organisations. As a consequence, release from work was a significant issue for participants in the programme[5] and resulted in the development of a best practice model in the form of a workplace learning agreement for establishing clarity in expectations. This clarity was seen as essential for new activists inexperienced in negotiations with managers who need their co-operation to facilitate their work. A series of forum meetings were organised for the LLAs by the project worker and it was anticipated that support would be sustained by the branch education officer after the end of the project funding. In 2002 UNISON was awarded a further ULF project to develop a regional support structure for lifelong learning and to disseminate this experience.

A number of key issues emerged from these early developments of the UNISON LLA role. These concerned the relationship between the LLA and management, on the one hand, and the relationship between the LLA and the local branch organisation, on the other. There were questions about the nature of support structures available to LLAs, their needs for further training and the types of learning that it was appropriate for them to promote.

Implications for recruitment and participation

UNISON has seen the workplace learning agenda as providing opportunities to recruit new members and to engage new union activists. This potential for organisational renewal relates to both the content and the process of union activity. Particular groups of workers, such as women and black workers, may perceive the content of union activity as lacking relevance to their experience of work (Waddington and Kerr 1999) and what unions do may have little resonance with their world (Munro 2001). Equally, some groups of workers may find the process of unions (the rules and procedures) alien to their experience and the place and timing of activities may make involvement difficult (Briskin and McDermott 1993; Munro 1999). In this context, the provision of learning opportunities which build self-confidence may contribute to members' ability to participate in the union.

The workplace learning agenda demonstrates how the content of union business can be widened to offer benefits to members. It can do this through creating access to learning opportunities to workers who have little access to employer-provided training. Local union representatives can provide a key role in facilitating participation by encouraging workers to take part in courses and in addressing issues of release from work. Evaluations of the UNISON programmes and the partnerships with employers have shown that many students gain promotion and move on to further training (Munro *et al*. 1997; Kennedy 1995). The range of joint provision is being extended into routes into professional training in multi-employer partnerships (Rainbird *et al*. 2002) and in the NHS through the Skills Escalator approach (Department of Health 2001), creating opportunities for job progression.

Where the union is seen to be concerned about the least powerful and often forgotten groups of workers, the process of recruitment to courses serves to raise the profile of the union in the workplace in a positive fashion. Where UNISON programmes are provided in partnership with employers, they are open to UNISON members, members of other unions and non-members. Therefore, it provides a possible route for unions to engage with groups of workers who were previously non-members or non-active members. Equally, it requires new ways of working co-operatively with other unions (cf. Calveley *et al*. 2003).

The extent to which the potential to develop new activists is realised in practice through the LLA role has not been researched on a systematic basis. Nevertheless, in our research on regulatory structures and access to learning, we have come across examples of learning advisers, which give an indication of how these roles are developing. The first of these was a former local authority catering assistant who had studied R2L as a member of NUPE, prior to the creation of UNISON in 1993. Enthused by her experience, she had then become a shop steward and had studied for a university degree as a mature student. Because there was a well-established partnership between UNISON and the employer in this local authority, she was given the role of acting as a role model and learning mentor to other members of staff. She was employed on a part-time basis in the Adult Education Department. In this instance, although she continued to be a union member, her learning mentor role was as a local authority employee.

In another case study organisation, former R2L students had taken on local branch posts despite the lack of a strong local organisation. One woman had become a learning representative and shop steward because a WEA tutor had suggested it. Most of her support and training had come from the training manager at the NHS trust where she worked and a WEA tutor organiser rather than from UNISON. She commented, 'if I'm stuck, I go to her [the training manager] and she will help'. Key issues, therefore, concern how unions can ensure that this potential is tapped and that new activists receive appropriate support and training *from within the union*.

These experiences demonstrate that the connections between different levels of UNISON's internal organisation and with providers of UNISON programmes, such as the WEA, are essential for capitalising on students' interest in taking on new activist roles. They point to the need for UNISON to hold and to make effective use of information about members taking courses so that branches have the capacity to respond to expressions of interest in relation to the LLA role. Where these activists are new to union activities and structures, the provision of networks of support within the branch and within the workplace are essential. These connections are already present for shop stewards taking on these roles but they have to be forged for LLAs coming through the new activist route. Interestingly, in both our examples, these new women activists had taken on shop steward roles, rather than opting solely for learning representative roles. In other words, participation in UNISON programmes, whether they were delivered through the union or in partnership with the employer, had contributed to an interest in traditional as well as new representative roles. As statutory rights for learning representatives heighten the significance of workplace learning within union branch structures, these developments may gain greater momentum.

Conclusion

In this chapter we have explored the development of the role of the union learning representative with special reference to the LLA role in UNISON. This role has evolved out of the enthusiasm generated by students' engagement in adult education opportunities provided through the union which have also formed the basis of UNISON's partnerships with public sector employers. It therefore demonstrates some features which distinguish it from developments in other TUC affiliates, whose ULR roles relate to other kinds of training provision.

We have compared and contrasted the role of learning representative with the more established roles of shop stewards and health and safety representatives in order to explore both its potential and areas of weakness. The potential of the lifelong learning agenda in the workplace lies in its capacity to demonstrate the significance of union organisation to groups of workers who are often marginalised in the workplace and in union structures. In a very concrete way it can include those who are often excluded from employer-provided learning, by creating a collective framework for workers who share the same workplace and conditions of employment. In building worker self-confidence, it also has the capacity to increase levels of participation in the union. Nevertheless, the development of the LLA role and its links into union structures still need to be forged. The extent to which the potential of the workplace learning agenda is realised depends on a number of different factors.

The first of these is the ability and willingness of branch officers and paid officials to engage with these workers who are potential members and activists. Many of the early UNISON/employer learning partnerships were established by national officials and national and regional officials still play a key role in setting them up (cf. Munro and Rainbird 2000). As a result learning partnerships may exist where there is weak local organisation. In this situation, workers taking part in the programmes may not realise that UNISON is involved in the partnership and opportunities for raising the profile of the union are lost. Course participants may be interested in becoming more active, but there is no one to capitalise on this interest and they may move on to activities outside the union. We have come across a number of cases where course participants spoke of being interested in the union, but no one had asked them if they wanted to become more involved. Both Fosh (1993) and Fairbrother (1996) have emphasised the significance of local union leaders in the process of union renewal. Here we have identified circumstances where branch officers may fail to build on 'surges of participation and interest' (Fosh 1993: 589).

Second, the response of local officers to the workplace learning agenda is also crucial. This is not just a case of weak branches failing to capitalise on potential members and activists. Officers may have little interest in workplace learning as a branch activity and the new learning representative role may not fit with their idea of an activist. A challenge to either the content or process of trade unionism may not be welcome to established branch officers. Existing Branch Education Officers may feel undermined or left behind with an influx of new learning representatives. It is not only branch officers who may not see benefits to engaging with potential new activists, but some paid officers may also be unenthusiastic or feel too busy for such activities. The development of new forms of activism relating to workplace learning offers the potential to revitalise workplace trade unionism, but this is by no means certain as many key players have an interest in retaining the status quo.

Third, the new statutory rights have made the role of union learning representatives too attractive for branches to ignore. This may provide an impulse for branches to take the workplace learning agenda seriously and for shop stewards as well as new activists to take on ULR roles. UNISON's policy of recruiting learning representatives from the ranks of new activists as well as from existing shop steward bodies implies some challenge to both the content and process of union business.

Finally, in contrast to the health and safety legislation, the new statutory rights do not provide the right to negotiate with the employer on workplace learning. Nevertheless, the transposition of the European Directive on Information and Consultation may provide the missing procedural basis for employers and unions to discuss training and development in the workplace. If this were the case, the LLA/ULR role might indeed provide UNISON and other trade unions with a basis for responding to the ' "qualitative" dimensions of contemporary managerialist discourse' (Hyman 1994: 127) as partners in workplace learning rather than representing an inexpensive source of expertise for the employer, the perspective emphasised by government departments.

Notes

1. This chapter draws primarily on two large-scale research projects. The first, 'The Future of Unskilled Work: Learning and Workplace Inequality' (1998/99) was based on six case studies in local authorities and NHS trusts, involving more than 330 face-to-face interviews and a survey conducted in two of the organisations which produced a similar number of responses. It focused on the opportunities and barriers to workplace learning for lower grade workers. All of the case studies selected had learning partnerships with UNISON and afforded the additional opportunity to assess the implications of such partnership arrangements as well as addressing the central research questions. This project was funded by the ESRC's 'Future of Work' programme (ref. L212 25 2017). The research team included Helen Rainbird, Anne Munro, Lesley Holly and Ruchira Leisten. The preliminary findings were published in Rainbird *et al.* (1999). The second project, 'Regulatory Structures and Access to Learning: Case Studies in Social Care and Cleaning Services', involved case studies of cleaning and care workers in the public and private sector and private contractors to the public sector. This was one of five related projects on the theme of, 'Improving Incentives to Learning at Work'. It was funded under the ESRC's Teaching and Learning Programme (L139 25 1005) and ran from 2000 to 2003. In addition, we have been involved in a number of research and evaluation projects related to UNISON's involvement in workplace learning over the last seven years. These have included an evaluation of some of the earliest partnerships with employers (Munro *et al.* 1997); an assessment of different models of the learning enthusiast role (Munro and Rainbird 1999), involvement in the management committee of a ULF project developing Lifelong Learning Advisers (Rainbird 2002), and evaluating multi-employer partnerships across health and social care (Rainbird *et al.* 2002).
2. The exception to this is where trade unions are recognised by employers under the statutory procedures of ERA 1999. In this instance, the employer must consult with trade unions on the company's training plan and report on training provided to workers on a six monthly basis. These provisions apply to a small minority of workplaces where trade unions are recognised under this procedure. When the provisions were introduced, the Department of Trade and Industry envisaged that they could provide a model to be adopted in other workplaces, the vast majority, where unions are recognised on a voluntary basis.
3. The following section draws on the background research that was conducted to identify the LLA role (see Munro and Rainbird 1999).
4. The following section is taken from the evaluation report on the project (Rainbird 2002).
5. This was a common finding in the evaluations of the ULF by other researchers (York Consulting 2001; Cutter 2000; Shaw 1999).

8

Partnership, Mutuality and the High-performance Workplace: A Case Study of Union Strategy and Worker Experience in the Aircraft Industry

Andy Danford, Mike Richardson, Paul Stewart, Stephanie Tailby and Martin Upchurch

Introduction

The adoption by firms of high performance work systems and supportive partnership relationships with their recognised trade unions is currently central to debates on Britain's productivity performance. It is also widely promoted as the preferred strategic option for firms that wish to take the so-called 'high road' to competitive advantage (DTI 2002b; TUC 2002a). The implied alternative option is a 'low road' characterised by short-term profit maximisation, low skill employment and low wages (Michie and Sheehan 2003).

In the context of the Western productivity crises of the 1970s and 1980s that arose from the limitations of Taylorised and Fordist mass production, a number of analysts have argued that many of the more 'progressive' manufacturing enterprises have been gradually developing new management techniques in labour deployment and employee participation. These can be collectively termed high-performance work systems (HPWS) (Bélanger, J. *et al.* 2002; Appelbaum *et al.* 2000). HPWS practices are assumed to increase organisational flexibility and efficiency by systematically mobilising workers' tacit knowledge and discretion in creative and participative work environments. Such practices include the provision of greater worker autonomy over questions of job task and method, the use of self-managed teams and worker participation in problem-solving groups, and more extensive communications between shop-floor workers, managers and technical specialists. It is argued that when these practices are used in work settings that provide intrinsically rewarding skilled jobs and real job security then greater employee commitment is likely to ensue (Appelbaum *et al.* 2000).

HPWS analysts also place considerable stress on the use of 'soft' human resource management and integrative industrial relations practices that promote social cohesion in the employment relationship (Bélanger, J. *et al.* 2002). The increase in worker commitment that is a critical feature of HPWS can be impaired by the presence of low-trust relations between managers and workers and antagonistic relations between managers and unions. Consequently, the development of new, co-operative partnership relationships between workers, unions and employers is deemed essential if high performance outcomes are to be achieved. In this context, partnership can be conceptualised as a combination of practices that promote the HPWS principles of joint management–employee commitment to the enterprise, employee participation in work decisions and greater involvement by both workers and their union representatives in organization-related decisions (Guest and Peccei 2001). Partnership would also be expected to foster employment security and to engender greater openness and transparency in decision-making by processes of information-sharing and genuine consultation (TUC 1999). It is the idea of 'mutuality' and the 'two-way street' that is perhaps central to this proposed shift in employment relations. That is, the proposition that if workers are expected to maximise their contribution to the firm then managers must offer meaningful work, meaningful participation and job security in return (Collins 2001).

To date, there has been insufficient examination of the impact of HPWS on workers themselves. Apart from the research that relies upon managers as inappropriate proxies for their employees' views the bulk of the worker-focused research has come out of the US. Much of this work has been underpinned by a perspective that assumes that HPWS must be inherently beneficial for both employers and workers alike. For example, Appelbaum *et al.* (2000) and Freeman and Rogers (1999) have used conventional survey techniques, involving structural mapping of employee attitudes, to argue for a positive link between co-operative work systems and employee commitment, trust and job satisfaction. Although we welcome the centrality of labour to these research agendas we do have severe reservations about the lack of critical space provided by these projects. This missing critique becomes more problematic in the light of alternative evidence from the US which suggests that employers that adopt high performance work practices are not necessarily making a progressive, 'strategic choice' that offers inherent advantages for labour. For instance, Cappelli (1999) has found that many American firms are frequently forced to adopt participative practices in conditions of tight labour markets in the belief that these will enhance job satisfaction and hence improve labour retention rates. Moreover, Cappelli notes that there is often a sting in the tail of these practices in that many are shaped to secure labour productivity gains for the firm at the expense of worker empowerment and job security. In return for more output and higher productivity workers are expected to manage their own careers and have an increasingly contingent relationship with their employer. As one of Cappelli's commentators colourfully puts it, 'without a reciprocal commitment by management to a long-term relationship, the employee who buys into the partnership model is being romanced for a one-night stand' (1999: 29).

North America is also one of the main sources of research on trade union partnership strategies in high performance work contexts. Much of this work tends to be sanguine and managerialist in its assumption that unions have much to gain and little to lose from co-operative engagement with the new management agendas. Commonly known as the 'mutual gains' approach, it argues that trade union participation in such management issues as work design and strategic planning offers a route to resolving opposing sets of interests between employers, workers and their unions. In other words, new forms of union participation and co-operation through partnership raise the prospects of organisational outcomes that benefit employers and their work-forces alike (Frost 2001b; Kochan and Osterman 1994). The new participa-tion may involve a weakening of those work practices that constrain managerial prerogatives. However, it also offers union involvement in joint committees that have as their objectives 'co-operative bargaining' over work organisation and the economic and financial management of the firm (Bélanger, P.R. *et al.* 2002).

In the UK, much of the current debate on workplace partnership has focused on its implications for current trends in the politics of management–union relations. The growing amount of published research in this area has provided important insights into management rationales and the nature of partnership agreements as well as the attitudes of union activists and the impact of partnership upon union influence at work (see e.g. Heery 2002; Martínez Lucio and Stuart 2002; Oxenbridge and Brown 2002; Tailby and Winchester 2002). There is also a growing body of work that offers an essen-tially pessimistic prognosis for the future of independent workplace union-ism in partnership environments. For example, both Terry (2003b) and Bacon *et al.* (1996) contend that union activists may have little option but to co-operate with managerial initiatives in the context of union weakness and management's ability to relocate production and either restructure or close existing workplaces in the UK. Equally, the dangers for unions of flirt-ing with partnership have been well documented. For instance, Kelly (1996a) and Taylor and Ramsay (1998) have both highlighted the risk that shop stewards may find themselves increasingly isolated from their rank and file members whilst their partnership agreements may often diminish union restraints on the imposition of managerial prerogatives.

Therefore, although the managerialist conceptualisations of workplace partnership have no difficulty in highlighting the potential of mutual gain in the employment relationship we are faced with either insufficient, or con-flicting, evidence of exactly what advantages unions might expect from the new conditions at work. Moreover, despite our knowledge that partnership will often involve changes to the labour process and employment relations through, for example, teamworking, pay incentives and dual communications structures (Oxenbridge and Brown 2002), there are few UK-based studies that consider union revitalisation strategies in the context of the reactions of those who have the most to gain or lose from these changes – workers themselves. This chapter addresses this question by presenting a factory case study of the impact of partnership and high performance work practices on British aircraft workers. The choice of sector is important for the following reasons.

The crude high road–low road dichotomy adopted by strategic choice theorists has been blamed for the failure of firms to sustain partnership and high performance work systems. For instance, Konzelmann and Forrant (2003) have argued that despite the inherent advantages of creative and co-operative work systems they inevitably operate in highly competitive free market conditions and high road firms are often undermined by low road competitors. Many advocates of partnership also adopt such an analytical framework (e.g. Appelbaum *et al.* 2000; Bélanger, P.R. *et al.* 2002). It assumes that if only new regulatory mechanisms could be introduced that somehow buffered high road employers from the perdition of profit maximisation and short-term shareholder interests then a new dynamic of progressive capitalism might be launched. If we were to accept this high road–low road terminology then the aerospace sector could be characterised as British manufacturing's premier high road sector, characterised by innovative work systems and high skill utilisation in both design and production. It is also a discrete sector that, although subject to global competition, has not been exposed to low cost competition to the extent seen in the mass production industries. Therefore, to adopt for the moment the assumptions of the high road–low road theorists, it is a sector in which we might expect to find positive worker outcomes from sustainable partnership programmes.

The case study provides a picture of the dynamics and politics of partnership in the high performance workplace as well as analysis of the underlying structural factors that shape partnership outcomes. We present qualitative data on the impact of different HPWS and partnership practices on skilled employees and their unions in a long-established aircraft design and assembly plant. There are three dimensions to our empirical analysis. First, we examine the different material and ideological components of management strategy and how these fit with the demands of capital accumulation. Second, we consider the strategic positions adopted by the plant's recognised unions. We explore the extent to which union influence changes in a partnership environment and whether partnership can foster or impair both the relationships between members and their representatives and between different unions in a multi-union workplace. And third, we explore the impact of HPWS and partnership on manual and non-manual workers, focusing on the extent of employee involvement, work intensification and job security. Specifically, we question whether affected workers really can secure meaningful participation in work and employment-related decisions – the essence of mutuality – or whether they are just as likely to become subject to a one way street of task accretion, work intensification and reduced job security. The chapter will argue that, on the basis of this case study of a high skill, creative work environment, there is no real dichotomy between high and low road management strategies. Instead, there is a single road towards greater flexibility, more systematic cost control and profit maximisation. It will also argue that trade union strategies based on partnership with management make no sense in the context of negative employee experience.

Research design

The case study factory is given the pseudonym Airframes. It is responsible for the design and assembly of different models of a particular type of aircraft that can be used for both civil and military purposes. The factory employs 4000 workers and is located in a small market town of 38 000 people. The relative size of the factory compared to alternative local employment means that it is virtually a single company town.

The workforce comprised 600 managers and supervisors; 1500 production workers (90 per cent skilled); and 1900 graduate, technical and administrative staff. Included in these figures are a significant number of temporary workers whose employment fluctuated in accordance with market changes. At the time of the research these numbered 300. The shop floor workforce was represented by the AMICUS–AEEU and TGWU. The non-manual workforce was represented by AMICUS–MSF and TGWU–ACTSS.

The chapter draws upon qualitative data that were collected at the factory in December 2000 and between the spring of 2001 and early 2002. During this time we carried out taped interviews with 70 staff. These comprised 13 senior and line managers, 9 union representatives, 20 production workers (nearly all of whom were skilled), 22 non-manual employees comprising design engineers, technical and administrative staff, and 6 temporary workers.

Management strategy: cost control in a velvet glove

The British aerospace industry has undergone radical change over the past two decades. The industry has always received unusually high levels of state support due to its importance for Britain's hi-tech manufacturing base along with its role as supplier of weapons equipment to the British armed forces. Although it still enjoys considerable state support the nature of this has shifted significantly since the mid-1980s as UK defence budgets declined and suppliers were expected to succeed in highly competitive export markets to a much greater extent than hitherto. As a result of these politico-economic changes all of the UK's indigenous aerospace manufacturers have undergone some form of restructuring. This has involved large-scale labour rationalisation, modernisation of management, flexibilisation of business organisation and reform of work practices and industrial relations (Danford *et al.* 2003; Lovering 1998).

The case of Airframes provides an example of these changes. The substitution of competitive tendering for 'cost-plus' defence contracts in the late 1980s and an intensification of global competition among aircraft suppliers combined to catalyse new directions in corporate strategy and widespread organisational restructuring. Different Airframes directors described the continual pressures to cut costs and improve lead times that resulted from engagement with competitive, fixed price equipment programmes both in the UK and abroad. One company director observed that, 'once you go beyond the MOD and you're more into military export, or civil business, it's very different, it's dog eat dog'. These politico-economic pressures meant that the Airframes plant had to continually improve its design to production lead times, product costs and product quality in order to remain competitive against American and European suppliers.

These exogenous factors were accompanied by changes in both the ownership of the firm and the nature of the management regime. Airframes was subject to a takeover by a large British-owned multinational manufacturing company in 1994. The management regime in the new company took a far greater interest in short-term profit generation and minimising costs than was the case previously and was concerned to engender a new business enterprise culture. The competitive drive for labour productivity and cost control – rather than engineering innovation – accelerated with the creation of a joint venture between Airframes and an Italian aerospace corporation early in 2001.

A multifaceted process of organisational change took hold during the years leading up to the period of research. Despite the plant's high skill base the basic pattern of reorganisation corresponded in many ways to Ackroyd and Procter's (1998) 'new flexible firm', the implications of which will be considered in the conclusion. This comprised new financial control techniques; the use of HPWS practices; and supportive partnership-based employee relations practices. Each of these will now be briefly described.

Financial control, labour deployment and cultural change

During the 1990s, the company developed a new financial control framework that was designed to secure the key objectives of lead-time improvements and reduced production costs. One key example of this was the substitution of 'systems integration' for conventional manufacturing. This involved sub-contracting the manufacture of large parts and assemblies to different firms in the supply chain and then acting as final assembler of these parts and providing post-sale services. In 1980 most part and sub-assembly manufacture was carried out in-house. By the time of the research in 2002, 85 per cent of the manufacturing operations required for aircraft assembly was outsourced to 1200 suppliers, many located overseas.

This process of cost reduction though dispensing with part manufacture was accompanied by a series of work reforms and changes to labour deployment that facilitated formal budgetary control techniques and precise performance measures. For example, the deployment of production workers into cells and of technical staff into matrix-based business streams created manageable units for the calculation of costs and productivity performance as well as increasing rates of labour utilisation.

These material changes were accompanied by cultural change at management level. The characteristic features of the previous management regime at Airframes were those associated with a traditional, paternalistic bureaucracy: a tall hierarchy; career progression on the basis of age and seniority; limited movement of staff across departmental boundaries; and formally at least, a reliance upon a comprehensive set of organisational procedures and engineering standards. A relatively high employment of ex-armed services personnel was an additional facet, particularly in such functions as customer support, and an informal convention of deference to rank was prevalent in these areas. The new economic conditions coupled with the change in ownership of the firm catalysed a gradual shift in this management culture. By 2002 the characteristics of the management regime had altered quite markedly. For example, individuals began to rise through a downsized managerial hierarchy on the basis of commercial awareness and degree qualifications rather than seniority. The plant's engineering director indicated that the majority of his managers now had business as well as engineering qualifications, their average age had reduced from the high fifties to the low forties, and they would be expected to move around the business every five years to gain in-depth experience of the different functions within the enterprise. This shift in management control and style became apparent in employee perceptions of management. For example, a number of employees complained during our interviews that the plant was being 'run by accountants rather than engineers' and that 'budgetary control rather than engineering innovation' seemed to be the guiding principle for management.

High performance work practices

The Airframes management introduced a series of work organisational changes in the three-year period leading up to the research. These took the form of different HPWS practices that sought to rationalise and flexibilise the design and production process whilst offering a degree of employee involvement. The most important of these were lean production control, teamworking, continuous improvement and a flexibilisation of employment contracts.

Lean production control involved a systematic reduction in the time required to build an aircraft through a combination of measures. These were the more efficient deployment of workers into teams (see below); the use of computerised just-in-time inventory control; the use of kanban production control techniques in some areas; and a re-organisation of workflow, stores and line-side part feeds. As a result of such measures the build hours required for completing each aircraft had been significantly reduced. For example, the build time for the plant's largest aircraft programme was reduced from 17 000 to 10 000 hours. During the first year of production of a new aircraft programme in 2001, total build was achieved in 5000 hours.

Teamworking involved a rationalisation of labour deployment through different types of cellular organisation in the production areas and the use of a matrix-based organisation in technical staff areas. In both cases, the objective was not to increase employee participation in the management of work but instead to establish more efficient and cost-accountable forms of labour utilisation. For example, in the production areas a tradition of relatively ample staffing levels and multi-skilled gangs working on a range of products was replaced by a system of discrete teams, each accountable for cost and performance. This had the effect of narrowing the range of workers' skills but increasing the volume of tasks and responsibilities. In the non-manual engineering areas traditional demarcations between the different engineering departments were replaced by a programme–centric matrix organisation. Programme managers, again accountable for performance and costs, were allowed to draw upon more mobile and flexible pools of technical staff to meet different project priorities. As a result, the engineering staff accumulated significant extra responsibilities and tasks.

The continuous improvement techniques provided the more participative dimension to the HPWS agenda although worker participation was restricted to narrow questions of team performance. In some areas of the plant continuous improvement was regarded as an informal and natural aspect of worker activity whereas in others local managers organised small, off-line problem-solving groups. In the latter cases, employee participation was voluntary and tended to be low.

The flexibilisation of employment contracts was an unusual development in the context of an aerospace industry that has traditionally relied upon large core workforces comprising skilled, permanent employees. It has long been common practice for aerospace corporations to utilise substantial numbers of sub-contract firms to supply parts for production and technical labour for some design work. In the late 1990s the Airframes management developed a new dimension to this flexibility practice. In order to emulate the lower cost employment practice in its Italian joint venture partner, and following a qualitative shift in senior management discussions on labour recruitment, the factory began to recruit large numbers of temporary agency staff in both design and production areas. The human resource director described the objectives:

> You get to a sort of core level, which if you like is your minimum core level to retain your expertise and competence and thereafter you manage everything else through outsourcing and temporary labour.

The number of temporary workers employed varied in accordance with fluctuations in project demands. For example, in 1999, the figure was as high as 750 manual and non-manual workers. By the end of 2002, this had reduced to 300 following the completion of a major production programme.

Social cohesion and workplace partnership

The introduction of different high performance work reforms embodied management's desire to establish a 'cost-efficient' work organisation that could more rapidly respond to market changes. Management also sought to develop a workplace partnership in order to secure employees' understanding, or even approval, of these changes. In other words, the promotion of partnership reflected the need to legitimise a process of continual improvement in organisational performance. There were two discrete relational facets of this partnership agenda: the first involved the plant's trade union representatives, the second involved employees directly.

Management's objective of securing a partnership with trade unions emerged in the context of a legacy of fairly adversarial management–union relations in both shop floor and technical areas. During the previous two decades the plant experienced recurrent industrial disputes over pay determination, working hours, new technology and representational rights. The aim of the partnership policy was not to enhance union rights *per se* but to reduce the likelihood of further union mobilisation and militancy against the effects of labour rationalisation, labour flexibility and cost reduction.

No formal partnership agreement existed at the plant. However, during the 1990s, the senior management had gradually developed a consultative architecture that comprised different forums for constructive dialogue with the trade unions. These operated outside of the conventional negotiating committees for collective bargaining on pay and conditions. For example, a company council of senior managers and union representatives met monthly to discuss strategic business issues and local grievances. A joint technical committee of engineering directors and staff representatives discussed workload, future projects and staffing levels in the non-manual areas. A manpower committee of production directors and manual shop stewards considered staffing levels and requirements for sub-contract and temporary labour. And a series of joint management–union working parties met to discuss specific issues such as new grading schemes. By the time of the research in 2001–02, the plant's senior management had begun promoting partnership in terms of a qualitative change in the nature of management–union interactions. With the architecture for union dialogue well established the management was seeking shifts in the *process* of bargaining and consultation towards one based on developing consensus. The plant's HR director explained:

> [It's] really about being as open and honest with each other as you can. Take the union guys in to your confidence and say, 'okay this is the business position, these are the issues that are facing us.' We want to work with you on this one. And then listen and not just hear what they come back with but to try and work together, to try and develop a joint plan on how you implement some of that.

The idea of cultivating consensus is also what framed management's approach to handling the contradictions between partnership, flexibility and organisational downsizing. It was hoped that a greater transparency in communications and decision-making would help unions and employees to recognise that although greater flexibility can help protect job tenure for some core workers, capitalist firms operating in global free markets do not offer job guarantees. As one senior manager put it:

> If you're having partnership, what is it the company should expect from its employees and what should employees expect from the company? We actually stated that, we've articulated that. One of the points in return for employees is security of employment. But then the acid test is, how do you actually bring that about? I've seen some organisations that have entered into guaranteed security. But who, hand on heart, can actually write that? We've always said we're not prepared to do that because we will be signing up to something that we know deep down we couldn't guarantee we could deliver. I think most places would recognize that as an honourable position.

The second facet of management's partnership policy involved the direct participation of employees through the integration of different communications techniques. Taken together these techniques were supposed to engender greater employee understanding of business changes and a new organisational commitment. The communications strategy comprised formal and informal elements. For example, monthly team briefing sessions with line managers, annual meetings between the workforce and the managing director, an intranet-based vox pop system and regular communications bulletins and newsletters. Whereas in the past some of these practices were used in an ad hoc manner the management was now attempting a more coherent and inclusive communications approach. This was aimed at incorporating employees with company objectives and engendering greater business awareness. The HR director summarised this:

> ...potentially there is a tension between stakeholders but I think that effective partnership will either facilitate that response to change, or you know, if the shareholders and the city say that it's got to be x, y and z and that has a negative impact on the organisation, at least if you've had that partnership arrangement, it will be better understood. I'm not saying it will be liked but it will be better understood. That to me would be the major benefit.

In many respects, therefore, management adopted an instrumentalist view of partnership. Trade union and employee participation in management decision-making was not supported for reasons of enhancing workers' rights *per se*; instead, participation was viewed as a means of enhancing efficient business and production methods and of improving business relations in more competitive environments (Allen 2001; Collins 2001). This should also be viewed in the context of the significant shifts in the politico-economic environment and changes in company ownership. These combined to engender a new type of management regime at Airframes, a regime that could be described as 'cost control wrapped in a velvet glove'. The 'hard' side to this was the new emphasis upon accountability, financial control and cost reduction by way of organisational restructuring and high performance work techniques. And the 'soft' side was the development of a partnership framework – an attempt to legitimise and facilitate change processes on management's terms by emphasising mutuality in the employment relationship. The extent to which the Airframes trade unions and workforce recognised this new mutuality is explored next.

Trade union response: disillusion and discord

The site unions were divided into two recognised bargaining groups – manual and non-manual. Although the two groups were, to varying degrees, cautious about many aspects of partnership they were both constrained by conditions of 'factory survival'. The Airframes factory was by far the biggest employer in its local community, an essentially rural community that most of its inhabitants felt strongly attached to. This meant that many workers were subject to a more acute dependency relationship than the norm, a relationship that shaped the behaviour of workers and union activists alike. For example, in the context of interview discussions on the pattern of incessant mass redundancies in the UK's aerospace industry, the AMICUS–MSF convenor reflected on the imperatives of factory survival in the following way:

> I will never forget how my father left his employer. He had worked for all of his life at Beesley's in the leather trades. The day he reached his retirement, aged 65, the factory announced it was closing down. This had a profound

effect on my dad. He came home that day in a state of shock. It was as if his whole life had amounted to nothing, that it had become meaningless. I've never forgotten that day. And as a senior union representative at this plant I've always been determined that it must never happen at *Airframes*. I see my prime role as doing everything possible to keep this factory running. Because the factory provides good employment for so many people in this town.

In this context, neither bargaining group eschewed management's overtures to partnership. Neither did they reject every aspect of the work organisational changes. For example, both groups implicitly supported the company's use of agency and sub-contract labour. This was on the condition that the length of employment contract was effectively policed and that, for agency workers, equal pay and conditions were applied so as to prevent the undercutting of core workers' conditions. In many respects, however, the policy of the union activists was to treat temporary staff as a 'necessary evil', as a means of protecting the job security of the unionised core workforce. The principle of 'last in first out' was replaced by 'temps in temps out'. The unions made little attempt to recruit agency workers and they were often described in derogatory terms. This dimension of 'partnership' amounted to little more than self-interested union collusion with the management's core–periphery, flexible employment strategy.

The unions' response to management's broader, 'participative' partnership agenda was marked by greater tension between the union groups and within the manual group. This was partly a function of the manual and non-manual group convenors' different interpretations of the partnership concept. The manual group convenor was a leading figure in regional Labour Party politics and a candidate at the 2001 general election. Although he voiced many misgivings over management's real commitment to partnership and felt that the manual unions had yet to secure any significant advantage from it he remained ideologically committed to the principle of joint co-operation in the interests of the survival of the firm:

> I hope that the directors of the company will see that there is something in this, we are positive, we aren't an "anti" organisation, we're not trying to slow the company, we're not trying to drag it. We're trying to move the company forward.

This commitment contrasted markedly with the views of the manual shop stewards. Whatever benefits accrued to the senior stewards through their participation in the different partnership committees, these did not percolate down to the shop floor. Every steward we interviewed indicated that the grass roots membership rejected management's version of partnership. It was felt that too many middle managers could not keep to their side of the bargain and showed no interest in compromising their perceived 'right to manage'. Moreover, this disjunction between the position of the rank and file and the group convenor reflected the latter's detached leadership style. As has been noted in other partnership case studies this disjunction threatened to isolate the plant's union activists (e.g. Danford *et al.* 2002; Taylor and Ramsay 1998). The following comment exemplified this:

> It's starting to come to a stage now where people are saying, 'well the union are saying yes all the time and getting nothing for it'. I mean, take my manager. We'll sit there and if I agree with what he's saying or he can agree with what I'm saying then fine. But we've also had a couple of situations where I've said 'no we're not doing that' and he's said 'oh well we'd better get Gary up [the convenor]'. So Gary comes and 'irons out the wrinkles' and in the end the manager gets what he wants. Because Gary says, 'well yes we've got to be a bit flexible'. So I go back to the workshop floor and they say to me 'what's the bloody point if you were going to turn around and say we're going to do it anyway'.

The response to partnership adopted by the non-manual bargaining group was more internally cohesive. Although the non-manual unions welcomed the potential of greater involvement both the convenor and the local staff representatives felt that the management's partnership agenda placed too much emphasis upon business interests alone. These activists sought an alternative partnership that focused more on the promotion of independent worker interests. For example, in 1997 the non-manual unions had launched their own partnership initiative. Succeeding in appropriating the company's own business rhetoric, the unions established a new forum entitled, Business Improvement Through People. This was initially supported by senior management and it required union representatives and company directors to discuss collective member concerns outside of the traditional bargaining framework, concerns such as employee morale and workplace stress. However, although these discussions did generate one or two examples of new company policy, the forum gradually atrophied as managers began to lose interest and prevaricate over policy implementation. As one ACTSS (Administrative, Clerical, Technical and Supervisory Staff) representative put it, 'it became in our opinion a talking shop – you would find one month the same thing would be discussed, what we were going to do, what we weren't going to do, but nothing ever was done about anything'.

By 2002, the non-manual unions' position on partnership was far more cynical, shaped by a belief that management's accommodating rhetoric in fact obscured widespread management resistance to notions of meaningful union or employee participation. As the non-manual group convenor commented:

> Yes. I think there is this bloody arrogance within management that says quite clearly, all the clever people are in management therefore nobody below management level can possibly have anything useful to offer. And

if you extrapolate that on to, say, where do unions fit in this then the position is even worse ... I think we certainly feel very frustrated in terms of the lack of what we've been able to deliver.

Our interviews with different local staff representatives identified the same frustrations and a much closer affinity between the non-manual convenor and local activists and members. This more cohesive opposition to partnership in turn created new tensions between the manual and non-manual bargaining groups. These manifested themselves in a number of ways during the period of the research. For example, different Human Resource (HR) and operations managers felt that the manual group leadership was far more supportive of management-led change compared to their 'difficult' and 'more distrustful' non-manual counterparts. Although the two bargaining groups traditionally worked together and co-ordinated their actions, by the time of the research this had reduced to a more pragmatic co-operation constrained at times by mutual suspicion. For instance, the 2002 annual wage negotiations were marked by a clear fracture between the two groups. Fairly early in the negotiating period the manual union convenor persuaded his members to accept what he termed 'a reasonably low percentage' in the interests of 'factory competitiveness'. By contrast, the non-manual union leadership strongly recommended rejection and this was overwhelming endorsed at a mass meeting. The non-manual bargaining group eventually succeeded in securing an improved offer whilst preparing a secret ballot for industrial action.

Therefore, in the context of the company's cost control strategy and extant management hostility to meaningful trade union participation, neither the manual nor non-manual union bargaining group had secured enhanced influence as a result of the management's introduction of partnership practices. Moreover, the quite different leadership orientations of the manual and non-manual unions meant that multiple divisions emerged within the workplace union organisation. For both groups the lack of mutuality in workplace partnership had engendered new tensions in inter-union and management–union relations.

The employees' perspective: cohesion or exclusion?

Advocates of partnership regard employee participation in management decision-making about work and organisation as central to the creation of more co-operative relations. If employees are given the opportunity to participate in matters affecting their work and employment then it is assumed that this will result in 'win-win' outcomes for employers and employees. That is, organisational performance will improve whilst employees benefit from enhanced trust and job satisfaction (Guest and Peccei 2001; Appelbaum *et al.* 2000; Kochan and Osterman 1994).

The Airframes management had introduced an extensive array of communications and involvement practices aimed, it was claimed, at increasing employee participation in organisational decision-making. Our interviews explored the impact of these practices in the office and on the shop floor. The first point to be noted is that most employees confirmed that the mass of company communications had increased significantly over recent years just as our management interviewees had suggested. However, when we explored the democratic dimensions of this new 'transparency' it became clear that the reality of unequal power in the employment relationship reduced the idea of employee participation through partnership to mere rhetoric. There were widespread feelings of 'them and us', evidence of a climate of fear, and a complete lack of influence over high-level decisions that affect job tenure and security.

Many employees articulated their resentment at what was described as a new managerial arrogance. It was felt that managers paid lip service to the participative agendas of partnership and instead felt the need to maintain their traditional power and status. In the engineering offices and on the shop floor the predominant view was that although the new involvement practices gave employees a limited voice, deep-seated class and status distinctions between managers and subordinates meant that this voice was rarely recognised. For example an engineer and a production inspector described relationships as follows:

> I believe that higher management are far less aware and responsive to employees' aspirations and are not in touch with the day to day feelings within the company. There is a pronounced 'us and them' culture fuelled by distrust and management arrogance.
>
> We are not all mushrooms and do not like to be kept in the dark and fed on shit – we are human beings with families and we need to know what our future job prospects are.

When discussing the need for two-way dialogue in the various communications settings, many employees voiced their concerns over the implications of heightened management power in an environment of insecurity. It was felt that this created a pervasive climate of fear that inhibited the articulation of an independent view. For example:

> ... they make sure they have a way of communicating as much as they can to every single person that works here. They should try and get more views back. A lot of people are scared of putting their views back because the people they're giving their views back to are the ones that can move them, shift them, even in some cases, get rid of them. At the moment the culture in engineering is of fear, driven by fear, disgusting because there's lip service to all the right ways of doing everything and

the people that are running it are absolutely not listening. (Data Analyst and AMICUS Rep)

This lack of meaningful voice and, in some cases, employee fear in this partnership environment was compounded by the fact that the substance of management's communications agenda rarely addressed the long-term interests of Airframes' employees. Theories of employee participation emphasise the requirement of employers to incorporate 'high level' business issues into their dialogue with employees (Boxall and Purcell 2003), issues that reflect employee concerns over job tenure and security. Yet, despite the fact that at the time of the research, and the period leading up to it, Airframes was subject to extensive re-organisation as a result of the Italian joint venture, nearly all of the employees we interviewed felt debarred from any discussion governing the implications of these changes for the workforce.

The treatment of the company's agency workers provided a further dimension to this pattern of exclusion. Every temporary worker that we interviewed articulated a surprisingly strong commitment to the company (a commitment tied to the hope of securing long-term employment) but in every case they reported feelings of formal disqualification from the practices of partnership and participation. This relational outcome of the market-based 'efficiency' of numerical flexibility policy was summed up by the following comment from a temporary staff employee:

> When things are being discussed that involve you, you will be missed out because you're temporary, but it affects you and you know how that process runs and everything but you will be left out ... When I first started, there was a guy that didn't speak to me for three months because he said that they'd had temps in here before and they don't last longer than three months and he said that he just about gets to speak to them and then they leave. So that made me feel really worthwhile as a human being!

Therefore, we could identify few gains for the different groups of employees in terms of the involvement and participation expected by the advocates of partnership relations. However, the process of rationalising labour deployment that was intrinsic to the work restructuring meant that many workers were expending more effort, working more flexibly and encountering a growing sense of job insecurity. In other words, the employer alone seemed to derive significant gains from this partnership.

In the production areas, labour intensification did not result primarily from speed-up – although some workers did report this – because unlike the conventional mass production of commodities, the small-batch manufacture of an aircraft is a slow, complex process that does not lend itself to the control techniques of the assembly line. Instead, many workers' experiences reflected Nichols' (1991) observation that the porosity of the working day is often reduced in more mundane ways by cutting idle time and by gradual task accretion. For example, many production workers described the increased workload and responsibility for quality control that the rationalisation of labour into teams required. The following view from an aircraft fitter was typical:

> Because of the additional responsibility I think that generally people do work harder but that doesn't mean to say it's terrifically harder, just harder. When I used to do just fitting I used to do a good days work, pack up, go home, come in the next morning and I didn't have to think, 'crikey I've got to do this or I've got to do that', it was just my job. Now to a certain extent some of the guys have to think about their work a lot more. Once they come into the realms of a fitter/inspector then you do take on extra responsibility and I think that job is quite hard to do properly.

In the non-manual areas, employees reported a pattern of increased effort caused by gradual staff reductions and the flexibility inherent in replacing function-based demarcations by the new programme–centric matrix model. And a good number reflected upon the health and stress implications of this:

> [The company] would say they've got all the things, occupational health and stress policies and this, that and the other. I think the company give the impression that they care about it all and try and help. But I haven't seen any evidence that they actually do care if people are over-stretched or overworked…I feel that we're all running around like loonies… because of the severe cutbacks. (Engineer)

Feelings of job insecurity are an additional indicator of stress because affected workers can sense a loss of certainty and personal control at work. Moreover, in environments of limited alternative job opportunities, such as the rural locality that Airframes was based in, workers who are compelled to cling to their jobs may suffer extra insecurity (Burchell 2002: 62). Our employee interviews confirmed such patterns. Although the plant had not experienced any mass redundancies since the early 1990s and, indeed, had experienced subsequent expansion, we discovered widespread unease and fears of job instability. Despite management's rhetoric of partnership and inclusion many employees felt that the new management regime, and its priorities of cost control, had substituted the principle of replaceability for the traditions of career path and stability. The following comment was typical:

> If you'd asked me whether job security is a factor ten years ago, or maybe even five years ago, I would have said I've got a job for life. Ask me that

now, no, absolutely not. And the company doesn't promote that image either. Whereas I think they used to, yes. You know I'm considered a Technical Specialist who are basically worth their weight in gold. Now you're just a number.

Early in 2002, these fears became fact when the management announced 600 redundancies. The scale of job loss came as a complete surprise to the plant's employees and trade union representatives. This in itself constituted a stark reminder of the myth of partnership. For many workers, therefore, the facile concept of 'mutual gain' actualised as a one way street: they experienced an intensification of labour and greater stress; they enjoyed little meaningful participation or influence over decisions that affected their core employment interests; their organisational loyalty was not reciprocated by management; and their confidence in long-term job tenure weakened – for some, it evaporated.

Conclusion

A checklist of management practices at Airframes would match most aspects of the HPWS-partnership model. A series of employee-centred measures was introduced that, ostensibly, aimed to increase organisational commitment and employee involvement, as well as labour productivity. Moreover, Airframes was a company operating in a discrete, high skill segment of Britain's manufacturing sector and, unlike firms operating in the mass production industries, was in many respects cushioned from the pressures of low-skill/low-wage competition. These were propitious environmental conditions that, for strategic choice theorists, would be expected to foster empowerment for workers and more influence for trade unions though partnership relationships (Konzelmann and Forrant 2003; Michie and Sheehan 2003; Appelbaum *et al.* 2000). And yet, worker and trade union outcomes were largely negative.

Why was this? A rudimentary starting point would be to attribute the negative patterns to the superficiality of the concept of 'mutual gain' in the workplace and to widespread management resistance to conceding any power or influence to workers or their union representatives. However, we would also argue that the study uncovers deeper problems for those regulationists who advocate new institutional arrangements and public policy to support fragile, creative work systems and 'high road firms' (Konzelmann and Forrant 2003; Bélanger, P.R. *et al.* 2002). Our analysis of the underlying dynamics of the new management practices found that in many respects this 'high road firm' was typical of the 'new flexible firm' that has become dominant in UK manufacturing (Ackroyd and Procter 1998). That is, in the context of the exigencies of Anglo-Saxon capitalism, where maximising profits and shareholder value remain paramount, many large British manufacturers are basing their capital accumulation strategies on new systems of financial control. Production and multi-tasked labour are reorganised into account-able units or cells that both contribute to flexibility and facilitate the calcu-lation of marginal costs; and core employees forego privileged status and job security as they compete with sub-contract labour and alternative suppliers in production operations that are treated as discrete, dispensable units. Such financial control regimes are able to monitor the performance of business units and indirectly control workers through the threat of rationalisation and downsizing (Ackroyd and Proctor 1998: 171, 176).

For most workers in these firms there is no high road or low road but instead a single road towards a new flexibility based on task accretion, reduced job security and the threat of competition between permanent and contingent workers. The case of Airframes exemplified this. In the context of new politico-economic pressures and intense global competition with other high skill aerospace firms, the Airframes management sought to squeeze design and production costs, improve lead times and maintain prof-itability. To do this it adopted a series of 'high road' practices that had two specific aims. First, to secure greater financial control and higher labour pro-ductivity through team accountability and task accretion. And second, to engender a new employee awareness of market realities through the prism of partnership. Our investigation into the impact of management's high per-formance practices found that many employees were delivering on their side of the mutuality 'bargain' in the form of effort intensification through creeping job rationalisation and task flexibility. However, they received very little in return. Many employees indicated a growing sense of job insecurity, a psychological state that was actualised in the final period of our research when 600 staff were made redundant.

Similarly, we found little evidence of two-way communications or employee influence over decision-making processes that affected their work-ing lives. Instead, in what some interviewees described as a climate of fear, we found consistent managerial opposition to meaningful employee partic-ipation and more than this, a pattern of exclusion from discussions and decisions that implicate job security and employee futures. Despite the rhetoric of 'social cohesion' in partnership debates, this pattern was espe-cially acute for the company's many temporary workers. Overall, for most workers, the outcome of partnership was communication without dialogue, consultation without influence.

Developments in industrial relations at the plant also followed a negative pattern. Despite the management rhetoric supporting partnership the man-ual and non-manual union representatives encountered extant managerial hostility to any notion of joint decision-making with trade unions. For many managers, union participation was fine so long as it was restricted to processes that engendered union support of business objectives rather than challenges to managerial authority. As a result, the partnership processes of consultation and dialogue were decidedly 'soft' on power. This in turn bred an increasing cynicism among the union activists and caused new antagonisms in management–union relations. At the same time, new fault lines on the basis of support or opposition to partnership opened up between the plant's manual union leadership and its members and between manual and non-manual unions. These divisions undermined the traditions of union solidarity that were characteristic of this multi-union plant.

This account of the politics and dynamics of the high performance workplace has clear implications for employee representation and trade union strategy. Advocates of HPWS in North America argue that trade union support for partnership is likely to redress the so-called 'representation gap' by encouraging employee participation and enhancing union influence over both local HPWS practices and employers' longer term strategic planning (Bélanger, P.R. *et al.* 2002; Frost 2001b; Appelbaum *et al.* 2000). In the UK, there is a similar body of work in a neo-pluralist vein which suggests that co-operation with management agendas might enable unions to regain a central place in the regulation of the employment relationship (e.g. Ackers and Payne 1998). Our case study highlights three flaws in these arguments. First, our analysis of worker outcomes in a densely unionised manufacturing plant showed that partnership may widen rather than narrow the representation gap by systematically denying worker aspirations for real influence and participation at work. Second, as Danford *et al.* (2003: 25) put it, 'meaningful partnerships require equal partners' and yet the case study reported here is by no means unique in highlighting the persistence of employer hostility to the prospect of surrendering any portion of their power to organised labour. The egalitarian rhetoric of partnership remains disconnected from the current reality of a profound imbalance of power between capital and labour. Third, the study shows that it is wrong to attempt to separate employment relations in so-called 'high performance', 'high road' firms from the degradation of work and employment conditions in other firms. The dominant pattern to emerge from our worker interviews was one of work intensification, workplace stress, job insecurity and feelings of disempowerment. Any trade union that ignores this rank and file experience risks becoming 'part of the problem' through incorporation in management. The likely consequence of such a stance would be a gradual decline in the union's collective base. As Kelly (1996a: 101) argues in his support for militant unionism, 'reliance on employer sponsorship and co-operation with consultative and advisory institutions can weaken or inhibit the growth of workplace union organisation and of any capacity to mobilize the union's membership for action against the employer'. High performance work systems and partnership do not resolve the structural antagonism between capital and labour. Union strategy in these work conditions needs to recognise this antagonism, and mobilise around the different dimensions of negative worker experience. Partnership does not negate Kelly's militant unionism, it demands it.

9

A Poisoned Chalice? Trade Union Representatives in Partnership and Co-operative Employer–Union Relationships

Sarah Oxenbridge and William Brown

Introduction

The growth in partnership arrangements in Britain has been widely chronicled in recent industrial relations literature. The number of meanings attached to the word 'partnership' reflects the variety of arrangements evident in workplaces today. Some writers restrict their interpretation of the concept to partnerships between employers and trade union representatives, while others encompass, within the definition, arrangements between employers and employees, without formalised union involvement (Guest and Peccei 1998).

But despite contrary views on the nature of the 'partner' on the employees' side, it is generally held that extensive consultation with the workforce by management is a key characteristic of genuine partnership relationships. The two concepts are linked, for example, in the discussion document issued by the Department of Trade and Industry (DTI) on the forthcoming Information and Consultation Directive (DTI 2002b). Within partnerships, a variety of mechanisms for consultation have been identified. In some cases, direct consultation and communication with individual employees is evident, rather than through representative bodies such as trade unions (Knell 1999).

Most studies of partnership, however, focus on those where employee representatives are the principal conduit for information-sharing and consultation. As Heery (2002) notes in his review of the partnership literature, a prominent feature of some partnerships is the creation of new consultative forums which may include both trade union and non-union employee representatives, and which serve as a vehicle for dialogue around change issues. And researchers such as Guest and Peccei (2001) identify certain positive impacts stemming from enhanced consultative processes within partnerships. In a survey of employers and employees in 54 partnership organisations (both unionised and non-union), the authors found that the expression of employee voice through representative participation in company-level decisions was a key partnership practice leading to more positive employee attitudes and behaviour. Enhanced employee attitudes in turn had a positive impact on employment relations outcomes, which were linked positively to organisational performance.

Indeed, some commentators position partnership as a strategy for trade union renewal and 're-legitimisation' precisely because it bolsters union influence in dialogue with management (TUC 2002b; Ackers and Payne 1998; IPA 1997). Others, conversely, argue that partnership benefits employers only, citing outcomes for unions including 'communication without dialogue, consultation without influence' (Danford *et al.* 2003: 68), and little or reduced union influence within relationships more generally (Kelly 2001).

This chapter draws upon case studies which highlight both positive and negative outcomes for union representatives of the shift to greater consultation. Some comparable studies identify positive impacts for unions resulting from strengthened consultation (either in place of or alongside, negotiation) within the context of partnership arrangements. In a study of two financial sector partnerships, Samuel (2001) found that the expansion of consultation machinery within partnership led to greater union influence over managerial decision-making for the benefit of members. In one of these companies – and in the Tesco–USDAW partnership relationship in supermarket retail – unions reported that prior to partnership, their relationship with management was confined to annual pay bargaining, with no influence over wider changes affecting staff (IRS 2000: 10; Samuel 2001: 131). However in both cases – as in cases profiled by Marks *et al.* (1998), Terry and Smith (2003) and Wills (2002b) – partnership enabled unions to extend their involvement from once-a-year pay bargaining to ongoing, broadened consultation around issues of business performance and change.

Moreover, Wills (2002b) and Marks *et al.* (1998: 219) described how partnership enables greater union influence at operational and corporate levels of organisations through union access to senior management and board-level decision-makers, rather than simply Human Resources personnel. Samuel (2001) and Wills (2002b: 11) also identified routine union involvement in the early stages of decision-making about employment issues and workplace changes as a characteristic of the finance sector partnerships they studied. Such efforts to broaden and deepen consultation – and negotiation – processes under partnership require managers to share more business, financial and strategic-level information and plans with representatives, as Bacon and Storey (2000), Haynes and Allen (2001) and Wills (2002b) all found. Likewise, in a study of DTI Partnership Fund recipients, Terry and Smith (2003) stressed the importance of management transparency in terms of sharing comprehensible and timely information, if consultation processes are to be effective.

If employers are to provide more information, then it follows that trade union representatives must be able to understand, use and respond to that information. In the case of Barclays Bank, Wills (2002b: 23) describes how union workplace representatives required expertise in interrogating corporate accounts, strategies and decision-making in order to assess the balance of interests between employees and the employer. Similarly, within the Tesco–USDAW partnership agreement, Union of Shop, Distributive and Allied Workers (USDAW) paid officers and workplace representatives were given training in business and financial matters to strengthen their influence during consultation and negotiation processes (IRS 2000).

The shift towards greater consultation that often accompanies partnership is not universally viewed as positive for trade unions. For instance, Marks *et al.* (1998: 220–1) argue that business-led consultative processes might displace plant level collective bargaining. As representatives' influence within corporate decision-making broadens, their authority at shopfloor level may be simultaneously weakened, with the balance of power shifting towards local management. Moreover as union paid officers shift their focus to strategic-level involvement rather than daily industrial relations matters, stewards' influence may be further reduced. Heery (2002: 23) concludes that in several partnerships, this 'de-emphasis' of bargaining and shift towards consultation has led to a weakening or abandonment of stronger, power-based forms of union influence such as collective bargaining.

Terry and Smith (2003: 57) take a counter view. They argue that while UK writers tend to view consultation as a weaker form of collective representation than negotiation, for workplace unions in many European countries consultation is routine and not a 'second-best' to negotiation. Consultation, they assert, should therefore not be seen as an attenuated form of 'real' bargaining in the UK context. Nonetheless, in order for consultation to be effective and mutually beneficial, it requires a similar degree of expertise and competence among the parties. They note that the development of such expertise may isolate workplace representatives from their members, who may view them as part of an 'elite' of management and senior representatives dominating decision-making processes. In some of their cases, union representatives outside of this group became suspicious that senior representatives involved in this elite had become too close to management, jeopardising the union's integrity. Martínez Lucio and Stuart (2000: 13) caution likewise that partnership may create a more 'managerial' local tier of union representatives who often appear at odds with the concerns of members.

Wills (2002b) describes further challenges to unions posed by greater involvement in decision-making. She reports how, through consultation with management, union representatives in Barclays are now compelled to publicly 'own' and endorse controversial or unpopular decisions that they might have condemned in the past. A further implication is that trade unions have historically used issue-based campaigning to recruit new members and strengthen their influence. However under partnership, conflict is kept behind managerial doors.

In essence, structures allowing for meaningful union involvement in organisational decision-making are positioned as one of several key characteristics of mutually beneficial partnerships. Much of the UK case study research and US mutual gains literature (e.g. Kochan and Osterman 1994) concludes that for partnership to yield benefits for all stakeholders, unions need to have meaningful voice, strong workplace representative structures and high membership levels (Oxenbridge and Brown 2002; Haynes and Allen 2001). These characteristics may be interlinked. Samuel (2001), for example, concluded that the longer a partnership based on strong unionisation endures, the greater the likelihood of union participation in senior level decision-making.

At its best, partnership enables the potential for union involvement in decision-making over a broader range of issues beyond traditional bargaining concerns, and input into decisions at the earliest stage of formulation. Yet this review of the research to date demonstrates that greater involvement in decision-making within partnership may also come at a price for union workplace representatives and their members.

Martínez Lucio and Stuart (2000: 21) contend that 'the study of partnership requires an approach that is sensitive to internal processes of decision-making, and the rationales that underpin the elaboration of strategies regarding work'. In this chapter we detail research where such an approach was taken. Our focus is on the role of workplace union representatives in cooperative relationships. We explore the dynamics of union involvement in decision-making and the behaviours of the parties in relationships by drawing on case studies of partnership and co-operative workplace agreements.

This chapter will set out the method by which the research was undertaken, before briefly describing the types or categories of partnership evident in the cases studied. The focus then shifts towards exploring the perceived benefits of union representatives' involvement in decision-making, before turning to the challenges that greater steward input and influence may bring. It ends with a discussion of strategies for countering the pitfalls and problems identified, and an assessment of whether partnership provides the key to trade union renewal.

Research methods

We report in this chapter on findings from an Economic and Social Research Council funded study of nine organisations conducted during 2001 and 2002. Four of the cases were studied as part of an earlier ESRC-funded project conducted during 1999 and 2000 (Oxenbridge *et al.* 2003). Five additional cases were selected with the help of trade union and Advisory, Conciliation and Arbitration Service (ACAS) officials. The cases represented three categories of relationship. Three were in organisations with formal partnership agreements, or where the parties were in the process of negotiating explicit agreements; three had informal partnership *relationships*, where the term was widely used but without any formalities; and three had co-operative relationships that were not described as partnerships. They were drawn from a variety of industry sectors. The four service sector cases were in the retail, insurance, office equipment servicing and outsourcing sectors. Four were from production industries: light engineering, heavy engineering, food processing and printing. The last was in rail transport.

All but one case involved interviews with the principal senior and Human Resources (HR) managers involved, the relevant union full-time official, one or more leading workplace union representatives and, in three of the case studies, trade union members who were not union activists. The prime concern was to obtain different perspectives on the co-operative relationship from within both management and the union in order to identify the nature of the relationship and its implications for the trade union. In total, 47 interviews were conducted with 52 individuals. This included: 16 managers; 16 paid trade union officers; 13 trade union workplace representatives; 4 trade union members and 3 ACAS and partnership advisors.

As this chapter focuses primarily on the experience of union representatives within partnership arrangements, it is useful to describe the characteristics of this group. The trade union representatives were primarily male, with only three women representatives among the 13. Five stewards (from three cases) held positions as full-time paid stewards at their workplaces. Stewards' average job tenure in their case study companies was 22 years, with almost all becoming union members when they joined the company. They had been union representatives for a period of between 2 and 24 years, with most (seven stewards) having held the position for between 10 and 20 years.

The nature of co-operative relationships

The research explored two key areas. The first was the extent to which each party – employers, union officials, union representatives and members – felt that they and other parties obtained benefits from the relationship. The second area was the rights afforded to trade unions within the relationship. This encompassed recognition, facilities and recruitment rights; the breadth and depth of information provision and consultation with union representatives; and the extent to which representatives had early and extensive involvement in decision-making.

Analysis of the nine case studies on this basis led us to conclude that two main types of relationship existed. We describe these as 'robust' and 'shallow' relationships. Robust relationships confer a range of benefits – though not necessarily (in any sense) equal benefits – to both parties. Within this grouping we distinguish between formal partnership, and informal (partnership and co-operative) relationships, of which our cases had three of each. Union density in these cases ranged from 40 to 90 per cent, with traditionally high membership levels. Unions negotiated with management over pay, terms and conditions and stewards had a strong, legitimate position in the organisation and extensive input into decision-making. Union interviewees in most robust cases were more likely than those in others to feel that the union had a high degree of influence at the early stage of decision-making processes, particularly over workplace-level decisions. In all of these cases, employers actively supported trade union recruitment of new members, providing unions with recruitment access rights at new starter inductions.

The second category, comprising three cases with 'shallow' arrangements, describes those relationships which confer fewer benefits to one party – the union – and are essentially shallow-rooted in terms of their formation, substance and potential longevity. There was a high degree of uniformity between the cases in this category, which encompassed both *formal* agreements and *informal* partnership relationships. These cases had low union density, of between 6 and 30 per cent, and managers prevented unions from extending their influence by allowing them only limited consultation and decision-making involvement, or by placing restrictions on union recruitment activity.

These findings indicate that the substance of the relationship, in terms of the rights afforded to unions and mutuality of benefit, is a more salient measure of robustness than the degree of formality in the relationship. Using this categorisation derived from analysis of the characteristics of relationships, we next explore perceived benefits stemming from relationships, in particular those relating to union representatives' roles within the relationship.

Union representatives and perceived benefits

Analysis of each party's perceptions of benefits flowing from the relationship showed a surprising degree of uniformity, with interviewees from both parties (employer and trade union) citing many of the same benefits. Some benefits were felt to accrue to both parties, and some to one party rather than the other. Each set of benefits is explored in turn in the following sections.

Jointly beneficial outcomes

Union representatives – and in some cases, managers – in just over half of the cases stated, unprompted, that a principal benefit of the partnership or co-operative relationship for both parties was an ability to discuss and resolve issues on an informal or 'off the record' basis. Interviewees in several robust cases highlighted the contrast with their past relationship, where formal complaints procedures were routinely used to resolve disputes or other issues.

Off the record dealings provided a means for managers and union representatives to resolve complaints and issues quickly and informally at the earliest opportunity, before the problem escalated to formal grievance or disciplinary procedures. As a steward in one case remarked, the co-operative relationship was of benefit to both parties because it enabled union representatives to 'address problems before they happen'. Likewise, when asked about the benefits flowing from their relationships, a manager and union paid official from the heavy and light engineering firms replied (respectively):

> We can deal with issues a lot earlier, and a lot less formal than what they used to be. If there's a concern now, the union will give me a ring – 'I need to have five minutes with you, can we discuss this?' – And nine out of ten times we can sort it.

> What we get out of [the relationship] is to be able to resolve issues quickly and easily. [The convenor] will have a problem, she'll go straight to whatever manager is involved and have a discussion and resolve it, without waiting for any formalised approach or JNCs and monthly meetings. It's very quick, either a telephone call, or, being a full-time convenor, that's important, just being able to walk across the factory, talk to a section manager.

Managers in robust cases also informed union representatives about ideas or future plans on an off the record basis either during the early stages of the decision-making process, or well in advance of their formal announcement, in order to seek representatives' input and advice. Some representatives therefore had considerable input into management decisions. A benefit for management was that representatives often highlighted potential problems or flaws in managers' proposals, and gave them guidance on how they might position issues or convey messages to the workforce so that they were more likely to gain workforce acceptance.

A second feature of relationships of benefit to both parties was the use of union channels for communication and consultation with the workforce. Managers in four mostly robust cases felt that an important advantage of their relationship with the union was the presence of consultative committees or representative bodies which provided employees with a confident 'voice', and managers with a formalised mechanism for consultation (Oxenbridge *et al.* 2003). Along with union structures serving as a means of *upward* communication (from the workforce, via union structures, to management), several managers, and union interviewees in most cases, described the advantages of union channels for downward communication. They emphasised the ease and speed with which the organisation could communicate with high proportions of the workforce via channels such as steward structures.

Benefits of the relationship for the company

Some perceived benefits were felt to accrue specifically to the employer. For example, both trade union and management interviewees described how union involvement 'softened' organisational change and restructuring processes. Workplace union representatives played a crucial role in legitimising change by acting as an 'intermediary' between management and the workforce in order to gain workforce co-operation, and by actively managing workforce morale. Interviewees described how union input at an early stage in the change process prevented managers from introducing changes in such a way as to damage employee morale. One full-time union convenor described how she was often required to convince managers to modify proposals so as to make them more palatable to employees. She explained:

> [The managing director] had to come here and make changes. My job is softening those changes, rounding the corners off. I mean if people knew what [the managing director's] first suggestions were every time, they'd be terrified.

According to managers, union representatives played a crucial role in 'smoothing the change process' by providing a gauge for workforce views and by communicating management change proposals to employees 'in their own language'. One manager, for example, described the value of the steward (who was quoted directly above) communicating proposed changes to employees:

> At the end of the day, if you need Mrs Mop on an assembly line to do something differently, she needs to do something differently. ... she needs to be told, honestly, fairly and straight, in simple language, 'You're going to have to change'. And you need someone to help you do that. Now hopefully your managers can do that. But everyone needs a logic check, and if Mrs Mop hears it from one of her own, so to speak, then fine.

Unions in retail and manufacturing sector cases played an important role in facilitating change around improving workforce flexibility. Workplace representatives worked closely with managers to introduce systems of banked or reserve (annualised) hours, job rotation, multi-skilling and teamworking. In the engineering firms, unions were involved in introducing changes on an almost constant basis to enhance competitive capabilities and thus ensure the companies' security, in light of threats of relocation of production offshore. Senior Amalgamated Engineering and Electrical Union (AEEU) (now Amicus) stewards in the two engineering cases were adherents of continuous change, towards more flexible working, and believed that this was a pivotal aspect of partnership working. One stated, '[In promoting partnership] we've said that these changes have to happen. In order to be successful you have to be flexible, you have to change'. Another, in a second case, was equally emphatic, 'We've got to keep changing. If we don't keep changing, the jobs are going to go to Poland. We've got to keep looking at ways of making it more efficient, which constantly means change.'

In six of the nine cases, trade unions were involved in organisational change programmes around harmonising terms and conditions and restructuring salary and grading schemes. In most cases, this occurred as a consequence of merger and acquisition activity, or efforts to integrate historically fragmented and devolved pay-setting systems. Restructuring of payment systems often occurred in conjunction with reviews of job evaluation schemes. Union involvement in these processes enabled managers to benefit from practical union knowledge of complex patterns of distribution of terms and conditions throughout the workforce. This was particularly the case where turnover of HR and line managers had resulted in a scarcity of management knowledge in this area. Employers also benefited from the union's ability to 'sell' the jointly designed changes to the workforce. One full-time steward in a 'shallow' case described how it became evident, during a harmonisation programme, that both trade union national officers, and company managers lacked basic knowledge of the terms and conditions which varied widely throughout the company's units. As a result, lay stewards were brought into the harmonisation process at the later stages, and played a crucial role. He described the situation:

> Where the company struggles, is they don't have managers or officials at [UK head office] who've got the knowledge of terms and conditions tucked in their head like the union reps have got. ... It was apparent that staff at union headquarters, or at [company head office], didn't know what our terms and conditions are. There are so many different sets. And that meant, in my members' case, that some of their terms were accidentally negotiated away.

Perceived benefits for the union and its members

Most union interviewees, and particularly workplace representatives, across the majority of robust *and* shallow cases felt that the partnership or co-operative relationship had resulted in union stewards and members having greater influence within the workplace, and greater input into company initiatives. Many of the perceived benefits they described echoed those described in the studies cited earlier (Wills 2002b; Samuel 2001). Union and management interviewees stressed the importance of union involvement in decision-making at an early stage in the process. One steward summed up the benefits for the union of their partnership relationship as 'learning about projects, sharing information at an early stage, having the ability to comment and change'. Managers in two robust cases described how a defining change in management's relationship with the union was that managers now 'try to talk to shop stewards early about things that affect their members', and that they introduce 'concepts' to the union, rather than presenting decisions as 'a *fait accompli*'.

Union interviewees in robust cases also described how under partnership, stewards and paid officers had influence over a broader range of workplace issues, such as the change initiatives described above, rather than simply pay. As in the research literature, partnership and co-operative relationships had resulted in more contact between the union and company, and greater union access to senior managers. In one case, this was a function of union representatives having frequent, direct access to senior managers through newly established high-level consultative structures. A union representative explained how this had increased stewards' influence vis-à-vis workplace personnel managers:

> Whereas before partnership, you went to see a personnel manager, and your rep training tells you that as a rep, you are speaking on an equal footing. And I felt that that was not really right before. I think that the difference now with the partnership is that [personnel managers] know you're seeing their boss's boss. And that makes a big difference.

Interviewees in nearly all robust relationships stated that a key feature of co-operative working was that the union representative's role and status within the organisation had been strengthened. This allowed them greater influence, and safeguarded them from discrimination or victimisation by managers. Where stewards felt that they were being undermined or mis-treated by managers, partnership arrangements provided them with a means of challenging managers on the basis that the company had committed to working in partnership. Alternatively, they referred managers back to formal partnership documents that stated this in writing. This greater sense of legit-imacy and security enabled representatives to speak their mind in dealings with management, without fear of retribution. A full time convenor in a robust case described this situation:

> I think that [the managing director] has a respect for me. I think he does respect my position. ... I think a lot of it is strength of personality, but also I'm in a privileged position. Because the managers don't like to say no to him – I told him that I'm the only person on this works who'll say 'No' to him. And the reason for that is, it's the position. What can he do to me?

Moreover because stewards' position was sanctioned and protected, unions in mainly robust cases experienced little difficulty filling representa-tive positions. A full-time officer stated, of the union:

> In a lot of companies we have great difficulties filling seats. [Recruiting representatives] has never been a particular problem in this company. ... I think it's [because of] the 'open and honest relationship' scenario. People don't feel that by putting themselves up as a rep, they're about to

be stitched up by the company. Whereas in some other companies there's a perception that 'If I become a rep, I might become targeted', and it might be difficult [to get] release time, whereas [this company] have been reasonable in terms of reasonable time off for trade union activity.

Even in those cases where a partnership arrangement was clearly not 'robust', representatives felt that it conferred similar benefits in terms of safeguarding stewards' role. A full-time steward in a case with a shallow partnership relationship stated, 'The attraction of partnership to a rep like me is that three or four years ago, I was terrified of getting sacked for doing what I do. And now that fear has been removed.'

In two robust cases, partnership agreements had been recently negotiated which contained explicit statements of company support for union representatives, and further strengthened their position through enhanced training and facilities rights. In these and other robust cases, managers provided support for union representatives in their role of representing individual members in grievance and disciplinary cases. One agreement contained statements requiring managers to support trade union activity and partnership working, and to value the role of worker representatives. A steward described how this new requirement had enhanced their legitimacy within the organisation as local managers now 'don't have an option' but to adhere to the new agreement in their day to day dealings with representatives. If managers refuse to comply, stewards may treat the matter as a dispute.

Summary

A range of benefits of partnership and co-operative working were identified by union and management interviewees. Both parties were felt to jointly benefit from informal 'off-the-record' discussions between managers and union representatives which enabled the resolution of problems before they escalated, and led to better quality decisions which were more likely to meet with workforce acceptance. Likewise, union channels for consultation and communication with the workforce were also positioned as advantageous. The main advantage of co-operative relationships for *employers* was felt to be union involvement in change programmes, particularly harmonisation of terms and conditions and reform of work practices. Lastly, benefits accruing to trade unions included enhanced influence in decision-making processes – in terms of both the scope and timing of consultation – and a strengthened position for representatives within the organisation, enabling them to advocate freely for members without fear of sanction.

Problems encountered by union representatives

While co-operative and partnership relations, where robust, led to greater management consultation with the union, they may also serve to isolate stewards from their membership. The following discussion explores the dilemma that union representatives face in having to prove to members that they are working on their behalf when subject to confidentiality constraints, or when there is no visible display of trade union strength.

Reconciling divergent views and expectations

This crucial challenge was described by stewards in some detail. Most stewards reported, for example, that their views were sometimes or often at odds with those of their members. Because they had access to management information during consultative and negotiation processes, stewards often had a deeper understanding of the business issues underlying management decisions than the membership at large. They described common situations where their members believed that one course of action should be pursued – for example, threatening industrial action – while stewards' views differed due to their greater awareness of the implications or penalties arising from this particular course of action.

Such divergences in views often arose in the context of pay negotiations, where stewards were apprised of financial or market information which informed managers' proposals for only moderate pay increases, while members had unrealistically high expectations. In the words of one works convenor, 'members want the earth, and you can't give them the earth'. Another stated:

> Because [members] don't see any of [the negotiation process], if you ask them 'What do you think a substantial pay increase is?', my answer is 'Anything above inflation that will fit in with what other retail companies are getting at the time', [but] they'd say 'Ten per cent.' And it's just that they don't get this information, so how are they going to make a good idea of what it is?

However, stewards in two robust manufacturing sector cases stressed that their positions on issues rarely diverged from that of their members because they based their stance on membership opinion, which they sought through comprehensive consultation with members and stewards' committees. They stressed that they made every effort to seek out and convey the majority membership position in dealings with management. Nonetheless, they had to balance this against their awareness of issues developed as a result of exposure to confidential information.

Isolation from members

When asked, most stewards stated that they felt isolated from their members because of their position as union representatives. In most cases, this was because they were required to withhold information from members. And because of the confidential nature of much information, they were unable to justify why certain decisions were taken, often in the face of considerable membership pressure. One steward commented that members constantly asked her about what was discussed in meetings with management, and that it was 'difficult to answer them without giving too much away'. Often, when stewards were unable to consult with members about management proposals due to confidentiality or time constraints, they faced uncertainty as to whether they had advocated the most representative stance that reflected the view of the membership majority.

Full-time stewards were particularly prone to feeling isolated from the workforce by virtue of the full-time nature of the position itself, and because they were more likely than other lay representatives to receive strategic, business or financial information pertaining to the organisation as a whole. One full-time steward described how, in some instances, he agreed with management proposals when presented with strategic-level information justifying such proposals. He also recognised that because he was removed from the daily work activity on particular sites, he had less of a personal stake in fighting to retain jobs affected by management proposals for workplace changes aimed at improving efficiency and workforce flexibility, and thus could take a stance from a position of some distance. He stated:

> Sometimes you can see the benefits of what the company's trying to do. Whereas someone who's particularly involved in that area feels sensitive about that – I think there's a natural reaction to want to kick back. So yes, you can [feel isolated]. ... In the seconded position you're seeing the national picture. Whereas if you're working in [a particular] section you're very much 'Oh, this is what we're doing in [that section]'.

Stewards in a second case sat on an ACAS-facilitated joint management/ union working party established to oversee the redesign and restructuring of work processes. Because of discussions with managers about the site's future, and management provision of financial and market information, stewards' awareness of the potential for production being relocated abroad and subsequent factory closure was much greater than that of their members. Stewards felt that closure was almost certain if changes to work processes were not made. Union members, by contrast, were aware of threats of closure but were not concerned, or believed that this might not necessarily happen. They were cynical in the face of management proclamations that the factory was under threat, as they had been told frequently in the past that closure may occur. In this and other cases, members believed that because stewards were advocating reform of working practices, they had been co-opted by management. As one steward stated of his relationship with members as a result of the change process:

> I have people that don't speak to me. I have ex-shop stewards who should know better, that say 'You've sold us down the river'. ... Being a shop

steward, or particularly convenor, you're treated a little bit like management, that sometimes they'll not talk to you.

As in Wills' (2002b) study, it was evident that a further difficulty of shifting from traditional bargaining modes to joint working is that union representatives may be required to agree to changes that they are personally uncomfortable with, and would have opposed in the past. Union representatives were also sometimes required to be the bearers of bad news, delivering decisions which proved detrimental to members. As one official remarked, 'That's the problem with partnership, is that in the old way [of working], we were expected to be on the receiving end of bad news. ... Now we've got to deliver it.' And in another case, a steward described the difficulties attached to her role in terms of having to persuade members to shift from one payment system to another, which led to reduced earnings for some:

> I had to help convince the people why we had to have it. That part of the job, you can't always be the hero. You have to take bad news back sometimes. That's quite hard. ... It *is* a hard job ... And when things aren't going well, when people don't like what's happening, the stewards do get a rough ride, on the lines.

Perceptions of co-option

Indeed all but two stewards stated that a minority of their members – those who were disgruntled, uninformed, or inactive, but nonetheless vocal – expressed views that the co-operative relationship had led to stewards being co-opted by management. One union officer painted a picture of membership fickleness, stating that members tended to be in favour of the union's partnership relationship with management '... when things are going well ... and you can help develop new reward structures and there's more money in the pot, and you can help to pay people, it's great.' However, he added that once the union has to deliver 'difficult' messages – for example, in relation to redundancies – members see the union as 'part of the company'.

Union interviewees in two robust cases described how a significant minority of their membership felt that the union had been co-opted because members believed that the union–management relationship should be one of confrontation rather than co-operation. This was the legacy of a tradition of adversarial dealings between the parties. In one such case, the workforce consistently rejected management's pay offers every year. However, during the most recent pay round, stewards accepted management's initial offer. Managers then refused to make further offers, insisting that the stewards 'sell' the deal to the workforce. According to one union member interviewee, this resulted in some union members voicing the view that the branch secretary was in management's back pocket. They believed that because she was recommending acceptance of the offer, she had engaged in trade-offs behind closed doors. A manager in this case alluded to the distance that had emerged between stewards and members, stating:

> The stewards recommended the settlement twice, and the workforce voted it out twice. Which is what I say about the stewards ... being moderate and sensible and they know a good deal when they see it. And maybe there's a bit of a gap developing between management and stewards, and the workforce.

Stewards also expressed frustration that members had little idea of the amount of work they put in behind the scenes to obtain the best deal. This was partly a function of consultation and negotiation processes being out of sight of members. Often, the only information divulged to members in the course of pay bargaining came in the form of a proposed pay deal at the end of lengthy negotiations – which then might be rejected by members. Stewards lamented the fact that members were unable to see the management claims put forward during the process, and thus did not realise the extent to which stewards negotiated deals which were often significantly better than management's initial offers. Stewards in several cases stated emphatically that members would not think that they had been co-opted if they were able to attend meetings and witness stewards' vigorous opposition to management proposals.

Proving independence and strength in a context of confidentiality

Several stewards described how they were often 'treated like management' by members. Most therefore strove to demonstrate to members that the co-operative relationship had not resulted in a loss of union independence, and that they had maintained their integrity in dealings with management. They did this by providing members with information that highlighted instances of union opposition to management plans and proposals, and detailed how disagreements were resolved. Many were regularly compelled to defend the co-operative relationship in the face of membership opposition.

In most of the robust cases, stewards and managers had recently worked together over years or months to negotiate formal partnership agreements or agreements committing the parties to joint working around workplace re-organisation. In all of these cases, the process of working closely together over lengthy periods allowed trust and understanding to grow between the individuals involved. One steward, for example, described the change in the steward/management relationship and the impact that this had had on steward relations with members:

> We've had [the] opportunity to get to know management better, management's had [the] opportunity to get to know us better. I was actually

arguing with [the manager] *against* some of our members the other day, because our members were wrong. That's the relationship we've got. Going back five years, we would have dug our heels in and sided with members, come hell or high water.

However the act of stewards and managers presenting a united front to the workforce has the potential to backfire. Members perceive stewards to be advocating for managers, rather than the membership. In a second case, managers and stewards together argued the case for workplace change, but this met with resistance from the workforce. A manager in this case explained the importance of bringing the union 'on-side':

> ... stewards have this crucial role in acting as intermediary in a lot of issues between the workforce and management. Management can go to the workforce, but what is important is that the union back up that message in their branch meetings and so on. Because if they say something different to what management is saying, then we'll never make progress. We're finding it easier to convince the stewards of what we're trying to do, and they agree with it, than [stewards] are, [in] trying to convince the workforce. So the model is that we're quite tight with the stewards. My worry is, there is this gap between us both and the workforce.

Both of these organisations were fairly traditional food processing and heavy engineering operations, located in the same region characterised by a tradition of union militancy. In each case, union members saw the union's role as one of consistent opposition to all management proposals. Accordingly, there was considerable scope for dissenting views between stewards and members.

Across most cases, stewards were required to tread a fine line between maintaining a constructive relationship with management to maintain their influence in decision-making processes, and proving to members that union independence had not been lost in the process. This was made all the more difficult when representatives and officials had to withhold information, which in turn prevented them from both proving to members that they were 'fighting their corner', and recruiting potential members on this basis. This issue was of much concern to many union interviewees.

In one case, stewards and paid officers debated the merits of entering into a formal partnership agreement, prior to negotiating an agreement with managers. They were concerned that the broadened consultation rights that would accompany partnership would reduce their ability to demonstrate union effectiveness to members. While they welcomed the potential for more extensive consultation over strategic issues, the confidential nature of such dealings prevented them from justifying to members why changes were needed, or, proving to members that the union has had an influence throughout a process that has taken place behind closed doors. Because discussions are confidential, representatives cannot consult with members at each stage of the consultation process. Consequently, when the company announces the outcome of the consultation process, union representatives may face difficulties proving that they have had influence on behalf of their members, who have no insight into the debates that have taken place in the course of reaching decisions. One officer stated:

> We can't explain it to people, so we might as well be the management in that case, because we've not been able to show any difference. It's not that we haven't made any difference, but we just can't *show* that we've made any difference.

In cases where members feel that representatives have had little or no influence throughout the process, they may conclude that the union would have had greater net influence by having had no involvement in a lengthy consultation process, and instead simply opposing ready-made management plans at the stage that they are made public. One officer stated, of the union, 'If we haven't delivered, or had influence, lay members could say "Weren't we better off being in the dark, and then fighting [management] when the plans come out?"'. He noted that the new mode of consultation within robust partnership involves the inclusion in decision-making processes of stewards and officers who are now 'almost part of the management team'. He added, 'It could be that you've only knocked a few rough edges off [management proposals]. On the other hand, if you hadn't been there, those changes wouldn't have been made. It's a real dilemma.'

Summary

Most union representatives highlighted a range of dilemmas presented by greater involvement in decision-making. They described how, in the course of decision-making processes, managers often discussed confidential strategic or financial information with them. This provided them with an understanding of the rationale behind management proposals, and led them to develop what they considered to be an informed stance on issues which on occasion differed from members' views. When challenged, however, stewards were sometimes unable to justify their stance to members because the information that informed their view was confidential. Members became dissatisfied, believing that stewards should reflect membership views by, for example, resisting management proposals for change. Moreover, because stewards could not tell members what was discussed with managers, they could not report back to them on progress made during consultation processes, nor prove that they were fighting on their behalf, or indeed that they had had any influence throughout the process. In the absence of information about discussions between the parties, members voiced suspicions that stewards had become co-opted by management. Resolving this dilemma presents a substantial challenge to those involved in partnership and co-operative relationships, and the implications of this challenge are discussed in the final section.

Conclusion

Can we conclude, in the light of this overview of the benefits and problems attached to partnership and co-operative relationships, that such arrangements offer the potential for union renewal? Certainly, if 'shallow' relationships predominate, there is little certainty of increased union power and a revival of strong and effective unionism. If, however, 'robust' relationships prosper, might we expect that enhanced decision-making involvement will provide a lever for revitalising workplace union organisation? In considering these possibilities, we should first contemplate the challenges that partnership and co-operative working presents for unions.

A central challenge relates to the resources unions must expend if representatives are to engage in constructive dialogue and debate with management. Terry and Smith (2003: 49) highlight the importance, within partnership, of providing training to allow union and employee representatives to contribute to consultative forums 'confidently and proactively'. However, a difficulty highlighted by interviewees relates to the inequality in knowledge and experience between the parties. Stewards may lack knowledge of strategic business and market issues simply because they do not deal with such matters on a day-to-day basis, while managers do. Indeed, managers in several robust cases expressed the desire for greater steward involvement in decision-making, but felt that stewards were hampered by a lack of business acumen and union backup and resources. They stated a preference for representatives proactively to *generate* ideas for change and business improvement, rather than simply commenting on or 'knocking the corners off' ready-made management decisions. If stewards are to play a more influential role in decision-making, the challenge for trade unions is to provide them with the skills and knowledge to do so, while weighing this against the resource outlay required.

But the greatest challenge for unions is the potential for a chasm to emerge between workplace representatives and their members. This study highlighted a growing disjunction between the views of union members, who believed that union strength is best demonstrated through confrontational means, and those of stewards, who had experienced the positive outcomes of co-operative working, including increased union influence at the workplace level. This was particularly the case where stewards acutely felt the need for workplace change, and became advocates for change, only to meet with membership opposition.

There is, of course, nothing new about the divergent frames of reference of shop stewards and their members. The classic observational study of shop steward leadership in a large engineering factory by Batstone and his colleagues (Batstone *et al*. 1977) provided many graphic instances of just the sort of frustrations and misunderstandings between stewards and members described above: accusations of 'selling out' and of undue sympathy for management's point of view arising from their gaining confidential information and a larger perspective. The big difference was that, in a context of trade union strength rather than weakness, the shop steward leaderships observed by Batstone and his colleagues could maintain their *bona fides* as being independent of management by mobilising aggressive collective action when they felt it necessary. Such demonstrations of independence are largely denied stewards in the context of Britain 30 years later. The key issue for them now is how they might prove to members that they are acting in their interests, despite agreeing to or endorsing management decisions that members disagree with.

Involvement in negotiating arrangements for improving organisational performance tended to isolate representatives. Although they grew in confidence and skills during the process, representatives' participation in change initiatives may come at a personal cost: they may be seen as an adjunct of management if they advocate unpopular decisions, and may be voted out of their position by members as a consequence. While turnover of activists is healthy, new representatives elected solely on the basis of an oppositional stance may destabilise co-operative relationships. Interviewees described how their constructive working relationship had taken time to build, and turnover of key actors within these relationships was felt to have the potential for instability.

Consultation processes – in particular, those involving issues of commercial sensitivity – may be invisible to the membership. One paradoxical consequence is that the gulf between representatives and members may be widened further by the increase in transparency, through greater management provision of information, that Terry and Smith (2003) advocate as necessary for robust consultation. The extra information may only extend as far as employee representatives, who are then required to withhold it from their members.

It is thus crucial that the parties to co-operative relationships work towards extending co-operative or partnership working throughout the organisation and develop means of making decision-making processes more transparent and open to union members. Given the growing preference among managers and representatives in our study for greater consultation over a wider range of non-pay issues, the challenge for unions in co-operative relationships is to find ways of proving to members, and to potential members, that the union has effective influence on employees' behalf during the decision-making process. This will be more difficult to prove in shallow relationships, where union involvement is severely curbed by management.

Closer relationships also require representatives to engage in more strenuous efforts to prove union independence. They must actively communicate to members points of difference between management and the union during decision-making and negotiation processes. It is important that managers develop an understanding of why unions need to prove independence to members, and support union efforts to do so. It was, for example, a feature of some robust relationships that straight pay rises were treated in a more traditional confrontational way than non-pay issues, as if a 'zero-sum' argument over pay was a way of signalling trade union independence of management. The maintenance of the co-operative bargaining relationship required the management to understand the importance of this for the union. Nor does the union representatives' need for support stop at the workplace entrance. Representatives must be able to show members that they have the backing of the wider union organisation in the decisions they make, with the active support of full-time officers where needed.

Co-operative working may offer a means for union renewal. But this may only be the case where union representatives are able successfully to reconcile their involvement in decision-making processes which were historically the sole domain of management with their role of representing often divergent membership interests. In recent years, trade unions have had little choice but to break with a tradition whereby employers were forced to listen to them through the underlying threat of collective action. In its place they are having to build on another tradition, never absent but never so conspicuous, whereby they earned the attention of management by the informed and co-operative representation of their members. If this is to provide a means of union renewal, careful attention has to be given to devising new ways of mediating unions' changed relationship with their members.

10
The Emerging System of Statutory Worker Representation

Mark Hall and Mike Terry

Introduction

The statutory regulation of employee representation is not confined to the union recognition provisions. Since the mid-1970s, UK employers have faced a growing number of statutory provisions, often driven by EU law, requiring them to inform and consult employee representatives on a range of issues. Crucially, following a key ruling of the European Court of Justice in 1994, EU information and consultation measures apply to employers whether or not they recognise trade unions, requiring UK law to provide for the election of issue-specific employee representatives in certain circumstances and overturning the UK's traditional reliance on recognised trade unions as the 'single channel' of employee representation.

While the existing statutory provisions requiring the election of employee representatives have been confined to specific issues (e.g. redundancies, transfers and health and safety) or, in the case of the Transnational Information and Consultation of Employees (TICE) Regulations 1999, a limited number of multinational enterprises, from March 2005, the UK will for the first time have a comprehensive, generally applicable statutory framework requiring employers to inform and consult employees or their representatives on a range of business, employment and restructuring issues, as a result of the 2002 EU Directive on the issue. The enactment of these Regulations a few years after the union recognition provisions of the Employment Relations Act (ERA) 1999 provides UK employees with two distinct legal routes to representation where a few years ago there were none. It is of fundamental importance for employees and trade unions to ask whether these two approaches may operate mutually to reinforce one another, and in so doing, to strengthen both employee representation systems and trade unions or whether, as some fear, the new European rights, deriving from very different legal and institutional origins to those of the UK, may serve to undermine the traditional mechanism of representation based in strong workplace-based trade unions.

This chapter aims to assess the impact of the new Directive, far more radical and substantial in its implications than the piecemeal measures that have preceded it, on systems of employee representation and workplace governance in the UK. Our assessment will be grounded in two main sets of data. First, we will review the nature and effect of existing legislation, paying particular attention to the experience of European Works Councils in UK companies. Second, we will summarise what is known about existing systems of employee information and consultation, paying particular attention to non-union firms, as the basis for assessing the implications of the Directive. While such evidence can provide only a starting point for such an analysis we will deploy it in the final section as a grounding for an assessment of the challenges and opportunities the new legislation will present to employers and trade unions.

Existing legislation and its impact

Historically, employee representation has not generally been regulated by the law in the UK, reflecting its 'voluntarist' industrial relations traditions. Public policy traditionally relied on 'single channel' representation via trade unions voluntarily recognised by employers. The initial focus of statutory intervention in the early 1970s was the promotion of trade union recognition. However, starting in 1975 with the redundancy consultation legislation, we have seen the development of statutory provisions requiring consultation with employee representatives on a range of issues.

Redundancies and business transfers

Under the UK's original statutory requirements concerning consultation in respect of impending redundancies (Employment Protection Act 1975) and business transfers (Transfer of Undertakings (Protection of Employment) Regulations 1981), introduced to implement EU Directives, the right to be consulted was confined to representatives of recognised trade unions. In 1994, however, infringement proceedings by the European Commission against the UK culminated in a landmark judgement by the European Court of Justice (ECJ) which ruled that the UK was in breach of the collective redundancies and transfer of undertakings Directives by failing to provide for the designation of employee representatives for the purposes of the consultation required by the Directives where an employer did not recognise unions (Hall 1996).

The UK was therefore forced to introduce supplementary statutory employee representation mechanisms to apply the Directives in the absence of union recognition. The then Conservative government introduced amending Regulations in 1995 requiring consultation on these issues either with representatives of recognised unions or with other representatives elected by employees.

These Regulations, however, were strongly criticised by trade unions and labour lawyers on the grounds that, since the choice of which type of representatives to consult lay with the employer, employers who recognised unions had the option of 'bypassing' existing union machinery and consulting elected employee representatives instead. Amending Regulations introduced by the Labour government in 1999 addressed this problem by providing that where an employer recognises an independent trade union in respect of employees affected by the proposed redundancies/transfer, consultation must take place with representatives of that union. In the absence of a recognised union the employer may choose to consult either appropriate existing elected employee representatives (e.g. a consultative committee) or employee representatives specially elected for statutory consultation purposes under election rules laid down by the Regulations. Employee representatives need only be elected on an ad hoc basis when such consultation is necessary. The use of standing bodies of employee representatives for consultation is permissible but not required.

In public policy terms, the reforms introduced by the 1995 Regulations refined by those of 1999 are of considerable significance. Traditionally, recognised unions have constituted the 'single channel' through which collective statutory employment rights have been applied. However, this policy was effectively overturned by the ECJ. Consequently, for the first time – and specifically for the purposes of consultation over redundancies and transfers – the UK introduced supplementary statutory employee representation mechanisms to fill the increasingly wide gaps left by reliance on employer recognition of trade unions (Hall and Edwards 1999).

Other issues

The piecemeal process of providing for issue-specific statutory employee representation mechanisms, applicable in the absence of recognised unions, continued with legislative developments in a number of other areas. The ECJ ruling prompted the introduction of the Health and Safety (Consultation with Employees) Regulations 1996. These 'top up' the Safety Representatives and Safety Committees Regulations 1977 by requiring employers to consult employees who are not covered by safety representatives appointed by recognised unions under the 1977 Regulations. The 1996 Regulations give employers the discretion to consult employees directly or through elected representatives (James and Walters 1997).

The Working Time Regulations 1998 make provision for the negotiation of 'workforce agreements' regulating working time issues between employers and elected employee representatives in respect of groups of employees not covered by collective bargaining (Hall *et al.* 1998). Their negotiation is voluntary: they are intended to offer employers without union recognition arrangements the same flexibility in the application of the Regulations as that available through collective agreements with trade unions.

The concept of workforce agreements was subsequently extended to the issue of parental leave. The Maternity and Parental Leave Regulations 1999 enable company-specific parental leave arrangements – which differ from but do not fall short of the statutory provisions – to be introduced by means of collective agreements with unions or workforce agreements with elected employee representatives in non-union situations.

European Works Councils

The Transnational Information and Consultation of Employees (TICE) Regulations 1999, introduced in response to the EU European Works Councils (EWCs) Directive, represent a significant further extension of the range of issues on which UK employees have statutory information and consultation rights, encompassing key business, employment and restructuring matters (Carley and Hall 2000). Most strikingly, for the first time in the UK, the Regulations provide for the establishment of a statutory standing works council-type body, where negotiations do not result in agreed, company-specific arrangements. However, the application of the 1999 Regulations is restricted to 'Community-scale' undertakings or groups (i.e. companies with at least 1000 employees across the European Economic Area, including significant operations in at least two member states), and the resulting EWCs are representative bodies of an international nature.

The policy of the EWCs Directive was to promote the negotiation of voluntary transnational information and consultation arrangements, via 'Article 13' agreements, which predated the implementation of the Directive, or 'Article 6' agreements reached under the 'special negotiating body' process established by the Directive. Only where the Directive's negotiating procedure is invoked (by either employees or management) and results in a failure to agree does a statutory model EWC become enforceable as a fallback.

In line with other EU measures, the information and consultation rights under the EWCs Directive apply to all employees within the enterprises concerned. The UK Regulations, rather than guaranteeing a role for existing union structures, require UK members of special negotiating bodies (SNBs) and statutory EWCs to be elected by workforce-wide ballot. Ballots are required, notwithstanding any existing trade union structures within the enterprise's UK operations, for selecting UK members of SNBs where there is no existing UK-wide consultative committee, and for selecting UK members of statutory EWCs where not all UK employees already have representatives. In most other countries covered by the Directive, SNB and statutory EWC representatives are drawn from existing workplace or company level representation structures, ensuring at least some degree of articulation between national and transnational levels of representation. In the UK, however, the balloting requirements could produce SNB negotiators or representatives on statutory EWCs who have no direct connection with domestic trade union or other existing representative structures.

Impact of existing measures

Other than in the area of EWCs, evidence of how the existing statutory employee representation provisions have worked is very sparse. All these provisions revolve around the election of employee representatives in non-union situations. A DTI-sponsored research project on redundancy consultation suggested that the organisation of elections for employee representatives is something which some employers may find difficult (Hall and Edwards 1999). In two of the three non-union companies investigated no employee representatives were elected for redundancy consultation. As regards the impact of the Health and Safety (Consultation with Employees) Regulations 1996, the WERS 1998 data show that elected safety representatives existed in 27 per cent of workplaces with no trade unions present, though consulting directly with employees is allowed under the Regulations.

The fact that the 1995 redundancies and transfers regulations and the 1996 health and safety Regulations gave no guidance to employers about the election procedures to be followed may be significant. Both were drawn up by the previous Conservative government with the objective of regulating as lightly as possible. But in the case of the 1995 Regulations, at least, the effect was of some uncertainty: managers indicated they would have preferred clearer guidance on how employee representatives should be elected (Hall and Edwards 1999). The 'second generation' of supplementary, issue-specific employee representation mechanisms introduced by the present Labour Government, that is, the 'workforce agreements' provisions for working time and parental leave, and the 1999 Regulations affecting redundancies and transfers, include more detailed provisions in the key area of election requirements. Whether these more detailed requirements have had any impact has so far gone largely un-researched, but initial indications concerning workforce agreements on working time were that compliance with the election requirements was still problematic (Neathy and Arrowsmith 2001).

It was also suggested at the time of the 1995 Regulations that such procedures might provide opportunities for trade union members to be elected as employee representatives and to build union influence within the company, and that redundancy consultation via elected representatives could lead to collective consultation on other matters and the establishment of more permanent consultation arrangements. But again there is no clear-cut evidence that this has happened. Hall and Edwards (1999) found little evidence that the need to consult over redundancies acted as a stimulus to unionisation, still less to recognition, nor that the existing, issue-specific mechanisms had been successfully exploited by unions to establish union organisation and influence within non-union workforces. In two of the three non-union case study companies, permanent consultation mechanisms were established or planned by management, but how far these decisions were a direct consequence of experience of the redundancy consultation provisions was unclear. Nevertheless, commentators have argued that the burgeoning range of issues on which consultation with elected employee representatives is required, or on which flexibility around statutory norms is possible via workforce agreements, may increasingly prompt employers to consider dealing with such issues via permanent standing consultative arrangements.

In contrast to this paucity of evidence on impact of these piecemeal measures we have considerable evidence of the UK's experience of EWCs. This may prove more relevant to assessing the likely impact of the information and consultation Directive than the operation of the one-off, issue-specific employee representation mechanisms.

Of the 232 UK-headquartered multinationals identified as being subject to the Directive in October 2002, 93 (40 per cent) have set up EWCs (Kerckhofs 2002). This is a slightly higher 'strike rate' than the global picture: the European Trade Union Institute (ETUI) puts the number of multinationals with EWCs at 639, that is, 34 per cent of the worldwide total of 1865 companies covered by the Directive. Nevertheless, despite the existence of the necessary statutory procedures, in 60 per cent of UK-based companies covered by the Directive neither management nor employees have initiated moves to set up an EWC. The bulk of the existing EWCs in UK-based companies were established on the basis of 'Article 13' agreements ahead of the Directive's implementation date. Relatively few are based on 'Article 6' agreements under the legislation's 'special negotiating body' procedure. In no known case to date has a fallback 'statutory model' EWC been imposed on a UK-based company. However, most agreements have been strongly influenced by the Directive's subsidiary requirements: virtually all provide for an EWC-type body rather than any alternative form of transnational information and consultation procedure, and in many cases, particularly Article 6 agreements, their provisions are modelled closely on the subsidiary requirements.

Research concerning the UK experience of EWCs presents a mixed picture. British companies were particularly apprehensive about the implications of EWCs. This was reflected in the 'damage limitation' provisions (in terms of restrictions on the remit of EWCs and detailed confidentiality clauses) which were widely incorporated in UK companies' EWC agreements (Marginson *et al.* 1998). A tendency towards 'containment' on the part of UK companies appears to be confirmed by research into employee representatives' experiences of EWCs which suggests that the provision of 'useful' information by management and the occurrence of consultation are less widespread amongst UK- and US-based multinationals than amongst companies headquartered in the continental European countries (Waddington 2001).

But both survey and case study evidence suggests that, in practice, EWCs have generally proved less of a threat than many managers originally feared. Wills' (1999) survey of British managerial opinion of EWCs found that managers in companies which had established EWCs had a much more positive view about the role of EWCs than those in companies without them, but saw the benefits of EWCs primarily in terms of reinforcing corporate communications rather than their wider consultative or representative role. Respondents saw EWCs as playing a useful role in terms of two-way communication (88 per cent), getting management views over to employees (63 per cent), hearing the voice of employees (56 per cent) and involving employees in the business (50 per cent). But only a minority of respondents associated EWCs with the more concrete outcomes of 'aiding organisational change' (25 per cent) and 'enhancing productivity through employee involvement' (6 per cent). A DTI survey (Weber *et al.* 2000) of managers in 10 companies with EWCs, six of them UK-based companies, produced similar results. Eight saw EWCs primarily as having 'symbolic value' and half the companies said that their EWCs had been beneficial in enabling them to exchange information with employee representatives and to involve employees more closely in the business. Again, few companies saw EWCs as 'aiding organisational change' or 'increasing productivity'. In terms of the major drawbacks of EWCs, other than the financial costs involved, the principal managerial concerns highlighted by both surveys included 'raised employee expectations' and 'increased bureaucracy'.

A more recent survey of 24 UK, US and Japanese multinationals (a third of which were UK-based companies) by the American management consultants Organization Resources Counselors Inc (ORC 2003) found that three-quarters of the companies said that EWCs had 'added value'. However, while 20 of the companies said they had informed and consulted their EWC over instances of company restructuring, and most regarded this as beneficial, its impact on the 'content of the decision' was generally described as 'low to non-existent'.

Case study research carried out in eight UK- and US-based companies (Marginson *et al.* 2004) shows that structural factors are a crucial element in explaining variations in the impact of EWCs on managerial decision-making. The key factors distinguishing those cases where the EWC had some impact from those where it had none relate essentially to company structure and the nature of the business portfolio. In those cases where the EWC had some impact, the companies shared a number of characteristics: they were strongly international in terms of the spread of their workforce across European countries; they tended to be focused on a single business; and production was integrated across borders. In the other companies, where no impact was detected, most or all of these factors were absent and, as a result, the EWC appeared much less relevant. Whether there was a European-level management structure, ensuring a close organisational 'fit' with the EWC, was also important in providing the basis for an effective relationship to develop.

On the employee side, IRRU's research suggests that UK workforce representatives tend not to 'punch their weight' within EWCs (Hall *et al.* 2003).

In six of the eight case study companies the UK was the 'home' or largest workforce yet conceded the employee-side leadership role to representatives of other nationalities in four. In each case, interviewees reported that the principal reason for this was British employee representatives' lack of familiarity with works council-type structures and consultation with senior management about corporate strategy, and their limited infrastructural support at the workplace. This reinforces similar findings by Wills (2000), whose study of an EWC in a company formed by an Anglo-French-American merger shows that, although the UK and France had the same number of EWC members, the employee-side tended to be 'dominated' by the French representatives due to their greater experience of consultation at national level in France.

Representation in non-union workplaces – the broader picture

The greatest impact of legislatively based systems of employee representation will be in those workplaces where no trade union is recognised. Some clues as to the operation of such systems, and in particular to managerial strategy with regard to their introduction, may be provided by considering what we know about those non-union workplaces that already have a system of indirect employee representation. Such systems (i.e. involving the agency of elected or nominated representatives acting on behalf of a constituency) are the exception rather than the rule in non-union workplaces. The 1998 WERS (see Cully *et al.* 1999: 95–6) reveals the presence of non-union representatives in only 11 per cent of such workplaces (47 per cent of all workplaces reported no trade union) and in 19 per cent of workplaces where a trade union was present but not recognised for collective bargaining (8 per cent of workplaces). Non-union representatives were also reported in 10 per cent of those workplaces where trade unions were recognised for collective bargaining (45 per cent of workplaces) where, presumably, they represent employees who are not members. Looking first at workplaces with no union recognition two immediate comments may be made. First, the overwhelming preference among non-union employers is *not* to create any formal indirect structure of employee representation. Second, the non-union representation phenomenon, where it exists, is overwhelmingly a private sector phenomenon.

The WERS data yield further useful findings. First, employers in non-union workplaces show a preference for obtaining employee representatives either through appointment by management or through seeking volunteers, such that '52 per cent of workplaces without [trade union] recognition had employee representatives whose only route to the [consultative] committee was appointment by management or as volunteers' (Cully *et al.* 1999: 101). As the authors comment; 'for these workplaces, there may be some doubts about the independence of the employee representatives'. Second, the statistics on employee representatives cited above specifically excluded health and safety representatives. When questioned specifically about such representatives, managers in workplaces with no union members reported a joint health and safety committee in 31 per cent of workplaces and elected safety representatives in 27 per cent (Cully *et al.* 1999: 96). While direct comparison with the earlier (1990) survey[1] is not possible on the basis of the published results, a plausible interpretation is that the 1998 figures reflect the impact of the Health and Safety (Consultation with Employees) Regulations 1996 which extended the legal requirement for consultation on these matters from workplaces with union recognition to all workplaces. However, the 1998 survey also found that where employers were required by law to consult with employees or their representatives over redundancy, over a third took advantage of the opportunity offered by the Collective Redundancies and Transfer of Undertakings (Protection of Employment) (Amendment) Regulations 1995 to 'bypass' recognised trade unions and utilise other consultative mechanisms (Cully *et al.* 1999: 97). Combining these two findings we can suggest that employers will comply with legal requirements to establish consultative systems in non-union workplaces, but may well be tempted to exploit them to weaken established union-based machinery if the law permits this. While the law on redundancy consultation has since been amended to prevent such 'bypassing' these two broad conclusions have considerable implications for our later analysis.

While survey data provide some useful starting points, greater clarity can be added by looking at the limited case study evidence available on non-union representation. Such systems have traditionally been perceived as, anomalous, partly because of their rarity, and partly because of the dominance of the union model of employee representation. Conventionally therefore non-union systems have been characterised as mechanisms for the deliberate *avoidance* of trade unions, established by managers opposed to trade union recognition (see Ramsay 1980). To achieve this, it is argued, such systems must 'mimic' the role normally played by trade unions, with a strong emphasis on processes of consultation and, in many cases, negotiation. Their staple fare is often similar to that of union-based bodies (pay, terms and conditions, etc.) and a number have provision for third-party intervention in the event of failure to agree. Where non-union representation is established in the wake of union derecognition this mimicking is at its clearest, as shown by Lloyd's research (2001) and, most starkly, Gollan's account of News International since the exclusion of trade unions in 1988 (Gollan 2002). As Butler comments, 'management's aim is to simulate pluralist industrial relations and the collective bargaining format – albeit decisively on management's own terms' (Butler 2003: 81–2). Not surprisingly, as an overview of the data suggests (Terry 1999), non-union representative systems established as union avoidance strategies are most likely to be found in workplaces with structural characteristics associated with trade union presence (large workplaces, manufacturing sectors), since such a strategy is, presumably, only worth implementing in workplaces otherwise prone to unionisation. The data suggest that union avoidance may be the dominant reason for the creation of most systems of non-union representation in the UK. However, it may not be the only one.

Case studies such as that of Broad suggest that representative participation may be established 'to provide a mechanism to rationalise the information and communications systems directed towards the achievement of a "consensus culture"' (1994: 27; see also Butler 2003). The establishment of systems of non-union representation may thus also be informed by considerations of enterprise performance and managerial control, rather than union avoidance.[2] While these two rationales may not be mutually exclusive they do suggest differences of emphasis, approach and agenda. On the one hand Broad's analysis suggests a managerial motivation for the introduction of employee representative structures other than the 'negative' exclusion of unions. On the other, the dominance of a managerial agenda and the emphasis on employee output suggests a highly constrained form of participation with little if any space for the expression of employees' collective interests. While such an approach may cut with the grain of modern management thinking and establish a 'business case' for employee representation, it stands in sharp contradistinction to the longstanding argument that the basis for employee participation lies in employee rights to have their views and interests taken into account in managerial decision-making; that is, that the fundamental point of employee participation is to shape *employer* rather than employee attitudes and behaviours.

The case study accounts we have of the operation of non-unionism also indicate further aspects of their operation relevant for a consideration of the impact of legislative innovation. First, management effectively controls the agenda of non-union representative structures, both the content and the timing of presentation of information. In particular there appeared to be a tendency for employers to be less forthcoming with information when the implications for the workforce appeared to be unpalatable – as with redundancies or pay freezes for example – and to revert to managerial unilateralism in such situations, leading to impotent frustration on the part both of representatives and those they sought to represent. Such 'consultation for the good times' (Terry 1999: 27) contributed to a second feature of non-union representation, namely its tendency to crisis. Examples were reported of the mass resignation of representatives, often out of frustration at their own ineffectiveness, perhaps leading to the abandonment of the system, to a period of inactivity, or to the recognition of trade unions and the 'unionisation' of the representative system. In several cases representatives sought to organise their workplaces, not always successfully. Trade unions thus remain in many cases the reference point. For employers, as we have seen, they are often the negative reason for the introduction of the system. At the same time for many non-union representatives trade unionism appears to hold the key to effectiveness. There is a widespread perception among such representatives that their trade union counterparts are more able, better-trained, and 'stronger' through their access to union resources and, ultimately, to the right to strike. On occasions this view is shared by employees in these workforces. Against this has to be set evidence of a preference for non-union forms of representation, particularly among white collar employees (see Lloyd 2001) provided they meet certain criteria of effectiveness.

In short, the evidence on indirect employee representation in non-union workplaces indicates that it is limited in its coverage and its effect. Its principal managerial justification appears to be as a bulwark against trade unionism, although it is also valued as a route to performance enhancement. From the perspective of employee representatives and those whom they represent, such systems are usually seen to lack effectiveness compared to unionised environments, principally as a consequence of managerial control of process and content, of representative inexperience and inadequate training and, in particular, of the absence of any recourse to sanction or effective 'pressure'.

'Hybrid' systems

Non-unionism is not, of course, confined to those workplaces with no trade union recognition. It is clear that in the great majority of unionised workplaces a proportion of the workforce – those employees in respect of whom no recognition agreement exists – do not enjoy access to representation through trade unions. In a small proportion of cases (10 per cent of workplaces with 25 or more employees and a recognised trade union) the presence of non-union representatives, presumably representing at least some of the excluded employees, was reported in 1998 (Cully *et al.* 1999: 96). The rarity of such 'hybrid' organisational forms indicates union (and often management) uncertainty as to how to deal with non-unionised groups in a unionised environment. It reflects a longstanding union commitment to the 'single channel' of representation and the view that if employees want to be effectively represented they should join a trade union. Nevertheless, there is some evidence that this principle may have been weakened. There is also some suggestion that hybrid structures have increased as a proportion of workplaces with recognised unions (in other words 'union-only' representation has decreased faster than mixed union and non-union representation (Millward *et al.* 2000: 122)). This is backed up by case study evidence of the recent establishment of universal systems of representation covering both union-recognised and non-union groups of employees, some undertaken by the Involvement and Participation Association (IPA 2001) who argue that consultative arrangements involving both union and non-union representatives are more common than previously. There is little research into how these bodies operate (one exception is Hall's (2003b) case study of the BMW Hams Hall plant council) but the IPA comments that such arrangements 'seem to have worked well' (IPA 2001). Their apparent growth suggests both a pragmatic rethinking of union hostility to the representation of non-organised groups and a managerial awareness of the value of universal as opposed to partial representation. Whether this represents a positive valuing of employee participation, an anticipation of legal pressures, or a desire to weaken the monopoly representation of trade unions is not clear.

One final consideration is relevant to both non-union and union-based forms of representation. It appears clear that the dominant mode of collective interaction between unions and employers has shifted from *negotiation* to *consultation*, a distinction never clearly specified in UK usage, but which tends to suggest a move from joint regulation to unilateral (employer) regulation incorporating union or employee opinions. It has been argued elsewhere (Terry 2003c) that this may have considerable significance for British trade unions, insofar as consultation, and especially consultation based on the deployment of legal rights, is a process based in advocacy and expertise rather than bargaining 'muscle'. This raises issues concerning the training and development of employee representative skills, and the managerial commitment to their provision, which appears to be increasingly weak. Since consultation is the mode prescribed by the existing and future legislation, arguments concerning representatives' ability to engage with this process may become more significant.

The evidence summarised above indicates that the emerging legal framework has significant implications for systems of employee representation and for the trade unions, traditional agents of such representation. But it also confirms that, as with EWCs it will be the attitudes and strategies of employers and managers that will most strongly influence the ways in which any new representative structures will emerge.

Draft Information and Consultation of Employees Regulations

The latest and most far-reaching development in the area of statutory employee representation stems from the adoption in March 2002 of the EU Directive on information and consultation in national undertakings.

A key element of the Commission's stated rationale for the information and consultation Directive was that one-off consultation exercises with hurriedly elected, ad hoc employee representatives (as under a number of the UK's statutory provisions outlined above) are unlikely to provide effective consultation. A central argument advanced by the Commission in support of its proposal was that:

> The absence of a general framework for information and consultation nationally results in the provisions of the [collective redundancies and transfer of undertakings] Directives having a limited impact. The preventive approach on

which they are based is difficult to implement in the context of information and consultation procedures that are isolated, fragmented and limited to cases of imminent collective redundancies and transfers of undertakings, and would be consolidated by the definition of more general and permanent information and consultation procedures. (European Commission consultation document, June 1997, quoted in *European Works Councils Bulletin* 10, 1997: 5)

Under the Directive, all undertakings with at least 50 employees (or, if preferred by a member state, establishments with at least 20 employees) must inform and consult employee representatives about a range of specified developments and decisions. Again, the Directive provides the scope for employers and employees to negotiate alternative, enterprise-specific information and consultation arrangements, provided these respect its broad principles. EU member states have until March 2005 to comply with the Directive. However, there are transitional arrangements allowing countries currently without 'general, permanent and statutory' systems of information and consultation and employee representation (effectively the UK and Ireland) to phase in the coverage of their implementation legislation, applying it to undertakings with at least 150 employees from March 2005, those with at least 100 from March 2007, and those with at least 50 from March 2008. Thus, by March 2005, the UK will have to legislate for substantially enhanced information and consultation rights for employees – a development which will take the UK further away from its voluntarist traditions and which has highly significant implications for UK industrial relations.

In July 2003, the government published a consultation document (DTI 2003) setting out how it proposed to implement the EU information and consultation Directive, based on an 'outline scheme' agreed between ministers, the Confederation of British Industry (CBI) and the Trades Union Congress (TUC), and inviting comments on draft Information and Consultation of Employees Regulations. The draft Regulations enable 10 per cent of the employees in an undertaking, or management themselves, to trigger negotiations about the introduction of agreed information and consultation arrangements. If management and representatives elected or appointed by the employees are unable to reach a negotiated agreement, a set of 'standard information and consultation provisions', based on the Directive's minimum requirements, will become enforceable via the Central Arbitration Committee (CAC). These require management to inform and consult employee representatives, elected in accordance with specified balloting procedures, about business developments, employment trends and changes in work organisation or contractual provisions.

Where there is an existing information and consultation agreement, but 10 per cent of the workforce still seek to trigger negotiations on new arrangements, employers will be able to hold a ballot in which at least 40 per cent of the workforce must endorse the request for new negotiations, otherwise existing arrangements can be maintained. But where employers seek to hold a ballot on existing arrangements which may not meet criteria laid down in the legislation (including that that they cover all the employees in the undertaking and have been approved by the employees), employee representatives or employees may challenge this before the CAC and, if their complaint is upheld, negotiations on new arrangements must take place.

Essentially, the draft Regulations mean that the options facing British companies and other undertakings falling within the requisite employment thresholds will be similar to those under the EWC Directive. Prior to the relevant commencement date (i.e. March 2005, March 2007 or March 2008, depending on the number of employees the undertaking has), undertakings will have the opportunity to establish information and consultation arrangements that cover all employees and have been approved by the workforce, with the aim of pre-empting the use of the Regulations. In many cases this may mean overhauling existing arrangements or underpinning them by formal agreements. Other companies may decide to introduce employee consultation arrangements for the first time. After the Regulations come into force, employers need not do anything unless employees trigger negotiations, but where this happens, the negotiation of an information and consultation agreement will take place against the benchmark provided by the 'standard information and consultation provisions' which may ultimately be enforced on the undertaking in the event of a failure to agree. Moreover, where a negotiated agreement is reached via the Regulations' procedures, or the standard information and consultation provisions apply, the Regulations' enforcement mechanisms involving the CAC and the Employment Appeal Tribunal (EAT) will become applicable. This does not apply to agreements reached before the Regulations come into effect.

The draft Regulations do however provide the scope for employers to pursue 'compliance' strategies based on securing employee agreement for relying on direct forms of information and consultation rather than informing and consulting via representatives. While the government has included such an option in response to employer lobbying, there would appear to be questions over its compatibility with the Directive which defines information and consultation as processes involving employee representatives (Hall 2003a) – and therefore over the long-term viability of employer strategies based on direct methods.

Likely impact

The new legislation in the area of information and consultation is likely to have a significant impact on workplace industrial relations in Britain, posing challenges for unions and management alike. The implications of the Regulations for the future shape of UK industrial relations in general and of systems of employee representation in the workplace in particular remain uncertain and speculative. However, on the basis of the data presented above some lines of probable development can be identified.

The 'representation gap'

The implementation of the Regulations will lead to an increase in the proportion of UK workplaces and employees with access to a formal system of indirect representation. The 'representation gap' will decrease at least in purely statistical terms. There is no suggestion from earlier evidence that employers will seek to frustrate the legal rights of employees in circumstances where the necessary numbers have indicated their wish to establish a representative structure. But there are a number of factors that may limit the impact of the Regulations. First, there is little reason to believe that most employers will actively seek to inform their employees of their rights to representation *unless* they believe that there may be advantage to be gained from so doing. In many workplaces with no trade union presence or contact, employees may remain ignorant of these new rights and the mechanism for their enforcement. The take-up rate may well be significantly lower than for EWCs, which have been established in large enterprises, in the great majority of cases with an active trade union presence to articulate and develop the rights available. Second, the level of employee support required to trigger negotiations about establishing information and consultation arrangements could prove to be a significant hurdle, especially in cases where agreed arrangements already provide for direct forms of information and consultation. Employee apathy, perhaps combined with an awareness of lack of employer enthusiasm, could limit the take-up rate. Third, in many workplaces it may prove difficult to find employees prepared or able to take the lead in organising an employee request, and to take on positions as representatives during and after negotiations. In enterprises and workplaces with no tradition of representation – the majority – it may prove problematic to identify the individuals necessary to articulate the case for representation especially in the face of employer hostility or indifference. While all these possible barriers to implementation might provide opportunities for trade union activity, they also indicate the crucial importance of managerial behaviour in assessing the likely impact of the Regulations.

The Directive and managerial strategy

There is no evidence of employer enthusiasm for the Regulations. The major employers' organisations lobbied for and supported the UK government's opposition to the Directive, and once it became clear that opposition was no longer tenable argued, successfully, for a flexible, minimalist approach to its implementation. It remains to be seen whether many employers will actively seek to introduce representative structures unprompted by employee demands. Nevertheless it is likely that it is managerial behaviour that will largely shape the nature of any emergent representative systems.

The earlier analysis suggests that in non-union firms the dominant managerial interest may lie in their potential for union avoidance. Following Sisson's (1993) categorisation between 'Human Resource Management' (HRM) non-union firms that displayed an interest in processes such as employee participation and involvement and had an effective personnel function, and 'Bleak House' firms characterised by an absence of both of these, we can suggest that this might well guide managerial behaviour, although for different reasons. Bleak House employers and managers are likely to be the least aware of the Regulations and, by implication, the least interested in their implementation. Their indifference to Human Resource (HR) techniques suggests that they are unimpressed by either of the motivations that induced the employers discussed above to introduce non-union systems of representations: they do not value representation systems either as bastions against union intervention or as sources of competitive advantage through enhanced employee engagement and motivation. These employers invest little resource in HR activity, and often lack managers with specialist HR skills and knowledge. The introduction of formal systems of representation under the Regulations may have a significant impact on industrial relations in such workplaces, since it would focus unprecedented attention on such issues and force management into taking seriously issues they had previously ignored. However, for the reasons cited, take-up is likely to be rare.

The second category to be considered is that smaller category of non-union workplaces Sisson has labelled 'HRM'. Some of these will consist of firms which invest time and money in sophisticated HR techniques, but whose approach is characterised by a strongly *individualist* approach. For these a formalised system of employee consultation and information may represent an unwelcome challenge to their managerial philosophy. Two comments may be made about such employers. First, they may well employ systems of 'direct' employee consultation and information dissemination which may constitute a 'defence' against approaches to establish an indirect system under the Regulations. Second, the opportunity presented to employees to establish a legally based system of collective interest representation provides a clear opportunity to test the case often made by such employers, that an effective system of direct employee voice reduces employee interest in indirect mechanisms. 'HRM' employers are frequently hostile to trade unions or argue that their employees do not wish or need them. While they may wish to avoid unionisation they are unlikely to perceive an alternative form of collective representation as an appropriate vehicle for such a strategy. Equally they will be interested in how sophisticated HR techniques can contribute to enhanced performance but again are unlikely to see the new mechanisms available as contributing to this. In non-union workplaces with an existing system of indirect collective representation the challenge is less radical; where union avoidance is the motivation the legal provisions may be welcomed as strengthening the legitimacy of the structures while leaving their operation largely unaffected.

Against this generally negative assessment must be set an apparent growth of employer interest in developing systems of employee consultation as a means towards improved corporate performance. The growth of employer interest in so-called 'partnership' approaches may be evidence of this (see Ackers and Payne 1998). While it is the case that most of these developments are taking place in unionised companies (Terry and Smith 2003), the recent establishment of elaborate systems of employee consultation in firms such as Pizza Express and B&Q (Hall 2003b) may be indicative of growing managerial interest in non-union firms. The dilemma that confronts such managerial initiatives is simply expressed: research evidence, in particular from continental Northern Europe, suggests that performance improvement is more likely to result from 'strong' than 'weak' forms of consultation, in other words from an approach that goes beyond the minimum framework established by the UK Regulations. To put it more strongly, the evidence suggests that effective participation rarely results from the enactment of legal rights alone; rather it emerges from systems of workplace consultation linked, directly or indirectly, to an active trade union presence (Terry 1994).

In unionised workplaces the challenge for employers lies in the requirement to extend consultation beyond those categories of employees that enjoy representation through trade union recognition into a system of universal representation. Here the Regulations may focus attention on the extent of employer support for union-based collective bargaining. Do they seek to protect the union channel, perhaps even extending representation, or will the temptation arise to develop alternative, parallel systems of representation, one union-based and the other not, with the potential to weaken both employer and employee commitment to union-based forms?

It appears inevitable that there will be a growth in 'hybrid' systems of representation as a consequence of the new legislation, but what these will look like, and how they will relate to and affect existing systems remains highly uncertain. Although the WERS data (see above) examine only workplaces where a non-union system for some employees coexists with union recognition for others, this is by no means the only possible version; representatives elected by all employees but with 'reserved seats' for trade unions is another. Nor is it clear whether structures for the representation of non-union employees will run in parallel to those for unionised employees, or whether a 'universal' system of representation that derives from the Regulations' fall-back 'standard information and consultation provisions' may provide a single forum and common agenda for both unionised and non-union employees. These and other different formulae offer different strategies for employers and different implications for trade unions.

Threat or opportunity for unions?

For trade unions, a general right to information and consultation is important for reasons of both principle and practice. The key point of principle is that the Directive gives legal authority to the notion of collective representation on which trade unions so depend. In practical terms, many commentators (e.g. Hall *et al.* 2002) see the Directive as an opportunity for unions to reinvigorate their organisation and membership.

Historically, many trade unions worried that a general right to information and consultation would undermine their single channel position. While the TUC strongly supported the adoption of the information and consultation Directive, there was relatively little discussion of its detailed implications for unions and the TUC's official position masked a degree of union ambivalence. The priority of most unions was to campaign for the introduction – and subsequently the strengthening – of statutory measures to support trade union recognition (introduced by the Employment Relations Act 1999 (ERA)). During a major TUC consultative exercise held in 1994–95 in response to the ECJ ruling, unions accepted that EU law meant that consultation with trade union representatives could no longer be regarded as the only available model in respect of redundancies and transfers, but were unenthusiastic about pursuing a wider universal consultation rights strategy involving proposals for statutory employee representation committees in non-union workplaces. The resulting policy statement *Your Voice at Work* (TUC 1995b) put forward a framework which included promoting *union-based* consultation machinery as the vehicle for a broader range of consultation rights.

The TUC exercise revealed considerable unease on the part of most major unions at the prospect of a radical departure from the traditional pattern of single-channel trade union representation. This reflects not only ideological qualms but also uncertainty about whether a broader range of universal consultation rights, and the emergence of consultation structures in the absence of recognised unions, would be an effective vehicle for extending union influence and organisation (Hall 1996; see also McCarthy 2000).

However, the experience of the 1980s and 1990s has demonstrated the fragility of a voluntarist system of trade union representation. The UK implementation of the Directive arguably offers unions their best prospect of making inroads into unorganised workplaces, providing the opportunity for union members to be elected as representatives with statutory rights to consultation on a range of key issues even though union recognition is refused by the employer. Organising the consultation committees that the Directive is likely to promote looks an easier proposition than recruiting individual members. Moreover, in unionised workplaces, as the TUC itself has emphasised, the Directive could also have profound implications. As summarised above, the 1998 WERS showed that the scope of bargaining/consultation where unions were recognised was often very narrow. Thus while at first glance it might appear unlikely that the implementation of these legislative rights has significant implications for organised workplaces, other than through the creation of new structures such as EWCs and, in some workplaces, more formalised arrangements for health and safety consultation, this is to ignore the implications of legislative rights as negotiating resources in their own right. The implications have been most clearly seen in unions' effective deployment of legal rights to redundancy consultation in high-profile restructuring cases such as BMW's break-up of the Rover Group (Batchelor 2001) and the ending of car production at Vauxhall's Luton plant. These examples, although rare and particular, nevertheless raise the possibility of legal rights being used to extend those available through traditional collective bargaining approaches. This has particular significance for a workplace unionism that, in general, has lost much of the bargaining strength and influence it enjoyed in earlier times. The work of Brown and his colleagues (Brown *et al.* 2000) using the 1998 WERS data clearly shows that, with regard to both wage and non-wage issues (workplace) unions' role has faded over two decades. Even where pay is still a subject of collective discussion, consultation appears to be displacing negotiation, and over a significant range of non-wage issues (recruitment, training, appraisal, even equal opportunities) the collective process cannot even be dignified by that term, since over half of employers and union representatives described it as either 'provision of information' or 'nothing' (Brown *et al.* 2000: 615–18; see also Cully *et al.* 1999: 103–5). The use made by UK trade unions of the opportunities provided by EWCs to obtain information and consultation access not available to them through national voluntary systems indicates a union preparedness to use opportunities deriving from legal rights. Such gradual 'juridification' of collective employee relations may be accelerated by the implementation of the new information and consultation legislation, with uncertain implications.

The introduction of new consultation rights under the Directive may thus enable unions to address a significantly broader agenda than is currently the case in many workplaces. Practically – and here the experience of working with employee representatives from other EU countries within the EWCs' has been important – a general right to consultation offers an opportunity to extend considerably the issues discussed with management, as well as securing better information about the organisation's business plans.

Opinions as to whether the opportunities for organisational development outweigh the risks of union weakening are divided (see e.g. the debate between Hyman 1996 and Kelly 1996b). The discussion above of the emergence of a range of possible 'hybrid' forms of representation suggests outcomes that may have very different potentials for union activity. But it is at the very least clear that if the new circumstances created by the regulations are to be exploited effectively by trade unions, they will need a well-resourced, proactive strategy for doing so.

Conclusion

Labour law developments at European Union level have exerted a profound influence on the growing statutory regulation of employee representation in the UK. The cumulative effect of EU policies based on the principle of universal employee representation, typical elsewhere in Europe, has been to change the traditional legislative policy in this country of recognised unions constituting the 'single channel' through which statutory collective employment rights are applied. The practical impact, however, has to date been limited. Though an under-researched area, there is little evidence of widespread consultation or workforce agreements with specially elected employee representatives under the current legislation on redundancies, working time and other issues. The EWCs' legislation applies only to multinational companies. But the practical impact of the information and consultation Directive will almost certainly be far more significant.

Even here, however, the proposed legislative framework for implementing the Directive's requirements is strongly influenced by the UK's voluntarist traditions. Far from imposing a single, works council-type structure as the vehicle for consultation, the draft Regulations seek to promote diversity by maximising the scope for agreed arrangements which may depart from the Directive's minimum requirements. (Indeed, as suggested above, to go as far as allowing agreed arrangements to take the form of direct forms of information and consultation rather than via employee representatives may prove to be incompatible with the Directive.)

Moreover, the experience of the existing statutory employee representation mechanisms suggests that a 'minimalist' implementation strategy is undesirable. Better regulation does not necessarily equate with minimal regulation. If there is to be regulation, employers are likely to prefer it to be systematic and sufficiently detailed so that they know what is expected of them (Hall and Edwards 1999). In particular, the bare bones of the draft Regulations' 'standard information and consultation provisions' would appear to need considerable fleshing out if they are to provide the basis for robust, authoritative structures of representation in the face of employer hostility or indifference.

The experience of both the EWCs' legislation and the UK's trade union recognition legislation suggests that there may be relatively few cases where the statutory fallback model is imposed on companies. The overall impact of the Regulations may be a kind of 'legislatively-prompted voluntarism' (Hall 2003a), similar to what has happened as a result of the EWCs and union recognition provisions, with the new legislation driving the spread of voluntary information and consultation agreements, reached either ahead of its entry into force or as a consequence of its trigger mechanism being used. Taken together the cumulative weight of EU legislation and the recognition provisions of the ERA provide an unprecedented set of legal frameworks for the establishment of employee representation rights, backed by legal legitimation and sanction. However, as argued above, there is still an open question as to whether the coincidence of the two sets of legal provisions will act to provide mutual reinforcement to effective employee representation, or whether the one may be deployed to weaken and undermine the other.

Whether the result of such new 'voluntarism', will cause the spread of a 'company-level council' model or a more diverse range of outcomes (as is the government's intention) remains to be seen. If the former, the new structures, as well as being important in their own terms, will also help fill an infrastructural gap in UK industrial relations by providing a bridge between local and European-level representation arrangements as well as providing a vehicle for meeting the current range of issue-specific employee representation requirements in UK law. The inability of UK employee representatives to 'punch their weight' within EWCs is a reflection of national industrial relations factors such as the lack of strong information and consultation rights and institutions in the UK and the decentralised, workplace focus of employee representation. UK implementation of the Directive on national information and consultation rules may help fill the infrastructural gap between EWC level and localised union structures but the development of a genuine consultation culture that may also facilitate the more effective participation of UK employee representatives within EWCs will inevitably take considerably longer.

For these potentialities to be realised in any significant way, much will depend on the attitudes and strategies of employers. On the one hand, we have the evidence of legislative avoidance, of 'Bleak House' employers, and of a minimal compliance with legal requirements; on the other, the apparent increasing interest in partnership, a process in which information and consultation are the bedrocks of the programme that the TUC has been eager to encourage. Likewise, for the IPA, information and consultation, along with representative employee 'voice', are seen as 'key building blocks' of 'partnership' and through that to effective performance. For many managers the gains may not be so immediately obvious – having to explain their position, take criticism and admit errors is something that few managers find easy; a right to representation will also change the power relationship with employees. Yet the considerable benefits far outweigh any disadvantages. Having to explain policies to employees obliges managers to allow time for a fuller consideration of their proposals than would otherwise be the case, helping to ensure that the wrong decisions are not rushed through. Moreover, effective information and consultation is a critical tool in obtaining the input of employees – the scrutinising of proposals by employees can lead to alternative and better decisions. The creation of effective and robust mechanisms through which employees can express views and help shape their working environment could, if the opportunities created by the Directive are acted upon, work to the benefit of unions, employees and employers.

Notes

1. The relevant data are discussed in Millward *et al*. (1992: 162).
2. Although, as Broad also notes, the more junior UK management saw it as a means of keeping the Transport and General Workers' Union (TGWU) out of the plant.

11
Agency Voice: The Role of Labour Market Intermediaries in Worker Representation

Janet Druker and Celia Stanworth

Introduction

The role of employment agencies dates back at least to the end of the nineteenth century, when they supplied both domestic labour and also staff to work in the growing number of clerical and office-based jobs (DTI 1999; McNally 1979: 105). From this time, agencies attracted an unenviable reputation for exploitative and unethical practices (McNally 1979) – a reputation that lingers despite the many changes that have taken place in recent years (NACAB 1997b). The expansion in the numbers both of agencies and of agency temps during the 1990s was premised on several different and contradictory factors including the pressures of technological change, internal financial controls limiting 'headcount' and the need to control labour costs (Ward *et al.* 2001). By the late 1990s, it was suggested that the 'temp' industry was polarising between low-paid and exploitative agencies on the one hand and those prioritising long-term client relationships with greater care for reputation on the other (Peck and Theodore 1998).

This chapter explores the ways in which workers' interests are represented where workers are engaged in a three-cornered employment relationship – being placed with a host employer by an intermediary. Most employment agencies facilitate placements both for temporary and permanent workers (Hotopp 2000), but we focus here on 'temps' who form the majority of placements and whose relationship with the agency is likely to be of longer duration than that of 'perms'.

In the employment agency environment, unions have only limited impact and agencies themselves may take on a representative role. The chapter commences with an overview of the impact and significance of trade union organisation for agency workers. Second, it considers in more detail the role of agencies and the ways in which they support and represent the individuals for whom they find work. Third, the chapter asks how the agency's representational role is framed and enacted, exploring the ambiguities inherent in the agencies' representative role. It concludes with some comments on the extent and limitation of the voice that is achieved by agency temps.

The chapter draws on research with two employment agencies (a term used here to denote both employment agencies and employment businesses); with clients, accessed through a postal survey and through face-to-face interviews; and with focus groups and interviews with agency temporary workers. Other interviews included officers of one of the unions that have been active in their support. We exclude from this discussion any consideration of the entertainment industry, where the role of the agency is rather different and distinct from the picture that has been presented above.

Trade unions and agency workers

The relationship between agency workers and trade unions has been under review in the UK for at least two decades (McNally 1979; Rothwell 1990). This can be summarised as a debate about whether trade unions should recruit agency workers and whether they can organise in a way that ensures they can effectively represent the interests of agency labour (Heery 2004b). Concerns about the conditions of engagement of employment agency workers and the abuses of 'flexible' labour encouraged the politics of resistance to the use of agency labour in the 1980s (TUC 1985: 35). Accordingly, unions sought to dissuade employers from using agencies and agency workers were widely perceived to be beyond the scope of collective regulation. Subsequently though, as resistance proved impractical, so the recruitment and representation of agency labour was accepted by TUC affiliates as the preferred option. In 1987 the TUC agreed upon a strategy to improve the pay and working conditions of part-time and temporary workers, based upon trade union organisation and collective bargaining (TUC 1988a: 32). From this time, unions have tended to endorse the recruitment and representation of temporary and agency labour through collective bargaining. However this too has proven difficult to implement effectively.

Only a small proportion of employment agency workers are union members. Studies undertaken at Cardiff University highlight the difficulties involved in trade union recruitment of temporary agency workers, contrasting the differences in approach that have been adopted (Heery *et al.* 2000). The transient situation of many agency workers diminishes both their prospect of job security and also the potential for their long-term identity with a union representing employees in a host workplace. This factor is important given the workplace focus of much trade union activity in the UK (Heery and Abbott 2000). Movement between different workplaces means that agency temps may experience both non-union and unionised work environments. Over time an individual may encounter different trade unions – but this experience does not enhance the possibility of union membership since no one union can claim the right to recruit agency temporary workers. 'There isn't a body (i.e., union) for temps', an agency worker from Leicester informed us. There is no consistent experience of trade unions then, for the agency temp.

Until recently, agency workers had very few statutory employment rights and our research suggests that their expectations of host employers are often low. Although there are exceptions, especially in relation to longer-term placements, agency workers may accept that their position is 'betwixt and between' organisations (Garsten 1999), a position that discourages allegiance with the workgroups that they encounter or with trade unions with whom these work colleagues are associated. Some agency temps who participated in our research were uncertain about whether they had the right to join a trade union – and whether there was a union that would accept them. Others simply felt it inappropriate. Asked whether they would join a trade union, the responses from office workers (including those in public sector, unionised workplaces) were, typically as follows:

> You don't generally think of it with temping. You think of it with permanent work. (Agency worker, Cardiff)

> I'm not aware of a trade union that deals with temping work. I don't know whether it would apply to you to join the trade union of the company if you're there for however long... You know you're not an employee of that company. I'm not certain what the rules are so.... (Agency worker, Leeds)

A different perspective might be expected in a unionised, manufacturing environment, but even in this context agency workers may feel that their position is differentiated from the more secure position of their colleagues who are permanent employees and who are union members. As one interviewee (non-union in a unionised workplace) said, she felt, 'less a person than the person next to you'. In this establishment, agency workers had been used as a buffer to protect the conditions of a diminishing permanent workforce over a period of more than 15 years – a position that was tacitly supported by the recognised union, the Amalgamated Engineering and Electrical Union (AEEU), which had, historically operated a closed shop. Permanent employees retained distinctive privileges as compared with the agency temps. 'Equal pay' was provided for agency workers as a consequence of the union's initiative. Yet despite 'equal pay', conditions were very different when the situation of the two groups was compared. Agency temps were vulnerable to a downturn in activity that could cut off their work and their income. They could more easily be transferred between jobs and across work teams. They were eligible for higher-grade posts only when no permanent employee was available. Whilst the AEEU was recognised and had workplace representation for permanent staff, the union's position in relation to the agency 'temps' was ambiguous. The union had been refused representation rights for agency temps and the workplace representatives had closer contact with members amongst the permanent staff, who were clearly their priority. Perhaps not surprisingly then, whereas 95 per cent of permanent staff were union members only 15–20 per cent of agency staff joined the union, even though some of them had long service both with the agency and with this client company.

The objective difficulties associated with union recruitment of agency workers may be actively fostered by the perceptions and interests of the other parties to this particularly complex set of work relationships. We look, first at the agency attitude towards trades unions. Then we consider the influence of their clients.

The major employment bureaux supply labour across many industries and for many occupations, shifting the focus of industrial or sectoral activity according to economic circumstances and business opportunities. The agency/union relationship is an instrumental one, serving as a marketing device to access and to sustain relations with unionised client organisations. The largest employment bureaux, notably Manpower and Adecco, sustain national level contacts with a number of trade unions (Storrie 2002: 24). These contacts serve to enhance the bureaux' access to commercial contracts (or at least to minimise in-house opposition) where an individual client recognises a trade union or unions. The agency relationship with individual unions may be framed as a 'recognition' agreement, but the relationship is different from the conventional recognition agreement because of the variable location and interests of the individual agency. New union relationships may be cultivated if circumstances require and 'recognition' of a particular union or group of unions lacks the exclusivity that is the norm in other employer/union recognition arrangements. Whilst Manpower has a long-established recognition agreement with the Transport and General Workers' Union (TGWU), for example, it continues to liaise with other trade unions – and would probably be prepared to open up discussions with any union that has a significant presence in the workplace of a major corporate client. The scope of collective bargaining is limited though and in general unions have little involvement in representing agency workers on pay or benefits.

The employment agency itself is most likely to encourage union membership with its recognised unions where a client – the host employer – has a prior relationship with a recognised trade union or unions and has agreed that the representational rights of the union should also encompass agency workers. Work candidates who are being placed by the agency may be advised as part of the placement process of the right to join a trade union and of the steps that should be taken to do so. In situations of this type the agency worker may be offered the opportunity to take part in union activities. More commonly though, it appears that host employers – even those with recognition agreements – are silent on this subject unless union activists amongst the permanent workforce actively champion the cause of agency workers.

The network of interactions that puts the agency temp into a job with a host employer may isolate the temp – even within a unionised workplace environment – from local union organisation. Client senior managers and team leaders in the host organisation represent the hub through which other relationships are significantly determined. The numerical balance between permanent and temporary staff is decided by client managers. The nature of the relationship (e.g. preferred or sole supply contract) with the employment agency is shaped by the client. The presence of union workplace representatives – and the choice of union too – is influenced by client attitudes and values. Union workplace representatives, who so often are subject to pressures in terms of the volume of work and the conflicts of demand associated with their role, may themselves see agency workers as a low priority. Client values are especially significant then in setting standards and expectations for the agency, for the trade union and for the agency workforce and even in the unionised workplace agency temps may be remote from union influence.

The position of the agency temp – isolated from mainstream union involvement – is illustrated in Figure 11.1. This shows that agency temps may be excluded from contacts with union representatives or from the possibility of union representation even in a workplace where the union is recognised. This is especially likely where an agency workgroup is isolated from the mainstream workforce and confined to a discrete and separate set of tasks. Agency workers may then be dependent on the flow of information and communication from agency branch staff and from workplace team leaders.

Our work suggests that long-service and closer familiarity with the work of a union encourages union membership amongst agency temps. In itself this is not surprising. If workers do not intend to remain at the plant – or if the future appears uncertain – then the motivation to join may be undermined. This is the case even where individuals with lower service levels are aware of positive work relations in the form of a partnership between the labour supplier and the union. It is an important point since the majority of assignments are very short-lived. Forde's (2001: 639) research for example, showed that 63 per cent of agency temps from his sample in Leeds and Telford, commenting on their current or most recent assignment, said that it had lasted less than one month. In itself this goes a long way to explaining why, in practice, a high proportion of agency temps will be operating without trade union support.

Local union representatives may endeavour to recruit from the agency workforce. However employment agencies – even those agencies that sustain national level compacts with trade unions – are unlikely to lend support for such initiatives if they jeopardise client relations. Union representatives may find that there are difficulties in terms of access to a section of

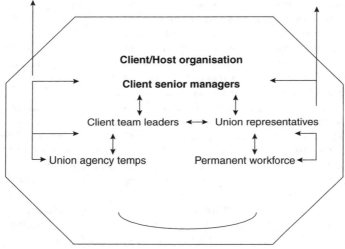

Figure 11.1   Agency temps in the unionised workplace

the workforce that is likely to have higher than average turnover and to be more than usually mobile within the plant. In practice – if not in theory – union representatives may accept that agency workers are not a priority in terms of recruitment. There may be significant differences of interest between the permanent workforce and agency temporary labour, most particularly where the host employer is using agency labour in order to provide a buffer for the permanent workforce – enhancing the job security of the latter at the expense of the former. Even negotiation around the principle of 'equality' of treatment may represent in practice a means of defending the jobs of permanent employees against the encroachment of agency labour.

The majority of employment agencies have no recognition agreement with a trade union or unions, however. The employment agency market is variegated and the largest agencies have a relatively small market share so in practice most agency workers are isolated and without recourse to union support at the workplace. Smaller agencies and those with specialist interests are those most likely to operate without trade union involvement. Where an agency hires out workers in an occupation with a low density of unionisation, for example in catering, agency workers are unlikely to encounter trade union representatives or activists. We conclude then that despite recent interest and some notable trade union campaigning initiatives, trade unions are not currently the main route to representation for agency workers. Given the mediating role of the employment agency, we must turn to an alternative possibility – namely that the employment agency itself provides a 'voice' for agency temps, representing their interests at the point of placement and articulating their views when there are problems.

Agencies, job search and worker representation

The relationship between the agency and the workers whom they place is defined in large measure by the business relations between client companies and the agency. In a quest for repeat contracts and bulk volume business, reputable employment agencies during the 1990s, emphasised a 'strategic' relationship with client employers and highlighted their capacity to recruit and manage staff on behalf of the client – a process that has been termed 'insourcing' (Purcell and Purcell 1999). Whether clients seek in-fill placements to cover occasional staff absence, repeat placements from the same worker or whether they are 'bulk-purchasing' with on-going labour supply contracts, there has been a growing emphasis on professionalism and on relational contracting especially amongst larger clients (Druker and Stanworth 2001).

Current business activities for the major players – including this emphasis on customer relationship management – encourage agency assignment co-ordinators to take a more positive approach to the relationship with individual workers. Agencies are increasingly interested in placing labour, with professional or specialist skills for which rewards are at a premium and professional or 'knowledge' workers command more choice and have greater independence than do their less skilled counterparts (Harvey and Kanwal 2000). When the labour market was tight, during the 1990s, employment agencies were keen to attract and to retain placeable workers. Even with the downturn in activity since the turn of the century, the demand for high level skills remains relatively buoyant. Agency consultants are likely, in this context, to foster relationships with those who are eligible for placement.

The fact that agency temps have seen improvements to their individual employment rights also encouraged agency managers and branch recruitment consultants in the late 1990s, to take greater care of their relationship with them. Employment legislation in that period gave rights to 'workers' as well as to 'employees', notably extending paid holiday entitlement to agency workers, diminishing the differences between their position and that of permanent employees (Druker and Stanworth 2001). Although the initiatives promised for agency temps in the 1998 Employment Act have not yet been implemented, the market leaders amongst the employment agencies, as well as their representative body, the Recruitment and Employment Confederation, are sensitive to the adverse publicity attracted by problems of legal compliance. This point should be qualified since it remains difficult for someone working as an agency 'temp' to win redress against a grievance or to pursue successfully a claim for improved working conditions. Moreover the pursuit of individual employment rights through an Employment Tribunal is becoming generally more complex since the Employment Act 2002 was passed (Hepple and Morris 2002).

The credibility of agencies as bona fide labour market intermediaries is, ultimately critical to their success. With an emphasis on 'human resource solutions' leading agencies are sensitive to the perceptions of client employers and also to the views of successive national governments, since legislation to regulate the industry appeared to be imminent both at the national and at the European level for several years. Agency representatives in the UK and in Europe are concerned to project a socially responsible role, one that focuses on the contribution to labour market lubrication, as they claim to up-skill the workforce, enhance the work experience of job candidates and contribute to economic growth (CIETT 2000). The relational marketing strategy of employment agencies is jeopardised if it appears that they intend only to capitalise on the labour market disadvantage of the workers that they place. To this end then, reputable employment agencies seeking a distinctive market position are increasingly likely to promote a form of relational contracting (or at least the rhetoric associated with relational contracting) with workers too – presenting the agency position as 'representative' of agency workers' interests.

There are certain common features to the activities of agencies placing temporary workers. The first is that, whatever their legal identity (employment agency or business), they operate as one corner of a three-cornered work relationship, with the 'agency' bringing a work-seeker into contact with a potential 'host' employer. This means that agencies take primary responsibility for recruitment – attracting candidates with appropriate experience and interests. The second is that agencies carry some responsibility (although this may be only partial) for selection, having already attracted a field of job candidates. Their role in selection may take the form of outright rejection of candidates who do not meet certain key criteria – with particular skills or qualifications, for example. It may require them to limit numbers, so that the host employer is offered a shortlist from which the final selection will be made. Alternatively the agency may take the full responsibility for selection, sending one candidate for a vacancy, with the premise that, if this person is not suitable, s/he may be rejected and replaced. Third, then, agencies share an interest with job candidates in ensuring that the candidate – or one of their candidates – is accepted by the host employer, since it is on this basis that the agency commission is paid and the agency sustains an on-going relationship with the host employer. Thus the agency provides some of the same functions as the union hiring hall in the USA, eliminating the cost for the employer of recruiting, screening and training temporary workers (Mangum *et al.* 1985).

In undertaking these activities, agencies provide a route through which the job candidate reduces the time and cost and enhances the potential opportunities and benefits of job search activities. It is difficult, of course to speak of a 'typical' job candidate, since agencies supply labour spanning a wide occupational and income range, from cleaning, catering and driving through to freelance providers of IT services and interim managers. However there are certain common assumptions that may be made by a job candidate who uses an agency as a means to finding work.

Through the agency a candidate can test out his or her labour market situation. The agency–job candidate relationship is not a mutually exclusive one since a candidate can register with more than one agency at any one time, maximising contact with potential employers. Agency registration enables a candidate to explore alternative work opportunities and the best available rates of pay with the minimum of personal involvement in the search process. This has real benefit for candidates with specialist skills or interests – for example in fields such as accountancy or IT – where the agency will have (or at least will appear to have) networks and contacts that maximise employment opportunities. It also benefits candidates where they are confident that a particular occupational route is most suitable (e.g. care homes). The use of an appropriate employment agency can reduce the amount of time that elapses between job search and work placement – a factor that is critical for job candidates who are without work. Moreover agency 'temping' is sometimes used by potential employers as a test ground for permanent employment – on a 'try before you buy' principle. This may be a positive feature of agency work for candidates who are searching for permanent employment. Indeed the agency with established contacts with high prestige local companies may be particularly attractive where it is perceived (sometimes erroneously) as offering a route into permanent employment with the 'best' local employers.

A high premium is attached to personal presentation and image in the process of job search – the 'personality market' described by C. Wright Mills (1956: 182–8) – and the employment agency may provide a form of personal 'branding' for the individual within the labour market. The agency offers a badge of identity and the appearance of corporate approval to the job candidate without any real commitment or engagement in this transaction on either side.

As a service organisation, the agency exists to supply labour. As a business organisation, the agency's interest is in ensuring access to credible job candidates and, wherever possible, that these candidates are placed in work for as long as possible. The agency is paid by the client employer (typically on a per capita per day basis) and the agency is legally precluded by law from levying a charge on individual job candidates. Since the agency's business centres on labour supply and since, too the individual recruitment 'consultant' working in the agency's offices may be paid according to performance, there is every interest in securing closure on the sale. In this way the agency's interests and those of job applicants are aligned.

The initial reception and responses of agency consultants in branch outlets are key to management of the perceptual and emotional responses of workers who are placed. As it is increasingly common for employers to use web-based recruitment and as high-street based agencies are now in competition with on-line placement providers, it is important for the high street agencies to distinguish their service through its 'personal' quality. The reception and greeting (branch staff are trained to smile and welcome people who enter the branch) decide whether or not an individual will remain. The physical environment and the layout of the reception area determine how comfortable people feel in the important early stages of their visit. Personal contact with a named assignment co-ordinator or recruitment consultant carries, implicitly, a promise that work will be found for the 'temp' – even though there is no such commitment in practice. At best, agency representatives may provide career advice, access to some training opportunities and discussion about options and possibilities, especially for new labour market entrants and for those who are in the aftermath of redundancy. Staff in the branches of the agency where our research was conducted were highly rated by temps and were perceived to be looking after their interests.

> ... the person who builds up a relationship with you and finds you work ... That is a busy and important person basically. (Agency worker, Manchester)
>
> You feel you're being looked after. (Agency worker, Cardiff)
>
> I have the confidence in them [agency consultants]. (Agency worker, Cardiff)

The employment agency – and especially staff at branch level – are the key in securing the role of the agency as representative of temp interests at the individual level. The emphasis on relational contracting with client businesses is mirrored in relations with stronger job candidates. There are many dimensions to the perception and experience of the 'agency' as it is almost invariably termed by temps. At one level the 'agency' gains in reputation as it seems to offer some protection against the behaviour of conventional employers – typified with the words: 'bullies, redundancy and boring jobs' (Agency worker, Bournemouth).

In reality, interests may be only partially aligned – since the agency's interests rest in a work placement being made, whereas the job applicant's interests are in the *best possible* placement being made. Where the agency has more than one suitable candidate or where it is envisaged that one post might be more easily filled than another, the agency may offer the job applicant a 'second best' option. In this respect then, the agency effects a compromise that provides partial and limited representation. A significant distinction must be made between representation of candidates who are perceived as potential placements and representation of those who, in some way, do not meet the agency's requirements. There is no obligation on agency consultants to inform a candidate where they will not offer work opportunities. Job candidates may leave the agency with the expectation that work will be forthcoming – only to find that they never hear again from the branch in question. Support and representation is not automatic, for the agencies – and the recruitment consultants who make placements – are selective. Workers in the agencies associated in our research were mostly well aware of the importance of developing an ongoing, positive relationship with agency consultants, as a way of being preferred for job placements.

The International Confederation of Private Employment Agencies (CIETT), the body that represents employment agencies in Europe, has argued on the basis of its own research, that many workers enrolling with employment agencies are 'outsiders' to the labour market who are integrated through the agency role (CIETT 2000: 6). It seems likely that the agency's support is especially important to candidates who are disadvantaged in the 'personality market' by employer perceptions and discrimination with respect to age, race, gender and disability. Our research was not geared to ascertain whether agencies were particularly effective in the placement of ethnic minority job applicants. Our 'temps' did suggest though that agencies provided a useful counter to age discrimination. Loss of confidence is a common problem where older people find themselves without work and contact with the agency and with assignment co-ordinators or consultants helped some of our research participants to re-establish perspective and re-enter the labour market.

The representative role of the employment agency was articulated most consistently by older workers, especially those who had experienced redundancy or problems at work in the past.

> There's a difference between 'agent' and 'agency'. Agent sounds grander. I treat (the agency) as my agent and they are tremendous for me. They are selling my skills and as a person. Without them there is an age discrimination barrier there. There is no age barrier with (the agency). They push my skills and experience. (Agency worker, London)

There may be tensions though in this role since the agency wishes to retain the client and to maximise placement opportunities.

Resolving workplace problems

The strengths of the relationship between the agency and the worker who is placed are tested most strongly when the agency is asked to tackle a problem encountered by the individual during a placement – for example relating to unsatisfactory pay levels or other workplace difficulties. Since the agency negotiates the terms on which a placement is made, the agency may be regarded as contributory to the problem but since the agency has the capacity to negotiate change, it is possible for the agency consultant to present his or her role as representative of the individual.

> If it's a grievance you'd come back to (the agency). If it's the scheme of things.... (Agency worker, Cardiff on short-term placement in an office environment)

Although it might be envisaged that workers on a long-term agency placement would have greater confidence in resolving problems individually in their host environment, the agency was often seen as sympathetic – and a source of advice and support.

Important to this perception was the fact that in a work environment, where the agency had an office on site, agency 'consultants' had personal contact with the staff that they placed and were accessible to them if there was a problem. One worker described the unsympathetic response of her host employer when she encountered childcare problems. She needed to arrive an hour later each morning for work and it was the agency that she turned to for support. The agency consultant shared an interest in her continuing presence at work as the local labour market was particularly tight and she would not easily be replaced. Hence the agency intervened to ensure that adjustments in working hours were accommodated.

Where the agency provides representation at the individual level during a placement, it has a strong interest in the perpetuation of established relations. The alternative to resolution of a problem might be for the 'temp' to quit – and there is a risk, in this eventuality, of the placement being terminated.

The most commonplace complaints made by 'temps' relate to pay and conditions – with the typical complaint directed at host employers, and agency intervention directed to the resolution of problems. Typically these problems were concerned with adjustments to pay to meet changes in job requirements or to provide for pay progression over a long placement. The agency's network of client contacts provides agency consultants with access to local labour market information and pay data, so that they are able to present as 'agent' to the client too, supporting job candidates by advising client employers of appropriate pay levels. The agency's interests rest initially in ensuring that the client specifies a realistic rate that will enable a job placement to be made. Since the agency is interested in retention once the placement is made, there is a continued concern to satisfy worker requests for an improvement in pay when the placement is established – and so the agency consultant may take on a representative role to seek an improvement to pay levels. Occasionally, the agency may accept a reduction in commission in order to ensure that a worker continues in a placement. This is viable since the agency's transaction cost is largely bound up with the initial placement arrangement: the longer the duration of the placement, the greater the return to the agency.

Unsurprisingly then, agency consultants were perceived as a means of advancing claims on pay and position, as the comments below suggest.

> I negotiated for more pay from a solicitor's assignment. (The agency) rang them up and kept the same commission but I got more pay. You raise the question with (the agency), not the employer. (Agency worker, Bournemouth)

> I tend to wait until I have been on the assignment for a while before I ask for more pay. If the job develops I go back to (the agency) to ask for more – the agency are fantastic about this. If the job description has changed they will negotiate more money. (Agency worker, Bournemouth)

A small minority of temps had encountered other problems in their placement (threatening behaviour in one case) with host organisations. They felt, for the most part, that they had been well supported by agency representatives with the agency providing voice and support – defined as a feeling of being 'looked after' – where circumstances were especially difficult. Even though temps were acutely aware of the commercial pressures influencing decision-taking by recruitment consultants, those who were well established in placements were confident of agency support in such circumstances.

Interestingly though, unless problems were severe, agency consultants were unlikely to move temps away from a job placement – especially if this threatened a long-term client relationship. Some temps acknowledged the ambivalence of agency representatives who were concerned to sustain a relationship with a client and to continue a placement with that client even when an individual temp was unhappy. One temp recalled a situation where she rang the agency consultant to report that she was unhappy with her placement, only to be told quite sharply that she should stop complaining (Branch interview, Guildford). Paradoxically, given their declared preference for moving on if problems became serious, temps gave accounts of placements where they had remained in a job, despite reservations, because of their own commitment to their agency. In this way relational contracting between the agency and the worker strengthened the agency's position in relation to client businesses.

Like any other representative, the agency cannot always resolve problems and may be accused of negligence in its failure to do so. The significance of failure in the representative role is highlighted in the remarks below, made by a 'temp' who abandoned a work placement because no remedy was found for the perceived inequities in her pay level.

> I have trained up five temps from (the agency) and we are all getting the same rate! All the temps where I am are getting the same rate – I would like an increase. I said to the client I must be valuable to you because you are using me to train up other staff now – I should be paid at least what your perm staff are getting. One ... agreed to pay more – as much as the full timer – we'll pay anything – I even had a copy of the newsletter with my new job title in it – but I heard nothing from the agency. I made numerous phone calls to (the agency) and then wrote a letter and a copy of the newsletter but it got lost in the post – and told them that the company were agreeable but got no response. I said that I wanted the higher rate and could not afford to work for the lower rate and that they wanted to take me on full-time but ... This has gone on for seven months now – I sent the letter again.... I am leaving this assignment now mainly because of this. If they had paid me the higher rate I would probably have stayed on .... (Agency worker, Leeds)

What is interesting in this case is the way in which dissatisfaction with the pay arrangements grew over time – eventually leading to the termination of the relationship.

It might be argued that, the failure of representation described above, suggests that the agency cannot really be the 'voice' for temp interests since the advocacy role requires consistency and predictability in terms of the capacity to meet expectations. Yet such criteria are not applied to trades unions even though it is common for trade union activists to suggest that it is inappropriate for union members to expect support from the union as a 'service agency' if they are not actively participating in union life (Munro 1999: 21).

The generally positive perceptions of the agency workers who participated in our research appear then to challenge the conventional and critical view of the employment agency as disadvantaging agency workers. Our 'temps' pointed to the benefits of a sympathetic 'agent' but a number of important qualifying points must be made.

First, our research was routed through larger and more reputable employment agencies, which are striving for a distinctive market position based upon relational contracting. It seems likely that the perception of agencies as representative of individual interests would be modified if research were conducted with agency workers across a wider range of employment agencies – where the traditional and critical perspective of the agency role may still be relevant. Second, we focussed on workers who were successfully placed. We had no access to those who were not placed or those who were placed but chose to move on, possibly because they were dissatisfied with the placement. We must conclude then, that the satisfaction that was expressed reflects placement experiences that, at least in part, have been positive. Third, it might be argued that the a-symmetry in power relations is a significant determinant of the perceptions of agency 'temps' who lack job security and the rights that accrue with service – most notably the rights to claim unfair dismissal and to challenge redundancy. The individuals who participated in our research understood the imperative of commercial inter- ests and were realistic about the implications for their own situation. The power imbalance that is inherent in every employment relationship is com- pounded by the dependency of the agency temp on the agency itself and by vulnerability to sudden change. Temps were acutely aware of the imminent possibility of termination of their work placement. Even those on long-term placements knew that their position was renewed on a week-by-week basis and could be terminated almost at any time. The good will and active com- mitment of the agency consultant could be key to assuring another place- ment and continuity of income – combating the insecurity of a job situation which provides no fallback payment. In this way, the positive perceptions of the agency (which is notably a positive perception of named individual consultants within an agency's branch) might be interpreted as an adjunct to a dependency relationship – rather than as a reflection of a fully repre- sentational role for the agency.

Finally we note the individual nature of the representation provided for temps. Whereas interest in union mobilization has focussed on the propen- sity for collective action (Kelly 1998), our research highlighted the distinc- tive and differentiated responses of individuals who did not 'connect' their own issues of concern with the experience of other workers – either in the same workplace or with the same agency. The agency may meet the need for a 'voice' for the individual – and may preclude the need for other forms of representation in some cases – but there is no question of emergent collective identity.

Conclusion

Our research uncovers significant evidence that leading employment agen- cies play a representative role on behalf of the workers they place, yet the agency relationship with job candidates remains in many respects ambigu- ous. It is clear that the role of agencies is concerned with recruitment and selection for work placement – developing and managing those who are selected in some cases, too. In selecting some individuals, others must be de-selected. So if the agency is representative it is also partisan, working to further the interests of particular groups and to exclude others. The agency is most strongly representative in the process of job search and negotiates the compromise between 'host' and job candidate on which a work place- ment is based. It may represent and support the individual over training and development needs too but always strictly within the confines of a commercial relationship. In the event of a work-based problem the agency or its staff may again speak for the aggrieved worker, acting as representative for the individual. The agency has an important vested interest in this situation – namely to ensure the continuity of the placement – either with the current worker or with a replacement if interests cannot be reconciled. The agency has dual commitments – to the client organisation and to the worker. In balancing those commitments, commercial interests ultimately will be paramount. The agency represents worker interests then, where they can be reconciled within the commercial imperative.

The representative role of the agency must be clearly distinguished from trade union representation to the extent that, with the former, advocacy is dependent upon commercial interest and relational contracting. In the case of trade union representation by contrast, advocacy is inherent in the very rationale for the union role. The individual worker has no democratic basis for influence within the employment agency, whereas the structure and organisation of trades unions – and indeed the membership base on which unions are founded – imply that there is room for democratic control for individual members in organisational life. It is relevant to our argument here that unions may not be effective in fulfilment of their role – so the attractions of other 'agents' may be enhanced. The erosion of trade union influence coupled with negative experiences of the unionised work environment amongst some of our research participants fostered their credence in alternative routes to representation.

The occupational and local labour market situation also influences the degree to which the agency will nurture relations with its workers. Tight labour markets and sharp competition between agencies to attract suitable workers will heighten this imperative. Significantly within this complex set of work relations, the worker may be represented to a client business by the agency but has no independent representative to mediate with the agency if the agency itself is the source of a problem. Employment agencies and businesses are taking on longer-term relations with workers. At the same time, individual statutory rights for workers are once again in question, following the passage of the Employment Act, 2002. For these reasons there continues to be scope for independent support and representation in addressing work-based problems in the relationship either with the 'host' organisation or with the commercial entity that places them.

12
Worker Representation through the Citizens' Advice Bureaux

Brian Abbott

Introduction

This chapter focuses on the Citizens' Advice Bureaux (CAB), a national charity that is becoming increasingly active in representing employees with work-related problems. The CAB undertakes a wide range of activities in the area of industrial relations, including lobbying, campaigning and promoting best practice. The main focus here, however, is on the employment advice provided to clients who contact CAB offices with work-related problems. In 1974–75, the CAB handled over 140 000 employment enquiries but by 2001–02 this figure had increased substantially to over 600 000. Enquiries of this kind account for 10 per cent of the workload of the CAB (NACAB 2002a: 10; 1975: 5) and are the third most common issue handled by bureaux after welfare benefits and consumer advice.

The increase in the employment work of the CAB has coincided with the decline in union membership and collective bargaining, the latter being the traditional source of employee representation and protection in the workplace (Brown 2000: 309; Cully *et al.* 1999). Some commentators argue that the absence of representative structures and opportunities for employees to express their voice has created a 'representation gap' in the workplace (Towers 1997; Freeman and Rogers 1993). At the same time, there has also been an increase in the number of small businesses and non-union firms, which are characterised by procedural informality and weak representative structures (Dickson *et al.* 1998; Gollan 2002; Scott *et al.* 1989). Given these shifts, the question arises of how, and where, workers are securing the resolution of workplace problems. A central argument of this chapter is that workers are increasingly seeking representation, and the enforcement of their rights, beyond the workplace through organisations like the CAB. The expansion of the employment work of the CAB and the growth of individual conciliation cases handled by Advisory, Conciliation and Arbitration Service (ACAS) reflect a shift away from collective expressions of conflict towards more individual expression.

Apart from brief references to the employment work of the CAB (Sisson 1993; Kessler and Bayliss 1995), there is a lack of information on its role in representing workers with employment problems (exceptions being Abbott 1998a; 1998b; Kelly 1998: 44). The account which follows seeks to fill this gap in our knowledge. It begins by providing a background to the CAB and describing the range of its employment work. It then focuses on the nature of the advisory process, the roles performed by advisers and their objectives when dealing with employers. The concluding parts seek to evaluate the work of the CAB, gauge its effectiveness and consider the nature of the organisation's relationship with trade unions. The questions addressed here are the extent to which the CAB competes with, or complements, the activities of union representatives.

The data for the chapter are taken from interviews with CAB advisers and their clients, workers who have sought advice. Interviews with advisers took place in 1996–97 and were arranged through ten bureaux, located in inner and outer London boroughs with varying industrial and occupational structures. Thirty-two in-depth interviews were conducted with 22 advisers, from a diverse range of industry and occupational backgrounds. The advisers interviewed were broadly representative of staff as a whole. Clients were contacted through the same bureaux and were selected, as far as possible, to reflect the composition of people seeking advice. A total of 40 semi-structured, face-to-face interviews were carried out in 1998–99 with CAB clients from a range of occupations and industries and with a variety of workplace problems.

The Citizens' Advice Bureau

The Citizens' Advice Bureau was established in 1939 and is a generalist advice agency providing free, impartial and confidential information on a range of issues, including debt, housing, immigration and employment, from over 2000 outlets across England, Wales and Northern Ireland. In addition to bureau offices, advice and information is provided at a variety of locations, such as hospitals, health and community centres and schools, to make advice as accessible as possible (NACAB 2002a: 10–11). Bureaux are independent charities run by a total of 5135 paid staff and 19 716 volunteers. Each bureau belongs to a national association, National Association of Citizens' Advice Bureaux (NACAB), which sets standards for the quality of advice and provides a range of services to bureaux, such as training and an electronic information system, which provides up-to-date information on the main areas of advice. In addition, NACAB co-ordinates social policy, publicity, parliamentary work and provides specialist support on complex advice issues, such as employment. The work of the CAB is supported by a central London office, a national office in Wales, a network of area field offices in England and Wales and the Northern Ireland Association of Citizens' Advice Bureaux.

Bureaux in Scotland are part of a separate organisation, Citizens' Advice Scotland (NACAB 2002a: 1).

The CAB service is dependent on a range of funders including the state, local authorities and the private sector. In 2001–02 the Department of Trade and Industry (DTI) provided funding totalling £17 140 000, accounting for 66 per cent of NACAB income. Approximately a third of NACAB expenditure is dedicated to supporting bureaux and conducting bureaux audits. Individual bureaux receive additional funding from a range of sponsors, including income from charitable trusts and the private sector. Local authorities, however, provide the bulk of bureaux funding; 53.8 per cent of total bureaux income of £103 397 in 2001–02 came from this source (NACAB 2002a: 16).

The employment work of the CAB

The CAB's involvement in the resolution of workplace problems is far from novel (Brasnett 1964). The organisation has provided advice and information on employment problems since its inception. However, the scale, volume and increasing complexity of workplace issues handled is new. Enquiries are often complex, relating to several employment jurisdictions and extend into other areas, such as debt (NACAB 2002a: 8). Increasingly, bureaux are undertaking the functions associated with traditional industrial relations actors, such as trade unions and ACAS, and an indicator of their growing significance is the range of employment work that is being undertaken. Today, this includes advice giving, campaigning, lobbying and promoting best practice.

Advice giving, which forms a key part of the employment work of the CAB, typically involves informing employees of their employment rights and how to enforce them. Advice is provided electronically and over the telephone, but predominantly in face-to-face interviews. The type of advice provided ranges from ongoing, in-depth casework, where the adviser gathers evidence in preparation for an employment tribunal hearing, and may even negotiate with the employer. Advice can also be of a 'one-off' nature. This is common where the enquiry deals with a point of fact and where the legal situation is clear; for example, clients enquiring about their holiday entitlements in law. Advisers may also refer workers with an enquiry to other more specialist organisations, such as a trade union or the Commission for Racial Equality.

The employment work of the CAB extends beyond advice giving to include campaigning, which involves advocating improvements to workers' rights and promoting an awareness of them. Campaigning includes exerting pressure from 'outside' through the publication of reports which typically identify the limitations of existing and proposed legislation and the abuse of management power. In 1993, NACAB published two research reports *Job Insecurity*, which focused on how the recession adversely affected CAB clients' experience of employment, and *Unequal Opportunities*, which explored issues around race and sex discrimination in the workplace (NACAB 1993; 1994).

Campaigning also involves collaborative work with traditional and non-traditional industrial relations actors, such as the Trades Union Congress (TUC), ACAS, the Low Pay Unit and the Maternity Alliance. In 1996, NACAB and the TUC participated in a campaign promoting greater awareness of part-time workers' rights. This involved distributing leaflets and providing information from diverse locations, such as shopping centres and outside schools (Abbott 1998a; Heery 1998: 353; NACAB 1996: 14). In 1999, NACAB, the TUC and the Greater Manchester Low Pay Unit jointly organised a conference on the minimum wage, which highlighted the reluctance of employees to make a complaint, where they had been denied their statutory rights and the methods adopted by employers to avoid payment (*The Guardian* 2 October 1999).

The CAB also performs a lobbying role, commenting on employment related Green Papers. Between 2001 and 2002, NACAB researched and compiled detailed responses to 66 consultations and select committees, providing various briefings for MPs and Assembly Members (NACAB 2002a: 11). Advisers are in a unique position when commenting on the operation of existing and proposed employment legislation as they encounter daily the types of problems clients experience when attempting to enforce their statutory rights, or when those rights have been eroded. For example, in 2002 NACAB produced *Routes to Resolution – Improving Employment Dispute Resolution*, which was highly critical of the Government's proposals for reform of the employment tribunal system. The government's proposal included a power for employment tribunals to reduce awards, where the employee fails to use internal procedures. The CAB argued that it was unrealistic and impractical for employees to use procedures in all cases, as there may be workplaces where the atmosphere is biased against a particular gender or ethnic group or the employee feels intimidated by their employer. In this type of environment an employee who feels discriminated against may feel entirely justified in believing that any discussion with management will be meaningless (NACAB 2002b).

The employment work of the CAB focuses almost exclusively on advising employees and campaigning for improvements in their employment rights. Advisers generally consider employers to possess greater resources and refer them to a solicitor or ACAS's Public Enquiry Points when they approach bureaux with employment problems. Bureaux, however, are concerned with the promotion of good employment practice, and in this area have greater contact with employers. For example, East Dorset CAB became aware of the increasing number of employment enquiries emanating from small firms within its catchment area. Consequently, the local CAB contacted the employers concerned and arranged a seminar, attended by ACAS, to discuss the issue and encourage the formalisation of employment practice (Abbott 1998a: 264; NACAB 1997a: 14).

Stages of representation

The previous section identified the range of employment activities undertaken by bureaux. This section concentrates on the advisory process and in particular casework, which was identified by 95 per cent of advisers, participating in this research, as the most common form of advice giving. Casework followed a standard approach and can be divided into three stages: identification of the problem, discussion of the options available and the goals/course of action to be pursued.

When a client approaches the CAB for employment advice, initial discussions focus on diagnosis. Advisers indicated that diagnosis could prove problematic, as clients often attended bureaux in a distressed state. Other studies have similarly documented the highly emotional state of clients seeking advice from ACAS in relation to employment issues (ACAS 2002: 12). Lack of documentary evidence demonstrating a connection to the firm, such as a contract of employment or wage slips, as the employment relationship was of an informal nature, could also make diagnosis difficult. More importantly, the presenting problem may not be of an employment nature, making identification of the problem difficult. For example, one adviser commented:

You see, the thing is not all people who come to you with an employment issue necessarily come in and say 'I've been dismissed' ... you get people that come in and say 'I want to know how to claim income support or whatever' ... and you fill it in for them and ... there will be a section about when did you last work and what your last job was and you would ask them ... and it might come out there [that the person had been unfairly dismissed].

To assist with the identification of problems and the options available an employment checklist was used by several bureaux. Checklists contained questions on whether clients had: a contract of employment, their length of service, whether they worked in a unionised environment and if they were a union member.

Once the nature of the complaint and the client's rights has been established the next stage of the casework role involved identifying the options available to the client. If it had been established that a client had been unfairly dismissed then one option that would be discussed would be submitting a claim to an employment tribunal. If workers had a complaint about their terms and conditions of employment, such as changes to their shift patterns they would be encouraged to discuss the issues with their employer, with the adviser remaining in the background advising and supporting the client.

The final stage of the casework role involved identifying the client's goals, how they wanted to resolve their grievance. Some of the literature relating to conflict resolution suggests that recourse to legal processes is increasing, and that employees are becoming increasingly litigious and prone to pursue their grievances at an employment tribunal (Dickens and Hall 2003: 136; Javaid 2000: 20; *The Guardian* 8 May 2000; Cully *et al.* 1999). Acceptance of this argument suggests that employees consider their goal to be 'having their day in court'. This research challenges this argument. Amongst clients there was a marked reluctance to pursue a tribunal claim, as many feared it might jeopardise their employment prospects as employers may label them troublemakers. Dickens (2000a: 76) also suggests that employees may be deterred from pursuing an employment tribunal case because of the stress and publicity involved. For example, one adviser commented:

> I think one of the problems with employment law is that your record goes with you, and for a lot of people going to an industrial tribunal leaves them with a black mark on their name and they are very concerned about that and will often settle for things that are not advantageous to them, because they don't want it to be put down 'he was dismissed for gross misconduct or he took us to an industrial tribunal and won'.

Similarly, another adviser reported:

> My personal experience is that I have had very few people who actually go to the tribunal, I don't know why that is. I have had several people who would have won tribunals, if they had gone, but haven't gone and we've managed to settle for them before [an employment tribunal hearing].

Goals pursued by clients often involved enforcing rights they had been denied. The methods used to attain these goals depended largely on the employer's response to the claim rather than the insistence of clients that legal action be used. As was indicated above, clients were often reluctant to pursue their case to a full tribunal hearing. In essence, 'litigious activity is as much determined by the propensity to settle as it is by the propensity of the public to use it' (Brown 2002: 24). Research conducted by Lewis and Legard (1998: 57) identified two broad strategies among employers towards settlement: those inclined to settle and those prepared to pursue a case to a hearing. The latter strategy was adopted to deter employees from making spurious claims in the hope of receiving financial compensation, and was associated with organisations with a high public profile.

Casework involves representation up to, and including, an employment tribunal hearing. Only one bureau taking part in this research provided its own tribunal representation. More typically, this function was provided by a Free Representation Unit (FRU), consisting of trainee barristers who provide free representation to needful clients as a means of gaining experience (Hepple 1987: 16). FRUs only become involved at the tribunal hearing as bureaux undertake all case preparation. According to one adviser, bureaux 'do most of the digging, the spade work, then pass it on to specialists', such as the FRU. Contacting a FRU did not guarantee representation and the client may only receive confirmation a day or two before the hearing. If the FRU was unable to provide assistance, the client could either seek an adjournment, clogging up an already over stretched system, or represent themselves.

The advisory process

The approach adopted by advisers, particularly in relation to casework, was one of individual empowerment. This involved encouraging clients to participate in the resolution of their workplace problems where this was possible. For example, one bureau adviser commented:

> One of the principles that we use, certainly in this bureau, is that we try to empower the client as much as possible, to give them the confidence and the inclination with which to go away armed and actually fight their own case, but with us in the background all the time.

Empowering was seen as a way of educating and helping clients understand what was happening to their case, so that if they or colleagues found themselves in a similar situation they would know how to respond. More practically, this approach enabled bureaux to manage their workloads and limited resources more effectively. This approach perhaps contrasts with the role of trade unions where 'empowerment' can involve developing collective workplace organisation as a means of equalising the employment relationship.

One possible weakness of the CAB approach is that it overestimates the extent to which clients, who predominantly contact bureaux individually, can deal with workplace problems on their own. Arguably, empowerment fails to recognise the impotence of the individual when negotiating in isolation with management, given the inherent power imbalance in the employment relationship (Heery *et al.* 2000: 39; Hepple 1987: 13). However, empowering did not mean abandoning clients once the options available had been identified. The articulacy and ability of the client along with the nature of the presenting problem influenced advisers' approach to empowering clients. Where possible, advisers encouraged clients to participate in the resolution of their own difficulties. This approach was characterised by a non-directive style with the adviser identifying the options, but the client collecting and completing any documentation and making the decisions.

A non-directive style was adopted when advisers believed that clients had the ability and confidence to pursue their case, with the adviser occupying a background, supporting role.

Where the adviser believed the client lacked the ability, confidence, knowledge and resources to pursue the case individually, the opportunities for empowering clients were limited. In this type of situation the adviser would adopt a directive style and be much more involved in negotiations and case preparation; for example, requesting documents and drafting letters on behalf of clients. Clearly, the nature of the CAB adviser's role is dynamic, shifting between a directive and non-directive role, in response to the presenting problem and the abilities of clients.

Dealing with employers

This section concentrates on identifying the objectives of advisers when representing clients and dealing with employers. Interview data demonstrates that negotiations between advisers and employers generally take place in writing, or by telephone, and that face-to-face contact rarely occurs. When negotiating with management 19 advisers (86 per cent) considered that their main role was to maximise the client's benefit. The latter referred primarily to financial compensation but could also include obtaining favourable references. In some cases though maximising benefits was interpreted more broadly to refer to the personal development of the client through participating in the resolution of their workplace problem. Thus, one adviser commented:

> I see our work primarily as empowering the client to learn through the procedure, to do it for themselves, if at all possible … I would see that as benefiting the client apart from the outcome of the actual case; getting the most money for the client. I think the benefit is very much more in those terms that they've actually done it.

Maximising benefits often went together with the notion of acting as the representative of clients. Indeed, 13 advisers (59 per cent) indicated that they considered this to be their key role when dealing with employers. However, there were some differences between advisers in how they conceived of their representative role. To some, being a worker representative meant actually that, championing their clients' interests. Advisers assuming this role adopted an unambiguously partisan stance, fighting hard for the client and with the client's interests being paramount. For example, one bureau volunteer commented that he found the:

> … notion of impartiality difficult [when dealing with employers]. Of course the bureaux are impartial, but it doesn't mean they are impartial

between the client and the other side: we are only on the client's side and I have never understood impartiality in that context.

Echoing this point another bureau worker commented:

Our [bureau's] main objective should be to be their [client] representative. We are acting for them. I do know that other bureaux don't see themselves in employment cases as being on the side of the employee, they see themselves as in the middle, as a facilitator between the two and I don't: I'm on the side of the employee. The employer has access to solicitor's advice, employers' associations, they've got all of that. What we're here to do is to help the employee sort something out.

In contrast, other advisers perceived the employee representative role in more neutral terms. Their task was to act as a bridge for the exchange of information between the client and the employer. In this respect, some advisers approximated to the conciliatory role adopted by officials of ACAS, while others were more openly partisan, acting more like union representatives.

Evaluating the employment work of the CAB

A key objective of CAB advisers, when negotiating with employers, was to maximise the benefits for clients. The lack of sanctions available to advisers might suggest that they are ineffective in resolving and representing workers with individual employment problems. Enforcement of employment rights through employment tribunals is the main sanction available to bureaux. To gauge the effectiveness of bureaux, in resolving employment problems, reference will be made to their success rate and the stage at which cases are settled. A further indicator of the significance of bureaux is the extent to which they can counteract the inequalities in the employment relationship.

Settlements, particularly those resolved without a tribunal hearing can be considered a desirable outcome for both parties, providing an important measure of the effectiveness of the CAB in resolving workplace conflict. For the client it means that they do not have to endure the costs, stress and acrimony of a tribunal hearing, as the problem is resolved at an early stage, before the two parties become entrenched. These benefits, which are often associated with Alternative Dispute Resolution mechanisms, have been well documented by other writers on conflict resolution (DeSouza 1998: 454; Lewis and Legard 1998: 55). Reaching a settlement is significant in itself. Without the support of advisers many of the clients participating in this research would not have pursued their grievance, because either they did not know their rights or how to enforce them. Therefore, the employer would have gone unchallenged and conflict would have remained implicit.

In this context, bureaux act as a channel transforming implicit conflict into explicit conflict and assisting in its resolution.

Of the 40 CAB clients interviewed 28 (70 per cent), indicated that their case had been settled. Of the 12 ongoing/unresolved cases five had submitted an application to an employment tribunal and were awaiting a hearing date, and, in the remaining seven cases, negotiations were continuing with the employer. The high settlement rate can be attributed to a range of factors. Advisers often filtered cases to distinguish between clients with a strong case and those with a weak case. In communications with employers advisers adopted a non-confrontational, factual approach, which may encourage the more reasonable employer to settle. The high settlement rate is also a reflection of the high legitimacy of the CAB in the wider society.

Of the 28 cases settled 57 per cent had been resolved without submitting an application to an employment tribunal. These cases revolved around monies owed, notice periods and redundancy enquiries, and involved negotiations either between the bureau and the employer or the employer and the client, with the CAB in the background. In some cases, it became apparent that the client had less than two years' service (the length of service requirement for protection from unfair dismissal at the time of the research) and therefore had no employment protection. Where this occurred the case could not proceed. Although the majority of cases were settled without recourse to an employment tribunal, advisers indicated that the threat of an employment tribunal, where appropriate, would have been highlighted in negotiations with employers. This may have accounted for the employer's decision to settle. Indeed, of the 28 cases settled 14 per cent were resolved after an IT1 form had been submitted but without a tribunal hearing. (If these cases are included in the pre-hearing settlement category then the pre-settlement rate increases from 57 to 71 per cent.) The pre-hearing settlement rate is consistent with other research indicating that approximately 60–75 per cent of cases are either settled or withdrawn before reaching a full tribunal hearing (ACAS 2002: 8; 2001: 34; Waterhouse and Lewis 1995: 47; Tremlett and Banerji 1994: 21; Dickens *et al.* 1985: 171).

The high pre-hearing settlement rate supports the advisers' comments that most employment enquiries were resolved without a tribunal hearing. Indeed, 64 per cent of advisers indicated that the bulk of employment enquiries were settled prior to a tribunal hearing. Although bureaux had no detailed records of the stage at which cases were settled, advisers commented that 'most', 'quite a lot' or the 'vast majority' were settled prior to a hearing. Some CAB advisers were more precise indicating that 50 per cent of cases were settled prior to a tribunal hearing while others suggested a higher figure of 90 per cent. The difference may simply reflect that some bureaux keep more accurate and up-to-date records than others. A more plausible explanation is that there is variation in the experience and knowledge of advisers, and therefore the quality of employment advice given.

The high success rate at tribunal hearings is a further indicator of the effectiveness of bureaux in helping workers with employment problems. It also highlights the importance of employees having access to a representative if they are to win their cases. Without representation employees will find it difficult to negotiate the employment tribunal system, given its increasingly legalistic nature and the complexity of employment legislation (Lewis and Legard 1998: 40; Waterhouse and Lewis 1995: 56). Given these developments it is imperative that employees have access to representation when they encounter workplace problems. Indeed, research suggests that users benefit significantly from representation to the extent that represented parties achieve a higher success rate compared with unrepresented parties (DTI 2002a: 27; Dickens *et al.* 1985). Reinforcing these findings, a recent report suggested that trade union supported cases outperformed non-union cases in terms of the nature of the settlement achieved (TUC 2001d: 8).

Recognising the pivotal role of the CAB in ameliorating the imbalance in the employment relationship provides a further way of gauging their effectiveness in resolving employment disputes. Reflecting the greater resources at the disposal of employers, a recent report suggested that employers were more likely than applicants to have discussed tribunal cases with a lawyer, with 63 per cent consulting a law firm compared with 49 per cent of employees (DTI 2002a: 25). 'Inequalities of representation' of this kind in turn result in an uneven approach to the resolution of claims that favours 'highly resourced legal firms over lay representatives as well as unrepresented users of the system' (DTI 2002c: 48). The first way in which the CAB helps offset the imbalance in the employment relationship, therefore, is by providing access to specialist advice in situations of conflict. Advisers inform clients of their employment rights and guide them through the different methods of enforcement. For example, one client working for a modelling agency reported:

> They [CAB] just go through like different systems, like small claims court, all the procedures, what's involved and everything and they also told me that there's another option which is the industrial tribunal...After weighing the pros and cons of both options I decided to go to the industrial tribunal. Had I not gone there [CAB] I probably wouldnt've known about the industrial tribunal until it was too late. I would have just used the small claims court, so it did help by telling me the other option.

Although clients were not asked directly whether or not they would have pursued a claim in the absence of the CAB, it came through strongly from related questions that if the CAB had not been available many clients would not have enforced their rights. This was either because they did not know their rights and how to enforce them, or because no other sources of advice and information were available. For example, a fast food store manager commented:

> I haven't got any alternative place to go. We [employees] haven't got anything. The only thing we have, if we want to get some advice is Citizens' Advice. We are expecting that much, it is a great help what they are doing.

An administrator, unsure of her employment rights and how to enforce them, commented:

> I would never have been able to do it, I wouldn't even've known what to do, wouldnt've understood any of it, if it wasn't for them [CAB] ... I wouldnt've pursued it; I would've let my horrible boss get away with it.

Consistent with the findings of Lewis and Legard (1998: 39), it was not only a lack of knowledge or familiarity with legislation and the tribunal system, which deterred applicants from pursuing an employment tribunal case. Some interviewees also mentioned a lack of self-confidence and an inability to cope with their problem alone. For example, one interviewee reported:

> I couldn't have dealt with fighting for anything myself, I would never have done it, let's put it that way. I would have just left everything ...

An important component of the advisory process is empowering clients to participate in the resolution of their problem as fully as possible. Advisers tended to stay in the background providing clients with the necessary information to challenge their employer. For example, a receptionist, with 20 years' service, who worked at a small optometrists', who was unsure of her redundancy entitlements, commented:

> Well, I knew that I was going to be made redundant and I wanted to know what benefits I could claim in the interim period between being made redundant and finding, hopefully, another job. I wanted to know what I could claim and they [CAB] told me ... I also wasn't quite sure how much I would be getting in redundancy and they sorted that out for me. They [CAB] gave me these booklets and we were able to work out how much I would be getting in redundancy.

When the receptionist discussed the redundancy settlement with her employer, she knew she was receiving what she was entitled to as the employer's offer corroborated the information that had been provided by the CAB. In this respect, the CAB was helping to offset the inequalities associated with the employment relationship by providing clients with information to check and challenge management to ensure that they receive their statutory entitlements. For example, the receptionist commented:

At least I had ammunition first, I got the figure [redundancy] first, so I thought now when he [employer] comes up with his figure, if its not like my figure I will say something, because this is my life here and I knew I got the correct figure.

The CAB also helped to redress the power imbalance in the employment relationship by helping clients overcome their feelings of isolation and powerlessness. This was achieved by providing clients with a voice and representation. In addition, the CAB also acted as a 'back-up', helping to reinforce the employee's position by ensuring that management took the client's complaint seriously. This is consistent with the findings of Cully *et al.* (1999: 296) who suggested that management take seriously employee grievances, when they are assisted by a trade union. For example, one CAB client, working for a contract cleaning firm, commented:

If I was on my own, I would've had a lot of problems with these people [employer]; they wouldn't have taken me seriously. First of all they didn't, for the first two, three weeks they didn't, so the Citizens' Advice Bureau really helped me.

In many respects, the CAB provides clients with the service and support traditionally provided by trade unions, particularly in relation to the 'sword of justice' role. Similarly, like trade unions, the CAB are helping to counter the inequalities in the employment relationship, providing clients with information and knowledge about their rights and how to enforce them. One outcome is greater equity in the workplace as advisers act as a check against the arbitrary use of management power. For example, one adviser commented:

Yes. When the employee as an individual faces the employer they are very weak, that is why the problem has arisen in the first place. The employer thinks he can get away with everything because the employee has no power and no knowledge. Once we [CAB] step in the employer feels that there is another side; can't just get away with mistreating people. The mere fact that we are there for the employee we are already influencing the situation... obviously by starting an IT, starting legal procedures the employee wouldn't be able to do it on their own and this will affect the employer.

Relations between bureaux and trade unions

It is evident from the discussion so far that bureaux are becoming increasingly active in industrial relations, which is illustrated by their lobbying, campaigning and advice giving activities. The section below focuses on the overlapping nature of the employment work carried out by the advisers and those traditionally performed by union shop stewards. The final part of this section concentrates on the extent to which the work of the CAB complements, or competes with, the work traditionally undertaken by trade unions.

Although CAB advisers and shop stewards provide advice and representation on a range of workplace issues there are a number of significant distinctions between them (see Table 12.1), a key difference being that advisers focus almost exclusively on the interests of isolated individuals. In contrast, shop stewards focus predominantly on the collective interests of their membership to whom they are directly accountable.

Advisers generally represent workers when they have been denied their rights. In this respect, they are ensuring the enforcement or implementation of legislation or company procedures, without having any direct input into the formulation of those procedures. Shop stewards, in contrast, are not only involved in ensuring procedural equity but they can be closely involved in the design and negotiation of organisational procedures.

Although a key role of CAB advisers is the enforcement of workers' rights, they have few sanctions at their disposal. Their main sanction is statutory enforcement of rights through employment tribunals. More generally, they seek to publicise abuses of workers' rights by lobbying and campaigning on local and national employment issues. Stewards and trade unions more generally can also engage in these activities, but they can also mobilise their membership to take industrial action. In this respect, stewards can have an immediate and direct impact on the organisations employing trade union members.

Table 12.1 Representative roles of CAB advisers and shop stewards

CAB advisers	Shop stewards
Representatives of an advocacy organisation	Representatives of a membership organisation
Individual representation	Collective representation
Individual empowerment	Collective empowerment
Maximise the benefits for the client	Maximise the benefits for the collective
Sanctions: enforce legislation, encourage best practice	Sanctions: employment legislation, mobilisation of the collective
External to the organisation	Internal to the organisation
Unconstrained by organisational considerations	Constrained by organisational/management considerations
Irregular contact with management	Regular contact with management
Enquiries/clients heterogeneous	Enquiries/clients homogeneous

Despite the bulk of advisers indicating that they were substituting for the functions traditionally carried out by trade unions, only three considered themselves to be undertaking a role directly analogous to that of a shop steward when providing employment advice. For example, one adviser commented:

> Yeah, I suppose I do in a way, people come to us and ask what their rights are in the workplace and I will tell them and I might even discuss it with the employer in certain circumstances and I suppose then I feel like I'm a shop steward representing the client on their employment rights...

Advisers who did not consider themselves to be acting in a manner similar to that of a shop steward generally commented that they lacked detailed and current information on the internal dynamics of the organisations with which they deal. This was attributed to the distance between themselves and the workplace, making it difficult for advisers to acquire the intimate local knowledge possessed by stewards of the industrial relations culture, working practices, procedures and management personalities. For example, one adviser commented:

> We [CAB] just fire-fight. We're just dealing with the individual issue at this time. You can't substitute for the internal knowledge and the ability to be around at all times is what unions have got.

Bureau workers viewed themselves as being 'outside' the workplace, whereas the steward was 'inside', in regular contact with management and employees. If bureau workers possessed this knowledge, which could be gained by closer co-operation with unions, then the view was strongly expressed that it would help them develop more appropriate negotiating tactics. These views are consistent with the work of Batstone *et al.* (1977: 64–6) who suggest that stewards, particularly those undertaking a leader role, needed up-to-date information on events in the plant and members' attitudes, to enable them to determine how to react to events and to the management personalities involved.

Acquiring this detailed knowledge is extremely difficult for advisers given the generalist nature of their work, and the diverse nature of their constituents. In contrast, a steward's constituents are likely to be more homogenous in terms of their characteristics, the nature of problems experienced and industry sector. Stewards have also traditionally provided advice on a narrow range of workplace issues. The CAB, however, deal with a broader range, extending beyond the workplace to include advice on debt, benefits, housing and immigration (NACAB 2002a).

Advisers rejecting the comparison with the role of shop steward also held stereotypical views of stewards perceiving them as ideologically driven, 'opposing' and 'fighting' management. This image has endured despite research identifying steward management relations as being more complex and not necessarily dominated by adversarial relations (Batstone *et al.* 1977: 26; Godfrey and Marchington 1996: 342). The average age of advisers participating in this research was 56: old enough to have lived through the heyday of union power an image that has proven difficult to dispel.

There is a growing interest in the emergence of new industrial relations actors and the extent to which they compete with, or reinforce, the activities of trade unions (Korczynski 2002; Osterman *et al.* 2001; Abbott 1998a). For example, Osterman *et al.* suggest that emerging industrial relations actors provide opportunities to unions for greater collaboration and alliance building, activities that can help reverse membership decline. The remainder of this section focuses on the extent to which the CAB is complementing or replacing activities traditionally undertaken by trade unions.

Fourteen advisers (64 per cent) considered themselves to be acting as a substitute or replacement for the work traditionally provided by trade unions. For example, one adviser commented:

> If you see unions as being something there to represent the client's interests then I suppose 'yes' we [CAB] are in a sense filling that role, though we don't represent in such an immediate way as a trade union rep. We are more likely to be guiding in the background than being on the spot.

Echoing this viewpoint, another adviser reported:

> I think generally the bureau does, 'yes'. Substitutes for the majority of people who come through that door who've got employment problems and they're not in a trade union 'yes' we're the next best thing for them. There's no one else to fight on their behalf, is there?

What advisers were substituting for was the presence of trade unions where they were absent rather than the role itself. Where unions are present managers tend to be much more careful when managing employees (Cully *et al.* 1999). In contrast, where there is no independent worker voice management can act more arbitrarily. It is in this context that bureaux increasingly work when dealing with employment problems.

It was less common for advisers to represent union members. This reinforces the point made above that, where unions have a workplace presence, bureaux had little if any role to play. If it emerged, during an interview, that a client was a union member they would usually be referred back to their union. For example, one adviser commented:

> Well, we would try and steer him back towards his steward if it was something that could be handled internally. Sometimes for some reason people

aren't always wanting to do this. I would certainly try and duck getting too far into representation if he had a union path which he could use because, after all he is paying a sub for that sort of service.

Similarly, if a client was a non-union member but worked in a unionised environment they would be encouraged to contact their union representative. Re-directing clients towards a union indirectly assists with union recruitment, particularly where the client has little knowledge or experience of trade unions. In this respect, advisers can help to generate a greater awareness of trade unions among workers with little understanding of their role. Substitution was not occurring because bureaux believed that they could replace or undertake the functions of a union more effectively. Neither were advisers trying to outmanoeuvre unions by expanding into another area of advice giving. The expansion of the employment work of the CAB was serendipitous and had not occurred because the organisation was anxious to develop new spheres of activity. Advisers often attributed the growth in employment advice-giving to the decline in union power and the erosion of their membership base. In this respect, the employment work of the CAB was demand driven. It was into this vacuum that CAB advisers were stepping. For example, one adviser recalled that she:

... first started work when trade unions were supreme and so you never even thought about advising clients who were union members at all ... So, 'yeah', in that way I suppose we're substituting for the downfall of the trade unions ...

In many respects, the explosion in the number of employment enquiries imposed further burdens on an already pressurised organisation. The view expressed by advisers was that they would prefer unions to be more effective in dealing with worker grievances, thereby relieving the pressure on the CAB. Advisers did not consider themselves to be functional equivalents to, or in direct competition with unions, seeking to replace the work of trade unions. In many respects, the work of the CAB complemented and reinforced the work of trade unions by providing advice and support to employees, who often had no internal mechanism for resolving their workplace grievances.

Will the expansion of the employment work of the CAB nevertheless lead to a reduced demand for the services traditionally provided by unions? This effect is likely to be confined to those employees who are more economically motivated, preferring to use the free services of the CAB rather than pay subscriptions to a trade union. Competition is not occurring at an institutional level in the sense that the respective organisations are attempting to attract more members/clients to increase their membership/client base, but from an individual level, as individuals select the course of action resulting in the minimum of costs to them. The issue here echoes the problem of the 'free rider' confronting unions, when employees want the advantages of being a trade union member without having to pay subscriptions.

Rather than competing with the work of trade unions the employment work of bureaux complements and reinforces the work of the labour movement on a number of levels. First, the volume of employment work handled by the CAB confirms the need for effective worker representation and greater employment protection. Second, the overlapping nature of the work of the CAB and trades unions, in the area of employment, provides opportunities for the two organisations to collaborate over issues of shared concern (see earlier). There could also be greater collaboration in relation to the exchange of information. For example, bureaux are particularly well informed in relation to the issue of welfare benefits. This type of information would be particularly valuable to employees who have been made redundant. Similarly, trade unions have greater industry knowledge and access to legal support. The exchange of information in this area may help advisers negotiate more effectively. Third, the increasing involvement of the CAB, an independent and impartial organisation, not traditionally associated with representing workers' interests, gives greater weight and legitimacy to union concerns for protection of workers. In this respect, the CAB reinforces and complements the work of trade unions.

Conclusion

The CAB has provided advice to citizens, often during periods of political and social upheaval, like the Second World War, when the organisation was first established. Its role has further evolved in response to economic, political and social changes, such as the creation of the welfare state and the growth of consumerism (Brasnett 1964: 15). Consequently, over time, bureaux have become established as important and credible sources of advice in areas where initially they had little knowledge or experience. The involvement of the CAB in employment issues is following a similar pattern. Crisis in the labour movement has resulted in the increasing participation of the CAB in the area of employment advice, a role that is unlikely to be reversed given the continued decline in union membership.

Given these developments, there is compelling evidence suggesting that some of the functions traditionally monopolised by trade union representatives, such as advice-giving, handling grievances and negotiating with management, are being performed by bureau advisers. However, despite the overlapping nature of the employment work of the two organisations CAB and trade unions are not functional equivalents. Indeed, there are a number of distinctions, the representative work of the CAB is primarily concerned with empowering employees with individual workplace grievances, and their resolution through the enforcement of individual rights. In contrast, unions are membership organisations, which emphasise the collective resolution of grievances through the mobilisation of their collective base.

Data gathered as part of this research revealed a high settlement rate, with most cases resolved without submitting a claim to an employment tribunal. Without the intervention of the CAB, employees, who often had very little awareness of their rights and how to enforce them, would simply be unable to effectively pursue their grievance. It is in this area that the CAB makes a significant impact, as their involvement encourages employers to take the concerns of employees seriously, without which many employees would remain isolated and unable to enforce their rights. Therefore, a key outcome of the intervention of the CAB is the amelioration of the inequalities in knowledge, information and power for the isolated employee, when faced with an employment problem. Given the positive outcomes associated with the employment work of the CAB, and their ability to influence other industrial relations actors, it is entirely appropriate to consider them as an important and effective industrial relations actor.

It is also important to recognise that bureaux are not competing against trade unions, or expanding deliberately, into areas normally the preserve of trade unions. They have serendipitously stepped into the vacuum created as a result of the decline of trade unions. Advisers are, therefore, substituting for the presence of trade unions, where they are absent, rather than acting as a replacement for them. Rather than competing against trade unions, the CAB complements their work through its campaigning, lobbying and advice giving activities. In this respect, the CAB provides the labour movement with a potential ally given the overlapping nature of their work and areas of shared concern. The two organisations, therefore, should build on their respective strengths and expand the areas of co-operation in the area of employment, so as to provide workers with greater protection and an enhanced voice in the workplace.

13
Organising the Low Paid: East London's Living Wage Campaign as a Vehicle for Change

Jane Wills

Introduction

In the summer of 2001, a team of researchers got together to gather information on the pay and conditions of almost 100 low-paid workers in East London. Working undercover to approach workers in hospital corridors, security offices, station platforms, canteens, public parks and the corporate splendour of Canary Wharf in the middle of the night, researchers used a simple questionnaire to expose the reality of low-paid work in one of the world's leading global cities. In the main, these workers were employed by private contractors to provide essential services such as cleaning, catering, portering, security and maintenance for a wide range of clients in both the public and private sectors. At the time, the national minimum wage was £3.70 an hour and most of those interviewed were found to earn around, or just above, this amount. More alarmingly, however, those who were not, or never had been, directly employed by the public sector were found to have minimal rates of overtime pay (if anything), no London Weighting, no sick pay, no company pension and no compassionate leave. Most had only the legal minimum of 20 days holiday a year (including eight national bank holidays) and very few were claiming the in-work benefits to which they were entitled. Those workers with dependent children were found to work long hours of overtime or at a second job to try and survive (for a fuller account of the data collected, see Wills 2001b).

Two years later in early June 2003, more than 300 of these low-paid workers, employed by ISS Mediclean to provide domestic, portering, catering, car parking, security and switchboard services at Whipps Cross Hospital in East London, were to be found on a lively picket line outside the hospital, demanding a living wage. After these workers had joined the East London Communities Organisation (TELCO) to take part in its living wage campaign, membership of the local branch of UNISON had increased by 300 per cent amongst contract workers (from 61 to about 350), the number of stewards had increased from none to four, and the union had submitted a claim for parity in terms and conditions with NHS staff. Contract staff employed by the same company at the Homerton and those employed by Medirest at Mile End and St Clement's Hospitals had settled their claims in the same week. Through their membership of TELCO and the living wage campaign, UNISON branches in East London had started to work together to support contract staff. This new activity, when coupled with the support of campaign organisers, meant that contract workers joined and took part in the union as never before. By working with the community, the union had gained much needed moral authority and media attention over an issue of social and economic injustice. This paper explores the development of this living wage campaign, the first of its kind in the UK, and puts it in the context of more extensive experience in the USA.

In what follows, this chapter explores the problem of low paid urban labour markets and the impact that can be made by living wage campaigns. The rest of the chapter then turns to the living wage campaign in East London, drawing on material collected through interviews, participant observation and close involvement throughout the campaign, to provide a brief overview of the campaign thus far, and the wider lessons it holds for those seeking to represent low-paid workers in Britain today.

Low-paid labour markets in the UK

It is now widely acknowledged that income inequality has widened in the UK since the 1980s. In contrast to the previous two decades, when differentials remained fairly constant, the wage gap increased very sharply after about 1979 (Gosling *et al.* 2000). For those in the upper echelons of the labour market, real wages have increased exponentially over this period, while for those at the bottom, there has been little real growth. Over time, such differences in pay have accumulated and further widened the gap between rich and poor. If we take London as an example, in 1979 the top 10 per cent of male full-time earners had 2.6 times more income than the bottom 10 per cent, but by 2000 this ratio had grown to 4.16 (Buck *et al.* 2002: 155). Despite dramatic increases in the costs of housing, childcare, transportation and living expenses over the past 20 years, wages for those at the bottom have not increased very much, if at all, in real terms.

Explanations for such widening inequality have focused on the impact of increased international competition (particularly in labour intensive manufacturing industries), the shift away from manufacturing towards service employment, and technological changes that have increased the premium on qualifications and reduced the opportunities for unskilled workers to find high-paying jobs (see Gosling *et al.* 2000). But in addition, the decline in labour market institutions has also left its mark on the low paid. In 1993, the Conservative Government abolished the 26 wages councils that had set minimum national standards of pay since 1909, leaving many of the most vulnerable workers without any floor to their wages and conditions of work until the Labour Government began to reverse this policy in 1999 (Machin 1997).

During the 1980s and 1990s trade unions were also assaulted with a series of legal changes designed to undermine their power and influence, and in conjunction with ongoing economic changes, this led to a major decline in their numerical strength and effectiveness, limiting their ability to regulate pay at the bottom. Moreover, those sectors of the service economy, which are prone to low pay, such as hospitality, retail and business support services are poorly unionised, the structure of the industries making it very difficult to organise those doing the work. It is well known that high labour turnover, fragmented workforces spread across many workplaces and shift working make it difficult for unions to organise, and there is growing evidence both from the USA and the UK that traditional models of 'industrial unionism' are poorly suited to workers in these low-paid service jobs (for the US, see Cobble 1999; Wial 1994; and for the UK, see Wills 2004; 2002c; 2001a).

Yet the subcontracting of support services, both through privatisation in the public sector and contracting practices in the private sector, has also had a great effect on the incidence of low pay. During the 1980s and 1990s public sector bodies were put under political and economic pressure to subcontract jobs like cleaning, catering, caring, maintenance and security in order to save money, and cost savings have come through the inferior terms and conditions on offer to staff. Sub-contracting tasks has effectively made low status work yet more inferior, further undermining terms and conditions of work. As Allen and Henry (1997: 189) put it:

> The nature of the work, the fact that it is routine service work and not work regarded as skilful or professional, does signify a subordinate status but it is reified when it becomes *contract* cleaning, *contract* catering and *contract* security. If the same functions were performed 'in house', the cleaners, the kitchen porters, the waiters and the security guards would share the same corporate identity as the rest of the firm's workforce and thus very likely the same employment rights and benefits. (Emphasis in the original)

Moreover, as Polly Toynbee points out in her book *Hard Work* (2003), such subcontracting also divides contracted workers from their colleagues on the same site. In the case of the hospitals in East London, for example, contracted staff have no direct managerial relationship with the NHS. Despite playing a vital role in hospital services, there is no mechanism for communicating with NHS staff and managers, leaving contract staff isolated from the rest of the team. Specialised skills, additional training and career development have also been lost.

The research conducted into low pay outlined in the introduction above, and additional research into homecare, has highlighted that such subcontracted relationships exist right across the public and private sectors in East London.[1] Since the introduction of market testing to the NHS in 1983 and the implementation of Compulsory Competitive Tendering by Local Authorities (following the 1988 Local Government Act), the NHS and Councils in the area have subcontracted large volumes of work (for more on the impact of privatisation in the public sector, see Reimer 1998; Sachdev 2001).[2] In East London's hospitals, the research conducted in 2001 found that support services were managed by ISS Mediclean, a Danish-owned multinational company in three locations, and by Medirest, a UK-owned subsidiary of the multinational company Compass in another. Local Councils had also subcontracted a large number of their services including school dinners (to Scolarest (Compass) in Hackney and Tower Hamlets), building cleaning (to Comatec (Onyx) and ISS in Hackney, and OCS and ISS in Tower Hamlets), refuse collection (to Service Team in Hackney and Onyx in Tower Hamlets) and leisure services (to Greenwich Leisure Ltd in Newham and Waltham Forest). In each case, the research identified a 'multi-tier' workforce, as staff who had been transferred from the public sector had their terms and conditions of work protected by Transfer of Undertakings (Protection of Employment) Regulations, 1981 (TUPE) whereas those employed since privatisation had inferior terms and conditions of work. UNISON officers at the Homerton argued that in just 5 years since the contract had been tendered out at their hospital, as many as 50 per cent of staff were on the new terms and conditions. Not only were wages lower for new starters, but these staff had very limited rates of overtime pay, no sick pay, no compassionate leave, no London Weighting and no pension. There were also fewer people employed to complete the work, using poor quality equipment with little opportunity for training and career development. Cost savings were clearly made at the expense of those doing the work *and* the quality of the service provided.

A similar process of subcontracting was identified in the transport sector as both public and private companies used a range of contractors to provide cleaning services for stations, buses and trains, again with very poor terms and conditions of work. And finally, the same companies were among those found to be providing services to the corporations housed at the prestigious Canary Wharf complex. Contractors such as ISS and OCS were employing cleaners on rates just above the minimum wage with no additional benefits. Moreover, in every case, the majority of workers were found to be from minority ethnic communities, many of them new immigrants from West Africa. Outside the public sector, most of these workers had no access to a trade union and even when contracted to work for the public sector, where various trade unions have recognition, many had opted to remain outside the union fold.

Subcontracting has made it more difficult for unions to organise workers as they are employed and managed by a separate company to many of their colleagues on the same site. In addition, the poor conditions of work increase staff turnover, reduce commitment and mean workers are less likely to stay and fight to improve their working conditions than move on elsewhere. In this way, subcontracting further undermines the position of workers who were already in a weak bargaining position, leaving them ill-equipped to organise for improvements in their conditions of work. Since the Labour Government came to power in 1997, privatisation has continued apace, and although the government has recently changed the law concerning Local Authorities, insisting that new contract staff cannot be employed on terms 'less favourable' than their ex-public sector colleagues, this does not cover those employed by contractors who have not taken on ex-public sector staff (known as spot-purchased services) nor does it cover the NHS and other public services.[3]

In addition, the Labour Government has sought to tackle some of the problems of low pay by introducing the National Minimum Wage in 1999 and paying tax credits to workers whose income falls below a recognised standard. These measures have, however, been insufficient to erode in-work poverty, or to 'make work pay', especially in a city as expensive as London (GLA 2002). While the minimum wage is not sufficient to support a household, the take up of in-work benefits has also been very low. The process of claiming benefits is complicated, many are ignorant of their entitlement and others are working in the 'unofficial' economy making it impossible to claim additional support from the state. Thus, even though progress has been made, it is not yet sufficient to end the problem of low pay in the UK.

The living wage campaign as a vehicle for change

In the USA over the past decade, a new weapon has been developed by community organisations, faith groups and trade unions to tackle these growing problems of low pay, poor conditions of work, subcontracting and weak labour organisations. Just as in the UK, sluggish rates of wage growth and weak wage regulation for those at the bottom end of the labour market have produced a 'wage gap' between the federal minimum wage ($5.15 an hour at the time of writing) and the amount required to actually live (and research usually puts this figure at something like 50 per cent higher than the minimum wage and up to 100 per cent higher in areas of California). New alliances of community, faith and labour organisations have worked together to put pressure on local politicians to promote a living, rather than a minimum wage for workers providing important local services in American cities. In the main, such ordinances have ensured that a living wage is paid to those providing contracted services for the public sector, but in some cases, this has been extended to those companies in receipt of concessions and subsidies from the state and even to City-wide ordinances (such as that proposed in New Orleans, Pollin *et al.* 2002; see also Pollin 2002; 2001; Luce and Pollin 1999; Pollin and Luce 1998). The first such living wage ordinance was secured in Baltimore in 1994 and at the time of writing, there are at least 80 ordinances in effect, covering half of America's 20 largest conurbations (including Los Angeles, Baltimore, San Jose, Boston, Milwaukee, San Francisco, New York and Detroit).

Drawing on arguments that stretch back beyond the New Deal of the 1930s, supporters of the living wage have made the case for wage increases in economic, political and moral terms (for an excellent historical overview of arguments for a living wage in the USA, see Glickmann 1997). A growing number of scholars have challenged the 'perversity thesis' that suggests increasing wages will have an unintended, harmful effect on the intended beneficiaries by reducing employment opportunities and incentives for the acquisition of skill. It is now more widely recognised that the laws of supply and demand do not apply to the labour market as they do elsewhere. When wages rise there is scope for companies to increase productivity or prices rather than reduce profits or jobs. Lower turnover also reduces spending on recruitment and training. And in addition, there is often very little scope for reducing employment in sectors that are already fully stretched to meet service standards (see Prasch and Sheth 1999; for the UK, see Dickens *et al.* 1999). Research into the actual costs of those living wage ordinances that are already in place has found remarkably few costs associated with the increased wages paid to those employed by contractors (for the case of Baltimore where contract costs increased by only 1.2 per cent, see Schoenberger 2000).

At a deeper level, however, there are also important arguments to be made about the costs that low pay incurs for the wider community. As Prasch and Sheth (1999: 470–1) put it, there are widespread economic advantages if firms are forced to pay well and invest in their staff:

> [F]irms that hire labor at below-subsistence wages, or maintain a dangerous or unhealthy workplace without paying a compensating wage, effectively transfer a portion of their production costs to the larger community. In this sense, low-wages or irregular employment generates a social cost of production that is not paid by the business enterprise. Labor, unless it possesses adequate bargaining power, cannot force firms to cover these costs. It follows that either these costs are borne by society at large, or society must tolerate the 'gradual diminishment' in the quality of its labor force.

Increasing the rate of pay provides an incentive for firms to provide training for staff, to secure staff loyalty and increase productivity, benefiting the wider society.

Moreover, paying living wages can be construed as an important aspect of a progressive economic development strategy, actually improving the competitiveness of an urban economy, making it more, rather than less, attractive to incoming firms. Better paid workers are healthier, more productive, their children are likely to do better at school, the city benefits from lower crime rates and more taxes are paid. As Schoenberger (2000: 435; see also Ambrose (2003) for arguments about the exported costs of poverty pay in the UK) suggests, poverty is not good for business success:

> Poverty, quite plainly, generates insecurity and difficulty for the rich and poor alike. It severely limits the local market which makes a city uninteresting to many kinds of business. It produces ill-prepared workers whose lives are easily disrupted by small catastrophes. If the car breaks down, if the kid gets sick, it suddenly becomes impossible to be a reliable worker. Poverty also generates poor health among workers, making them less reliable still and raising the cost of employing them ... it produces also a meagre tax base and poor physical infrastructure and public services.

Such arguments have allowed living wage coalitions in the USA to engage in deliberations about the evolution of local political-economy, ranging far beyond the confines of debates about the particular wages paid to particular staff.

Politically, living wage campaigns have also contributed to re-energising the labour movement in the USA. Those areas of the labour market that had proved hardest for unions to organise and regulate in recent years have again become viable territory through the alliances built over living wage campaigns. Although contract workers have little bargaining power on their own, alliances with community and faith organisations have helped to apply political and moral pressure on public authorities to ensure that justice is done (see Walsh 2000). Arguments have been made to 'see that public money is not used to create or subsidize "working poverty"' (Nissen 2000: 30). And in so doing, unions have the chance to take part in new successful social movements that are able to reach and mobilise new groups of workers, address the need for social and economic justice and attempt to democratise local political economy. In a number of cities, unions are now acting as part of wider social movements for change and in these cases, new organisations have been established to cement relationships on a more permanent basis. Innovative examples include the Los Angeles Alliance for a New Economy (LAANE), and the Campaign for a Sustainable Milwaukee (Reynolds 2001). Unions in these locations have begun to address labour–market wide issues such as training, housing, transport and the environment (for the case of LA, see Pastor 2001).

In practice, however, American unions have not necessarily seized the opportunities that living wage campaigns and associated coalitions pose to work in this way. Indeed, Nissen uses the case of Miami to demonstrate that it has been possible for unions to take part in living wage campaigns *without* transforming themselves into social movement organisations. Despite leadership from the local American Federation of Labour–Congress of Industrial Organizations (AFL–CIO), via the Central Labor Council (the equivalent of a UK trades union council) on the issue, Nissen found that local unions in Miami saw little immediate advantage, and were reluctant to get more involved in the campaign, as he explained:

> Living wage issues were not being approached by unions primarily from a point of view of seeking to raise the floor of all wages in the local labour market, but from a viewpoint seeking first and foremost immediate institutional advantage. Seeing none, most unions chose to play little or no role in the earlier stages of the campaign, despite general sympathy for the cause. (Nissen 2000: 45)

The living wage ordinance in Miami was thus passed without involving a transformation in trade union activity or the development of a permanent coalition between labour and community in the city, despite the best hopes of the AFL-CIO at both national and city-wide scales.

Moreover, even in Baltimore, the union–community alliance behind the first successful living wage campaign only involved one trade union, American Federation of State, Country and Municipal Employees (AFSCME). Through an alliance built on the common ground shared by the union and the local Industrial Areas Foundation (IAF) body called BUILD (Baltimoreans United in Leadership Development), the living wage campaign began to evolve. Indeed, as Walsh (2000: 1600) points out:

> BUILD and AFSCME shared similar concerns about the proliferation of low-wage jobs in the city, the same constituency of low and moderate (largely African-American) workers, a common interest in city and state politics, and a commitment to experimental organizing techniques.

BUILD and AFSCME had concrete reasons for working together. On the one hand, BUILD was concerned about the plight of the working poor in the city and the lack of 'trickle-down' that had resulted from massive economic investment in the city, and recognised the need for improved city-wide wage regulation and the redistribution of wealth. While on the other hand, AFSCME was suffering the fall in membership that comes with privatisation and the move of their members into the private sector, and the union needed to find new mechanisms to organise and regulate ex-public sector employment. The idea of a living wage campaign emerged from this set of mutual interests, only later becoming a model for the rest of the USA and beyond. Moreover, through their experiences, BUILD and AFSCME established a new organisation for low-paid workers in the city, the Solidarity

Sponsoring Committee, providing low-cost membership benefits to workers in high turnover and non-union recognised jobs, which has not been replicated elsewhere (Walsh 2000).

In the UK, the concept of a living wage is certainly not new, and the origins of the phrase are said to rest with a group of striking miners in England during the 1880s (see Glickmann 1997; Webb and Webb 1897). As early as 1891, trade union pressure forced Parliament to address the problems of subcontracting, and a fair wages clause was implemented in all Government contracting after this date. Local authorities such as the London County Council took up this approach and adopted fair wages clauses in contracting construction and engineering, ensuring 'no less favourable' terms and conditions of work (Citrine 1935). At this time, the London Trades Council established its own contracts committee to monitor the allocation of contracts, carefully reviewing the wages and conditions paid and highlighting any violations (even if the workers concerned did not belong to the trade union movement). As the trade union movement grew during the twentieth century, it continued to use both economic and political pressure – via the organised workplace and the Labour Party – to secure advances in the pay of those at the bottom. Indeed, it was not until the 1980s, and the advent of a neo-liberal Conservative Government, ongoing trade union decline and the expansion of the low-wage service sector, that wage inequality really started to rise. As might be expected, such conditions have made it difficult for unions to survive, let alone find the reserves to tackle the more difficult reaches of the low-paid labour market. It is only in recent years, and particularly in the light of American experiences and in the shadow of a Labour Government, that the unions have looked more closely at organising and that the concept of living wage/fair wage clauses in public contracting have re-surfaced as a political tool. In this regard, the following section of the paper explores the East London living wage campaign in more depth.

TELCO's living wage campaign

TELCO was established in 1995, in four Boroughs in East London, through the work of the Citizen Organising Foundation (COF), a body that seeks to develop the political skills of community leaders in order to empower communities to take greater control over their lives. At present, TELCO is a coalition of about 40 local organisations including churches, mosques, schools, community centres and trade union branches representing at least 50 000 people. In the early years, TELCO led local campaigns on supermarket pricing in poor communities, the quality of local hospital services, sites for travelling people and the paucity of labour market opportunities for local people. In leading such campaigns, TELCO employed up to three full-time organisers but always lay great store on finding leaders within affiliate members and developing their role through training and support. In philosophy and practice, COF and TELCO follow the model of the American Industrial Areas Federation (IAF), established in the 1950s by Saul Alinsky, to develop broad-based collective organisation for community empowerment and progress (see Warren 2001; Alinsky 1971).

Drawing on the experiences of their sister organisation BUILD in Baltimore, TELCO started work on an East London living wage campaign in early 2001. This initiative represented a major new campaign for an organisation as small as TELCO, and it was viewed in part, as a means to develop new relationships with the trade unions in London's East End. Indeed, the public sector trade union, UNISON, funded the important research that kick-started the campaign and UNISON and TELCO have since continued to work very closely together. In 2001, the Family Budget Unit was commissioned to measure the essential expenditure incurred by various family units in East London and thus establish the income needed to support a family with a 'low cost but acceptable' standard of living.[4] Despite the conservative assumptions made in these calculations (such as the absence of debt, no special needs and the availability of local authority housing), the research produced a figure of £6.30 an hour as East London's living wage (see Parker 2001; and in 2003 this figure was increased to £6.50 due to inflation). At the time, the Labour Government's Low Pay Commission had set a National Minimum Wage of £3.70 an hour, as much as £2.60 short of the living wage target. Moreover, despite increases which took the minimum wage to £4.50 by October 2003, this national rate remained £2 short of anything like a real living wage.

East London's living wage campaign was officially launched at a large meeting of up to a thousand people from TELCO's affiliates, official guests and the media in Walthamstow Assembly Halls in April 2001. Since then, the campaign has developed by using a combination of academic research and events to outline the scale of the problem; holding large public meetings to put direct and mediated pressure on local politicians and officials who are able to implement change; and directing trade union, community and media pressure on very particular targets (the hospitals, Local Authorities, Strategic Health Authorities and HSBC's global headquarters at Canary Wharf). Such pressure has involved mass attendance at the board meetings of NHS Trusts at the hospitals, demonstrations outside the hospitals to mark particular events during the campaign, demonstrations and share-holder attendance at HSBC's Annual General Meetings and the mass occupation of an HSBC branch in a central part of the City at a busy time of the year. Although it is difficult to capture such a multifaceted campaign, some of the key events are presented chronologically in Table 13.1.

During the first year of the campaign, seven local UNISON branches were convinced to join TELCO, representing most of the major health and local government branches in East London (covering the Boroughs of Hackney, Newham, Tower Hamlets and Waltham Forest). In addition, the campaign has developed good working relationships with the finance union UNIFI

Table 13.1 A chronology of the East London living wage campaign, April 2001–June 2003

Date	Events
April 2001	Campaign launched at large public assembly. Announced living wage figure of £6.30 an hour (£6.50 at the time of writing). Invited local MPs,Council, trade union and community leaders to sign up to a living wage.
September 2001	Published *Mapping Low Pay in East London*, documenting the extent to which low-paid workers are in the gap between the minimum and living wage, with very poor conditions of work. Launched at a conference held at Queen Mary, University of London.
November 2001	Public assembly of up to 1000 held at York Hall, Bethnal Green, attended by local MPs, officials and John Monks (General Secretary of the TUC), restated the case for a living wage.
December 2001	Occupied a branch of HSBC in Oxford Street to protest at the low pay and poor conditions of cleaners at the Canary Wharf site.
April 2002	Parliamentary hearing for the living wage campaign, held at the House of Commons with invited MPs and a guest speaker from Baltimore.
May 2002	At least 40 ISS workers, along with representatives from local mosques, churches, colleges and the media attended a meeting of the NHS Trust board at the Homerton Hospital, made a presentation and handed over a petition with 600 signatures from hospital staff.
May 2002	Attended AGM of HSBC to demand a meeting with the Chairman, Sir John Bond, to discuss contracting arrangements at Canary Wharf.
July 2002	UNISON/TELCO submitted a claim for improved conditions for staff working for the contractors ISS Mediclean and Medirest at 5 East London's hospitals.
Autumn 2002	Living wage campaign supported by Billy Bragg's tour, raising the profile and finance from gigs across the country.
November 2002	Held living wage march involving local schools along the Mile End Road before large public assembly at the People's Palace, Queen Mary, University of London. Led by black Pentecostal churches from the area.
March 2003	Held academic conference at the London School of Economics to make the case for a living wage, drawing on US experience.
April 2003	Public rally of 200 contract workers involved in the East London claims held in Stratford, addressed by the General Secretary of UNISON and workplace activists, building for industrial action in pursuit of the claim.
May 2003	Public assembly of about 500 held in Stratford, to confirm support for a strike of contract staff in the hospitals. New aspect of the campaign also developed to work on better ethical standards in UK contracting practice.
May 2003	Demonstration outside and inside HSBC's AGM, again putting pressure on the bank over contracting arrangements at Canary Wharf.
June 2003	Improved offer accepted by contract staff at the Homerton and Mile End/St Clements Hospitals, to secure immediate improvements and parity with NHS conditions by 2006. Strike and large demonstration held to try and increase the wage level and improve the offer at Whipps Cross Hospital.

(who have members at the Canary Wharf complex including the banks HSBC and Barclays), but other unions and the regional TUC have been very slow or even reluctant to get more involved. These developments relate, at least in part, to the strong common ground shared by TELCO and UNISON. Just as in Baltimore, both organisations have an interest in the impact of subcontracting on pay and conditions of work, both have a deep interest in the provision and quality of local public services, both focus their attention on local and city-wide politics and the actions of public sector organisations, and both represent large numbers of locally resident workers. Most significantly, however, UNISON also had some key officers and lay officials who were willing to take a risk by supporting this innovative strategy. Without the intervention of one national officer in particular, who encouraged local branches to get more involved, it would have been difficult to win over UNISON branches to the campaign.

Indeed, building such relationships has proved much more difficult in the private sector, not least because the contract workers who are employed at business centres like Canary Wharf are not unionised. While white collar banking staff do belong to Unifi, a union that has showed solidarity with the plight of the low paid and TELCO's campaign, the unions that would be expected to organise cleaners, catering and security staff in the private sector, such as the TGWU and the GMB, have been reluctant to get more involved. These unions have stronger traditions in manufacturing and the limited resources that they have devoted to organising have been spent there, rather than on hard-to-reach service-based workers.

Thus it is perhaps no surprise that the activities of the campaign have had greatest impact on UNISON's health branches, and it is here that the benefits of working together are most clearly displayed. At the Homerton Hospital in Hackney, about 200 domestic, catering and portering staff are employed by ISS Mediclean; at Whipps Cross in Waltham Forest, ISS Mediclean employs about 360 staff as porters, domestics, caterers, switchboard, security and car parking staff; and at Mile End and St Clements Hospitals, Medirect (Compass) employs about 140 staff to do similar tasks.[5] In each case, the local UNISON branch found it increasingly difficult to retain union membership amongst these workers after privatisation. Once the work shifts to the private sector and new workers are employed on inferior terms and conditions, turnover increases and staff commitment falls. Moreover, new employees who have never worked for the NHS have much less inclination to join UNISON than those who were once part of the NHS team. In addition, privatisation has tended to involve major reductions in the facility time available to shop stewards and branch officials, increasing the informality of arrangements and removing the opportunity to negotiate or even contact the NHS managers in charge of the Trust. Likewise, stewards employed by the NHS are often refused facility time to deal with contract staff as they have different employers. Not surprisingly then, during the 1990s, UNISON membership amongst contract staff had declined in each branch. Getting involved in TELCO has allowed these UNISON branches to turn this around. By working with a representative body from the local community, UNISON has found a new mechanism to communicate directly with the NHS Trust about this group of staff. The fact that a community body is raising issues of low pay and poor conditions, the implications for service delivery and social justice, has strengthened UNISON's case. In effect, TELCO has recast trade union issues as being critical to the well-being of the whole community, not just workers, making it harder for a public body like an NHS Trust to ignore. TELCO has pointed out that the hospitals are public bodies charged with looking after the health needs of the local community in these poor inner-city locations, yet managers are ignoring the health effects of the employment provided on site. Workers who don't earn enough to eat well, who have to work long hours and/or more than one job to survive upon, who don't have sick pay or leave to attend medical appointments and who receive no thanks for their work, are much more likely to present serious health challenges to the NHS. In addition, poor service delivery caused by cuts in staffing, inadequate equipment and low staff morale in cleaning and domestic work can increase the level of hospital-acquired infections, and imperil the wider community. And although the local branches of UNISON have raised this injustice in the past, only to be told that the hospitals had to save money on 'hotel' services in order to put resources into front line healthcare, the living wage campaign has given the union a much more powerful voice to start to agitate around these concerns. Moreover, the campaign has boosted the morale of staff to know that others are concerned about their plight, as a UNISON branch official from the Homerton explained:

> The campaign has been good because it has shown the staff – the NHS staff and the new ISS staff – that there are other people and other organisations out there who have an interest and concern... It gives us that extra dimension of moving it [the debate about low pay] out from the hospital where it seems to get trapped in negotiations that never get anywhere... so it gives it that boost, it adds an external force to it.

Examples of community–union pressure include a lobby of a meeting of Homerton's NHS Trust Board in May 2002. TELCO and UNISON successfully mobilised at least 40 ISS workers along with representatives from local mosques, churches, colleges and the media to this event. After handing over a petition with 600 signatures from hospital staff, the case for a living wage was presented with quiet passion by a nun from a religious community in Hackney. The Trust was forced to concede the moral case for improved pay and conditions but restated the financial limitations they faced. Similar initiatives at the other hospitals in the area resulted in UNISON activists deciding to submit a detailed claim for improved wages and conditions (a living wage), across the contractors at five East London hospitals in July 2002. This unique initiative sought immediate improvements in pay and conditions, leading contract workers closer to parity with NHS terms and conditions, with the ultimate goal of full parity. Launched with a demonstration at Whipps Cross Hospital, the claim featured on the BBC television news and in the local press, increasing interest in the campaign.[6]

But six months later and despite promises from the contractors to move forward in negotiations, no progress had been made at any of the hospitals. Although they were now well organised, UNISON members employed by the contractors at the Homerton, Whipps Cross, Mile End and St Clements hospitals became increasingly frustrated and decided to pursue ballots for industrial action. In each case, the ballots were successful and UNISON moved towards strike action. At the eleventh hour, the NHS Trust Boards, ISS and Compass put together improved offers that were accepted at the Homerton and Mile End and St Clements Hospitals, but rejected at Whipps Cross. In the latter case, two days of very successful strike action in June 2003 led to new talks and an improved offer being made. At each hospital, sustained action by TELCO's living wage campaign together with strengthened negotiations by UNISON had secured immediate increases in pay and conditions, and parity with NHS staff by 2006 (for the details of the offers made, see Table 13.2).[7] Rather than working outside trade union channels, the campaign had given UNISON and their members in contract services the confidence they needed to pursue a living wage claim.

Table 13.2 The improved wages and conditions secured at East London's hospitals by the living wage campaign (June 2003)

Hospital (contractor)	New wages and conditions secured
Homerton (ISS Mediclean)	Immediate: 13 per cent pay increase to £5 an hour minimum; 3 days compassionate leave; 22 days annual leave entitlement (after 3 years' employment); ISS sick pay scheme (12 days a year max.); enhanced Sunday hours of £1.20 an hour. By April 2006 parity with NHS pay rates and all conditions of work except pensions (binding on all contractors in future).
Mile End and St Clements (Medirect)	Immediate: pay increase to £5.16 an hour and 10 days' sick leave a year. By April 2006 parity with NHS pay rates and all conditions of work except pensions (binding on all contractors in future).
Royal London (ISS Mediclean)	Despite not taking an active part in the campaign at the time, staff were awarded the same offer as that at the Homerton.
Whipps Cross (ISS Mediclean)	As at the Homerton, with the addition that those staff already in receipt of £5 an hour or more had a small lumpsum payment at the time of the agreement.

As part of this action it was essential to increase membership of UNISON and to develop new leadership amongst contract staff. TELCO's living wage organiser worked closely with a UNISON-employed organiser to develop relationships with UNISON branch officials and workers at each site. These organisers spent many hours in each hospital, meeting workers, listening to their stories and encouraging them to get involved in the campaign and the union. At the Homerton, UNISON's membership increased from 100 to nearly 200, at Whipps Cross from 61 to 340, and at Mile End and St Clement's from 70 to 140 over the two years of the campaign (generating more than 400 new members across the three sites). Moreover, in each case, new shop stewards were identified and developed during the campaign. Workers initially recruited through the living wage campaign were able to develop their interests and leadership skills. Some of these new union members found the inner strength to speak at TELCO assemblies, in front of hundreds of people, developing into new union leaders at work. Whereas these workers had been seen as difficult, if not impossible, to organise in the past, they had become the best organised section of each revitalised branch just two years after joining the campaign. As the UNISON organiser explained: 'TELCO have used a new approach to engage people, to inspire, to get people active, to give people things to do and so teach them to take responsibility for their own situation. Now UNISON is getting involved in developing the activists that have come forward to find out what they can do.'

In very different circumstances, TELCO has also taken the living wage campaign to the prestigious office complex at Canary Wharf. Since it was built in 1980s with massive public subsidy, Canary Wharf has come to symbolise the social and economic inequality of London's East End. Whereas financial and media professionals work there during the day, often for huge salaries and lavish benefits, low-paid cleaners labour during the night, for as little as £4.50 an hour without any additional perks. Even though these workers do not have union recognition, TELCO has sought new points of leverage to try and ensure that cleaning contracts are only awarded to those contractors who pay a living wage to their staff.

To focus the campaign, TELCO targeted the new global headquarters of HSBC that opened in mid-2002, demanding that the tower be cleaned by those earning a living rather than a minimum wage. By picketing a retail bank branch on Oxford Street and lobbying the company's AGM with the media present, they have forced the company to at least meet and discuss the plight of the low paid. Indeed, those cleaners employed by OCS at the HSBC Tower are now the best-paid contractors on the Canary Wharf site, even if pay and conditions are still below living wage standards. As at the hospitals, the campaign has thrown up new leaders from amongst the workers, helping to identify those who are willing to speak out and talk to the press. Despite efforts to develop a relationship with the TGWU, however, TELCO has not yet found a trade union partner with whom they can organise workers at this key site. The TGWU has made promises but in practice the union has been reluctant to commit the necessary time and resources to organise workers who are only present at nights, with the additional problems of high turnover, English language difficulties and trouble paying union dues. Without trade union organisation on the inside, it has been difficult to wield community and media pressure to greatest effect.

In the latest stage of the campaign, TELCO is focusing more explicitly on the private sector, talking to those involved in the contract cleaning industry, in the City and in the world of Corporate Social Responsibility about setting a new standard for employment practices in business support services in the UK. Just as they are under pressure to audit their international supply chains for ethical practice, large companies will be asked to support good practice in contracting at home, covering wages, conditions and training. Although trade union organisation at the workplace will be essential to ensure compliance with good employment standards, TELCO has been able to bring community and media pressure to bear on leading corporations at locations like Canary Wharf, making it easier to defend the space to unionise on the ground.[8]

Conclusion

It is clear that trade unions face a real challenge in trying to tackle the problems faced by low-paid service workers, and subcontracted workers in particular. The old workplace-focused models of trade union organisational practice and structures are ill-suited to the service sector where workers are spread across a number of sites, labour turnover can be high, shift working is common, workplace commitment is weak and managerial control is off-site. Living wage campaigns provide a new vehicle to intervene in these situations. As this paper has outlined, workers can be mobilised to take part in a campaign involving trade unions and the community acting together for change. Indeed, one of the key lessons of the East London living wage campaign has been the need for an alliance between trade unions acting *inside* a workplace or the bargaining unit and community and media pressure acting *outside*. Where this has worked well, as in the East London hospitals, the campaign has made major progress in securing new gains *and* organising workers. But where it has been difficult to forge an alliance with a trade union acting to organise workers from within, as at Canary Wharf, it has been harder to apply sufficient pressure for change.

UNISON has a strong tradition of forging these kinds of alliances over particular campaigns against service closures and cuts. Indeed, a community–union alliance was formed to try and prevent the extension of privatisation at Whipps Cross Hospital in April 1997. Called *Health in Crisis*, the campaign brought together local community groups concerned with care for the elderly and the disabled along with UNISON and other trade unionists in the Borough. The campaign called a strike and demonstration on the eve of the privatisation extension but once it had failed to reverse the decision, the campaign petered out. What is new in the living wage case is the union's willingness to build a long-term sustainable alliance which will continue once the immediate issue is resolved (see Littman and Wills 2002; Wills 2001a).

Of course, in London there is still a lot more to be done. Other public sector bodies such as the Local Authorities, Transport for London, the Post Office, the Civil Service and Police have hardly been touched by the campaign. Moreover, there are large numbers of private sector organisations, including those in receipt of public subsidies (such as the companies at Canary Wharf) that could also be targets in future. In addition, there is scope for the living wage initiative to be more firmly implanted in the work of the mayor's office and in the policy development of the Greater London Authority (GLA).

In many ways, the East London living wage campaign is still in its infancy, and even where the campaign has been most successful, UNISON branches have been slow to get involved in TELCO's other activities. There has been little cross-fertilisation between union and community issues, people and interests. As a national officer from UNISON explained, this is partly due to the novelty of this approach but it is also due to local branch activists being over-stretched:

I'm not sure that they [the UNISON branches] really understand what they are part of, and I think that is part of the problem. But in addition, the branches are tremendously stretched, they're being asked to do huge amounts of work, partly because the organising model is only really beginning to penetrate and most branches are still operating on the servicing model. So, what you get is branch officers running around like chickens with their heads cut off, trying to do absolutely everything and this is an addition.

This officer went on to highlight the importance of doing educational work with the UNISON branches to explain more about TELCO, the principles of broad-based organising and how it might help the branch (and indeed, a number of the leading UNISON activists have taken up COF's leadership development courses in recent times). But in addition, there is scope for increasing direct participation by all members of TELCO. Asking the union branches to get more involved in decision-making, not just over the living wage campaign, but over matters such as the ongoing campaign over the care and dignity of elders that would help to promote more two-way dialogue and relationship building. Whereas there is a stronger tradition of community and faith-based activism in the USA, this is much weaker in the UK and in some ways TELCO and COF have yet to fully adapt the IAF model to the different circumstances of the UK.

In summary, the UK's first experiment with a living wage campaign demonstrates that there is scope to develop new ways of organising British workers that are more akin to a traditional social movement. In East London, workers have been mobilised around the demand for a living wage through community, as much as, union leadership. However, rather than *replacing* unions, the campaign has demonstrated that unions and community-based organisations can work together for mutual advantage. The living wage campaign illustrates the ways in which union and community alliances can generate momentum, even amongst workers employed in the most disempowering reaches of the labour market. In this case, the campaign has made real gains for workers while also building organisation and developing leadership. This model of organisation points to new ways of organising low-paid service workers in future, even if the specifics of each campaign and the alliances on which it was based, would vary as they evolved across the UK.

Acknowledgements

I am grateful to the ESRC for financial support in order to conduct this research (fellowship number R000271020). I would also like to thank all those who were interviewed formally for the research. The ideas presented have developed through ongoing discussion and debate with Deborah Littman, Catherine Howarth, Neil Jameson, Lina Jamoul, Jane Holgate and Anibel Ferus-Comelo to whom I am very grateful.

Notes

1. The research into low pay is more fully reported in Wills (2001b) and that concerning homecare services can be found in Wills (2004).
2. In 1983 the Conservative Government reversed its support for the Fair Wages Resolution that had been in place since 1891, violating standards set at the ILO since 1946, and making it possible to subcontract work without protecting the wages and conditions of staff for the first time in almost 100 years (UNISON, undated b).
3. The 'Code of Practice on Workforce Matters in Local Authority Service Contracts' issued by the Labour Government in 2002 is an attempt to clarify the situation in regard to the impact of privatisation on employees' terms and conditions. In the case of contracting-out, when council staff are transferred to another employer, the code insists that TUPE should always apply, protecting the existing wages and conditions of staff. Moreover, according to the new code, any new staff that are employed by the contractor to provide council services should be employed 'on fair and reasonable terms and conditions which are, overall, no less favourable that those of transferred employees'. Such conditions are to include the provision of a pension scheme to which the employer will also make a contribution. It is claimed that this code will effectively end the problem of the 'two-tier workforce' which affects all contracted out public services in the UK, eroding many of the cost advantages of privatisation in the first place. Under Ken Livingstone's control, the GLA became the first public body to declare its support for this approach, acting in 2002 to ensure that GLA employment conditions were matched by contractors.

However, there are many cases where this new code will have no impact on the pay and employment conditions of workers. Where there has been a gradual development of a mixed economy through buying services from outside providers, rather than directly transferring council staff, this code will not apply. Moreover, the same situation will remain unchanged in the NHS and other public services.

4. There is no official national or regional measurement of a 'low cost but acceptable' family income, and the living wage campaign thus had to start by commissioning original research on this front. Calculating the wider costs of inadequate income, to health, educational performance, long-term productivity loss, crime rates, community participation and the wider social fabric is a task yet to be undertaken (see Ambrose 2003).

5. Contracting first took place at Whipps Cross Hospital when domestic staff were transferred to RCO in 1985. In April 1987 this contract was enlarged to include portering, switchboard, security and car parking staff and was secured by Tarmac Service Master who held the contract for only six months. After this time the contract was managed solely by Tarmac until 1 year later when it was passed to ISS Mediclean. Likewise, at the Homerton Hospital, the contract for hotel services was first awarded to *RCO* in 1996 before transferring to ISS Mediclean at a later date. In both cases, as can be seen, subcontracting has greatly increased the insecurity in employment arrangements.

6. UNISON has had enquiries from other branches to work on similar claims, and progress has been made following action in Swansea and Glasgow during 2002/3.

7. Similar progress has also been made with the North East London Strategic Health Authority who have promised an end to the two-tier workforce and full parity between contracted and NHS staff by 2006 across 15 hospitals in the region.

8. It is interesting that very similar arguments are current in debates about international labour standards. While organisations like the Ethical Trading Initiative have set important benchmarks of good practice, and try to ensure their corporate members improve labour standards along the supply chain, many NGOs and Global Union Federations argue that labour organisation at the workplace is essential to ensure compliance and the proper monitoring of corporate codes (see Wills 2002a; Hale and Shaw 2001). Moreover, internationally, labour issues are increasingly being taken up by NGOs and community groups, due to the prevailing weakness of trade union organisation, just as demonstrated by living wage campaigns here and in the USA (see Waterman and Wills 2001).

References

Abbott, B. (1998a) 'The emergence of a new industrial relations actor', *Industrial Relations Journal*, 29, 6: 257–69.

Abbott, B. (1998b) 'The new shop stewards – the Citizen's Advice Bureaux', *Employee Relations*, 20, 6: 610–27.

ACAS (2001) *Annual Report, 2000–01*, London: Advisory, Conciliation and Arbitration Service.

ACAS (2002) *Annual Report, 2001–02*, London: Advisory, Conciliation and Arbitration Service.

Ackers, P. and Payne, J. (1998) 'British trade unions and social partnership: rhetoric, reality and strategy', *The International Journal of Human Resource Management*, 9, 3: 529–50.

Ackers, P., Marchington, M., Wilkinson, A. and Dundon, T. (2004) 'Partnership and voice, with or without trade unions: changing British management approaches to participation', in M. Stuart and M. Martínez Lucio (eds) *Partnership and Modernisation in Employment Relations*, London: Routledge.

Ackroyd, S. and Procter, S. (1998) 'British manufacturing organisation and workplace industrial relations: some attributes of the new flexible firm', *British Journal of Industrial Relations*, 36, 2: 163–83.

Adams, R. (1995) *Industrial Relations under Liberal Democracy*, Columbia SC: University of South Carolina Press.

Alferoff, C. and Knights, D. (2002) 'Quality time and the "Beautiful Call"', in U. Holtgrewe, C. Kerst and K. Shine (eds) *Re-organizing Service Work: Call Centres in Germany and Britain*, Aldershot: Ashgate.

Alinsky, S. (1971) *Rules for Radicals: A Pragmatic Primer for Realistic Radicals*, New York: Vintage Books.

Allen, J. and Henry, N. (1996) 'Fragments of industry and employment: contract service work and the shift towards precarious employment', in R. Crompton, D. Gallie and K. Purcell (eds) *Changing Forms of Employment: Organisations, Skills and Gender*, London: Routledge.

Allen, J. and Henry, N. (1997) 'Ulrich Beck's risk society at work: labour and employment in the contract services industry', *Transactions of the Institute of British Geographers*, 22: 180–96.

Allen, M. (2001) 'Stakeholding by any other name: a third way business strategy', in A. Giddens (ed.) *The Third Way: Global Agendas?*, Cambridge: Polity.

Almond, P. and Rubery, J. (1998) 'The gender impact of recent European trends in wage determination', *Work, Employment and Society*, 12, 4: 675–93.

Ambrose, P. (2003) *'Love the Work, Hate the Job': Low Cost but Acceptable Wage Levels and the 'Exported Costs' of Low Pay in Brighton and Hove*, Brighton: University of Brighton.

Appelbaum, E. (2002) 'The impact of new forms of work organisation on workers', in G. Murray, J. Bélanger, A. Giles and P-A Lapointe (eds) *Work and Employment Relations in the High Performance Workplace*, London and New York: Continuum.

Appelbaum, E. and Batt, R. (1994) *The New American Workplace*, London and Ithaca, NY: ILR Press.

Appelbaum, E., Bailey, T., Berg, P. and Kalleberg, A.L. (2000) *Manufacturing Advantage: Why High Performance Work Systems Pay Off*, Ithaca, NY: Cornell University Press.

Arzbacher, S., Holtgrewe, U. and Kerst, C. (2002) 'Call centres: constructing flexibility', in U. Holtgrewe, C. Kerst and K. Shine (eds) *Re-organizing Service Work: Call Centres in Germany and Britain*, Aldershot: Ashgate.

Bacharach, S.B., Bamberger, P.A. and Sonnenstuhl, W.J. (2001) *Mutual Aid and Union Renewal: Cycles of Logics of Action*, Ithaca, NY and London: ILR Press.

Bacon, N. and Storey, J. (1996) 'Individualism and collectivism and the changing role of trade unions', in P. Ackers, C. Smith, P. Smith (eds) *The New Workplace and Trade Unionism*, London: Routledge.

Bacon, N. and Storey, J. (2000) 'New employee relations strategies in Britain: towards individualism or partnership?', *British Journal of Industrial Relations*, 38, 3: 407–27.

Bacon, N., Blyton, P. and Morris, J. (1996) 'Among the ashes: trade union strategies in the UK and German steel industries', *British Journal of Industrial Relations*, 34, 1: 25–50.

Bain, G.S. (1970) *The Growth of White-collar Unionism*, Oxford: Clarendon Press.

Bain, G.S., Coates, D. and Ellis, V. (1973) *Social Stratification and Trade Unionism*, London: Heinemann.

Bain, P. and Mulvey, G. (2002) 'Workforce flexibility in call centres: stretching to breaking point?', Paper to *20th Annual International Labour Process Conference*, University of Strathclyde, Glasgow, 2–4 April.

Bain, P. and Taylor, P. (2000) 'Entrapped by the electronic panopticon? Worker resistance in the call centre', *New Technology, Work and Employment*, 15, 1: 2–18.

Bain, P. and Taylor, P. (2001) 'Seizing the time? Union recruitment potential in Scottish call centres', *Scottish Affairs*, 37: 104–28.

Bain, P. and Taylor, P. (2002) 'Ringing the changes? Union recognition and organisation in call centres in the UK finance sector', *Industrial Relations Journal*, 33, 3: 246–61.

Bain, P., Watson, A., Mulvey, G., Taylor, P. and Gall, G. (2002) 'Taylorism, targets and the pursuit of quality and quantity by call centre management', *New Technology, Work and Employment*, 17, 3: 170–85.

Barrett, R. (2001) *Symbolic Analysts or Cyberserfs? Software Development Work and Workers*, Working Paper, Melbourne: Monash University.

Bartlett, D., Corrigan, P., Dibben, P., Franklin, S., Joyce, P., McNulty, T. and Rose, A. (1999) 'Preparing for best value', *Local Government Studies*, 25, 2: 102–18.

Batchelor, J. (2001) *Employment Security in the Aftermath of the Break-up of Rover Group*, University of Warwick: Warwick Papers in Industrial Relations.

Batstone, E., Boraston, I. and Frenkel, S. (1977) *Shop Stewards in Action*, Oxford: Basil Blackwell.

Batstone, E., Boraston, I. and Frenkel, S. (1978) *The Social Organisation of Strikes*, Oxford: Basil Blackwell.

Batt, R. (2000) 'Strategic segmentation in front-line services: matching customers, employees and human resource systems', *International Journal of Human Resource Management*, 11: 540–61.

Beirne, M., Ramsay, H. and Panteli, A. (1998) 'Developments in computing work: control and contradiction in the software labour process', in P. Thompson and C. Warhurst (eds) *Workplaces of the Future*, Basingstoke: Macmillan Business.

Bélanger, J., Giles, A. and Murray, G. (2002) 'Towards a new production model: potentialities, tensions and contradictions', in G. Murray, J. Bélanger, A.Giles and P.A. Lapointe (eds) *Work and Employment Relations in the High-performance Workplace*, London and New York: Continuum.

Bélanger, P.R., Lapointe, P.A. and Lévesque, B. (2002) 'Workplace innovation and the role of institutions', in G. Murray, J. Bélanger, A. Giles and P.A. Lapointe (eds) *Work and Employment Relations in the High-performance Workplace*, London and New York: Continuum.

Belt, V. (2002) 'A female ghetto? Women's careers in call centres', *Human Resource Management Journal*, 12, 4: 51–66.

Benner, C. (2002) *Work in the New Economy: Flexible Labor Markets in Silicon Valley*, Oxford: Blackwell.

Benner, C. and Dean, A. (2000) 'Labor in the new economy: lessons from labor organizing in Silicon Valley', in F. Carré, M.A. Ferber, L. Golden and S.A. Herzenberg (eds) *Nonstandard Work: The Nature and Challenges of Changing Employment Arrangements*, Champaign, IL: Industrial Relations Research Association.

Bennett, J. (2000) 'Safety in numbers: educating safety representatives in the 1970s', *History of Education Society Bulletin*, 66: 71–9.

Bett, M. (1999) *Independent Review of Higher Education Pay and Conditions*, Report of Committee chaired by Sir Michael Bett, London: The Stationery Office.

Beynon, H. (1984) *Working for Ford*, second edition, Harmondsworth: Penguin.

Birkinshaw, J. and Hagstrom, P. (eds) (2000) *The Flexible Firm: Capability Management in Network Organizations*, Oxford: Oxford University Press.

Blackburn, R.M. and Prandy, K. (1965) 'White-collar unionization: a conceptual framework', *British Journal of Sociology*, 16: 111–22.

Booth, A.L., Dolado, J.J. and Frank, J. (2002) 'Symposium on temporary work: introduction', *The Economic Journal*, 112: F1–8.

Boxall, P. and Purcell, J. (2003) *Strategy and Human Resource Management*, Basingstoke: Macmillan.

Bradley, H. (1999) *Gender and Power in the Workplace*, London: Palgrave.

Bradley, H., Erickson, M., Stephenson, C. and Williams, S. (2000) *Myths at Work*, Cambridge: Polity Press.

Bradley, H., Healy, G. and Mukherjee, N. (2002) *Inclusion, Exclusion and Separate Organisation – Black Women Activists in Trade Unions*, ESRC Future of Work Programme, Working Paper No. 25.

Bradley, H., Healy, G. and Mukherjee, N. (2004) 'Multiple burdens: the problems of work-life balance for ethnic minority trade union activist women', in D. Houston (ed.) *The Future of Work Life Balance*, London: Palgrave.

Brasnett, M.E. (1964) *The Story of the Citizens' Advice Bureaux*, Plymouth: Latimer, Trend and Co. Ltd.

Brecher, J. and Costello, T. (1990) *Building Bridges: The Emerging Grassroots Coalition between Labor and Community*, New York: Monthly Review Press.

Briskin, L. (1999) 'Autonomy, diversity and integration: union women's separate organizing in North America and Western Europe in the context of restructuring and globalization', *Women's Studies International Forum*, 22, 5: 545–54.

Briskin, L. and McDermott, P. (eds) (1993) *Women Challenging Unions*, Toronto: University of Toronto Press.

Bristow, G., Munday, M. and Griapos, P. (2000) 'Call centre growth and location: corporate strategy and the spatial division of labour', *Environment and Planning A*, 32: 519–38.

Broad, G. (1994) 'Japan in Britain: the dynamics of joint consultation', *Industrial Relations Journal*, 25: 26–38.

Bronfenbrenner, K. and Juravitch, T. (1998) 'It takes more than house calls: organizing to win with a comprehensive union-building strategy', in K. Bronfenbrenner, S. Friedman, R.W. Hurd, R.A. Oswald and R.L. Seeber (eds) *Organizing to Win: New Research on Union Strategies*, Ithaca, NY: ILR Press.

Brown, T. (2002) 'The social costs of a compensation culture', in E. Lee (ed.) *Compensation Crazy*, Institute of Ideas, London: Hodder and Stoughton.

Brown, W. (2000) 'Putting partnership into practice in Britain', *British Journal of Industrial Relations*, 38, 9: 299–316.

Brown, W., Deakin, S., Hudson, M., Pratten, C. and Ryan, P. (1998) *The Individualisation of Employment Contracts in Britain*, Employment Relations Research Series, London: Department of Trade and Industry.

Brown, W., Deakin, S., Nash, D. and Oxenbridge, S. (2000) 'The employment contract: from collective procedures to individual rights', *British Journal of Industrial Relations* 38: 299–316.

Brown, W., Deakin, S., Nash, D. and Oxenbridge, S. (2000) 'The employment contract: from collective procedures to individual rights', *British Journal of Industrial Relations*, 38, 4: 611–29.

Brown, W., Marginson, P. and Walsh, J. (2003) 'The management of pay as the influence of collective bargaining diminishes', in P. Edwards (ed.) *Industrial Relations: Theory and Practice*, second edition, Oxford: Blackwell Publishing.

Buck, N., Gordon, I., Hall, P., Harloe, M. and Kleinman, M. (2002) *Life and Labour in Contemporary London*, London: Routledge.

Burchell, B. (2002) 'The prevalence and redistribution of job insecurity and work intensification', in B. Burchell, D. Ladipo and F. Wilkinson (eds) *Job Insecurity and Work Intensification*, London: Routledge.

Butler, P. (2003) *Employee Representation in Non-union Firms: A Critical Evaluation of Managerial Motive and the Efficacy of the Voice Process*, PhD thesis: University of Warwick.

Caldwell, P. (2000) 'Adult learning and the workplace', in H. Rainbird (ed.) *Training in the Workplace: Critical Perspectives on Learning at Work*, Basingstoke: Macmillan.

Callaghan, G. and Thompson, P. (2001) 'Edwards revisited: technical control and call centres', *Economic and Industrial Democracy*, 22, 1: 13–37.

Calveley, M. and Healy, G. (2003) 'Political activism and workplace industrial relations in a UK "failing" school', *British Journal of Industrial Relations*, 41, 1: 97–113.

Calveley, M., Healy, G., Shelley, S., Stirling, J. and Wray, D. (2003) *Union Learning Representatives – A Force for Renewal or 'Partnership'*, Employment Studies Working Paper No. 48, University of Hertfordshire.

Cappelli, P. (1999) *The New Deal at Work. Managing the Market-driven Workforce*, Boston, MA.: Harvard Business School Press.

Carley, M. and Hall, M. (2000) 'The implementation of the European Works Councils Directive', *Industrial Law Journal*, 29: 103–24.

Carter, B. (2000) 'Adoption of the organizing model in British trade unions: some evidence from Manufacturing, Science and Finance (MSF)', *Work Employment and Society*, 14, 1: 117–36.

Casey, B., Metcalf, H. and Millward, N. (1997) *Employers' Use of Temporary Labour*, London: Policy Studies Institute.

Castells, M. (1996) *The Rise of the Network Society*, Oxford: Blackwell.

Castells, M. (2000) *The Rise of the Network Society*, Vol. 1, second edition, Oxford: Blackwell.

Census (2001) http://www.statistics.gov.uk/census2001

Charlwood, A. (2002) 'Why do non-union employees want to unionize?', *British Journal of Industrial Relations*, 40, 3: 463–91.

Charlwood, A. (2004) 'Annual review article 2003: the new generation of trade union leaders and the prospects for union revitalisation', *British Journal of Industrial Relations*, 42, 2: 379–98.

Child, J. and Faulkner, D. (1998) *Strategies of Co-operation: Managing Alliances, Networks and Joint Ventures*, Oxford: Oxford University Press.

CIETT (2000) *Orchestrating the Evolution of Private Employment Agencies: Towards a Stronger Society*, Brussels: International Confederation of Private Employment Agencies (CIETT).

Citrine, W. (1935) *The Case for Fair Wages*, London: Trades Union Congress.

Clawson, D. (2003) *The Next Upsurge: Labor and the New Social Movements*, Ithaca, NY and London: ILR Press.

Clegg, H.A. (1976) *Trade Unionism under Collective Bargaining: A Theory Based on Comparison of Six Countries*, Oxford: Basil Blackwell.

Clough, B. (2002) *Time Off for Union Learning Representative Duties and Activities. Briefing for Union Learning Representatives*, London: Trades Union Congress.

Coates, K. and Topham, T. (1980) *Trade Unions in Britain*, Nottingham: Spokesman.

Cobble, D.S. (1991) 'Organizing the post-industrial workforce: lessons from the history of waitress unionism', *Industrial and Labor Relations Review*, 44, 3: 419–36.

Cobble, D.S. (1999) 'Making postindustrial unionism possible', in S. Friedman, R.W. Hurd, R.A. Oswald and R.L. Seeber (eds) *Restoring the Promise of American Labor Law*, Ithaca NY: ILR Press.

Cobble, D.S. and Vosko, L.F. (2000) 'Historical perspectives on representing nonstandard workers', in F. Carré, M.A. Ferber, L. Golden and S.A. Herzenberg (eds) *Nonstandard Work: The Nature and Challenges of Changing Employment Arrangements*, Champaign, IL: Industrial Relations Research Association.

Cockburn, C. (1983) *Brothers: Male Dominance and Technical Change*, London: Pluto Press.

Cockburn, C. (1989) 'Equal opportunities: the long and short agenda', *Industrial Relations Journal*, 20, 3: 213–25.

Colgan, F. and Ledwith, S. (1996) 'Sisters organising – women and their trade unions', in S. Ledwith and F. Colgan (eds) *Women in Organisations: Challenging Gender Politics*, Basingstoke: Macmillan.

Colgan, F. and Ledwith, S. (2000) 'Diversity, identities and strategies of women trade union activists', *Gender, Work and Organisation*, 7: 242–57.

Colgan, F. and Ledwith, S. (2002) 'Gender, diversity and mobilisation in UK trade unions', in F. Colgan and S. Ledwith (eds) *Gender, Diversity and Trade Unions: International Perspectives*, London: Routledge.

Colling, T. (1995) 'Renewal or *rigor mortis*? Union responses to contracting in local government', *Industrial Relations Journal*, 26, 2: 134–45.

Colling, T. (2000) 'Personnel management in the extended organisation', in S. Bach and K. Sisson (eds) *Personnel Management in Britain*, Oxford: Blackwell.

Colling, T. and Claydon, T. (2000) 'Strategic review and organisational change in UNISON', in M. Terry (ed.) *Redefining Public Sector Unionism: UNISON and the Future of Trade Unions*, London: Routledge.

Colling, T. and Dickens, L. (1989) *Equality Bargaining – Why Not?*, Equal Opportunities Commission Research Series, London: Her Majesty's Stationery Office.

Colling, T. and Dickens, L. (1998) 'Selling the case for gender equality: deregulation and equality bargaining', *British Journal of Industrial Relations*, 36, 3: 389–411.

Colling, T. and Dickens, L. (2001) 'Gender equality and trade unions: a new basis for mobilisation?', in M. Noon and E. Ogbonna (eds) *Equality, Diversity and Disadvantage in Employment*, Basingstoke: Palgrave Macmillan.

Collins, H. (2001) 'Is there a third way in labour law?' in A. Giddens (ed.) *The Third Way: Global Agendas?* Cambridge: Polity.

Cooke, F.L., Earnshaw, J., Marchington, M. and Rubery, J. (2004), 'For better and for worse? Transfers of undertakings and the reshaping of employment relations', *International Journal of Human Resource Management*, 15, 2: 276–94.

Corby, S. (1999) 'Equal opportunities: fair shares for all?', in S. Corby and G. White (eds) *Employee Relations in the Public Services: Themes and Issues*, London: Routledge.

Cornfield, D. and McCammon, H. (eds) (2003) *Labor Revitalization: Global Perspectives and New Initiatives. Research in the Sociology of Work*, Vol. 11, Amsterdam: Elsevier.

Coupar, W. and Stevens, B. (1998) 'Towards a new model of industrial partnership: beyond the "HRM versus industrial relations" argument', in P. Sparrow and M. Marchington (eds) *Human Resource Management: The New Agenda*, London: Financial Times/Pitman.

Crain, M. and Metheny, K. (1999) ' "Labor's divided ranks": privilege and the united front ideology', *Cornell Law Review*, 84: 1542–626.

Cully, M., Woodland, S., O'Reilly, A. and Dix, G. (1999) *Britain at Work: As Depicted by the 1998 Workplace Employee Relations Survey*, London: Routledge.

Cutter, J. (2000) *A Second Evaluation of the Union Learning Fund*. DfEE Research Report No. RR208, Nottingham: Department for Education and Skills.

D'Alessio, N. and Oberbeck, H. (2002) 'Call centres as organizational crystallisation of new labour relations, working conditions and a new service culture?' in U. Holtgrewe, C. Kerst and K. Shine (eds) *Re-organizing Service Work: Call Centres in Germany and Britain*, Aldershot: Ashgate.

Daft, R. and Lewin, A. (1993) 'Where are the theories for the new organizational forms? An editorial essay', *Organization Science*, 4, 4: i–iv.

Danford, A. (2003) 'Workers, unions and the high performance workplace', *Work, Employment and Society*, 17, 3: 569–73.

Danford, A., Richardson, M. and Upchurch, M. (2002) ' "New Unionism", organising and partnership: a comparative analysis of union renewal strategies in the public sector', *Capital and Class*, 76: 1–27.

Danford, A., Richardson, M. and Upchurch, M. (2003a) *New Unions, New Workplaces*, London: Routledge.

Danford, A., Richardson, M., Stewart, P., Tailby, S. and Upchurch, M. (2003b) *Partnership, Mutuality and the One-way Street: A Case Study of Aircraft Workers*, Paper presented to the 21st International Labour Process Conference, Bristol.

Darlington, R. (1994) *The Dynamics of Workplace Unionism*, London: Mansell.

Darlington, R. (1998) 'Workplace union resilience in the Merseyside Fire Brigade', *Industrial Relations Journal*, 29, 1: 58–73.

Darlington, R. (2001) 'Union militancy and left-wing leadership on London Underground', *Industrial Relations Journal*, 32, 1: 2–21.

Dawson, P. (2003) *Reshaping Change: A Processual Perspective*, London: Routledge.

Dean, A. (2002) 'The view from Silicon Valley', in P. Auer and C. Daniel (eds) *The Future of Work, Employment and Social Protection*, Geneva: International Institute for Labour Studies.

Deery, S., Iverson, R. and Walsh, J. (2002) 'Work relationships in telephone call centres: understanding emotional exhaustion and employee withdrawal', *Journal of Management Studies*, 39, 4: 471–96.

Deery, S. and Kinnie, N. (2002) 'Call centres and beyond: a thematic evaluation', *Human Resource Management Journal*, 12, 4: 3–13.

Deery, S. and Walsh, J. (1999) 'The decline of collectivism? A comparative study of white-collar employees in Britain and Australia', *British Journal of Industrial Relations*, 37, 2: 245–69.

Department of Health (2001) *Working Together – Learning Together: A Framework for Lifelong Learning in the NHS*, London: Department of Health.

DeSouza, R. (1998) 'Alternative dispute resolution: methods to address workplace conflict in health services organizations', *Journal of Health Care Management*, 43, 5: 453–66.

Dex, S., Willis, J., Paterson, R. and Sheppard, E. (2000) 'Freelance workers and contract uncertainty: the effects of contractual change in the television industry', *Work, Employment and Society*, 14, 2: 283–305.

DfEE (2001) *Consultation on the Impact of Statutory Recognition for Union Learning Representatives*, www.dfee.gov.uk/ulf.

Diamond, W.J. and Freeman, R.B. (2002) 'Will unionism prosper in cyberspace? The promise of the internet for employee organization', *British Journal of Industrial Relations*, 40, 3: 569–96.

Dickens, L. (1998) *Equal Opportunities and Collective Bargaining in Europe: 4. Illuminating the Process*, Dublin: European Foundation for the Improvement of Living and Working Conditions.

Dickens, L. (2000a) 'Doing more with less: ACAS and individual conciliation', in B. Towers and W. Brown (eds) *Employment Relations in Britain: 25 years of the Advisory, Conciliation and Arbitration Service*, Oxford: Blackwell.

Dickens, L. (2000b) 'Still wasting resources? Equality in employment', in S. Bach and K. Sisson (eds) *Personnel Management*, third edition, Oxford: Blackwell.

Dickens, L. and Hall, M. (2003) 'Labour law and industrial relations: a new settlement?', in P. Edwards (ed.) *Industrial Relations: Theory and Practice*, second edition, Oxford: Blackwell.

Dickens, L., Jones, M. Weekes, B. and Hart, M. (1985) *Dismissed: A Study of Unfair Dismissal and the Industrial Tribunal System*, Oxford: Basil Blackwell.

Dickens, R., Machin, S. and Manning, W. (1999) 'The effects of minimum wages on employment: theory and evidence from Britain', *Journal of Labor Economics*, 17: 1–22.

Dickson, T., McLachlan, H.V., Prior, P. and Swales, K. (1998) 'Big Blue and the unions: IBM, individualism and trade union strategy', *Work, Employment and Society*, 2, 4: 506–20.

Druker, J. and Stanworth, C. (2001) 'Partnerships and the private recruitment industry', *Human Resource Management Journal*, 11, 2: 73–89.

Druker, J. and Stanworth, C. (2004) 'Mutual expectations: a study of the three-way relationship between employment agencies, their client organisations and white-collar agency temps', *Industrial Relations Journal*, 35, 1: 58–75.

DTI (1999) *Regulation of the Private Recruitment Industry: A Consultation Document*, London: Department of Trade and Industry.

DTI (2002a) *Findings from the 1998 Survey of Employment Tribunal Applications (Surveys of Applicants and Employers)*, Employment Relations Research Series 0. 13, London: Department of Trade and Industry.

DTI (2002b) *High Performance Workplaces: The Role of Employee Involvement in a Modern Economy*, London: Department of Trade and Industry.

DTI (2002c) *Moving Forward: The Report of the Employment Tribunal System Taskforce*, London: Department of Trade and Industry.

DTI (2003) *High Performance Workplaces – Informing and Consulting Employees*, London: Department of Trade and Industry.

Duncan, C., Loretto, W. and White, P. (2000) 'Ageism, early exit, and British trade unions', *Industrial Relations Journal*, 31, 3: 220–34.

Dyer, J. and Singh, H. (1998) 'The relational view: cooperative strategy and sources of interorganizational competitive advantage', *The Academy of Management Review*, 23, 4: 660–79.

Earnshaw, J., Rubery, J. and Cooke, F.L. (2002) *Who Is the Employer?*, London: The Institute of Employment Rights.

Erickson, C.L., Fisk, C.L., Milkman, R., Mitchell, D.J.B. and Wong, K. (2002) 'Justice for janitors in Los Angeles: lessons from three rounds of negotiations', *British Journal of Industrial Relations*, 40, 3: 543–68.

Fairbrother, P. (1994) *Politics and the State as Employer*, London: Mansell.

Fairbrother, P. (1996) 'Workplace trade unionism in the state sector', in P. Ackers, C. Smith and P. Smith (eds) *The New Workplace and Trade Unionism: Critical Perspectives on Work and Organisation*, London: Routledge.

Fairbrother, P. (2000) *Trade Unions at the Crossroads*, London: Continuum.

Fairbrother, P. and Stewart, P. (2003) 'The dilemmas of social partnership and union organisation: questions for British trade unions', in P. Fairbrother and C.A.B. Yates (eds) *Trade Unions in Renewal: A Comparative Study*, London: Continuum.

Fairbrother, P. and Yates, C.A.B. (eds) (2003) *Trade Unions in Renewal: A Comparative Study*, London: Continuum.

Findlay, P. and McKinlay, A. (2003) 'Organizing in electronics: recruitment, recognition and representation – shadow shop stewards in Scotland's "Silicon Glen" ', in G. Gall (ed.) *Union Organizing*, London: Routledge.

Fiorito, J. (2001) 'Human resource management practices and worker desires for union representation', *Journal of Labor Research*, 22, 2: 335–54.

Fiorito, J., Jarley, P. and Delaney, J.T. (2002) 'Information technology, union organizing and union effectiveness', *British Journal of Industrial Relations*, 40, 4: 627–58.

Fitzgerald, I. and Stirling, J. (1999) 'A slow burning flame: organisational change and industrial relations in the fire service', *Industrial Relations Journal*, 30: 46–60.

Forde, C. (2001) 'Temporary arrangements: the activities of employment agencies in the UK', *Work, Employment and Society*, 15, 3: 631–44.

Fosh, P. (1993) 'Membership participation in workplace unionism – the possibility of union renewal', *British Journal of Industrial Relations*, 31: 577–92.

Freeman, R.B. (1995) 'The future for unions in decentralised collective bargaining systems: US and UK unionism in an era of crisis', *British Journal of Industrial Relations*, 33, 4: 519–36.

Freeman, R.B. and Rogers, J. (1993) 'Who speaks for us? Employee representation in a non-union labor market', in B.E. Kaufman and M.M. Kleiner (eds) *Employee Representation Alternatives and Future Directions*, Madison: Industrial Relations Research Association.

Freeman, R.B. and Rogers, J. (1999) *What Workers Want*, Ithaca, NY and London: Cornell University Press.

Frege, C.M. (2002) 'A critical assessment of the theoretical and empirical research on works councils', *British Journal of Industrial Relations*, 40, 2: 221–48.

Frege, C.M., Heery, E. and Turner, L. (2004) 'The new solidarity? Trade union coalition-building in five countries', in C.M Frege and J. Kelly (eds) *Varieties of Unionism: Labour Movement Revitalization in a Globalizing Economy*, Oxford: Oxford University Press.

Frege, C.M. and Kelly, J. (2003) 'Introduction: union revitalization strategies in comparative perspective', *European Journal of Industrial Relations*, 9, 1: 7–24.

Frege, C.M. and Kelly, J. (eds) (2004) *Varieties of Unionism: Labour Movement Revitalization in a Globalizing Economy*, Oxford: Oxford University Press.

Frenkel, S., Korcyznski, M., Shire, K. and Tam, M. (1999) *On the Front Line: Organization of Work in the Information Society*, Ithaca, NY: Cornell University Press.

Frost, A.C. (2001a) 'Creating and sustaining local union capabilities: the role of the national union', *Relations Industrielles*, 56, 2: 307–33.

Frost, A.C. (2001b) 'Reconceptualising local union responses to workplace restructuring in North America', *British Journal of Industrial Relations*, 39, 4: 539–64.

Fryer, R., Fairclough, A. and Mason, T. (1978) 'Facilities for female shop stewards: the Employment Protection Act and collective agreements' *British Journal of Industrial Relations*, 16: 101–74.

Gall, G. (1997) 'Developments in trade unionism in the financial sector in Britain', *Work, Employment and Society*, 11: 219–35.

Gall, G. (2001) 'The organisation of organised discontent: the case of the postal workers in Britain', *British Journal of Industrial Relations*, 39, 3: 393–410.

Gall, G. (ed.) (2003) *Union Organizing: Campaigning for Trade Union Recognition*, London: Routledge.

Gall, G., Taylor, P., Baldry, C. and Bain, P. (2004) ' "Striving under chaos": the effects of market turbulence and organizational flux on call centre work', in P. Stewart (ed.) *Emerging Patterns of Work and Employment*, London: Routledge.

Gallie, D., White, M., Cheng, Y. and Tomlinson, M. (1998) *Restructuring the Employment Relationship*, Oxford: Oxford University Press.

Garsten, C. (1999) 'Betwixt and between: temporary employees as liminal subjects in flexible organizations', *Organization Studies*, 20, 4: 601–17.

Gilbert, E. (2002) *Organising Homeworkers in the UK*, Leeds: National Group on Homeworking.

GLA (2002) *London Divided*, London: Greater London Authority.

Glickmann, L.B. (1997) *A Living Wage: American Workers and the Making of Consumer Society*, Ithaca, NY and London: Cornell University Press.

Godfrey, G. and Marchington, M. (1996) 'Shop stewards in the 1990s: a research note', *Industrial Relations Journal*, 27, 4: 339–44.

Goldthorpe, J., Lockwood, D., Bechhofer, F. and Platt, J. (1968) *The Affluent Worker: Industrial Attitudes and Behaviour*, Cambridge: Cambridge University Press.

Gollan, P. (2002) 'So what's the news? Management strategies towards non-union employee representation at News International', *Industrial Relations Journal*, 33, 4: 316–31.

Gosling, A., Machin, S. and Meghir, C. (2000) 'The changing distribution of male wages in the UK', *Review of Economic Studies*, 67: 635–66.

Gospel, H. and Palmer, G. (1993) *British Industrial Relations*, second edition, London: Routledge.

Gospel, H. and Pendleton, A. (2003) 'Finance, corporate governance and the management of labour: a conceptual and comparative analysis', *British Journal of Industrial Relations*, 41, 3: 557–82.

Gospel, H. and Willman, P. (2003) 'Dilemmas in worker representation: information, consultation and negotiation', in H. Gospel and S. Wood (eds) *Representing Workers: Union Recognition and Membership in Britain*, London: Routledge.

Green, F., Machin, S. and Wilkinson, D. (1996) *The Determinants of Workplace Training*, Leeds: University of Leeds, School of Business and Economic Studies Discussion Paper.

Greene, A.M. and Kirton, G. (2002) 'Advancing gender equality: the role of women-only education', *Gender, Work and Organization*, 9, 1: 39–59.

Greene, A.M., Black, J. and Ackers, P. (2000) 'The union makes us strong? A study of the dynamics of workplace leadership at two UK manufacturing plants', *British Journal of Industrial Relations*, 38, 1: 75–93.

Guest, G. and Peccei, R. (1998) *The Partnership Company: Benchmarks for the Future*, London: Involvement and Participation Association.

Guest, D. and Peccei, R. (2001) 'Partnership at work: mutuality and the balance of advantage', *British Journal of Industrial Relations*, 39, 2: 207–36.

Hale, A. and Shaw, L. (2001) 'Women workers and the promise of ethical trade in the globalised garment industry: A serious beginning?', *Antipode*, 33: 510–30.

Hall, M. (1996) 'Beyond recognition? Employee representation and EU law', *Industrial Law Journal*, 25: 15–27.

Hall, M. (2003a) 'Draft information and consultation legislation published' *European Industrial Relations Observatory*: http://www.eiro.eurofound.eu.int/2003/07/feature/uk0307106f.html.

Hall, M. (2003b) *Informing and Consulting Your Workforce: The BMW Hams Hall Plant Council*, Involvement and Participation Association Case Study, No. 4, Series 4.

Hall, M. (2003c) *Informing and Consulting Your Workforce: B&Q – Listening to the Grass Roots*, Involvement and Participation Association Case Study, No. 3, Series 4.

Hall, M. and Edwards, P. (1999) 'Reforming the statutory redundancy consultation procedure', *Industrial Law Journal*, 28: 283–302.

Hall, P.A. and Soskice, D. (2001) 'An introduction to varieties of capitalism', in P.A. Hall and D. Soskice (eds), *Varieties of Capitalism: The Institutional Foundations of Comparative Advantage*, Oxford: Oxford University Press.

Hall, M., Broughton, A., Carley, M. and Sisson, K. (2002) *Works Councils for the UK? Assessing the Impact of the EU Employee Consultation Directive*, London: Eclipse.

Hall, M., Hoffmann, A., Marginson, P. and Müller, T. (2003) 'National influences on European Works Councils in UK- and US-based companies', *Human Resource Management Journal*, 13: 75–92.

Hall, M., Lister, R. and Sisson, K. (1998) *The New Law on Working Time: Managing the Implications of the 1998 Working Time Regulations*, London: Eclipse.

Harvey, C. and Kanwal, S. (2000) 'Self-employed IT knowledge workers and the experience of flexibility: evidence from the United Kingdom', in K. Purcell (ed.), *Changing Boundaries in Employment*, Bristol: Bristol Academic Press.

Haynes, P. and Allen, M. (2001) 'Partnership as union strategy: a preliminary evaluation', *Employee Relations*, 23, 2: 164–87.

Healy, G. (1997) 'Gender and the unionisation of professional work – the case of teachers', in B. Fitzpatrick (ed.) *Bargaining in Diversity: Colour, Gender and Ethnicity*, Dublin: Oakwood Press.

Healy, G. and Kirton, G. (2000) 'Women, power and trade union government in the UK', *British Journal of Industrial Relations*, 38, 3: 343–60.

Hebson, G., Grimshaw, D., Marchington, M. and Cooke, F.L. (2003), 'PPPs and the changing public sector ethos: case-study evidence from the health and local authority sectors', *Work, Employment and Society*, 17, 3: 481–501.

Heery, E. (1996) 'The new new unionism', in I. Beardwell (ed.) *Contemporary Industrial Relations: A Critical Analysis*, Oxford: Oxford University Press.

Heery, E. (1998) 'Campaigning for part-time workers', *Work, Employment and Society*, 12, 2: 351–66.

Heery, E. (2000) 'Trade unions and the management of reward', in G. White and J. Druker (eds) *Reward Management, a Critical Text*, London: Routledge.

Heery, E. (2002) 'Partnership versus organising: alternative futures for British trade unionism', *Industrial Relations Journal*, 33, 1: 20–35.

Heery, E. (2003) 'Trade unions and industrial relations', in P. Ackers and A. Wilkinson (eds) *Understanding Work and Employment: Industrial Relations in Transition*, Oxford: Oxford University Press.

Heery, E. (2004a) 'Sources of change in trade unions', *Work, Employment and Society*, forthcoming.

Heery, E. (2004b) 'The trade union response to agency labour in the United Kingdom', *Industrial Relations Journal*, forthcoming.

Heery, E. and Abbott, B. (2000) 'Trade unions and the insecure workforce', in E. Heery and J. Salmon (eds) *The Insecure Workforce*, London: Routledge.

Heery, E. and Adler, L. (2004) 'Organizing the unorganized', in C. Frege and J. Kelly (eds) *Varieties of Unionism: Labour Movement Revitalization in a Globalizing Economy*, Oxford: Oxford University Press.

Heery, E. and Kelly, J. (1988) 'Do female representatives make a difference? Women full-time officials and trade union work', *Work, Employment and Society*, 2, 4: 487–505.

Heery, E. and Kelly, J. (1995) 'Conservative radicalism and nostalgia: a reply to Paul Smith and Peter Ackers', *Work, Employment and Society*, 9, 1: 15–64.

Heery, E. and Simms, M. (2004) *Bargain or Bust? Employer Responses to Union Organising*, London: Trades Union Congress.

Heery, E., Conley, H., Delbridge, R. and Stewart, P. (2000) *Beyond the Enterprise: Trade Unions and the Representation of the Contingent Workforce*, ESRC Future of Work Programme, Working Paper No. 7, Cardiff: Cardiff Business School.

Heery, E., Conley, H., Delbridge, R. and Stewart, P. (2004a) 'Beyond the enterprise: trade union representation of freelance workers in the United Kingdom', *Human Resource Management Journal*, 13, 2: 20–35.

Heery, E., Conley, H., Delbridge, R. and Stewart, P. (2004b) 'Seeking partnership for the contingent workforce', in M. Stuart and M. Martínez Lucio (eds) *Assessing Partnership: The Prospects for and Challenges of Modernization in Employment Relations*, London: Routledge.

Heery, E., Delbridge, R., Simms, M., Salmon, J. and Simpson, D.H. (2003) 'Organising for renewal: a case study of the UK's Organising Academy', in D. Cornfield and H. McCammon (eds) *Labor Revitalization: Global Perspectives and New Initiatives. Research in the Sociology of Work*, 11: 79–110.

Heery, E., Kelly, J. and Waddington, J. (2003) 'Union revitalization in Britain', *European Journal of Industrial Relations*, 9, 1: 79–97.

Heery, E., Simms, M., Conley, H., Delbridge, R. and Stewart, P. (2002) *Trade Unions and the Flexible Workforce: A Survey Analysis of Union Policy and Practice*, ESRC Future of Work Programme, Working Paper No. 22, Cardiff: Cardiff Business School.

Heery, E., Simms, M., Delbridge, R., Salmon, J. and Simpson, D. (2000a) 'Union organising in Britain: a survey of policy and practice', *International Journal of Human Resource Management*, 11, 5: 986–1007.

Heery, E., Simms, M., Simpson, D., Delbridge, R. and Salmon, J. (2000b) 'Organising unionism comes to the UK', *Employee Relations*, 22, 1: 38–57.

HELA (Health and Safety Executive Local Authority Unit) (2001) *Advice Regarding Call Centre Working Practices*, Local Authority Circular 94/1 (rev), Sheffield: Health and Safety Laboratory.

Heller, F., Pusic, E., Strauss, G. and Wilpert, B. (1998) *Organizational Participation: Myth and Reality*, Oxford: Oxford University Press.

Hepple, B. (1987) *Industrial Tribunals*, London: Justice.

Hepple, B. and Morris, G. (2002) 'The Employment Act 2002 and the crisis of individual employment rights', *Industrial Law Journal*, 31, 3: 245–69.

Herzenberg, S.A., Alic, J.A. and Wial, H. (1998) *New Rules for a New Economy: Employment and Opportunity in Post-industrial America*, Ithaca, NY and London: ILR Press.

Heyes, J. and Stuart, M. (1998) 'Bargaining for skills: trade unions and training in the workplace', *British Journal of Industrial Relations*, 36, 6: 459–67.

Hibbett, A. (2002) *Ethnic Minority Women in the UK*, http://www.cabinet office.gov.uk/womens-unit/research/gender_briefing/home.htm

Hoddinott, S. (2000) 'The worker basic skills "crisis": some industrial relations implications', in H. Rainbird (ed.) *Training in the Workplace: Critical Perspectives on Learning at Work*, Basingstoke: Macmillan.

Holgate, J. (2003) *Black Workers and Trade Unions in London and the South East: Focus on Effectiveness of Organising and Recruitment Strategies*, London: South East Region of the Trades Union Congress.

Hotopp, U. (2000) 'Recruitment agencies in the UK', *Labour Market Trends*, October: 457–63.

Howell, C. (1999) 'Unforgiven: British trade unionism in crisis', in A. Martin and G. Ross (eds) *The Brave New World of European Labor: European Trade Unions at the Millennium*, New York and Oxford: Berghahn Books.

Hunter, L., Beaumont, P. and Sinclair, D. (1996) 'A "partnership" route to human resource management', *Journal of Management Studies*, 33, 2: 235–57.

Hurd, R.W., Milkman, R. and Turner, L. (2003) 'Reviving the American labour movement: institutions and mobilisation', *European Journal of Industrial Relations*, 9, 1: 99–117.

Hyman, R. (1989) 'The politics of workplace trade unionism: recent tendencies and some problems for theory', in R. Hyman (ed.) *The Political Economy of Industrial Relations: Theory and Practice in a Cold Climate*, Basingstoke: Macmillan.

Hyman, R. (1991) 'European unions: towards 2000', *Work, Employment & Society*, 5, 4: 621–39.

Hyman, R. (1994) 'Changing trade union identities and strategies' in R. Hyman and A. Ferner (eds) *New Frontiers in European Industrial Relations*, Oxford: Basil Blackwell.

Hyman, R. (1996) 'Is there a case for statutory works councils in Britain?' in A. McColgan (ed.) *The Future of Labour Law*, London: Pinter.

Hyman, R. (1999) 'Imagined solidarities: can trade unions resist globalization?', in P. Leisink (ed.) *Globalization and Labour Relations*, Cheltenham: Edward Elgar.

Hyman, R. (2003) 'The historical evolution of British industrial relations', in P. Edwards (ed.) *Industrial Relations: Theory and Practice*, Oxford: Blackwell.

Hyman, J. and Mason, B. (1995) *Managing Employee Involvement and Participation*, London: Sage Publications.

Hyman, J., Baldry, C., Scholarios, D. and Bunzel, D. (2003) 'Work-life imbalance in call centres and software development', *British Journal of Industrial Relations*, 41, 2: 215–39.

IDS (1973) 'Part-time work', *IDS Study*, 62.

IDS (1976) 'Part-time work', *IDS Study*, 118.

IDS (2003) *Pay and Conditions in Call Centres*, London: Incomes Data Services.

IPA (1997) *Towards Industrial Partnership: A New Approach to Relationships at Work*, London: Involvement and Participation Association.

IPA (2001) *Sharing the Challenge Ahead: Informing and Consulting with Your Workforce*, London: Involvement and Participation Association.

IRRR (1991) 'New bargaining agenda for unions', *Industrial Relations Review and Report*, 492: 9–14.

IRS (2000) 'Buy in or sell out?', *IRS Employment Trends*, 716: 6–11.

Jackson, N. (2000) 'Writing up people at work: investigations of workplace literacy', *Literacy and Numeracy Studies*, 10, 1 and 2: 5–22.

James, P. and Walters, D. (1997) 'Mixed responses to new safety consultation rights', *Industrial Law Journal*, 26: 35–50.

Jarley, P. (2002) 'American unions at the start of the twenty-first century: going back to the future?', in P. Fairbrother and G. Griffin (eds) *Changing Prospects for Trade Unionism: Comparisons between Six Countries*, London: Continuum.

Javaid, M. (2000) 'Hearing impairment', *People Management*, 6, 26 October: 21.

Johnston, P. (1994) *Success While Others Fail: Social Movement Unionism and the Public Workplace*, Ithaca, NY: ILR Press.

Katz, H. and Darbishire, O. (2000) *Converging Divergences: Worldwide Change in Employment Systems*, Ithaca, NY: ILR Press.

Kaufman, B.E. and Taras, D.G. (2000) 'Nonunion employee representation: findings and conclusions', in B.E. Kaufman and D.G. Taras (eds) *Nonunion Employee Representation: History, Contemporary Practice, and Policy*, Armonk, NY: M.E. Sharpe.

Kelly, J. (1990) 'British trade unionism 1979–89: change, continuity and contradictions', *Work, Employment and Society*, Special Issue: 29–65.

Kelly, J. (1996a) 'Union militancy and social partnership', in P. Ackers, C. Smith and P. Smith (eds) *The New Workplace and Trade Unionism: Critical Perspectives on Work and Organisation*, London: Routledge.

Kelly, J. (1996b) 'Works councils: union advance or marginalization?' in A. McColgan (ed.) *The Future of Labour Law*, London: Pinter.

Kelly, J. (1998) *Rethinking Industrial Relations: Mobilization, Collectivism and Long Waves*, London: Routledge.

Kelly, J. (1999) 'Social partnership in Britain: good for profits, bad for jobs and unions', *Communist Review*, 30: 3–10.

Kelly, J. (2001) *Social Partnership Agreements in Britain: Union Revitalization or Employer Counter-Mobilization?*, Paper at the 'Assessing Partnership' conference, Leeds University Business School, Leeds.

Kelly, J. (2004) 'Social partnership agreements in Britain: labour cooperation and compliance', *Industrial Relations*, 43, 1: 267–92.

Kelly, J. and Heery, E. (1994) *Working for the Union: British Trade Union Officers*, Cambridge: Cambridge University Press.

Kennedy, H. (1995) *Return to Learn: UNISON's Fresh Approach to Trade Union Education*, London: UNISON.

Kerckhofs, P. (2002) *European Works Councils: Facts and Figures*, Brussels: European Trade Union Institute.

Kessler, I. and Purcell, J. (1995) 'Individualism and collectivism in theory and practice: management style and the design of pay systems', in P Edwards (ed.) *Industrial Relations: Theory and Practice in Britain*, Oxford: Blackwell.

Kessler, S. and Bayliss, F. (1995) *Contemporary British Industrial Relations*, Basingstoke: Macmillan.

King, D. (1993) 'The Conservatives and training policy 1979–1992: from a tripartite to a neo-liberal regime', *Political Studies*, XLI, 2: 214–35.

Kinnie, N., Hutchinson, S. and Purcell, J. (2000) 'Fun and surveillance: the paradox of high commitment management in call centres', *International Journal of Human Resource Management*, 11, 5: 967–85.

Kirton, G. (1999) 'Sustaining and developing women's trade union activism: a gendered project?', *Gender, Work and Organization*, 6, 4: 213–23.

Kirton, G. and Greene, A.M. (2002) 'The dynamics of positive action in UK trade unions: the case of women and black members', *Industrial Relations Journal*, 33, 2: 157–72.

Kirton, G. and Healy, G. (1999) 'Transforming union women: the role of women trade union officials in union renewal', *Industrial Relations Journal*, 30, 1: 2–15.

Kirton, G. and Healy, G. (2004) 'Shaping union and gender identities: a case study of women-only trade union courses', *British Journal of Industrial Relations*, 42, 2: 303–23.

Klandermans, B. (1986) 'Psychology and trade union participation: joining, acting, quitting', *Journal of Occupational Psychology*, 59, 3: 189–204.

Knell, J. (1999) *Partnership at Work*, Employment Relations Research Series 7, London: Department of Trade and Industry.

Knox, B. and McKinlay, A. (2003) 'Organising the unorganised: union recruitment strategies in American multinationals, c.1945–1977', in G. Gall (ed.) *Union Organizing: Campaigning for Trade Union Recognition*, London: Routledge.

Kochan, T.A. (1980) *Collective Bargaining and Industrial Relations*, Illinois: Richard D Irwin.

Kochan, T.A. (2003) 'A US perspective on the future of trade unions in Britain', in H. Gospel and S. Wood (eds) *Representing Workers: Union Recognition and Membership in Britain*, London: Routledge.

Kochan, T.A. and Osterman, P. (1994) *The Mutual Gains Enterprise*, Boston, MA.: Harvard Business School Press.

Konzelmann, S. and Forrant, R. (2003) 'Creative work systems in destructive markets', in B. Burchell, S. Deakin, J. Michie and J. Rubery (eds) *Systems of Production. Markets, Organisations and Performance*, London: Routledge.

Korczynski, M. (2002) *Human Resource Management in Service Work*, Basingstoke: Palgrave.

Kraft, P. and Dubnoff, S. (1986) 'Job content, fragmentation and control in computer software work', *Industrial Relations*, 25, 2: 184–96.

Kunda, G. Barley, S.R. and Evans, J. (2002) 'Why do contractors contract? The experience of highly skilled technical professionals in a contingent labor market', *Industrial and Labor Relations Review*, 55, 2: 234–61.

Lash, S. and Urry, J. (1987) *The End of Organized Capitalism*, Cambridge: Polity Press.

Ledwith, S. and Colgan, F. (2002) 'Tackling gender, diversity and trade union democracy: a worldwide project?', in F. Colgan and S. Ledwith (eds) *Gender Diversity and Trade Unions: International Perspectives*, London: Routledge.

Ledwith, S., Colgan, F., Joyce, P. and Hayes, M. (1990) 'The making of women trade union leaders', *Industrial Relations Journal*, 21, 2: 112–25.

Lee, G. and Loveridge, R. (1987) 'Black members and their unions', in G. Lee and R. Loveridge (eds) *The Manufacture of Disadvantage*, Buckingham: Open University Press.

Lewin, A., Long, C. and Carroll, T. (1999) 'The co-evolution of new organizational forms', *Organization Science*, 10, 5: 535–50.

Lewis, J. and Legard, R. (1998) *ACAS Individual Conciliation: A Qualitative Evaluation of the Service Provided in Industrial Tribunal Cases*, Research Paper No. 1, London: Advisory, Conciliation and Arbitration Service.

Littman, D. and Wills, J. (2002) 'Community of interests', *Red Pepper*, February: 23–5.

Lloyd, C. (2001) 'What do employee councils do? The impact of non-union forms of representation on trade union organisation', *Industrial Relations Journal*, 18: 313–27.

Lockyer, C., Scholarios, D., Watson, A. and Bunzel, D.I. (2002) *Career and Commitment in Call Centres*, Future of Work Programme, Working Paper No. 19, London: Economic and Social Research Council.

Lovering, J. (1998) 'Opening Pandora's Box: de facto industrial policy and the British defence industry', in R. Delbridge and J. Lowe (eds) *Manufacturing Transition*, London: Routledge.

Luce, S. and Pollin, R. (1999) 'Can US cities afford living wage programs? An examination of alternatives', *Review of Radical Political Economics*, 31, 1: 16–53.

Ludlam, S. and Taylor, A. (2003) 'The political representation of the labour interest in Britain', *British Journal of Industrial Relations*, 41, 4: 727–49.

Lupton, T. (1963) *On the Shop Floor*, Oxford: Pergamon.

Machin, S. (1997) 'The decline of labour market institutions and the rise of wage inequality in Britain', *European Economic Review*, 41: 647–57.

Machin, S. (2000) 'Union decline in Britain', *British Journal of Industrial Relations*, 38, 4: 631–45.

MacPherson, W. (1999) *The Stephen Lawrence Inquiry*, London: The Stationery Office.

Mangum, G., Mayall, D. and Nelson, K. (1985) 'The temporary help industry: a response to the dual internal labour market', *Industrial and Labor Relations Review*, 38, 4: 599–611.

Marchington, M., Cooke, F.L. and Hebson, G. (2003) 'Performing for the "customer": managing housing benefit operations across organisational boundaries', *Local Government Studies*, 29, 1: 51–74.

Marginson, P., Gilman, M., Jacobi, O. and Krieger, H. (1998) *Negotiating European Works Councils: An Analysis of Agreements Under Article 13*, Luxembourg: Office for Official Publications of the European Communities/European Foundation for the Improvement of Living and Working Conditions.

Marginson, P., Hall, M., Hoffmann, A. and Müller, T. (2004) 'The impact of European Works Councils on management decision-making in UK- and US-based multinationals: a case study comparison', *British Journal of Industrial Relations*, 42, 2: 209–34.

Marks, A., Findlay, P., Hine, J., McKinlay, A. and Thompson, P. (1998) 'The politics of partnership? Innovation in employment relations in the Scottish spirits industry', *British Journal of Industrial Relations*, 36, 2: 209–26.

Martínez Lucio, M. and Stuart, M. (2000) *Swimming against the Tide: Social Partnership, Mutual Gains and the Revival of 'Tired' HRM*, Working paper 00/03, The Centre of Industrial Relations and Human Resource Management, Leeds University.

Martínez Lucio, M. and Stuart, M. (2002) 'Assessing the principles of partnership. Workplace trade union representatives' attitudes and experiences', *Employee Relations*, 24, 3: 305–20.

Mason, B. and Bain, P. (1993) 'The determinants of trade union membership in Britain: a survey of the literature', *Industrial and Labor Relations Review*, 46, 2: 332–51.

May, T.Y., Korczynski, M. and Frenkel, S. (2002) 'Organizational and occupational commitment: knowledge workers in large corporations', *Journal of Management Studies*, 39, 6: 775–801.

McAdam, D. (1988) 'Micromobilization contexts and recruitment to activism', *International Social Movement Research*, 1: 125–54.

McBride, A. (2000) 'Promoting representation of women within UNISON', in M. Terry (ed.) *Redefining Public Sector Unionism: UNISON and the Future of Trade Unions*, London: Routledge.

McBride, A. (2001) 'Making it work: supporting group representation in a liberal democratic organisation', *Gender, Work and Organisation*, 8, 4: 411–29.

McCarthy, W. (2000) 'Representative consultations with specified employees – or the future of rung two', in H. Collins, P. Davies and R. Rideout (eds) *Legal Regulation of the Employment Relation*, The Hague: Kluwer.

McIlroy, J. (1995) *Trade Unions in Britain Today*, second edition, Manchester and New York: Manchester University Press.

McIlroy, J. (1997) 'Still under siege: trade unions at the turn of the century', *Historical Studies in Industrial Relations*, 3: 93–122.

McIlroy, J. and Campbell, A. (1999) 'Organizing the militants: the Liaison Committee for the Defence of Trade Unions, 1966–1979', *British Journal of Industrial Relations*, 37, 1: 1–31.

McKenzie, R. (2003) *Black Self-organising Groups*, Paper Presented to Working Lives Institute, London Metropolitan University.

McLoughlin, I. and Gourlay, S. (1994) *Enterprise without Unions*, Buckingham: Open University Press.

McNally, F. (1979) *Women for Hire: A Study of the Female Office Worker*, London and Basingstoke: Macmillan.

Meghnagi, S. (2004) 'The quality of work and workers' competences in Italian small firms', in H. Rainbird, A. Fuller and A. Munro (eds) *Workplace Learning in Context*, London: Routledge.

Michie, J. and Sheehan, M. (2003) 'Labour "flexibility" – securing management's right to manage badly?', in B. Burchell, S. Deakin, J. Michie and J. Rubery (eds) *Systems of Production. Markets, Organisations and Performance*, London: Routledge.

Middlehurst, R. and Kennie, T. (1997) 'Leading professionals: towards new concepts of professionalism' in J. Broadbent (ed.) *The End of the Professions? The Restructuring of Professional Work*, London: Routledge.

Millward, N., Bryson, A. and Forth, J. (2000) *All Change at Work?*, London: Routledge.

Millward, N., Stevens, M., Smart, D. and Hawes, W. (1992) *Workplace Industrial Relations in Transition*, Aldershot: Dartmouth.

Modood, T., Berthoud, R., Lakey, J., Nazroo, J., Smith, P., Virdee, S. and Beishon, S. (1994) *Ethnic Minorities in Britain*, London: Policy Studies Institute.

Morgan, P., Allington, N. and Heery, E. (2000) 'Employment insecurity in the public services', in E. Heery and J. Salmon (eds) *The Insecure Workforce*, London: Routledge.

Morris, T., Storey, J., Wilkinson, A. and Cressey, P. (2001) 'Industry change and union mergers in British retail finance', *British Journal of Industrial Relations*, 39: 237–56.

Munro, A. (1999) *Women, Work and Trade Unions*, London and New York: Mansell.

Munro, A. (2001) 'The feminist trade union agenda? The continued significance of class, race and gender', *Gender, Work and Organization*, 8, 4: 454–71.

Munro, A. and Rainbird, H. (1999) *Creating Lifelong Learning Advisers: Project for UNISON Supported by the DfEE's Union Learning Fund*, Northampton: University College Northampton.

Munro, A. and Rainbird, H. (2000) 'The New Unionism and the new bargaining agenda: UNISON-employer partnerships on workplace learning in Britain', *British Journal of Industrial Relations*, 38, 2: 223–40.

Munro, A., Rainbird, H. and Holly, L. (1997) *Partners in Workplace Learning: A Report on the UNISON/Employer Learning and Development Programme*, London: UNISON.

NACAB (1975) *Annual Report, 1974–75*, London: National Association of Citizens' Advice Bureaux.

NACAB (1993) *Job Insecurity*, London: National Association of Citizens' Advice Bureaux.

NACAB (1994) *Unequal Opportunities*, London: National Association of Citizens' Advice Bureaux.

NACAB (1996) *Annual Report, 1995–96*, London: National Association of Citizens' Advice Bureaux.

NACAB (1997a) *Annual Report, 1996–97*, London: National Association of Citizens' Advice Bureaux.

NACAB (1997b) *Flexibility Abused: A CAB Evidence Report on Employment Conditions in the Labour Market*, London: National Association of Citizens Advice Bureaux.

NACAB (2002a) *Annual Report, 2001–02*, London: National Association of Citizens' Advice Bureaux.

NACAB (2002b) *Routes to Resolution – Improving Employment Dispute Resolution – the CAB Service's Response*, London: National Association of Citizens' Advice Bureaux.

Neathy, F. and Arrowsmith, J. (2001) *Implementation of the Working Time Regulations*, Employment Relations Research Series 11, London: Department of Trade and Industry,

Nichols, T. (1991) 'Labour intensification, work injuries and the measurement of Percentage Utilisation of Labour (PUL)', *British Journal of Industrial Relations*, 29, 4: 569–92.

Nissen, B. (2000) 'Living wage campaigns from a "social movement" perspective: the Miami case', *Labor Studies Journal*, 25, 3: 29–50.

Nolan, P. and Slater, G. (2003) 'The labour market: history, structure and prospects', in P. Edwards (ed.) *Industrial Relations: Theory and Practice*, second edition, Oxford: Blackwell.

Nolan, P. and Wood, S. (2003) 'Mapping the future of work', *British Journal of Industrial Relations*, 41, 2: 165–74.

ONS (2001) *Annual Business Inquiry*, London: Office of National Statistics.

ORC (2003) *European Works Councils Survey 2002*, London: Organization Resources Counsellors Inc.

Osterman, P., Kochan, T.A., Locke, R.M. and Piore, M.J. (2001) *Working in America: A Blueprint for the New Labor Market*: Cambridge MA.: The MIT Press.

Oxenbridge, S. and Brown, W. (2002) 'The two faces of partnership? An assessment of partnership and co-operative employer/trade union relationships, *Employee Relations*, 24, 3: 262–76.

Oxenbridge, S., Brown, W., Deakin, S. and Pratten, C. (2003) 'Initial responses to the Employment Relations Act 1999', *British Journal of Industrial Relations*, 41, 2: 315–34.

Parker, H. (ed.) (2001) *Low Cost but Acceptable: A Minimum Income Standard for Households with Children in London's East End*, London: UNISON.

Pastor, M. (2001) 'Common ground and ground zero? The new economy and the new organising in Los Angeles', *Antipode*, 33: 259–88.

Peck, J. and Theodore, N. (1998) 'The business of contingent work: growth and restructuring in Chicago's temporary employment industry', *Work, Employment and Society*, 12, 4: 655–74.

Perlow, L.A. (1998) 'Boundary control: the social ordering of work and family time in high-tech corporations', *Administrative Science Quarterly*, 43: 328–57.

Phan, T. (1999) 'ILO Convention on private employment agencies (No.181)', in R. Blanpain (ed.) *Private Employment Agencies*, The Hague: Kluwer International.

Phelps Brown, H. (1990) 'The counter-revolution of our time', *Industrial Relations*, 29, 1: 1–14.

Pollin, R. (2001) 'Time for a living wage', *Challenge*, 44, Sept.–Oct.: 6–18.

Pollin, R. (2002) 'What is a living wage? Considerations from Santa Monica CA', *Review of Radical Political Economics*, 34: 267–73.

Pollin, R., Benner, M. and Luce, S. (2002) 'Intended versus unintended consequences: evaluating the New Orleans living wage ordinance', *Journal of Economic Issues*, XXXVI: 843–75.

Pollin, R. and Luce, S. (1998) *The Living Wage: Building a Fair Economy*, New York: New Press.

Prasch, R.E. and Sheth, S.A. (1999) 'The economics and ethics of minimum wage legislation', *Review of Social Economy*, LVII: 466–87.

Premack, S.L. and Hunter, J.E. (1988) 'Individual unionization decisions', *Psychological Bulletin*, 103: 223–34.

Purcell, J. (1987) 'Mapping management styles in employee relations', *Journal of Management Studies*, 23: 205–23.

Purcell, K. and Purcell, J. (1999) 'Insourcing, outsourcing and the growth of contingent labour as evidence of flexible employment strategies', *Bulletin of Comparative Labour Relations*, 35: 161–81.

Purcell, J. and Sisson, K. (1983) 'Strategies and practice in the management of industrial relations', in G. S. Bain (ed.) *Industrial Relations in Britain*, Oxford: Blackwell.

Purcell, J., Purcell, K. and Tailby, S. (2004) 'Temporary work agencies: here today, gone tomorrow?', *British Journal of Industrial Relations*, 42, 4, forthcoming.

Rainbird, H. (2002) *Evaluation of the Union Learning Fund Project 'Developing Support for Lifelong Learning Advisors'. Project Partners UNISON and Birmingham City Council*, Northampton: University College Northampton.

Rainbird, H. and Munro, A. (2003) 'Workplace learning and the employment relationship in the public sector', *Human Resource Management Journal*, 13, 2: 30–40.

Rainbird, H., Fuller, A. and Munro, A. (eds) (2004) *Workplace Learning in Context*, London: Routledge.

Rainbird, H., Holly, L. and Munro, A. (2002) *Learning Partnerships in Health and Social Care: An Evaluation of Partnership Initiatives in Health and Social Care*, London: UNISON.

Rainbird, H., Edwards, P.K., Sutherland, J., Holly L. and Munro, A. (2003) *Employee Voice and Its Influence over Training Provision*, London: Department of Trade and Industry.

Rainbird, H., Munro, A., Holly, L. and Leisten, R. (1999) *The Future of Work in the Public Sector: Learning and Workplace Inequality*, ESRC Future of Work Programme Working Paper No. 2, University of Leeds.

Rainbird, H., Sutherland, J., Edwards, P., Holly, L. and Munro, A. (2003) *Employee Voice and Training at Work: An Analysis of Case Studies and WERS98*, Employment Relations Research Series, No. 21, London: Department of Trade and Industry.

Rainnie, A. (1989) *Industrial Relations in Small Firms*, London: Routledge.

Rainnie, A. (1998) 'The inevitability of flexibility?', *Work, Employment and Society*, 12, 1: 161–7.

Ramsay, H. (1977) 'Cycles of control: workers' participation in sociological and historical perspective', *Sociology*, 11, 3: 1–22.

Ramsay, H. (1980) 'Phantom participation: patterns of power and conflict', *Industrial Relations Journal*, 11: 46–59.

Ramsay, H. (1999) *Close Encounters of the Nerd Kind*, Paper presented to the Worklife 2000 Programme, Sweden.

Reed, C.S., Young, W.R. and McHugh, P. (1994) 'A comparative look at dual commitment: an international study', *Human Relations*, 47, 10: 1269–91.

Reimer, S. (1998) 'Working in a risk society', *Transactions of the Institute of British Geographers*, 23: 116–27.

Reynolds, D. (2001) 'Living wage campaigns as social movements: experiences from nine cities', *Labor Studies Journal*, 26, 2: 31–65.

Roche, W.K. (2000) 'The end of new industrial relations?', *European Journal of Industrial Relations*, 6, 3: 261–82.

Rock, M. (2001) 'The rise of the Bangladeshi Independent Garment-Workers' Union (BIGU)', in J. Hutchinson and A. Brown (eds) *Organising Labour in Globalising Asia*, London: Routledge.

Rose, E. (2002) 'The labour process and union commitment within a banking services call centre', *The Journal of Industrial Relations*, 44, 1: 40–61.

Rose, F. (2000) *Coalitions across the Class Divide: Lessons from the Labor, Peace and Environmental Movements*. Ithaca, NY: Cornell University Press.

Rothwell, S. (1990) *Changing Labour Markets: What Is the Role for Employment Agencies?*, Henley Management College Working Paper Series, Henley-on-Thames: Henley, The Management College.

Rubery, J., Cooke, F.L., Earnshaw, J. and Marchington, M. (2003) 'Inter-organisational relations and employment in a multi-employer environment', *British Journal of Industrial Relations*, 41, 2: 265–89.

Rubery, J., Earnshaw, J., Marchington, M., Cooke, F.L. and Vincent, S. (2002) 'Changing organisational forms and the employment relationship', *Journal of Management Studies*, 39, 5: 645–72.

Rundle, J. (1998) 'Winning hearts and minds in the era of employee involvement programs', in K. Bronfenbrenner, S. Friedman, R.W. Hurd, R.A. Oswald and R.L. Seeber (eds) *Organizing to Win: New Research on Union Strategies*, Ithaca, NY and London: ILR Press.

Sachdev, S. (2001) *Contracting Culture from CCT to PPPs: The Private Provision of Public Services and Its Impact on Employment Relations*, London: UNISON.

Samuel, P. (2001) *Partnership Efficacy: Some Preliminary Evidence from Trade Union Officials*, Paper presented at the 'Assessing Partnership' Conference, Leeds University Business School.

Samuel, P. (2005) 'Partnership working and the cultivated activist', *Industrial Relations Journal* (forthcoming).

Saundry, R. (1998) 'The limits of flexibility: the case of UK television', *British Journal of Management*, 9, 1: 151–62.

Schoenberger, E. (2000) 'The living wage in Baltimore: impacts and reflections', *Review of Radical Political Economics*, 32: 428–36.

Scott, M., Roberts, I., Holroyd, G. and Sawbridge, D. (1989) *Management and Industrial Relations in Small Firms*, Research Paper No. 70, London: Department of Employment.

Scottish Enterprise (2001) *A National Strategy for Scotland*, Glasgow: Scottish Enterprise.

Selmi, M. and McUsic, M.S. (2002) 'Difference and solidarity: unions in a postmodern age', in J. Conaghan, R.M. Fischl and K. Klare (eds) *Labour Law in an Era of Globalization*, Oxford: Oxford University Press.

SERTUC (2000) *New Moves Towards Equality: New Challenges*, London: South East Region of the Trades Union Congress.

Shaw, N. (1999) *An Early Evaluation of the Union Learning Fund*, Research Report RR113, London: Department for Education and Employment.

Sisson, K. (1993) 'In search of HRM', *British Journal of Industrial Relations*, 31, 2: 201–10.

Sisson, K. and Marginson, P. (2003) 'Management: systems, structure and strategy', in P. Edwards (ed.) *Industrial Relations: Theory and Practice*, second edition, Oxford: Blackwell.

Smith, C. (1987) *Technical Workers: Class, Labour and Trade Unionism*, Basingstoke: Macmillan.

Smith, M., Fagan, C. and Rubery, J. (1998) 'Where and why is part-time work growing in Europe', in J. O'Reilly and C. Fagan (eds) *Part-time Prospects: An International Comparison of Part-time Work in Europe, North America and the Pacific Rim*, London: Routledge.

Smith, P. (2001) *Unionization and Union Leadership: The Road Haulage Industry*, London: Continuum.

Stanworth, C. and Stanworth, J. (1997) 'Managing an externalized workforce: freelance labour use in the UK', *Industrial Relations Journal*, 30, 2: 101–17.

Storey, J. and Bacon, N. (1993) 'Individualism and collectivism into the 1990s', *International Journal of Human Resource Management*, 4: 665–84.

Storey, J., Bacon, N., Edmonds, J. and Wyatt, P. (1993) 'The "New Agenda" and human resource management: a roundtable discussion with John Edmonds', *Human Resource Management Journal*, 4, 1: 63–70.

Storrie, D. (2002) *Temporary Agency Work in the European Union*, Dublin: European Foundation for the Improvement of Living and Working Conditions.

Streeck, W. (1989) 'Skills and the limits to neo-liberalism: the enterprise of the future as a place of learning', *Work, Employment and Society*, 3, 1: 89–104.

Streeck, W. (1992) 'National diversity, regime competition and institutional deadlock: problems in forming a European industrial relations system', *Journal of Public Policy*, 12: 301–30.

Streeck, W. (1994) 'Training and the new industrial relations: a strategic role for unions?', in M. Regini (ed.) *The Future of Labour Movements*, London: Sage.

STUC (2000) *Annual Conference Agenda*, Composite R, Edinburgh: Scottish Trades Union Congress.

Tailby, S. and Winchester, D. (2002) 'Management and trade unions: towards social partnership?', in S. Bach and K. Sisson (eds) *Personnel Management: A Comprehensive Guide to Theory and Practice*, Oxford: Blackwell.

Tarrow, S. (1998) *Power in Movement: Social Movements and Contentious Politics*, second edition, Cambridge: Cambridge University Press.

Taylor, P. and Bain, P. (1999) '"An assembly line in the head": work and employee relations in call centres', *Industrial Relations Journal*, 30, 2: 101–17.

Taylor, P. and Bain, P. (2001a) *Call Centres in Scotland in 2000*, Glasgow: Rowan Tree Press.

Taylor, P. and Bain, P. (2001b) 'Trade unions, workers' rights and the frontier of control in UK call centres', *Economic and Industrial Democracy*, 22, 1: 39–66.

Taylor, P. and Bain, P. (2003a) *Call Centres in Scotland and Outsourced Competition from India*, Stirling: Scotecon Network.

Taylor, P. and Bain, P. (2003b) 'Call centre organizing in adversity: from Excell to Vertex', in Gall, G. (ed.) *Union Organizing: Campaigning for Trade Union Recognition*, London: Routledge.

Taylor, P. and Bain, P. (2003c) ' "Subterranean worksick blues": humour as subversion in two call centres', *Organization Studies*, 24, 9: 1487–1509.

Taylor P. and Ramsay, H. (1998) 'Unions, partnership and HRM: sleeping with the enemy?', *International Journal of Employment Studies*, 6, 2: 115–43.

Taylor, P., Baldry, C., Bain, P. and Ellis, V. (2003) ' "A unique working environment?" Health, sickness and absence management in UK call centres', *Work, Employment and Society*, 17, 3: 435–58.

Taylor, P., Mulvey, G., Hyman, J. and Bain, P. (2002) 'Work organisation, control and the experience of work in call centres', *Work, Employment and Society*, 16, 1: 133–50.

Taylor, S. (1998) 'Emotional labour and the new workplace', in P. Thompson and C. Warhurst (eds) *Workplaces of the Future*, Basingstoke and London: Macmillan.

Terry, M. (1994) 'Workplace unionism: redefining structures and objectives', in R. Hyman and A. Ferner (eds) *New Frontiers in European Industrial Relations*, Oxford: Blackwell.

Terry, M. (1995) 'Trade unions: shop stewards and the workplace', in P. Edwards (ed.) *Industrial Relations – Theory and Practice in Britain*, Oxford: Blackwell.

Terry, M. (1999) 'Systems of collective employee representation in non-union firms in the UK', *Industrial Relations Journal*, 30: 16–30.

Terry, M. (2000) 'UNISON and the quality of public service provision', in M. Terry (ed.) *Redefining Public Sector Unionism: UNISON and the Future of Trade Unions*, London: Routledge.

Terry, M. (2003a) 'Can partnership revive the decline of British trade unions?', *Work, Employment and Society*, 17, 3: 459–72.

Terry, M. (2003b) 'Employee representation: shop stewards and the new legal framework', in Edwards, P. (ed.) *Industrial Relations: Theory and Practice*, second edition, Oxford: Blackwell.

Terry, M. (2003c) 'Partnership and the future of trade unions in the UK', *Economic and Industrial Democracy*, 24: 485–507.

Terry, M. and Smith, J. (2003) *Evaluation of the Partnership at Work Fund*. DTI Employment Relations Research Series No. 17, London: Department of Trade and Industry.

Thelen, K. (2001) 'Varieties of labor politics in the developed economies', in P.A. Hall and D. Soskice (eds) *Varieties of Capitalism: The Institutional Foundation of Comparative Advantage*, Oxford: Oxford University Press.

Tilly, C. (1978) *From Mobilization to Revolution*, New York: McGraw-Hill.

Tilly, C. (1996) *Half a Job: Bad and Good Part-time Jobs in a Changing Labor Market*, Philadelphia, PA.: Temple University Press.

Towers, B. (1997) *The Representation Gap: Change and Reform in the British and American Workplace*, Oxford: Oxford University Press.

Toynbee, P. (2003) *Hard Work: Life in Low Pay Britain*, London: Bloomsbury.

Tremlett, N. and Banerji, N. (1994) 'The 1992 survey of Industrial Tribunal applications', *Employment Gazette*, Employment Department: 21–8.

TUC (1985) *Report of the 117th Annual Trades Union Congress*, London: Trades Union Congress.

TUC (1988a) *Report of the 120th Annual Trades Union Congress*, London: Trades Union Congress.

TUC (1988b) *Special Review Body Report*, London: Trades Union Congress.

TUC (1994) *Involvement of Black Workers in Trade Unions – A Survey of Union Policies and Strategies*, London: Trades Union Congress.

TUC (1995a) *Report of Congress*, London: Trades Union Congress.

TUC (1995b) *Your Voice at Work: TUC Proposals for Rights to Representation at Work*, London: Trades Union Congress.

TUC (1996) *Part of the Union? The Challenge of Recruiting and Organising Part-time Workers. A Report for the TUC by the Labour Research Department*, London: Trades Union Congress.

TUC (1999) *Partners for Progress: New Unionism in the Workplace*, London: Trades Union Congress.

TUC (2000a) *Annual Conference Agenda*, London: Trades Union Congress.

TUC (2000b) *Partnership: A Boost to Business*, London: Trades Union Congress.

TUC (2001a) *General Council Report*, London: Trades Union Congress.

TUC (2001b) *Report of Congress*, London: Trades Union Congress.

TUC (2001c) *Rights not Favours: Submission to 'Work and Parents' Green Paper*, London: Trades Union Congress.

TUC (2001d) *Trade Union Trends, Focus on Employment Tribunals*, London: Trades Union Congress.

TUC (2001e) *TUC Directory 2001*, London: Trades Union Congress.

TUC (2002a) *High Performance Workplaces. TUC Submission on the Government's Discussion Document*, London: Trades Union Congress.

TUC (2002b) *Partnership Works*, London: Trades Union Congress.

Turnbull, P., Blyton, P. and Harvey, G. (2005) 'Cleared for take-off? Management–labour partnership in the European civil aviation industry', *European Journal of Industrial Relations* (forthcoming).

Turner, L. (2003) 'Reviving the labor movement: a comparative perspective', in D.B. Cornfield and H. McCammon (eds) *Labor Revitalization: Global Perspectives and New Initiatives. Research in the Sociology of Work*, 11: 23–58 Amsterdam: Elsevier JAI.

Turner, L., Katz, H.C. and Hurd, R.W. (eds) (2001) *Rekindling the Movement: Labor's Quest for Relevance in the 21st Century*, Ithaca, NY: ILR Press.

Twomey, B. (2002) 'Women in the labour market: results from the spring 2001 LFS', *Labour Market Trends*, Mar.: 109–27.

Undy, R., Ellis, V., McCarthy, W.E.J. and Halmos, A.M. (1981) *Change in Trade Unions: The Development of UK Unions since 1960*, London: Hutchinson.

Undy, R., Fosh, P., Morris, H., Smith, P. and Martin, R. (1996) *Managing the Unions: The Impact of Legislation on Union Behaviour*, Oxford: Clarendon Press.

UNISON (undated a) *Developing Support for UNISON Lifelong Learning Advisers – Report of a ULF Project by UNISON, Birmingham City Council and the WEA*, London: UNISON.

UNISON (undated b) *A Fair Wages Strategy*, London: UNISON.

UNISON (undated c) *The New Learning Agenda: UNISON's Approach to Lifelong Learning in the Workplace*, unpublished discussion document.

Upchurch, M. and Danford, A. (2001) 'Industrial restructuring, globalisation and the trade union response: a study of MSF in the south west of England', *New Technology, Work and Employment*, 16: 100–17.

Verma, A., Kochan, T. and Wood, S. (2002) 'Editors' introduction', Special Edition on Union Decline and Prospects for Revival, *British Journal of Industrial Relations*, 40, 3: 373–84.

Virdee, S. (2000) 'Organised labour and the black worker in England: a critical analysis of postwar trends', in J. Wets (ed.) *Cultural Diversity in Trade Unions: A Challenge to Class Identity?*, London: Ashgate.

Virdee, S. and Grint, K. (1994) 'Black self-organisation in trade unions', *Sociological Review*, 42, 2: 202–26.

Visser, J. (2002) 'Why fewer workers join unions in Europe: a social custom explanation of membership trends', *British Journal of Industrial Relations*, 40, 3: 403–30.

Voss, K. and Sherman, R. (2003) 'You just can't do it automatically: the transition to social movement unionism in the United States', in P. Fairbrother and C.A.B. Yates (eds) *Trade Unions in Renewal: A Comparative Study*, London and New York: Continuum.

Wacjman, J. (2000) 'Feminism facing industrial relations in Britain', *British Journal of Industrial Relations*, 38, 2: 183–201.

Waddington, J. (2001) 'What do EWC representatives think? Views from five countries', *European Works Councils Bulletin*, 33: 12–16.

Waddington, J. (2003) 'Trade union organisation', in P. Edwards (ed.) *Industrial Relations: Theory and Practice*, second edition, Oxford: Blackwell.

Waddington, J. and Kerr, A. (1999) 'Trying to stem the flow: union membership turnover in the public sector', *Industrial Relations Journal*, 30, 3: 184–96.

Waddington, J. and Kerr, A. (2000) 'Towards an organising model in UNISON? A trade union membership strategy in transition', in M. Terry (ed.) *Redefining Public Sector Unionism: UNISON and the Future of Trade Unions*, London: Routledge.

Waddington, J. and Whitston, C. (1996) 'Empowerment versus intensification: union perspectives on changes at the workplace', in P. Ackers, C. Smith and P. Smith (eds) *The New Workplace and Trade Unionism*, London: Routledge.

Waddington, J. and Whitston, C. (1997) 'Why do people join trade unions in a period of membership decline?', *British Journal of Industrial Relations*, 35, 4: 515–46.

Waldinger, R., Erickson, C., Milkman, R., Mitchell, D.J.B., Valenzuela, A., Wong, K. and Zeitlin, M. (1998) 'Helots no more: a case study of the Justice for Janitors campaign in Los Angeles', in K. Bronfenbrenner, S. Friedman, R.W. Hurd, R.A. Oswald and R.L. Seeber (eds) *Organizing to Win: New Research on Union Strategies*, Ithaca, NY and London: ILR Press.

Walsh, J. (2000) 'Organizing the scale of labour regulation in the United States: Service sector activism in the city', *Environment and Planning A*, 32: 1593–1610.

Ward, K., Grimshaw, D., Rubery, J. and Beynon, H. (2001) Dilemmas in the management of temporary work agency staff', *Human Resource Management Journal*, 11, 4: 3–21.

Warren, M. (2001) *Dry Bones Rattling: Community Building to Revitalize American Democracy*, Princeton, NJ: Princeton University Press.

Waterhouse, P. and Lewis, T. (1995) *Improving the Quality of Employment Advice*, London: National Association of Citizens' Advice Bureaux.

Waterman, P. and Wills, J. (eds) (2001) *Place, Space and the New Labour Internationalisms*, Oxford: Blackwell.

Webb, S. and Webb, B. (1897) *Industrial Democracy*, London: Longmans, Green.

Weber, T., Foster, P. and Levent Egriboz, K. (2000) *Costs and Benefits of the European Works Councils Directive*, Employment Relations Research Series 9, London: Department of Trade and Industry.

Weiss, D.J., Dawis, R.D., England, G.W. and Lofquist, L.H. (1967) *Manual for the Minnesota Satisfaction Questionnaire*, Industrial Relations Center: University of Minnesota.

Whitehouse, G. (1992) 'Legislation and labour market inequality', *Work, Employment and Society*, 6, 1: 65–86.

Wial, H. (1993) 'The emerging organizational structures of unionism in low wage services', *Rutgers Law Review*, 45, 1: 671–738.

Wial, H. (1994) 'New bargaining structures for new forms of business organisation', in S. Friedman, R.W. Hurd, R.A. Oswald and R.L. Seeber (eds) *Restoring the Promise of American Labor Law*, Ithaca, NY: ILR Press.

Williams, S. (1997) 'The nature of some recent trade union modernization policies in the UK', *British Journal of Industrial Relations*, 35: 495–514.

Willman, P. (2001) 'The viability of trade unionism: a bargaining unit analysis', *British Journal of Industrial Relations*, 39, 1: 97–117.

Wills, J. (1999) 'European Works Councils in British firms', *Human Resource Management Journal*, 9: 19–38.

Wills, J. (2000) 'Great expectations: three years in the life of a European Works Council', *European Journal of Industrial Relations*, 6: 85–107.

Wills, J. (2001a) 'Community unionism and trade union renewal in the UK: moving beyond the fragments at last?', *Transactions of the Institute of British Geographers*, 26: 465–83.

Wills, J. (2001b) *Mapping Low Pay in East London*, London: TELCO.

Wills, J. (2002a) 'Bargaining for the space to organise in the global economy: a review of the Accor–IUF trade union rights agreement', *Review of International Political Economy*, 9: 675–700.

Wills, J. (2002b) *Partnership and Trade Unionism in Practice: An Overview of the Barclays/UNIFI Partnership Agreement*, Working Paper Five, Geographies of Organised Labour, Queen Mary College, University of London.

Wills, J. (2002c) *Union Futures: Building Networked Trade Unionism in the UK*, London: Fabian Society.

Wills, J. (2003) *On the Front Line of Care: A Research Report to Explore Home Care Employment and Service Provision in Tower Hamlets*, London: UNISON.

Wills, J. (2004) 'The geography of union organising in the private services sector in the UK: lessons from the T&G's campaign to unionise the Dorchester Hotel, London', *Antipode* (forthcoming).

Wright Mills, C. (1956) *White-collar: The American Middle Classes*, New York: Oxford University Press.

York Consulting (2001) *Evaluation of the Union Learning Fund in Year 3*, DfES Research Report No. 283, London: HMSO.

Index